FUNCTIONAL GRAMMATICS

This book provides a re-conceptualization of grammar in a period of change in the communication landscape and widening disciplinary knowledge. Drawing on resources in systemic functional linguistics, the book envisions a 'functional grammatics' relevant to disciplinary domains such as literary study, rhetoric and multimodality. It re-imagines the possibilities of grammar for school English through Halliday's notion of grammatics.

Functional Grammatics is founded on decades of research inspired by systemic functional linguistics, and includes studies of grammatical tools useful to teachers of English, research into visual and multimodal literacies and studies of the genre–grammar connection. It aims to be useful to the interpretation and composition of texts in school English, portable in design across texts and contexts and beneficial for language development.

The book will be of interest to researchers and teacher educators, as well as undergraduate and postgraduate students and practicing teachers committed to evidence-based professional development.

Mary Macken-Horarik is a Senior Research Fellow in the Learning Sciences Institute Australia (LSIA) at the Australian Catholic University, Australia.

Kristina Love is a Professor of Education at the Australian Catholic University, Australia.

Carmel Sandiford is a Lecturer in Language and Literacy Education at the Melbourne Graduate School of Education, The University of Melbourne, Australia.

Len Unsworth is Professor in English and Literacies Education at the Learning Sciences Institute Australia (LSIA) at the Australian Catholic University, Australia.

FUNCTIONAL GRAMMATICS

Re-conceptualizing Knowledge about Language and Image for School English

Mary Macken-Horarik, Kristina Love, Carmel Sandiford and Len Unsworth

LONDON AND NEW YORK

First published 2018
by Routledge
2 Park Square, Milton Park, Abingdon, Oxon OX14 4RN

and by Routledge
711 Third Avenue, New York, NY 10017

Routledge is an imprint of the Taylor & Francis Group, an informa business

© 2018 Mary Macken-Horarik, Kristina Love, Carmel Sandiford and Len Unsworth

The right of Mary Macken-Horarik, Kristina Love, Carmel Sandiford and Len Unsworth to be identified as authors of this work has been asserted by them in accordance with sections 77 and 78 of the Copyright, Designs and Patents Act 1988.

All rights reserved. No part of this book may be reprinted or reproduced or utilised in any form or by any electronic, mechanical, or other means, now known or hereafter invented, including photocopying and recording, or in any information storage or retrieval system, without permission in writing from the publishers.

Trademark notice: Product or corporate names may be trademarks or registered trademarks, and are used only for identification and explanation without intent to infringe.

British Library Cataloguing in Publication Data
A catalogue record for this book is available from the British Library

Library of Congress Cataloging in Publication Data
Names: Macken-Horarik, Mary, author.
Title: Functional grammatics: re-conceptualizing knowledge about language and image for school English/Mary Macken-Horarik, Kristina Love, Len Unsworth and Carmel Sandiford.
Description: Abingdon, Oxon; New York, NY: Routledge, [2018] | Includes bibliographical references.
Identifiers: LCCN 2017020762| ISBN 9781138948044 (hbk) | ISBN 9781138948051 (pbk) | ISBN 9781315669731 (ebk)
Subjects: LCSH: English language–Grammar–Study and teaching (Primary) | English language–Grammar–Study and teaching (Secondary) | Language arts (Primary) | Language arts (Secondary)
Classification: LCC LB1528 .M282 2018|DDC 372.61–dc23
LC record available at https://lccn.loc.gov/2017020762

ISBN: 978-1-138-94804-4 (hbk)
ISBN: 978-1-138-94805-1 (pbk)
ISBN: 978-1-315-66973-1 (ebk)

Typeset in Bembo
by Deanta Global Publishing Services, Chennai, India

CONTENTS

Preface ix
Acknowledgements xi

1 Negotiating the territory of English through functional grammatics 1
   The problem of grammar 1
   Re-imagining grammar through systemic functional grammatics 4
   *Finding directions in the territory using four points on
      a theoretical compass 10*
   Preview of chapters 25
   Notes 26
   References 27

2 True North: investigating a grammatics for narrative 32
   Exploring the interface between grammatics and narrative 32
   Grammatics and genre 39
   Grammatics, meaning and metafunctions 44
   Applying an ideational lens to narrative 50
   Conclusion 62
   Notes 63
   References 64

3 'The Wild West': understanding resources for meaning in narrative 67
   Moving into the sometimes forbidding territory of language and image 67

Exploring interactive systems of choice in verbal texts 69
Exploring interactive systems of choice in images 76
Managing interaction in narrative composition 79
Exploring stratification in language and image 81
A step into more delicate regions of the interpersonal territory – APPRAISAL 86
Concluding remarks 96
Notes 98
References 98

4 Moving South: teaching narrative in classrooms — 101
Introduction to the teachers and the teaching and learning cycle 101
Three scenarios in teaching a grammatics for narrative 104
Scenario 1 – teaching narrative in a primary classroom 106
Building the context for work on narrative 107
Modelling features of narrative (setting and dialogue) 108
Guided practice – joint construction of a new narrative 112
Independent composition of narratives 114
Extension work – other possibilities for work with functional grammatics 115
Scenario 2 – teaching narrative in a secondary classroom 115
Reviewing and consolidating students' understandings of narrative viewpoint 116
Building the context for work on narrative 118
Modelling the text 119
Guided practice 123
Independent writing and reflection 124
Scenario 3 – multimodal narrative interpretation and text creation with Year 7 124
Planning for teaching 125
Building the context for work on multimodal narrative 128
Modelling the text – from teacher to small groups 129
Guided practice – applying the tools to composition of a multimodal narrative 135
Independent composition of multimodal narratives 136
Conclusion 136
Notes 138
References 138

5 True North: investigating a grammatics for persuasion — 141
Exploring the interface of grammatics and persuasion 141

Rhetoric and grammatics: the case of one young orator   148
Rhetoric and logogenesis: the case of a political orator   155
Grammatics and rhetoric in the broader civic domain   164
Multimodal forms of persuasion   165
Note   172
References   172

6 **'The Wild West': understanding resources for meaning in persuasion**   176
Moving into the territory of persuasive resources in school English   176
Written expositions in schooling: a developmental perspective   182
Written analytical expositions in the secondary school   193
Resources for expanding and contracting argumentative positions   203
Expositions: a multimodal focus   205
References   207

7 **Moving South: teaching persuasion in classrooms**   211
Scenarios in teaching a grammatics for argument   212
Scenario 1 – exposition in a primary (Year 5/6) classroom   215
Scenario 2 – multimodal composition in the primary classroom   226
Composing a multimodal text   230
Building shared understandings about images in advertisements   230
Scenario 3 – Mood and Modality in a secondary classroom   235
Conclusion   240
Notes   240
References   240

8 **Tracking East: exploring narratives of many kinds (and modes)**   242
Introduction   242
The challenge of diverse multimodal narratives   242
The Great Bear   246
The Tunnel   252
The Lost Thing   255
Transforming meanings   259
Notes   269
References   270

9 **Envoi**   272
The problems of grammar reprised   272

What we did about the problems 273
Negotiating the terrain in English – potentials and problems of grammatics 277
References 279

Index 281

PREFACE

Our aim in writing this book is to illustrate how meaning-oriented grammatical study can be an exciting and vital field of inquiry both in itself and as it contributes to students' deepened appreciation and composition of the verbal and multimodal texts of contemporary subject English. In this intention, we speak to English/Language Arts teachers and researchers alike. While drawing largely on our research and teaching experiences in the Australian context, and particularly on our recently completed four-year Australian Research Council (ARC)-funded project, we have taken care to connect with teachers and researchers in North America, the UK, New Zealand and other Anglophone contexts.

Each of the authors has taught in English classrooms and their research as academics has closely connected with teachers' work. We are keenly aware of the challenges teachers face as they incorporate research-informed insights about grammar in its various forms into their daily practice and the obstacles, both personal and institutional, to realize the best outcomes for their students. Indeed the metaphor of the compass that underpins this book has its genesis in our own struggles: as teachers seeking to chart the ever shifting terrain of grammatical knowledge as we seek the best literacy outcomes for our diverse students; as curriculum advisors and developers seeking to support the design and national implementation of meaningful English/Language Arts curricula; and as researchers connecting with international colleagues to investigate what teacher knowledge about language really makes a difference to student literacy outcomes. In each of these fields, the challenge is heightened and enlivened by the widening purview of contemporary subject English to include appreciation and production of multimodal texts. Here, meanings are made through the interplay of intra- and inter-textual choices from visual as well as verbal systems, and we need a compass to guide us in these crucial excursions into this new and emerging territory of subject English.

Halliday's meaning-oriented grammar has been the magnet that activates our compass, guiding our pedagogies with teachers, and their pedagogies in turn with their students, in a deeply enriched study of the narrative and persuasive texts that underpin the disciplinary practices of English. This 'grammatics' has allowed the teachers we have worked alongside over various research projects to re-engage with knowledge about language, not as a set of dry, prescriptive rules, but as a resource for meaning, supporting the practical tasks of comprehension, critical analysis and composition of the increasingly complex texts (including multimodal texts) of their twenty-first-century classrooms. Our 'elbow to elbow' work with these teachers, and most recently those in our four-year ARC research project, left us deeply impressed with their resilience as they engaged with the intellectual challenges of learning a grammatics 'good enough' for school English. We learnt much from them as they implemented contextualized, meaningful and creative approaches to grammar in classrooms that ranged from middle primary to the senior years of secondary school. It was these teachers who both tested and helped shape the theoretical compass with which we could navigate the different regions in the territory of English: its distinctive texts, their functions and associated practices; the organization of the meaning-making (semiotic) resources involved; its requirement to build students' repertoires over time; and its broader purview towards texts of many kinds and many modes, both within school and in wider social, civic and personal spaces.

The research and publication outputs generated from our collaboration with teachers committed to this meaning-oriented grammatics have opened up conversations with like-minded colleagues in the UK and the US. Through such conversations, clear evidence is emerging of the positive effects of contextualized or 'rhetorical' grammar teaching on students' engagement with English/Language Arts and on the quality of their writing. We hope this book continues those dialogues, while inviting other teachers and researchers into the conversation.

Mary Macken-Horarik, Kristina Love,
Carmel Sandiford and Len Unsworth

ACKNOWLEDGEMENTS

The authors and publisher wish to thank the following for permission to use previously published material:

For excerpts:

Blueback by Tim Winton © (1997), London. Reproduced with permission by Penguin Australia Pty Ltd.
Fantastic Mr Fox by Roald Dahl © (1974), London. Reproduced with permission by Penguin Australia Pty Ltd.
Unhappily Ever After in *Quirky Tails* by Paul Jennings (1999). Ringwood, Victoria: Penguin Books. Reproduced with permission by Lockley Lodge Pty Ltd.
Jenny Balcombe for her permission to use her writing on the dangers of mobile phone.
Janicka Horarik for her permission to use a dialogic extract from her draft novel
The Great Bear. Text © 1995 Libby Gleeson. Illustrations © 2010 Armin Greber. From *The Great Bear* by Libby Gleeson, illustrated by Armin Greder. Reproduced by permission of Walker Books Ltd, London SE11 5HJ: www.walker.co.uk.
The Lost Thing by Shaun Tan © (2000), Lothian Children's Books, an imprint of Hachette Australia.
The Lost Thing Animated Movie (2010) – Directors: Shaun Tan and Andrew Ruhemann; Producer: Sophie Byrne; Production Company: Passion Pictures Australia. © Passion Pictures Australia & Screen Australia.
From *The Tunnel* by Anthony Browne. Copyright © 1989 Anthony Browne. Reproduced by permission of Walker Books Ltd, London SE11 5HJ: www.walker.co.uk.
The Weapon by Fredric Brown. © 1951 by Street & Smith Publications, renewed 1979 by the Estate of Fredric Brown. Originally appeared in *Astounding Science*

Fiction, April 1951 and reprinted by permission of the Estate and its agent, Barry N. Malzberg.

For the following Figures:

Figure 2.2 and Figure 5.5
Text © 1995 Libby Gleeson
Illustrations © 2010 Armin Greder
From *The Great Bear* by Libby Gleeson, illustrated by Armin Greder
Reproduced by permission of Walker Books Ltd, London SE11 5HJ
www.walker.co.uk

Figures 2.3, 2.4, 3.3, 3.4
Copyright © 1989 Anthony Browne
From *The Tunnel* by Anthony Browne
Reproduced by permission of Walker Books Ltd, London SE11 5HJ
www.walker.co.uk

Figures 4.4, 4.5, 4.6, 4.7, 4.8
From *Grandad's Gifts* by Paul Jennings and Peter Gouldthorpe
Copyright © Paul Jennings and Peter Gouldthorpe, 1992. Reprinted by permission of Penguin Random House Australia Pty Ltd

Figure 5.1 – Mobile Recycle (Gorilla), Melbourne Zoo, Elliott Avenue Parkville VIC 3052

Figure 5.2 – Aboriginal and White Boys, Fairfax Media Limited, Sydney

Figure 5.3 – Aboriginal Man + baby, Fairfax Media Limited, Sydney.

Figure 8.3 – Finn's visualization of the scene from Blueback, reproduced with permission of Finn Barry

Figures 8.4, 8.5, 8.6, 8.7, 8.8
Humpty Dumpty, reproduced with permission of Rali Beynon

1
NEGOTIATING THE TERRITORY OF ENGLISH THROUGH FUNCTIONAL GRAMMATICS

The problem of grammar

For decades now, school English has had a contentious relationship to grammar and perhaps never more so than in the current era with its constantly morphing digital media and new forms of textuality and a simultaneous pressure to 'deliver' quality outcomes for students in high stakes national and international tests. In many Anglophone countries, teachers are working with expanded notions of text and their disciplinary practices require a rethinking of available metalanguages. In this communicative environment, calls for a return to 'the basics' so students can succeed on high stakes tests appear anachronistic at best, misguided at worst. Instruction narrows to accommodate superficial grammatical rules and conventions; grammatical terminology is restricted to forms of standard English; interesting grammatical study of 'textese', non-standard forms in beat poetry, news captions or tweeting are abandoned. As one student put it, "Grammar has an air of unhappiness about it."

Could it be different? Could grammatical study become not only a valid avenue of study but an exciting field of inquiry? Could it play a vital role in the interpretation and composition of texts? Might it be extended to images and multimodal texts? This book responds in the affirmative. It argues for a conception of grammar – what Halliday has come to call 'grammatics' – that is adequate both to the study of texts of many kinds and to crucial disciplinary practices in English (Halliday, 2002). It images this field of practices as territory that makes distinctive demands on grammatical study. In particular, it aims to show that a grammatics good enough for English will have four attributes: It will be relevant to disciplinary practices with narrative and persuasion; it will contribute to knowledge of language (and image) as a resource for meaning; it will be relevant to practical tasks in teaching of writing; and it will offer interesting 'ways in' to texts of all kinds. Happily for us (and for the profession), new descriptions are emerging that deal with images and other resources for meaning in picture books, graphic novels, posters and movies. Our hope is that the excursions we undertake in this book will encourage teachers to explore the possibilities of grammatically informed knowledge for interpreting and composing texts of all kinds.

Re-imagining grammar in these ways is difficult however, not least because subject English is more vulnerable than other school subjects to the expectations and anxieties of those beyond the school walls: it is the lingua franca in Anglophone countries, the primary means for learning most other school subjects and (for many students) the basis on which lives beyond the school can be optimised. Knowledge of language (and of grammar within this) is both important and unfamiliar territory for many in English and in the broader community. If collocation is the study of 'the company a word keeps' (Carter, 1998, p. 38), the noun 'grammar' often conjures adjectives like 'correct', 'good' and 'bad'. Such associations reinforce a view of grammar as a standard against which language use (and user) is judged. For many, it evokes memories of the red pen on the margins of written work, comments about unsatisfactory forms of expression and 'correctionist' impulses that seek to erase rather than understand non-standard wordings. It is closer to the kill-joy than to the expressive gesture.

If grammar has an image problem, it is partly the result of a brace of studies that appear to have confirmed its adverse consequences (Braddock, Lloyd-Jones & Schoer, 1963; Hillocks, 1984; Wyse, 2001). For example, a meta-analysis conducted by Andrews and colleagues revealed that grammar instruction has either a negligible or (worse) a negative effect on student writing, if only by virtue that it takes up time that could be spent on more profitable tasks (Andrews, 2005; Andrews *et al.*, 2006). Perhaps because they were based on traditional or transformational generative models of grammar (the latter of which was never intended for education), studies like this are limited by the familiar assumption that grammar instruction "is about the avoidance or remediation of error" (Myhill, Jones, Watson & Lines, 2013, p. 104). Furthermore, the research was mostly conducted in classrooms in which grammatical instruction was conducted separately from work on composition. The implicit assumption is that disciplinary relevance is unnecessary to the study of grammar. Professionally influential research into effects of grammar instruction has entrenched anachronistic views of grammar.

And yet knowledge of language as system and structure *is* important to teachers. And they are worried about their lack of knowledge about grammar. In the United Kingdom, for example, studies of teachers' grammatical knowledge either confirm gaps in understanding (e.g. Cajkler & Hislam, 2002; Hudson & Walmsley, 2005; Watson, 2015) or report higher levels of confidence than can be demonstrated in tests of knowledge amongst primary and secondary teachers (e.g. Sangster, Anderson & O'Hara, 2012, p. 18). A similar picture has emerged in Kolln and Hancock's historical review of grammar within English teaching in the United States. They note a general unpreparedness to teach grammar across the profession, underpinned by a "general public failure to recognize grammar as anything but a loose collection of prescriptive mandates" (Kolln & Hancock, 2005, p. 11). Comparable profiles of fragmentary linguistic knowledge amongst teachers have been detected in Canada (Williams, 2009) and New Zealand (Gordon, 2005; Meyer, 2008). In Australia, several studies have identified gaps in teachers' linguistic knowledge (Commonwealth of Australia, 2009; Hammond & Macken-Horarik, 2001; Harper & Rennie, 2009; Jones & Chen, 2012; Louden *et al*., 2005). One recent study undertaken by two authors uncovered high levels of 'avowed confidence with grammar' amongst Australian teachers and profound uneasiness with specifics of grammatical knowledge (Love, Macken-Horarik & Horarik, 2015). Like others, these teachers have an ambivalent relationship to grammar.

These are important questions to explore that have not yet been taken up in previous research into grammar, despite claims of empirical robustness. For example: Just how is identification of grammatical forms to be related to descriptions of their function? How do teachers interpret these in larger patterns of meaning in texts? In what ways can they relate descriptions of verbal texts to multimodal texts? More generally, how far can they stretch grammatical descriptions in this vastly expanding digital world? A crucial starting point in addressing such questions rests on the assumption that grammar is about meaning. However, understanding *how* grammar makes meaning is too difficult if one's conception of it is too narrow. The results for teaching can be grim, as Myhill and colleagues point out:

> Weak linguistic knowledge can lead to an over-emphasis upon identification of grammar structures without fully acknowledging the conceptual or cognitive implications (Myhill 2003) of that teaching. Equally, it can lead to sterile teaching, divorced from the realities of language in use.
> *(Myhill, Jones, Lines & Watson, 2012, p. 142)*

A pattern of weak linguistic subject knowledge presents an intellectual challenge for a subject dedicated to the study of language *and* historically resistant to its re-imagining. In reality, the approach to grammar that many in subject English eschewed decades ago was too limited to serve the demanding tasks of the discipline. In reflecting on the wholesale rejection of grammar in English during the sixties, Halliday argues that "Grammar had largely been disappeared from the curriculum, because teachers in the schools found the traditional grammar boring and useless; but nothing had come in in its place" (Halliday, 1991/2007, p. 283). For Halliday, responding to this difficulty means that grammatical instruction should be a properly constructed avenue of study rather than "a kind of linguistic nature study, with lists of parts of speech and rules of behavior" (Halliday, 1991/2007, p. 288). Re-conceptualizing grammar is vital if teachers are to invest in and profit from its study.

But there is a third problem for the re-imagining of grammar, this time emerging from neo-conservative forces in the socio-political environment. Grammar is always a fraught issue in public discourse, particularly in times of great change. At times of curriculum renewal, we often find political leaders offering opinions about the curriculum of English that will win them the support of disaffected popular opinion. As Deborah Cameron observes of this period in the United Kingdom, public debates about grammar quickly descended into a preoccupation with 'the particular values and standards the idea of grammar has been made to symbolise" (Cameron, 1995). Five years later, Myhill was led to claim that rational argument about grammar "had been hijacked to support political arguments concerning the decline of moral standards and the need for order and authority" (Myhill, 2000, p. 152). Similar forces emerged in Australia during the development of the national curriculum, championed by Murdoch press journalists at *The Australian* newspaper such as Luke Slattery and Kevin Donnelly (see Macken-Horarik, 2009 and 2011 for discussion). In the United States, a period of ferment followed standards-based reforms like 'No Child Left Behind' that was signed into law by George Bush in 2002. In contexts such as these, talk of grammar is never *just* about grammar. It is about anxieties originating elsewhere and favours metaphors such as 'grammar wars' that bear little relationship to teachers' everyday work (Snyder, 2008; Locke, 2010).

In sum, re-conceptualizing grammatical instruction in English is problematic for several reasons. Here we have outlined three factors that make this enterprise more challenging: the 'aura of unhappiness' that grammar has accumulated in discourses of deficit (an image problem), a pattern of weak linguistic knowledge across the profession (a knowledge problem) and the controversies that grammar constellates in public media (a distractor problem). In addressing such challenges, we need to begin with meaning making to develop a principled and coherent knowledge of language in the profession and to find ways to demonstrate the power of this in students' literacy practices.

Re-imagining grammar through systemic functional grammatics

There are hopeful signs emerging in recent studies of meaningful approaches to grammatical instruction. The work of Myhill and colleagues in England has presented clear evidence of the positive effects of contextualized grammar teaching on students' writing (Jones, Myhill & Bailey, 2013; Myhill, Jones, Lines & Watson, 2012; Myhill & Watson, 2014). This parallels interesting work in the United States on 'rhetorical grammar' (e.g. Kolln & Hancock, 2005; Hancock, 2009) and 'contextualized grammar' instruction (Weaver, 2010). Despite decades of dismissal of a role for grammar in English by the National Council of Teachers of English, there are signs that teachers are moving from 'error to pattern' in approaches to grammar (Gartland & Smolkin, 2016, p. 395). Teaching inspired by functional linguistics continues to improve academic learning for English Language Learner (ELL) students (e.g. Brisk, 2015; Moore & Schleppegrell, 2014; Schleppegrell, 2013).

In New Zealand, functional approaches have informed critical approaches to grammar instruction (e.g. Locke, 2005, Locke, 2010) even if many teachers lack a secure base in linguistic knowledge (Gordon, 2005; Meyer, 2008). A little way across the Pacific, Australian educators have long been conversant with the notion of grammar as a resource for meaning in texts (Christie & Derewianka, 2008; Derewianka, 2012; Humphrey, Love & Droga, 2011). It is the home of genre-based approaches to literacy teaching, inspired by decades of 'Sydney School' work (Christie, 2002; Axford, Harders & Wise, 2009; Rothery, 1989, 1994; Rose & Martin, 2012). The national survey referred to above revealed an extremely high percentage (93.5%) of teachers expressing confidence in knowledge of, and capacity to teach, text types (Love *et al.*, 2015).

Because of decades of such work, it is easier to situate grammatical study within meaningful frames of reference such as genres. Even so, English teachers need principled ways of relating grammar and genre. This book is founded on insights generated in a four-year project[1] that attempted to theorise the conditions of a grammatics 'good enough' for English – contextualized, meaningful and creative. This research project will be referred to throughout the book as 'The Grammatics Project'. The intellectual challenges of the new curriculum called on teachers not only to 'develop students' understanding about how the English language works', and progress this in a 'coherent and cumulative' way from Foundation (Kindergarten) to Year 10, but to promote portable learning 'applicable to new settings across the school years and beyond' (Commonwealth of Australia, 2009, p. 6). Most tellingly they were now expected to develop 'an increasingly broad repertoire of spoken, written <u>and</u> multimodal texts' (Commonwealth of Australia, 2009, p. 5). On each of these four challenges, our project aimed to investigate the potential of systemic functional grammatics to key tasks of English and unearth the conditions that made it 'good enough' for ordinary teachers working at four different stages of schooling (see Macken-Horarik, Love & Unsworth, 2011 for a full account of this context).

An immediate problem in tackling these issues was the term 'grammar' itself, which has a double meaning. In the Australian curriculum, grammar is defined as "the language we use <u>and</u> the description of language as a system" (Commonwealth of Australia, 2009, p. 5). Talk of grammar tends to obscure the nature of the object of reflection. Are we referring to language usage or to the description of this? Observing the difficulties created by such confusion, Michael Halliday wrote:

> All systematic knowledge takes the form of 'language about' some phenomenon; but whereas the natural sciences are language about nature, and the social sciences are language about society, linguistics is language about language – 'language turned back on itself' in Firth's oft-quoted formulation. … How does one keep apart the object language from the metalanguage – the phenomenon itself from the theoretical study of that phenomenon?'
>
> *(Halliday, 2002, p. 384)*

Halliday has attempted to resolve the category problem by distinguishing between 'grammatics' (as metalanguage) and grammar (as language). In an essay co-authored with Christian Matthiessen, he explains this distinction:

> So as to maintain the distinction between grammar and theories of grammar, we shall call theory of grammar 'grammatics'. The distinction is analogous to that between language and linguistics, or between society and sociology. The difficulty is that people often use the same term for both the phenomenon and its study: e.g. we speak of the 'grammar of English' (the phenomenon) but also of 'traditional grammar' (one theory of the phenomenon). We could clarify this situation if we called the second 'traditional grammatics'. Our concern here is thus with systemic-functional grammatics.
>
> *(Halliday & Matthiessen, 2009, p. 1)*

This clarifies the relationship between the two categories: grammar is the resource we use when we produce (or interpret) wordings in a language and grammatics is the theory we use to reflect on this. Of course, like other phenomena of study, grammar is interpreted differently within distinctive theories of language. There are different kinds of grammatics – traditional school grammatics, structuralist grammatics and transformational (generative) grammatics, along with others having a functional orientation. Systemic functional grammatics is one of the latter: it takes the size, complexity and multifaceted nature of language in the everyday life of society as its starting point, including what Halliday often calls 'the mess'.

Systemic functional theory has a powerful set of affordances in addressing such phenomena. All grammarians pay special attention to units of form at the level of sentence and clause. In this sense, they 'turn language back on itself' to describe regularities in linguistic forms. For this reason, some degree of slippage between usage and label is probably inevitable. But systemic functional grammatics interprets form in functional ways. For example, within the system of TRANSITIVITY, it labels nominal groups in a **Material Process** clause such that their role as **Actor** or **Goal** is clear.[2] A Material Process is a verbal group that 'does' something while a **Mental Process** is a verbal group that 'senses' something. The same approach is applied in other systems like **Mood**. A clause is a means not only for representing experience but of interacting with others – for proposing courses of action, expressing opinions, asking questions, commanding another, offering a service. These mini speech acts are managed through the predicative power of a grammatical **Subject** and a **Finite verb**, along with additional elements like a **Complement** or **Object**. In simple clauses like 'She stood on the headland' or 'She watched the sea', the Subject is the third person pronoun ('She') and 'agrees' with each of the finite verbs ('stood' and 'watched'). If we turn these statements into questions, we change the order of Subject and finite verb and, in the process, change the nature of the exchange they initiate. Interrogative question forms begin with the finite verb, which precedes the Subject, as in '<u>Did</u> she stand on the headland?' and '<u>Did</u> she watch the sea?' Managing Subject verb agreement and word order is crucial both to the formal arrangement of sentences and to the speech acts these enact. If we ask a question, we position our listener as informant whereas if we make a statement, we establish the other in our dialogue as 'receiver' of information. We manage our interactions in part through control of clause structure and its functions.

While control of grammatical structure is crucial, it is not the starting point in a functional grammatics. In studies of sentence combining in writing instruction, for example, students are often asked to integrate material in a series of simple sentences into the one macro-sentence (Graham & Perin, 2007). In a functional grammatics, the same task would have a more rhetorical orientation, with students introduced to resources for expanding clauses such as **Elaboration**, **Enhancement** and **Extension** (Halliday & Matthiessen, 2004, p. 395–396). Elaboration is favoured in reformulating a clause message, perhaps making it more concrete or abstract; Enhancement provides temporal, spatial, causal details in a new clause; Extension is used to provide additional or alternative information. In other words, it is not just the combination of clauses that matter but their semantic role in building meaning within a sentence. In combining clauses and (later) learning to integrate them through nominalization, students come to exploit the formal and functional significance of grammar.

This is not to suggest that functional grammatics is the only theory with a semantic orientation, but that this is elevated to a principle of design in its conceptual architecture. Control of grammatical structure *is* important. However, as Halliday explains, grammar is first and foremost a meaning-making resource. He elaborates on this stance in the third edition of *Introduction to Functional Grammar* (revised by Christian Matthiessen):

> The perspective moves away from structure to consideration of grammar as system, enabling us to show the grammar as a meaning-making resource and to describe grammatical categories by reference to what they mean. This perspective is essential if the analysis of grammar is to be an insightful mode of entry to the study of discourse.
>
> *(Halliday & Matthiessen, 2004, p. 10)*

Systemic functional theory offers much to the process of re-imagining the potential of grammatical instruction for school English. In reviewing current models of linguistics for education, Hancock has argued that it holds promise because it "heals the split between grammar and meaning" (Hancock, 2009, p. 201). But its nature and scope cannot be taken as 'given'. In fact, Halliday maintains that grammatics "has no domain until it defines one for itself (or until one is defined for it within general linguistics – exactly at what point the term grammatics takes over from linguistics is immaterial)" (Halliday, 2002, p. 386). Defining the scope of grammatics in a text-centred discipline like English is crucial. But of course, this raises the question of how far we can stretch a grammatical metalanguage. For Halliday, having a base in wording is a crucial feature of grammatics:

> Now one special kind of semiotic system is one that has a grammar in it: such a system 'means' in two senses, having a distinct phase of wording serving as the base for the construction of meaning. In other words, its 'content plane' contains a grammar as well as a semantics.
>
> *(Halliday, 2002, pp. 387–388)*

If wordings are crucial to a grammatics, to what extent can we draw on it to explore multimodal texts? It is important that students learn to enjoy and understand the comic force of parallel narratives in picture books like *Rosie's Walk* (Hutchins, 1968), gender reversals in *Piggybook* (Browne 1986/1996) and (probably in senior years) the combined action of image, verbiage and layout in graphic novels like *Maus* (Spiegelman, 1980). In consequence, teachers who introduce students to the semiotic workings of such texts need metalanguages adequate to these. If this is a curricula demand, it takes us beyond questions of teacher preference and puts creation of an adequate metalanguage firmly on the agenda.

The Australian curriculum for English (AC:E) is ambitious about study of images and multimodal texts generally (ACARA, 2009, 2012). As early as Year 2, for example, children are expected to "identify visual representations of characters' actions, reactions, speech and thought processes in narratives, and consider how these images add to or contradict or multiply the meaning of accompanying words" (ACELA 1469).³ By Year 5, they "Explain sequences of images in print texts and compare these to the ways hyperlinked digital texts are organized, explaining their effect on viewers' interpretations" (ACELA 1511). And expectations of metalanguage continue to rise in high school. In Year 7, for example, students are expected to "compare the ways that language and images are used to create character" (ACELT 1621). In Year 8, they "explore and explain the ways authors combine different modes and media in creating texts and the impact of these choices on the viewer/listener" (ACELY 1735). Then in Year 9, they "analyse and explain the use of symbols, icons and myth in still and moving images and *how these augment meaning*" (ACELA 1510).

Our highlighting of augmentation in the content description above is deliberate. It draws attention not just to the ambition of the curriculum when it comes to multimodality but to the limits of current understanding about just how readers draw on and integrate meaning cues in different modes in interpreting texts (see Unsworth, 2014 and Unsworth & Chan, 2009 for discussion). A multimodal metalanguage is not only a disciplinary (and arguably an ethical) responsibility, but a semiotic one. We use the word 'semiotic' advisedly. Semiotics is the study of meaning and meaning making in texts. This includes but transcends linguistically-mediated meaning. It creates immediate problems for our extension of grammatics to analysis of non-linguistic modes. As a key theorist of multimodality argues:

> [A] linguistic theory cannot provide a full account of what literacy does or is; language alone cannot give us access to the meaning of a multimodally constituted message; language and literacy have to be seen as the partial bearers of meaning only.
>
> *(Kress, 2003, p. 35)*

In developing a grammatics 'good enough' for English (Macken-Horarik, 2012), we needed to recognize that we were expanding the toolkit beyond the purview of verbal communication. We felt that this was necessary in The Grammatics Project if we were to engage with the communicative modes that are now part of English (ACARA, 2012). If we adopted a different metalanguage for each mode, we risked over-crowding, even atomizing, interpretation of texts. Theo van Leeuwen contextualizes the issue this way:

> Traditionally words and pictures have been analyzed in quite different ways. Different disciplines, different terminologies, different methodologies, and different criteria of relevance grew up for each: linguistics for language, art history for pictures – and for children's drawings mostly Piaget-inspired developmental psychology. … This made it difficult to compare the two, to investigate, for instance, whether a text and its illustration, or a photo and its caption derive from the same underlying construction of the reality that is being represented.
>
> *(van Leeuwen, 2005, p. 276)*

The question is whether we can develop common principles, common semiotic functions and even a common terminology for multimodal analysis in school English. Research informed by systemic functional theory has pursued this line of inquiry in analysis of images (Kress & van Leeuwen, 2006), artworks (O'Toole, 1994) and even film narratives (Bateman, 2013). These excursions have been promising and, as we revealed above, profoundly influenced curriculum development in Australia and other countries. However, their implications for interpretation and composition need consideration. If students are asked to compare meanings made in photo and caption, text and illustration and perhaps music and montage in film narration, they require a common terminology to integrate their analyses in an interpretive response in ways acceptable to English teachers. In the domain of literary study, for example, the principle of metafunction (which we explain below) can be brought to bear on interpretation of narrative and on questions of ethos, logos and pathos in persuasion. Within the interpersonal metafunction, we can move between modes to explore point of view, voicing and attitude. As we hope to show in chapters to come, a common terminology can differentiate and enrich interpretation of multimodal communication.

It *is* possible to widen the purview of a grammatics once we accept a meaning-centred view of language. In fact, discourse theorists like Jim Martin have extended systemic functional principles like system, stratification and metafunctions to larger frames of meaning – what Martin calls 'discourse semantics' (Martin, 1992). In this interpretation, sentences are not studied in isolation but 'as part of the text' (Halliday & Matthiessen, 2009). It is our view that without this perspective, we cannot move in a principled way from study of grammar to interpretation of the patterns of meaning these make in texts. This is not to suggest that Martin would endorse the view we have taken – that the principles of grammatics can be extended to an exploration of texts. In his book with Matthiessen and Painter, Martin maintains:

> [A]n analysis based solely on grammar, however rich, is not a complete analysis, since relationships between sentences (between clause complexes) still have to be accounted for. To interpret these relations beyond the clause, we need a model of text structure, and a model of social context.
>
> *(Martin, Matthiessen & Painter, 2010, p. 272)*

In a text-based discipline like English, the role of grammar needs to be conceptualized so as to link forms not just to functions, but to patterns of meaning in texts. But as Martin argues, it also needs to be related to text structure and to the social contexts in which it is used. And the social environment is becoming increasingly complex, requiring a new grammatics.

Not only are young people more intensively engaged with multimodal communication in everyday interactions, the texts themselves exist in different versions. We are seeing works of literature for children and young people simultaneously available in paper and digital multimedia in the form of books, graphic novels and live action and animated movies. Even when the versions of these stories in different modes are ostensibly very similar, there are significant differences in the interpretive possibilities of each version (Unsworth, 2006, 2013, 2014a, 2014b, 2014c). Authors of literature for children and young people are now beginning to publish their works simultaneously in book format and as iPad apps (Zhao & Unsworth, 2017). For at least a decade, many young people have become online authors, constructing their identities in various social contexts: social, fantasy, role-playing; and for various social purposes through images and language to develop a full sense of presence online and to communicate with their peers (Chandler-Olcott & Mahar, 2003; Hansford & Adlington, 2009; Thomas, 2007; Unsworth & Thomas, 2014). Engaging with the texts of this digital environment and new forms of textuality cannot be left for later days and future teachers.

The teachers who joined The Grammatics Project in 2011 were being asked to implement a national curriculum with a vastly expanded purview and to teach a grammatics relevant to this multimodal environment. In the process of finding their way through this new territory, they were asking questions like: What is the role of formal, functional and semantic knowledge about language in this context? How do we develop shared understandings with learners so they can innovate on these resources in their composition of texts? Answering such questions requires a lot of any grammatics. Posing them is a crucial starting point if teachers and students are to navigate this territory effectively.

Finding directions in the territory using four points on a theoretical compass

It is one thing to assert that school English is currently morphing in contact with a rapidly expanding digital and curriculum environment; it is quite another to develop navigational tools to explore this (relatively) unfamiliar territory. And of course, much of the English curriculum is not new. Study of literary texts is a constant, along with the expectation that students will produce coherent, well-reasoned and apposite responses to these. The literary canon may have expanded to include new works in a range of modes but exploration of highly valued texts is central to the work of English. New literacies may have begun to penetrate classroom work, making it likely that students will produce blogs, contribute to wikis and Facebook pages, even YouTube videos on topics of interest. But students are still expected to answer comprehension questions, identify problems in spelling, punctuation and grammar in written texts and generally manage traditional literacies. Our challenge is to develop a toolkit for exploring the grammar of traditional and digital literacies, canonical and new works of literature and familiar and unfamiliar forms of textuality. This book represents one step in this direction, re-imagining the possibilities of grammatically informed instruction.

Our strategy in undertaking this task is to orient each chapter towards some point on a theoretical compass that helps 'wayfarers' find directions to different regions in the territory of English. We introduce each compass point briefly below, touching on some of the tools in functional grammatics that (we think) help make the journey more manageable. In this task, we attempt to introduce key principles of systemic functional grammatics and to show how they can be adapted to the demands and possibilities of English.

'True North' – English and its disciplinary practices

The first point on our compass concerns disciplinary practices. But what is distinctive about the practices of English? Communication surely – lots of textual practices. More precisely, English focusses on key domains of textual practice – narrative, argument and interpretation. In the first of these, we know that narratives are temporally organized texts that focus on problems in human experience. They include a diverse family of texts, including fables, short stories, novels, picture books, graphic novels, feature films. And narratives vary in the nature of experience they explore (whether character or plot-driven), point of view, textual organization and mode. In the second domain, persuasion, we include political speeches, editorials, expository essays, advertisements, campaign brochures, blogs or expert panels on television. As key genre within this family, argument is often the focus of national tests of literacy. In preparing for such tests, teachers often teach students about the structure of **Exposition** – how to develop an opening paragraph that contains a thesis (or position on an issue), to back up claims with evidence and accumulate points in the re-iteration stage of the argument. But, as students go on in English, the nature of argumentation changes or, perhaps better, develops. Students not only learn about the features of Discussions and Critiques, they explore new forms of reasoning and learn how to integrate arguments in essayist texts. English students profit hugely from understanding the language features of texts produced in civic, promotional and academic domains (Humphrey, 2017).

So here is the first point on the compass: the demands and possibilities of English as a discipline, its 'true north'. The word discipline suggests singularity, but there are many ways of reading and writing narratives – hence our emphasis on the plural form of 'practices'. For example, as Chapter 8 shows, students can read a picture book like Anthony Browne's *The Tunnel* (1989) in terms of its storyline, its theme or its semiotic character as a multimodal artefact. In looking closely at the semantic features of responses, the grammatics can shed light on pedagogic practices that shift students into more productive readings of literary texts. In this role, it must be attuned to concepts in literary theory, in this case narratology. Its role is to inform intuitions about point of view, dialogue, metaphor, plotting or characterization in narrative, showing how these are 'grammaticalised'. A verbal text is, after all, made of language, so to speak, and the grammatics must provide insight into its workings, at least if it is to be useful to literary study. A key theoretical resource is the principle of *metafunctions*.

Early in his development of systemic functional theory, Halliday observed that certain language features tended to cluster together depending on their sensitivity to contextual parameters. Some language features were called forth by social roles and relationships (interpersonal meanings), some by social activity (ideational meanings) and others to the channel of communication adopted (textual meanings). Halliday proposed a 'hook-up' between contextual variables and meanings and argued that our implicit awareness of the connection between context and meaning enables us to predict with a reasonable expectation of success what is to come in the flow of discourse (Halliday, 1978). Like the rainbow with its diverse spectrum of colours, a text is a construct that refracts (and constructs) meanings about experience, engages an audience interpersonally and embodies design features of composition. But the same applies to the individual messages that make up a text. Each message is meaningful such that "you can put any spin (interpersonal) on any topic (experiential) at any discursive moment (textual)" (Halliday, 2008, p. 47).

In The Grammatics Project introduced above, we generated an interface with disciplinary practices through the notion of metafunctions. We suggested that teachers think of each metafunction as a different lens on meaning in a text. An ideational lens reveals meaning as content (what the text is about) and as logic (how the messages of the text are developed). An interpersonal lens brings interactive and evaluative meanings into view (how a text positions an audience to see, feel or judge things). A textual lens highlights composition (how texture, balance and signposting and salience work).

The concept of metafunctions is not limited to linguistic meanings. As a portable tool it has been applied to semiotic systems like art (Kress & van Leeuwen, 2006; O'Toole, 1994), music (van Leeuwen, 1999), action (Martinec, 2001), body language (Hood, 2010), picture books (Painter, Martin & Unsworth, 2013) and cultural systems generally (see, for example, Lemke, 1990, 1995). Though in some cases it is more difficult to apply the lenses (e.g. ideational meaning in music), the meanings made in each practice can be probed from the point of view of ideational, interpersonal and textual meaning. This is not to suggest that these modes are 'the same' but that we can draw on analogies between strategies used in one mode and similar strategies in another. We can apply this notion to the concept of internal focalization, for example. Focalization is a narrative strategy for representing experience through the eyes of a character (Genette, 1980). In a verbal narrative, authors manage this grammatically through resources like Mental Processes, the **Projection** of **Ideas** and attitudinal language associated with this character. Visually, internal focalization is achieved through aligning the viewer's gaze with that of a given character (Painter *et al.*, p. 137). Perception is common to both modes and we can exploit the presence of the perceiving gaze in our metalanguage, bringing depth of understanding to meaning making and to the grammatics.

The 'Wild' West – understanding the organization of semiotic resources

No one can doubt that English teachers need to pay attention to narrative and to both meaning and form in narrative and persuasion. But *which* aspects of the giant resource that we call the English language are relevant to *which* aspects of texts? Here we touch on the second point on our compass – language and image as resources for making meaning. For many teachers of English, this is where the territory becomes far more complex and the technical demands of any grammatics more forbidding. For some, this is the equivalent of the wild west of school English, which is, as Shakespeare wrote, 'the undiscovered country, from whose bourn no traveller returns'! But of course, this fear is wildly overstated. It is often as simple as a lack of instruction in language as system and of how to relate grammatical forms to their function and from there to 'step up' to higher levels of organization in texts. For most high school English teachers, pre-service training featured a limited (and often narrowly conceived) introduction to linguistic subject knowledge. And study of grammar was the poor relation. It is important to note, however, that the situation was not the same for teachers of English as an additional language or dialect. In fact, important research is emerging in contexts where English Language Learners (ELLs) learn academic language (e.g. Brisk, 2015; Moore & Schleppegrell, 2014; Schleppegrell, 2013).

For teachers of English in mainstream classrooms, even knowing 'where they are' in the complex architecture of language can be a problem. For example, just how do they distinguish between open class words like verbs, nouns, adjectives and adverbs and closed class words like prepositions, articles, conjunctions and pronouns? How do they describe the work these words do in larger constituents like groups, phrases and clauses? More ambitiously, how do they move from lower levels of description, explaining the contribution of grammatical choices to higher order meanings of texts? Systemic functional grammatics builds form, function and pattern into its account of language through the principle of *stratification*. Language is organized on several planes or strata and grammar has a special place in the content stratum of language. Halliday explains:

> We use language to make sense of our experience, and to carry out our interactions with other people. This means that the grammar has to interface with

what goes on outside language: with the happenings and conditions of the world, and the social processes we engage in. But at the same time it has to organize the construal of experience, and the enactment of social processes, so that they can be transformed into wording. The way it does this is by splitting the task into two. In step one, the interfacing part, experience and interpersonal relationships are transformed into meaning; this is the stratum of semantics. In step two, the meaning is further transformed into wording: this is the stratum of lexicogrammar. This is, of course, expressing it from the point of view of a speaker, or writer; for a listener, or reader, the steps are the other way round.

(Halliday & Matthiessen, 2004, pp. 24–25)

A stratified model of grammar is powerful because it is open to the environment through its interface with social realities (and theories of these). At the same time, it is internally organized: the semantic stratum transforms meanings into wordings (what Halliday calls lexicogrammar) which are realized through phonology (for speech) and graphology (for writing). The word 'realize' is a technical term in functional grammatics. It is intended to communicate the fact that language is a multiply-coded system with each level related symbolically. Grammatical forms 'realize' grammatical functions and both 'realize' experiences and interactions in the social environment. It is important to understand both the interface and the organization of language. Students must use grammar to build linguistic meanings and English teachers help them to do this in their daily interactions with learners. But they typically manage their acts of meaning intuitively, as experienced speakers and writers of English. Like mothers, teachers tend to mediate 'native' understandings of the relationship between meaning and wording rather than introducing students to grammatically informed understanding of language. But such knowledge is both crucial and problematic for the profession as we indicated earlier. It is not just important in its own right though. It is pertinent to big questions in the study of narrative and rhetoric. For example, understanding the system of TENSE is relevant to questions like why present tense is a marked option in narrative; the system of PERSON enables us to tackle differences between third-person and first-person narration; the system of PROJECTION is relevant to analysis of how 'free indirect discourse' insinuates readers into the consciousness of characters without doing so explicitly. It is also crucial to an understanding of how citation works in argument.

In a stratified account of language, answering such questions means adopting what Halliday calls 'trinocular vision':

When we are observing and investigating language, or any other semiotic system, our vision is essentially *trinocular*. We observe the phenomenon we want to explore – say, the lexicogrammar of a language – from three points of vantage. We observe it from above, in terms of its function in various contexts. We observe it from below, in terms of its various modes of expression.

And thirdly, we observe it from its own level: from within or round about, according to whether we are focusing on the whole or on some of its parts.

(Halliday, 2008, p. 141)

In The Grammatics Project, we introduced teachers to the principle of stratification using the metaphor of 'landing places'. It is common in much curriculum parlance to refer to language study at three levels – text, sentence and word. This is a handy rule of thumb for managing the reality of different levels of organization in language. But it is perhaps more useful to refer to the kinds of work that we undertake on each level – the ability to identify a grammatical unit; the ability to describe the function or role of this unit in a 'stream' of sound or writing; and the ability to interpret and explain the patterns into which this and other units fall in (a phase or stage of) text. All three landing places are important in distributing the study in functional grammatics and shifting gears from lower to higher levels of organization in language. But they involve different kinds of work (and different metalanguages).

Table 1.1 presents one adaptation of the principle of stratification using the metaphor of 'landing places' in study of texts. For purposes of explication, we suggest the kinds of talk that would be common at each level, based on work we did with teachers on the novel *Blueback* by Tim Winton (1997).

Of course, we have already taken for granted that teachers and students can recognize a unit of form and meaning in a stream of wordings, and this is not very fair, especially given that many are not sure about the basis on which units can be identified. We have referred to **Finites** and **Subjects** without really stopping to check that all those on the journey can distinguish a verb from a noun or, at a higher rank, a verbal group from a nominal (or noun) group. A map to guide processes of exploration in unfamiliar territory (what we are calling 'the wild west' should enable wayfarers to find a location using coordinates on different axes (X and Y perhaps), drawing on agreed conventions for representing scale or distance between one point and another on the map. We need to ensure we can calibrate our

TABLE 1.1 Applying the notion of stratification to narrative grammatics

Three steps in using grammatics

- **Identification** of a unit of form and meaning in the stream of writing (or speaking). Knowing <u>what</u> you are looking at: Is it a verb group, a noun group, an adverbial or prepositional phrase?
- **Description** of the function of the unit in a clause or sentence – <u>how</u> it works (e.g. the verb group tells us about the character's feeling, action, state or saying).
- **Interpretation and Explanation** of the patterns of choice in a text – <u>why</u> it might work this way (e.g. "I notice that in this narrative, there is a back and forth pattern between doing and saying or doing and sensing (action and reaction)" or "You can see that the author relies mostly on subtle covert attitude to shape our response to Abel's undersea world" or "Look at this evaluation stage! It halts the action and lets us in on Abel's love of his mother".

readings of a feature and its distance from us or from another feature. This is part of the process we go through when we begin orienteering: we learn to read the conventions that indicate a copse of trees and distinguish these from a rock form or a river and thus more quickly apprehend how to get from one point to another in minimum time. The same thing applies to grammatical analysis: we need a map of language that will "enable us to locate exactly where we are at any point along the route" (Halliday & Matthiessen, 2004, p. 19). The principle of stratification locates us in the general territory of language and other semiotic resources, whether in context, in semantics, in grammar or in the output in speech or writing (or signing in fact). But even more precision is required because lexicogrammar is not all of a piece. It is internally differentiated, like other features in a landscape that need a closer look. In order to explore this, we make use of the principle of *rank*.

Despite the appeal of simple rules of thumb in curriculum documents such as 'the level of the sentence', it does not take us very far in grammatics. A sentence is often defined as a string of written words that communicates a message and makes complete sense. This is useful as far as it goes, but really it is the clause that is central to syntactic 'sense'. In fact, in any grammatics, we begin with the clause and its constitutive features rather than the sentence. Every clause contains a verbal group that consists of one or more verbs and these 'realize' different processes in experience that we referred to earlier. The following examples are single clause (simple) sentences with verbal groups underlined:

> Down in the valley there <u>were</u> three farms.
> The room <u>was</u> quiet in the darkness of early evening.
> Great, round boulders and dark cracks <u>loomed</u> below.

A sentence often contains more than one clause and these can be independent (able to stand alone) or dependent (unable to stand alone). A sentence that contains two or more independent clauses is called a compound sentence with clauses joined by a **Co-ordinating Conjunction**, e.g. *and, or, either/neither, but, yet, so, then*. The compound sentences below display co-ordinating conjunctions in italics and verbal groups underlined.

> He <u>was</u> as thin as a pencil *and* (was) the cleverest of them all.
> Abel <u>screamed</u> in his snorkel *and* <u>pushed</u> hard off the bottom *but* the big blue shadow suddenly <u>had</u> him by the hand.
> It <u>would be</u> an embarrassing interview, *yet* only rudeness <u>was</u> effective.

A sentence that contains one or more dependent clauses is called a complex sentence. The dependent or subordinate clause is joined by **Subordinating Conjunctions** such as *when, while, before, after, because, if, although, unless, since, that* and *whether*. The dependent clause can be introduced by either a **Finite** or **Non-Finite** verb (underlined), explained further in Chapter 3. In the following examples, we have indicated clause boundaries with a double slash, as in || ... ||.

English through functional grammatics 17

> Every evening *as soon as* it <u>got</u> dark, || Mr Fox would ask Mrs Fox for her order.
> It was so still || that he <u>could hear</u> the turning of pages in the next room || *as* his son <u>leafed</u> through a picture book.

And, of course, a sentence can include both kinds of clauses – dependent and independent. The compound-complex sentence is common in literate discourse, even in texts for younger readers. In the example below, the embedded clause is indicated with double square brackets, as in [[...]].

> And *when* Mrs Fox <u>had told</u> him [[what she <u>wanted</u>]], || Mr Fox <u>would creep</u> down into the valley in the darkness of the night || *and* <u>help</u> himself.

Although we have been talking about relationships *between* clauses in sentences, it may be useful to explain another kind of relationship *within* clauses that is a feature of written language – what Halliday calls **Embedding**. Systemic functional grammatics interprets embedded clauses as different from dependent clauses. An embedded clause is down-ranked, operating at the same or a lower rank in a group or phrase. It is a powerful strategy for boosting the information load of a clause and often qualifies a nominal group, providing additional information about the head noun. Sometimes an embedded clause stands in place of a group at clause rank. Here are examples of a clause or clauses embedded in a nominal (noun) group, with verbal groups in italics:

> All three of them were about as nasty and mean [[as any men you *could meet*]].
> You *are* the man [[whose scientific work *is* more likely than that of any other man || *to end* the human race's chance for survival]].
> [[What this *means*]] is [[that science *is* the only concern]].

In this last example, we have a sentence that consists of two embedded clauses, with most of the 'meat' compressed into the nominal group and its embedded material. Often one embedded clause is equated with another as in the final example above. Such grammatical patterns are typical of literate, abstract and scientific discourse and can be very challenging to process for young readers. If teachers are to be able to recognize the source of the difficulty, and to exploit the potential of nominalization in teaching writing, they need to know that clauses consist of groups or phrases that themselves consist of words and that sometimes a unit from a higher rank (like a clause) can be embedded in a lower one (like a group or phrase). In other words, when looking closely at wordings in written language, teachers need to know about the rank scale.

Some teachers (and some approaches to grammar) argue that this complicates grammar too much and that we can identify the components of a sentence by simply pointing to the individual words, as in the following sentence from *Blueback*:

> He   fell   back   into   the   water   with   a   cold   crash

However, we miss so much meaning if we ignore how words work together in this sentence and the functions the groups and phrases serve in the clause. A 'words-in-sentences' model of grammar ignores important aspects of meaning and can lead to impossible complexity in analysis of real-life discourse. "Describing a sentence as a construction of words is rather like describing a house as a construction of bricks, without recognizing the walls and the rooms as intermediate structural units" (Halliday & Matthiessen, 2004, p. 310). Grouping the words in functional ways makes it easier to show how they create meanings about action but also about the circumstances surrounding actions (e.g. where they occur and how in the sentence above).

We can only skate across the surface of the architecture of grammar within the content strata of language in this chapter. A simpler, more parsimonious, model may be easier to learn, and more familiar to teachers of English, but as Halliday states:

> (L)anguage is complicated and there is no point in pretending that it is simple. The problem is to recognize which aspects of the theory are relevant to a given task; and that does entail having some acquaintance with the whole.
>
> *(Halliday, 2009, p. 61)*

Our concern in the introduction to grammatics here is to balance adequacy to 'the whole' of language against the practical needs and starting points of teachers who often have a fragmentary knowledge of language. A working knowledge of design principles like stratification and rank should help make the journey into language knowledge more tractable and the features of the environment recognisable. The principle of stratification enables us to locate ourselves in the territory ('where we are' in our work on text, sentence or word levels of organization, or, as we showed above, in the intermediate levels of clause, group or phrase). The principle of rank enables us to identify units of form and meaning in a string of wordings and to label these appropriately. This is so important if we want to explore the effect of a description in a nominal group, a powerful verb or a circumstantial meaning in a prepositional phrase. It focusses our attention precisely on the unit of meaning and form we need to discuss. Managing the complexity of language as a vast resource for meaning has meant attempting to translate such principles into accessible (even metaphoric) categories like landing places, viewpoints and lenses. This work of translation is only at a beginning but we take it up greater detail in the Chapters 3 (for narrative) and 6 (for persuasion).

Moving South – building students' repertoires over time

The south point of our compass moves from the territory of disciplinary practices to the development of students' repertoires. This is the region where teachers turn knowledge into know-how, attuned to "the ongoing process in which this is used, transformed, enhanced, and attuned to situations" (Bereiter & Scardamalia, 1993, p. 46). It can take place over a shorter or a longer time frame. In our book, we focus on the longer time frame of schooling, often a hard trudge for many teachers. The practical and rhetorical relevance of grammatical knowledge is captured well in a paper framing development of the AC:E:

> The goal of teaching grammar and textual patterns should *go beyond* students' labelling of various grammatical categories; it should centre on goals such as clearer expression of thought, more convincing argumentation, more careful logic in reasoning, more coherence, precision and imagination in speaking and writing, and knowing how to choose words and grammatical and textual structures that are more appropriate to the audience or readership. The goal here centres on the gradually more powerful conversion of 'knowledge about' language into a resource for effective reading listening, writing, speaking and designing.
>
> *(ACARA, 2009, p. 6)*

A repertoire is a stock or store of songs, plays, or routines that we can access and 'perform' when called upon. In the world beyond work, most people have hobbies – things we love to do and want to get better at. Often, we enrol in classes – music lessons, choirs, art classes, dance – just because we enjoy the activity. Over time, as we participate in communities of practice focussed on this activity, we build our repertoire. In the same way, students' literacy repertoires expand as they practice doing things in writing and reading, drawing on expert guidance in the process. But what kind of guidance do we need to provide as teachers? And what do we look for in our students' writing? Perhaps the first thing is that learners need to be motivated to begin a task – much like we are when we sign up for a class – fitness, yoga, pottery, karate, trombone or choir. Only if there is desire are they really motivated to learn something new. Stimulating this kind of motivation however, is something most English teachers are really good at. As a major study of the practices of Queensland teachers found, English teachers tend to be strong on 'social support' and on managing learning environments so students feel inclined to participate. But they are not often strong on 'intellectual challenge' (Luke, Ladwig, Lingard, Hayes & Mills, 1999). Another Australian study by Ken Johnston and Deb Hayes (2008) revealed that many classrooms are 'orderly restricted'; routines are clear and safe but challenges remain low. In this book, we assume that a learning task informed by grammatics should be interesting in its own right *and* challenging for learners as they learn to read and write texts in English.

There are at least two aspects to repertoire development – a *creative* aspect – where students try new things, elaborate or innovate on an idea, for example; and there is a *control* aspect – where they learn how to manage and direct the flow of ideas. Learning to tell or write engaging narratives involves development of an interest in the potential of the genre – how to create a gloomy setting, make a reader or listener empathize with a character or hate him or her, build a mythical world which is both credible *and* fantastic, generate funny dialogue and so on. But it is also about coherent compositions, sentences that make clear propositional sense, dialogue where readers understand who is saying what to whom, descriptions that create a vivid and clear picture of a character and so on. In short, repertoire growth is a matter of experiment (creative excursions of different kinds) and control (management of excursions in the interests of clarity, sense and coherence). And teachers have a crucial role to play in development of both aspects.

In our work with teachers, we drew productively on the teaching learning cycle first popularised in genre-based approaches to literacy teaching (Rose & Martin, 2005; Rose & Martin, 2012; Rothery, 1989 & 1994). This pedagogy is informed by principles of scaffolding associated with the socio-cultural model of development associated with Lev Vygotsky and Jerome Bruner (1986). In this approach, a teacher selects an age-appropriate text for ongoing classroom work. The text is typically beyond what the student can read independently, with the steps within the sequence structured to support students so that they can successfully work within their 'zone of proximal development' (Vygotsky, 1978). Using the selected text, the cycle provides predictable teaching-learning routines for both teacher and student, moving from co-contextualisation, modelling, fluent reading, grammatically-informed analysis, guided practice (sometimes called 'joint construction') and then into independent writing.

Teachers begin by building the context of learning, orienting students to the disciplinary knowledge relevant to the focal or mentor text. A key aim of scaffolding pedagogy is to bridge any cultural and semantic gaps between the text content and learners' experiences. Rather than relying upon more familiar pre-reading prediction strategies such as questioning "What do you think this story is about?" or "What do you think will happen next?", students are 'told' the text in a story telling mode. When it comes to multimodal texts, teachers typically draw children's attention to the images and what they contribute to the text's meaning. In orienting the students to the text, teachers are encouraged to use the wordings of the text, especially those likely to be difficult for students. In this way, they are supported in their text predictions, better able to 'participate in the meanings of the text' (Freebody & Luke, 1990).

Any pedagogy that aims to engage learners with challenging texts needs to be maximally supportive especially in early phases of repertoire building. It is important to use a predictable teaching sequence that sets all students up for success in their reading and writing by making the 'ground rules' for participation in classroom interactions very explicit. This has been a guiding principle of the pedagogy known as Accelerated Literacy, which has informed our pedagogy chapters (Cowey, 2005, p. 4). Adequate orientation to meaning is essential if students are going to be able to decode, understand and later 'appropriate' language patterns in their own writing (Axford *et al.*, 2009; Rose & Martin, 2012).

Once a disciplinary context has been built, students are exposed to a model or mentor text in which key features to be explored through grammatics are on display. For example, having planned which aspects of narrative or rhetorical technique are to be taught, teachers typically use strategies such as highlighting of texts, identification of choices carrying focus meanings, even comparison of one text with others where different choices are made. The point here is to ensure that the text is not only accessible to all students but that key choices are visible to all. Teachers might assist students to identify and talk about parts of a text that contain focus features. Some will use a technical metalanguage and others will talk about the features in commonsense ways. What is crucial is that teachers can identify, describe and interpret the significance of the choices themselves. Their linguistic knowledge needs to be greater than that of their students, whether this is made explicit during modelling or not. In some classrooms, we have observed teachers inviting children up to a white board to underline words, phrases or sentences. In others, students work with a copy of the extract and highlight choices or even patterns of choice in texts. The key is to ensure that students cannot just recognize a grammatical unit in focus, but describe its function and interpret its contribution to patterns of meaning in the text as a whole.

Following modelling of features in the mentor text with attention to key extracts and opportunities to look closely at these, perhaps putting on different metafunctional lenses, students prepare for collaborative work on a new text (or part of a text). In this stage, students are supported to build knowledge of a new context so that they can jointly compose a text in the focus genre. In this task, they will be learning to incorporate the resources they have learned about earlier, with the teacher drawing on the grammatics to guide this work. For example, if the focus is on plotting, students might use a template prepared earlier as they mapped stages of narrative and identified key events occurring at each stage of the text. They may focus on techniques such as creation of suspense or handling of the crisis stage of a narrative. The plotting of events will support the class or group text, enabling learners to draw on this in suggesting wordings in the creation of the group narrative. A related strategy is used in producing an exposition in work on persuasion. Perhaps the students focus on citation of authorities using what they know of Projection; or they focus on inclusion of evidence using Expansion. The point is that guided practice depends on shared understandings about the genre to be produced and the purpose of the activity (including which aspects of the grammatics they need to focus on in their learning).

Once students are in a position to work independently, they can be encouraged to compose their own text. At this phase, they can draw freely on language (or image) patterns they have been exposed to in earlier phases of learning or they may prefer to experiment with the possibilities of the genre or a technique. Reflection on learning is central to this phase and can be undertaken in a range of ways – through classroom discussion, feedback on individual texts, conferences between teacher and student or student and other writers. At the heart of the learning is an invitation to discipline knowledge that counts and literacies that enable students to access this. There have been different versions of the teaching learning cycle. One we find particularly helpful is the model used by Sally Humphrey and Susan Feez (2016) and a recent publication by Humphrey that reports on research into disciplinary literacies. The following figure (Figure 1.1) represents the pedagogy we use in our work in this book.

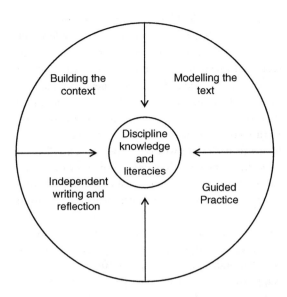

FIGURE 1.1 A text-based teaching learning cycle (adapted from Humphrey & Feez, 2016 and Humphrey, 2017).

It goes without saying that a grammatics that is going to foster students' literacy repertoires cannot be relegated only to the correction (control) side of the writing equation – checking sentences for sense, punctuation, paragraphing and so on. It should also lead to the development of ideas and to awareness of grammar as a resource for meaning in this enterprise. This is new territory for any grammatics – becoming associated with the development of meaning. Grammar and creativity – a new collocation for school English perhaps! But this is not really a matter for levity. It is hard to imagine that anyone composes a text thinking about subject–verb agreement, consistent use of tense, pronoun reference, nouns and verbs and adjectives. Such matters come into play post-fact, once a first draft is produced. As they move into independent work on writing, students learn to revise their writing, checking that it makes sense, works well. They can share with a fellow student, asking for feedback on it, focussing on the aspects of the task that have been the subject of earlier classroom work.

In sum, the grammatics has a role at both the creative and the control stages of independent writing. During a first draft stage, students need to be free to try our ideas, to expand a point, cite an authority, find a metaphor, produce an image based on the text. What matters at the message development stage are the ideas, the meanings, the direction of a composition. This is the point at which it gets interesting for students – where their narrative can take off in unexpected directions, a character can 'take over' and lead the writer down unplanned paths.

In this book, we assume that the grammatics needs to begin with meaning in its various aspects. In the case of narrative, this means consideration of how we build a plausible 'possible world' in which characters confront challenges in experience and try to resolve them; how to engage our readers with this world so they understand what is going on, empathize with the right characters, see the beauty of the world we are creating, feel scared when we want them to feel 'afraid, very afraid' and get the jokes in our character's dialogue; and beyond the experiential and the interpersonal, there is the textual aspect of meaning – how to produce a text that makes sense and hangs together. In the creative moment, a grammatics is simply attentive to the emergent meanings a student is working with. English is great at this – alive to the sudden joke, the unusual device, the quirky turn of phrase in a dialogue, the pathos in a character's reaction to loss or to the expression of intimacy. The first task for teachers is one of recognition – aliveness to meaning in its early phases of development in a text. Coming in too strongly with a red pen here often stifles the creative drive here and is likely to cruel the student's expressive and sometimes risky exploratory moves. The second is intervention – knowledge of how to open possibilities for meaning in a text through supportive and challenging pedagogy.

Tracking East – exploring texts of many kinds (and in different modes)

The East position on the compass points to where the sun rises and the new day is heralded by morning light. It suggests renewal, enlightenment. It orients us to a territory in school English where students engage with texts of many kinds and new experiences beckon. The East point on the compass indicates a domain often disconnected from grammar – texting, tweeting, googling and participating in other forms of social media. It's a familiar and sweet space for many children and young adults in the culture. But the visual and multimodal texts produced and consumed so continuously on Facebook, YouTube and Instagram do require scrutiny as well as participation. In this terrain, the grammatics can become a theoretical and metalinguistic resource for reflecting on wordings and images in texts. This is not a trivial matter, even if the texts are ubiquitous. World changing events are often mediated through texts that appear relatively mundane. One thinks of presidential tweets disclosing controversial changes to policy in the United States, of the photos appearing to provide 'evidence' of the preparation of weapons of mass destruction in Iraq and justify the disastrous US-led invasion of Iraq and of momentous WikiLeaks disclosures. Critical scrutiny of such texts and of the social conditions which give them salience is a vital aspect of the enlightenment possible in the territory of the East. Our book cannot of course deal with all such matters. But it does acknowledge the importance of a socially responsive (and responsible) grammatics in probing the choices made in such texts and exploring the implications of choices made (and how they could be made differently).

In a world of digital media, we deal with the everyday textual practices of citizens (snapchats with friends, 'likes' on Facebook, sharing of tweets). In this region, the grammatics must abandon a preoccupation with the forms of standard English and take on a research orientation to changes in grammar, observing, tracking, seeking understanding of choices and arrangements and patterns. The centrality of the notion of choice has become a feature of the design of systemic functional grammar. Halliday explains this as follows:

> In a systemic representation of language, the basic organizing concept is that of choice. A choice has two components: it consists of (1) a set of 'things', of which one must be chosen; and (2) an entry condition – the environment in which the choice is made. The environment of a choice could be thought of as a structural setting or background; but it can equally be represented as the combined outcome of a range of other choices. The formal representation of a choice is called (following Firth) a 'system'; hence, a choice network is a system network. The description of a language takes the form of system networks.
>
> *(Halliday, 1984, p. 7)*

The grammatics is predicated on the assumption that resources for meaning are organized into contrastive choices activated in particular environments. They represent differences in meaning 'that make a difference'. Whenever we communicate, we make selections from available options for meaning and give expression to these through forms like wordings or images (which are the focus in this book). In the system of TRANSITIVITY at clause rank, verbal groups give expression to (realize) processes of doing, sensing, saying or relating. It makes a difference to the experience we create whether we choose a Material Process (doing) or a Mental Process (sensing). In narrative, the latter is crucial to representation of a character's feelings, perceptions or thoughts, just as Verbal Processes (saying) are crucial to representation of what a character says. As Chapter 2 reveals, grammatical systems of MOOD, MODALITY and POLARITY enact options for interaction in the environment of the clause. **Declarative Mood** contrasts with **Interrogative Mood** and this difference is grammaticalised through the ordering of Subject and Finite verb.

The same principle of systemic contrast operates in visual communication. In the interpersonal domain, for example, we consider systems like FOCALIZATION, SOCIAL DISTANCE and ATTITUDE for enacting image-viewer relations. Understanding the distinctive either/or nature of choices in wordings and images is crucial to analysis of choices. It enables us (and our students) to see options for meaning that are available and then which ones are selected in particular texts (and social contexts). Alternative choices are represented in the form of system networks, revealing options that may be available but have not been taken up. This representation of choice has resonance for English teachers, albeit one that is more systematic than many everyday notions of choice as list or menu. Even if this is unconscious, teachers invoke the idea of available options whenever they invite students to reflect on and discuss a composer's choices in literary or persuasive texts. The system network is a powerful heuristic for exploring lexical, grammatical and semantic options. The following chapters present further details on systems deployed in the grammatics project and the ways in which teachers and students worked with them.

English is a field of diverse texts and ways of interpreting these. In this territory, we acknowledge the impact of new approaches to textuality, pedagogies of multiliteracies and the requirements that a grammatics be honed to deal with image and verbiage and their interplay in texts and with different versions of the same 'story'. Not only are young people more intensively engaged with multimodal communication in everyday interactions, the texts themselves exist in different versions. We now see works of literature for children and young people simultaneously available in paper and digital multimedia in the form of books, graphic novels and live action and animated movies. Even when versions of these stories in different modes are ostensibly similar, there are significant differences in the interpretive possibilities of each version (Unsworth, 2006, 2013, 2014a, 2014b, 2014c). Authors of literature for children and young people are now beginning to publish their works simultaneously in book format and as iPad 'apps' (Zhao & Unsworth, 2017). For at least a decade, many young people have become online authors, constructing their identities in various social contexts: social, fantasy, role-playing; and for various social purposes through images and language to develop a full sense of presence online and to communicate with their peers (Chandler-Olcott & Mahar, 2003; Hansford & Adlington, 2009; Thomas, 2007; Unsworth & Thomas, 2014). The grammatics aims to be relevant to texts (and different versions of the 'same' story) and to shed light on choices made in the texts and how their readers take them up.

Our focus on readers is deliberate there. The East is a territory not just of new experiences, but of transformations. At this point, we explore students' experiments with visualizations of verbal narrative like Winton's *Blueback* and even the nursery rhyme, *Humpty Dumpty*. It is in these less intensively monitored regions of semiosis that we find perhaps the most unexpected work with texts.

Preview of chapters

The following chapters represent our working out of the issues raised in an introductory way in this introduction. There are two major sections in the book, the first dealing with the domain of narrative and the second with persuasion. Each chapter deals with a key aspect of work in English related to that domain and indicated by the compass points.

The first section deals with the grammatics of narrative. Chapter 2 explores disciplinary practices around narrative and the necessary interface of a functional grammatics with investigation of narrative craft. The focus in this chapter is on published narratives. Chapter 3 looks closely at the grammatical organization of written narratives and adaptation of the grammatics for study of images. It focusses on how such knowledge can aid in understanding students' narrative compositions. Chapter 4 takes up the matter of pedagogy and how primary and secondary teachers can use grammatics in teaching narrative. The material here is based on data gathered over the course of the four-year grammatics project along with supplementary material where necessary.

26 English through functional grammatics

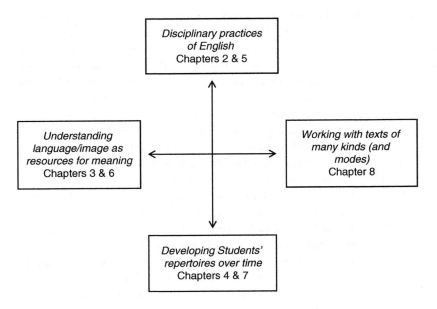

FIGURE 1.2 The territory of school English.

The second section deals with the grammatics of persuasion. Chapter 5 opens up disciplinary practices around persuasion and the interface of a functional grammatics with the rhetoric of young citizens and older leaders. Chapter 6 looks closely at grammatical organization of resources related to persuasion and focusses on the contribution this knowledge can make to an understanding of students' development in expository writing. Chapter 7 takes up the matter of pedagogy and how primary and secondary teachers can deploy the grammatics in teaching persuasion. Chapter 8 deals with some of the excursions possible with grammatics, particularly how we can use it to track students' transformations of meaning in visual, verbal and multimodal responses to texts.

Figure 1.2 presents the heuristic we use to explore the territory of school English through grammatics and the chapters that deal with each point on the compass.

Notes

1. The authors wish to acknowledge support from the Australian Research Council that funded a Discovery project from 2011–2014 (DP110104309) on which many insights in this book are based.
2. In systemic functional theory, when a functional technical term is used for the first time, initial letters are capitalised and the term is highlighted in bold. When a system within language or image is identified, it is put in small caps and when a systemic functional principle is first introduced, it is put in italics. Class labels are not distinguished in this way.
3. The acronyms in brackets following content descriptions refer to content strands and associated numbers for each aspect of the AC:E (2012). ACELT refers to literature; ACELA refers to language; and ACELY refers to literacy.

References

Andrews, R. (2005). Knowledge about the teaching of (sentence) grammar: The state of play. *English Teaching: Practice and Critique*, 4(3), 69–76.

Andrews, R., Torgerson, C., Beverton, S., Freeman, A., Locke, T., Low, G., Robinson, A. & Zhu, D. (2006). The effect of grammar teaching on writing development. *British Educational Research Journal*, 32(1), 39–55.

Australian Curriculum, Assessment and Reporting Authority (ACARA, formerly National Curriculum Board) (2009). *The shape of the Australian curriculum: English*. Retrieved from www.acara.edu.au.

Australian Curriculum Assessment and Reporting Authority (ACARA) (2012). *Australian curriculum: English*. Version 3.0. Sydney: ACARA. Retrieved from www.australiancurriculum.edu.au/English/Curriculum/F-10.

Bateman, J. (2013). Multimodal analysis of film within the GEM framework. *Ilha Do Desterro: A Journal of English Language, Literatures in English and Cultural Studies*, 64, 48–84.

Bereiter, C. & Scardamalia, M. (1993). *Surpassing ourselves: An inquiry into the nature and implications of expertise*. Chicago, IL: Open Court.

Braddock, R., Lloyd-Jones, R. & Schoer, L. (1963). *Research in written composition*. Urbana, IL: National Council of Teachers of English.

Brisk, M. (2015). *Engaging students in academic literacies: Genre-based pedagogy for K-5 classrooms*. New York: Routledge.

Browne, A. (1986/1996). *Piggybook*. London: Walker Books Ltd.

Browne, A. (1989). *The tunnel*. London: Julia McRae Books.

Bruner, J. (1986). *Actual minds, possible worlds*. Cambridge, MA: Harvard University Press.

Cajkler, W. & Hislam, J. (2002). Trainee teachers' grammatical knowledge: The tension between public expectations and individual competence. *Language Awareness*, 11(3), 161–177.

Cameron, D. (1995). *Verbal hygiene*. London: Routledge.

Carter, R. (1998). *Vocabulary: Applied linguistic perspectives* (2nd edition). London & New York: Routledge.

Chandler-Olcott, K. & Mahar, D. (2003). 'Tech-saviness' meets multiliteracies: Exploring adolescent girls' technology-related literacy practices. *Reading Research Quarterly*, 38(3), 356–385.

Christie, F. (2002). *Classroom discourse analysis*. London: Continuum.

Christie, F. & Derewianka, B. (2008). *School discourse: Learning to write across the years of schooling*. London: Continuum.

Commonwealth of Australia, 2005: Teaching Reading: Report and Recommendations [National Inquiry into the Teaching of Literacy]. Department of Education, Science & Training.

Commonwealth of Australia. (2009). *The shape of the Australian curriculum*. ACT, Australia: National Curriculum Board.

Cowey, W. (2005). A brief description of the National Accelerated Literacy Program. *TESOL in Context*, 15(2), 3–14.

Derewianka, B. (2012). Knowledge about language in the Australian Curriculum: English. *Australian Journal of Language and Literacy*, 35(2), 127–146.

Freebody, P. & Luke, A. (1990). Literacies' programs: Debates and demands in cultural context. *Prospect*, 5 (3), 7–15.

Gartland, L. B. & Smolkin, L. B. (2016). The histories and mysteries of grammar instruction: Supporting elementary teachers in the time of the Common Core. *The Reading Teacher.* 69(4), 391–399.

Gordon, E. (2005). Grammar in New Zealand schools: Two case studies. *English Teaching, Practice and Critique*, 4(3), pp. 48–68.

Graham, S. & Perin, D. 2007. A meta-analysis of writing instruction for adolescent students. *Journal of Educational Psychology*, 99, 445–476.

Gray, B. (2007). *Accelerating the literacy development of Indigenous students*. Darwin, Australia: CDU Press.

Halliday, M. A. K. (1978). *Language as social semiotic: The social interpretation of language and meaning*. London: Edward Arnold.

Halliday, M.A. K. (1984). Language as code and language as behaviour: A systemic-functional interpretation of the nature and ontogenesis of dialogue. In M.A.K Halliday, R. P. Fawcett, S. Lamb & A. Makkai (Eds.), *The semiotics of language and culture (Vol. 1)* (pp. 3–35). London: Frances Pinter.

Halliday, M. A. K. (1991/2007). The notion of 'context' in language education. In J. Webster (Ed.), *The collected works of M. A. K. Halliday: Language and education (Vol. 9)* (pp. 269–290). London & New York: Continuum.

Halliday, M. A. K. (2002). On grammar and grammatics. In J. Webster (Ed.), *The collected works of M. A. K. Halliday: On language and linguistics (Vol. 3)* (pp. 384–417). London: Continuum.

Halliday, M. A. K. (2008). *Complementarities in language*. Beijing: The Commercial Press.

Halliday, M. A. K. (2009). Methods-techniques-problems. In M.A.K. Halliday & J. Webster (Eds.), *Continuum companion to systemic functional linguistics* (pp. 59–86). London: Continuum.

Halliday, M. A. K. & Martin, J. (1993). *Writing science: Literacy and discursive Power*. London: Falmer.

Halliday, M. A. K. & Matthiessen, C. (2004). *An introduction to functional grammar* (3rd edition). London: Edward Arnold.

Halliday, M. A. K. & Matthiessen, C. (2009). *Systemic functional grammar: A first step into theory*. Beijing: Higher Education Press.

Hammond J. & Macken-Horarik, M. (2001). Teachers' voices, teachers' practices: Insider perspectives on literacy education, *Australian Journal of Language and Literacy*, 24(2), 112–132.

Hancock, C. (2009). How linguistics can inform the teaching of writing. In R. Beard, D. Myhill, J. Riley & M. Nystrand (Eds.), *The Sage handbook of writing development* (pp. 194–208). London: Sage.

Hansford, D. & Adlington, R. (2009). Digital spaces and young people's online authoring: Challenges for teachers. *Australian Journal of Education*, 32(1), 55–68.

Harper, H. & Rennie, J. (2009). "I had to go out and get myself a book on grammar": A study of pre-service teachers' knowledge about language. *Australian Journal of Language and Literacy*, 33(1), 22–37.

Hillocks, G. (1984). What works in teaching composition: A meta-analysis of experimental treatment studies. *American Journal of Education*, 93(1), 133–170.

Hood, S. (2010). *Appraising research: Evaluation in academic writing*. London: Palgrave, Macmillan.

Hood, S. (2011). Body language in face-to-face teaching: a focus on textual and interpersonal meaning. In S. Dreyfus, S. Hood and M. Stenglin (Eds), *Semiotic Margins: Meaning in Multimodalities*. London and New York: Continuum.

Hudson, D. & Walmsley, J. (2005). The English patient: English grammar and teaching in the twentieth century. *Journal of Linguistics*, 41(3), 593–622.

Humphrey, S. (2017). *Academic literacies in the Middle Years: A framework for enhancing teacher knowledge and student achievement*. New York & London: Routledge.

Humphrey, S. & Feez, S. (2016). Direct instruction fit for purpose: Applying a metalinguistic toolkit to enhance creative writing in the early secondary years. *Australian Journal of Language and Literacy*, 39(3), 207–219.

Humphrey, S., Love, K. & Droga, L. (2011). *Working grammar: An introduction for secondary English teachers*. Port Melbourne, Victoria: Pearson.

Hutchins, P. (1968). *Rosie's walk*. New York: Macmillan.
Johnston, K. & Hayes, D. (2008). "This is as good as it gets": Classroom lessons and learning in challenging circumstances. *Australian Journal of Language and Literacy*, 31(2), 109–127.
Jones, P. & Chen, H. (2012). Teachers' knowledge about language: Issues of pedagogy and expertise. *Australian Journal of Language and Literacy*, 35(2), 149–174.
Jones, S., Myhill, D. & Bailey, T. (2013). Grammar for writing? An investigation into the effect of contextualised grammar teaching on student writing. *Reading and Writing*, 26(8), 1241–1263.
Kolln, M. & Hancock, C. 2005. The story of English grammar in United States schools. *English Teaching: Practice and Critique*, 4(3), 11–31.
Kress, G. (2003). *Literacy in the new media age*. London & New York: Routledge.
Kress, G., & van Leeuwen, T. (2006). *Reading images: A grammar of visual design* (2nd edition). London & New York: Routledge.
van Leeuwen, T. (1999). *Speech, music, sound*. London: Macmillan.
van Leeuwen, T. (2005). *Introducing social semiotics*. London & New York: Routledge.
Lemke, J. (1990). *Talking science: Language, learning and values*. Norwood, NJ: Ablex.
Lemke, J. (1995). *Textual politics: Discourse and social dynamics*. London & Bristol (US): Taylor & Francis.
Locke, T. (2005). Editorial: Grammar in the face of diversity. *English Teaching: Practice and Critique*, 5(1), 1–15.
Locke, T. (Ed.) (2010). *Beyond the grammar wars: A resource for teachers and students on developing language knowledge in the English/literacy classroom*. New York & London: Routledge.
Louden, W., Rohl, M., Gore, J., Greaves, D., McIntosh, A., Wright, R., Siemon, D. & House, H. (2005). *Prepared to teach: An investigation into the preparation of teachers to teach literacy and numeracy*. Mount Lawley, Western Australia: Edith Cowan University.
Love, K., Macken-Horarik, M. & Horarik, S. (2015). Grammatical knowledge and its application: A snapshot of Australian teachers' views. *Australian Journal of Language and Literacy*, 38(3), 171–182.
Luke, A., Ladwig, J., Lingard, B., Hayes, D. & Mills, M. (1999). *Queensland school reform longitudinal study*. St Lucia: University of Queensland.
Macken-Horarik, M. (2009). Grammar needs hip operation. *The Australian*. Retrieved from www.theaustralian.news.com.au/story/024971662-12332.
Macken-Horarik, M. (2011). Building a knowledge structure for English: Reflections on the challenges of coherence, portability, cumulative learning and face validity. *Australian Journal of Education*, 55(3), 183–278.
Macken-Horarik, M. (2012). Why school English needs a 'good enough' grammatics (and not more grammar). *Changing English: Studies in culture and education*, 19(2), 179–194.
Macken-Horarik, M., Love, K. & Unsworth, L. (2011). A grammatics 'good enough' for school English in the 21st century: Four challenges in realizing the potential. *Australian Journal of Language and Literacy*, 34(1), 9–21.
Martin, J. R. (1992). *English text: System and structure*. Amsterdam: Benjamins.
Martin, J. R. (2010). Discourse semantics. In Wang, Z (Ed.), *The collected works of J. R. Martin (Vol 2)*. Shanghai: Shanghai Jiao Tong University Press.
Martin, J. R. & Rose, D. (2003). *Working with discourse: Meaning beyond the clause*. London: Continuum.
Martin, J. R., Matthiessen, C. & Painter, C. (2010). *Deploying Functional Grammar*. Beijing: The Commercial Press.
Martinec, R. (2001). Interpersonal resources in action. *Semiotica*, 135, 117–145.
Meyer, H. (2008). It's sort of intuitive, isn't it? *English in Aotearoa*, 65, 59–76.

Moore, J., & Schleppegrell, M. (2014). Using a functional linguistics metalanguage to support academic language development in the English Language Arts. *Linguistics and Education* 26, 92–105.

Myhill, D. (2000). Misconceptions and difficulties in the acquisition of metalinguistic knowledge. *Language and Education*, 14(3), 151–163.

Myhill, D. (2003). Principled understanding? Teaching the active and passive voice. *Language and Education*, 17(5), 355–70.

Myhill, D. & Watson, A. (2014). The role of grammar in the writing curriculum: A review of the literature. *Child Language Teaching and Therapy*, 30(1), 4–62.

Myhill, D., Jones, S., Lines, H. & Watson, A. (2012). Re-thinking grammar: The impact of embedded grammar teaching on students' writing and students' metalinguistic understanding. *Research Papers in Education*, 27(20), 139–166.

Myhill, D., Jones, S., Watson, A. & Lines, H. (2013). Playful explicitness with grammar: A pedagogy for writing, *Literacy*, 47(2), 103–111.

O'Toole, M. (1994). *The language of displayed art*. London: Leicester University Press.

Painter, C. (1986). The role of interaction in learning to speak and learning to write. In C. Painter & J. R. Martin (Eds.), *Writing to mean: Teaching genres across the curriculum* (pp. 62–97). Applied Linguistics Association of Australia (Occasional Papers 9).

Painter, C., Martin, J. R. & Unsworth, L. (2013). *Reading visual narratives: Image analysis of children's picture books*. London: Equinox.

Perera, K. (1984). *Children's writing and reading: Analyzing classroom language*. New York: Blackwell.

Rose, D. (2011). *Reading to learn: Accelerating learning and closing the gap*. Sydney: Reading to Learn. Retrieved from www.readingtolearn.com.au.

Rose, D. and Martin, J. R. (2005). Designing literacy pedagogy: Scaffolding democracy in the classroom. In R. Hasan, C. Matthiessen, C. J. Webster, J. (Eds.), *Continuing discourse on language: A functional perspective (Vol. 1)* (pp. 251–280). London: Equinox.

Rose, D. & Martin, J. R. (2012). *Learning to write, reading to learn: Genre, knowledge and pedagogy in the Sydney School*. London: Equinox.

Rothery, J. (1989). Learning about language. In R. Hasan and J. R. Martin (Eds.), *Language development: Learning language, learning culture* (pp.199–256). Norwood, NJ: Ablex.

Rothery, J. (1994). *Exploring literacy in school English (Write it right resources for literacy and learning)*. Sydney: Metropolitan East Disadvantaged Schools Program.

Sangster, P., Anderson, C. & O'Hara, P. (2012). Perceived and actual levels of knowledge about language amongst primary and secondary student teachers: Do they know what they think they know? *Language Awareness*, 22(4), 1–27.

Schleppegrell, M. (2013). The role of meta-language in supporting academic language development. *Language Learning*, 63(1), 153–170.

Snyder, I. (2008). *The literacy wars: Why teaching children to read and write is a battleground in Australia*. Crows Nest, NSW: Allen & Unwin.

Spiegelman, A. (2003). *Maus I: A survivor's tale: My father bleeds history: Maus II and here my trouble began*. London: Penguin Books.

Thomas, A. (2007). *Youth online: Identity and literacy in the digital age*. New York: Peter Lang.

Unsworth, L. (2006). *e-literature for children: Enhancing digital literacy learning*. London & New York: Routledge/Falmer.

Unsworth, L. (2013). Point of view in picture books and animated movie adaptations. *Scan*, 32(1), 28–37.

Unsworth, L. (2014a). Interfacing visual and verbal narrative art in paper and digital media: Recontextualizing literature and literacies. In G. Barton (Ed.), *Literacy in the Arts: Retheorising learning and teaching* (pp. 55–76). Cham, Heidelberg, New York, Dordrecht, London: Springer.

Unsworth, L. (2014b). Investigating point of view in picture books and animated movie adaptations. In K. Mallam (Ed.), *Picture books and beyond: Ways of reading and discussing multimodal texts* (pp. 92–107). Sydney: PETAA.

Unsworth, L. (2014c). Point of view in picture books and animated film adaptations: Informing critical multimodal comprehension and composition pedagogy. In E. Djonov & S. Zhao (Eds.), *Critical multimodal studies of popular culture* (pp. 201–216). London: Routledge.

Unsworth L. & Chan E. (2009). Bridging multimodal literacies and national assessment programs in literacy. *Australian Journal of Language and Literacy*, 32(3), 245–257.

Unsworth, L. & Thomas, A. (Eds.) (2014). *English teaching and new literacies pedagogy: Interpreting and authoring digital multimedia narratives*. New York: Peter Lang Publishing.

Vygotsky, L. (1978). *Mind in society*. Cambridge, MA: Harvard University Press.

Watson, A. M. (2015). Conceptualisations of 'grammar teaching': L1 English teachers' beliefs about teaching grammar for writing. *Language Awareness*, 24(1), 1–14.

Winton, T. (1997). *Blueback*. London: Picador.

Weaver, C. (2010). Scaffolding grammar instruction for writers and writing. In Locke, T. (Ed.), *Beyond the grammar wars: A resource for teachers and students on developing language knowledge in the English/literacy classroom* (pp. 185–205). New York & London: Routledge.

Williams, G. (2009). Learning to know about language. Unpublished paper for *Australian Systemic Functional Association Conference*, September 30–October 2. Brisbane: Queensland University of Technology.

Wyse, D. (2001). Grammar for writing? A critical review of empirical evidence. *British Journal of Educational Studies*, 49(4), 411–427.

Zhao, S. & Unsworth, L. (2017). Touch design and narrative interpretation: A social semiotic approach to picture book apps. In N. Kucirkova & G. Falloon (Eds), *Apps, technology and younger learners* (pp 89–102). London: Routledge.

2
TRUE NORTH

Investigating a grammatics for narrative

Exploring the interface between grammatics and narrative

Narrative is at the heart of children's lives and cultures from earliest years. They are exposed to countless anecdotes in family interactions and neighbourhood talk, they hear stories and tell them, developing a feel for the culturally distinctive ways of structuring narratives and keeping listeners interested. In later years, children growing up in literate cultures will read (or have read to them) picture books, fairy tales and 'chapter books', possibly engaging with complex fiction in time. Their interest in multimodal narratives will often extend to graphic novels, video or computer games, television cartoons and films. Narrative is central to the life-worlds of students and prodigious in its variety. As Roland Barthes once observed:

> (N)arrative is present in every age, in every place, in every society; it begins with the very history of mankind (sic) and there nowhere is nor has been a group of people without narrative. All classes, all human groups, have their narratives, enjoyment of which is very often shared by men with different, even opposing, cultural backgrounds. Caring nothing for the division between good and bad literature, narrative is international, transhistorical, transcultural: it is simply there, like life itself.
>
> *(Barthes, 1977, p. 79)*

If narrative is there 'like life itself', it is also a crucial site of specialised study in school English. In this subject, children learn to read stories, learn *through* stories and learn *about* the structure and nature of different story genres. They may be taught that personal recounts differ from anecdotes and both from narratives. They will probably learn to distinguish a narrative complication (or problem) from a relatively unproblematic sequence of events in a recount. Later, they will learn about how different kinds of narrative innovate on the structure of genre – how crime fiction often begins with a complication (like a murder) and works backward through events leading to the crime and how crime fiction differs from romance or fantasy fiction. Beyond differences of structure or content, as they begin to study literary craft, students learn about techniques like characterization, plotting, first and third person point of view, suspense and so on. When they come to study the short story, they may learn to distinguish its intensive and compact forms (Cox, 2011). Some may speculate about telling 'gaps' in a narrative that help them interpret a 'twist' at its end (Trimarco, 2011). In all these tasks, they discover the nature of narrative through a combination of immersion in stories and explicit teaching. It is the latter that demands most of them. Narrative may be there 'like life itself', but study of its aesthetic patterning calls for a more conscious apprenticeship.

And yet, even though grammar is central to narration and its interpretation in English, it is not often based on explicit study of grammatics. As we argued in our introductory chapter, grammar is often taught at a distance from other tasks like interpretation and composition in English classrooms. Teachers fail to make an impact through teaching grammar, because grammar and writing "do not share the same instructional context" as Fearn and Farnan (2007, p. 16) observed in their US research. The strategy in many Australian classrooms is to teach 'grammar at the point of need' (Doecke, Howie and Sawyer, 2006, p. 7) which begs the question of whether teachers with a weak linguistic knowledge can recognize a need. It is more likely to lead to ad hoc responses, cursory attention to grammatical features and lost opportunities to understand the language patterning of narrative texts.

In this chapter, we reveal more about how systematic study of grammatical choices can shed light on such patterning and ground intuitions about the impact of grammatical choices and arrangements on readers. For example, within the system of TRANSITIVITY outlined in systemic functional (SF) theory (Halliday & Matthiessen, 2004), analysis can reveal how Material and Behavioural Processes (verbs that communicate action) alternate with Mental Processes (verbs that communicate feeling or perception) in many narratives. This knowledge supports insights into the action–reaction patterns in children's novels like Roald Dahl's *Fantastic Mr Fox*, Tim Winton's *Blueback* and short stories like *The Weapon,* by Fred Brown. Of course, these are not the only choices recruited in creating particular phases of narrative. As Martin and Rose point out:

> (R)eactions may take many forms, including attitudinal attributes: *I was too terrified to move*, by ideas and locutions: *I wished the moon would go in, we both screeched ... 'Run!'* or by actions involving intensified processes: *We tore through the waist high rubbish.*
>
> (Martin & Rose, 2008, p. 87)

While "types of phases are not determined by grammatical categories" as Martin and Rose argue (2008, p. 87), a grammatics in support of interpretation does provide a more secure footing in recognition of diverse grammatical choices in a text. It offers a grammatically informed metalanguage for exploring phases of action and reaction, dialogue and response or expectancy and counter-expectancy in narratives.

The issue of metalanguage needs airing, especially given that application of grammatical knowledge is not a standard part of technical talk when it comes to literary interpretation in school English. And of course, metalanguage is only part of learning when it comes to narrative and other genres. We may be able to produce a powerful narrative without a technical vocabulary to describe what we are doing. We may also be able to respond to a literary text (or indeed any text) without a specialised metalanguage. But if we are to investigate wordings (or images) in narratives in rigorous and systematic ways, we need access to a shared metalanguage for talking about aspects of their construction. It is our view that producing insightful (shared) talk about narrative depends on a metalanguage attentive to meaning, function and form in texts of all kinds – verbal, visual <u>and</u> multimodal. Explicitness of this kind depends on shared understandings about the precise character of these choices:

> Teaching language explicitly means bringing unconscious knowledge to consciousness. To do this, teachers and students need to be able to <u>name what they are talking about</u>, and this involves a systematic understanding of how language works.
>
> *(Rose & Martin, 2012, p. 236, emphasis added)*

As we indicated in the introductory chapter, a functional grammatics should provide a basis for identification of a constituent in a stretch of wordings and even to bracket and label it formally and functionally. It should enable students to answer questions like the following: "Is this a verbal group?" or "Is this a conjunction?" and related questions about grammatical units. But it should do more than this too. Because it is oriented to function, it must enable students to describe the function or role of such constituents in a clause or a longer phase of text. Here the questions have to do with the role or work of the constituent, as in "Is this verbal group communicating a Mental, Material or Behavioural Process?" or more colloquially (drawing on the metalanguage of a teacher we worked with when teaching her children about adversative conjunctions, "Is this one of those 'big buts' that signal the beginning of the Complication?"). Once learners can identify the 'what' of grammatical choices in a phrase, group or clause, they can more easily discuss the 'how' of its workings in longer stretches of text.

Sharing a precise metalanguage for naming 'what is talked about' in language is a crucial aspect of consciousness-raising and ensuring our intuitions are grounded in close study of the grammatical choices that produce particular effects. The 'pay off' is that study of narrative grammar can deepen children's appreciation of highly valued classics of junior secondary English like the *Harry Potter* series, *The Hunger Games*, *Blueback* or *Coraline* as well as other cultural narratives that they will encounter in print, graphic and digital formats within and beyond classrooms.

As later chapters will show, this meaning-oriented metalanguage can become a resource for composing narratives (Macken-Horarik & Sandiford, 2016; Unsworth & Macken-Horarik, 2015).

Appreciation of literature and close study of its craft is central to the vertical direction of our theoretical compass – the demands and possibilities of the discipline, what we call its 'true north'. The word 'discipline' suggests singularity. But there are many ways of interpreting and composing narratives, just as there are many varieties of narrative, as Barthes (1977) claimed. Hence our emphasis on the plural form of 'practices' in labelling of the northern compass point. Thinking about narrative practices can lead to questions like the following: How do composers create plausible 'possible worlds' of experience for readers (or viewers)? Why do we laugh, shudder or even weep at a particular point in a narrative? How does dialogue contribute to characterization? How does an enigmatic ending to a story relate to its opening moments? Of course, it will be obvious that these are also questions posed by literary theorists – people with an interest in the workings of narrative. Our challenge here is to construct a metalanguage that interfaces with vital concerns of narrative study. As will be seen, a Janus-facing account of metafunctions is crucial to this enterprise because we can use it to face towards literary and linguistic accounts of meaning.

Linguistically informed study of literature is not new. It has a long history, notably in – "a method of textual interpretation in which primacy of place is assigned to language" (Simpson, 2004, p. 2). But it also applies to semiotic patterning in multimodal literature, as we will show. Like those working in stylistics (focussed on literature proper), narratologists draw attention to features of narrative craft. They may highlight creative deployment of metaphor in literary and everyday narratives (Carter, 2004), relationships between different levels of narration such as story and discourse (Bal, 1985; Genette, 1980; Prince, 1982), transitivity and agency in narrative (Burton, 1982) and how point of view works in narratives of different kinds (Genette, 1980; Simpson, 1993; Toolan, 1988).

Narratology is a rich seam of work emerging from linguistically informed study of narrative, much of it inspired by systemic functional theory. Its emphasis on choice and on motivated patterns of choice in texts has even informed studies of the ideological role of children's fiction (Knolwes & Malmkjaer, 1996; Stephens, 1992). These studies are important because they demonstrate the power of grammatical analysis to unearth semantic patterns in literary texts – patterns that would otherwise remain hidden from view. For example, in a seminal paper about patterns of grammatical choice in *The Inheritors*, by William Golding, Halliday (1971/2002) established a link between transitivity choices and the contrasting worldviews of two stone-age tribes fighting for dominance in the world of the novel. The key to this analysis is Halliday's exploration of deep patterns in processes and agency in the experience of the two groups of early humans. A meaningful grammatics is crucial if it is to serve the needs of literary study. We need to be able to discern the 'semantic drift' of an ensemble of choices in literary texts, whether classics like *The Inheritors*, the poetry of Wallace Stevens (Butt, 1983) and even the multimodal power of a graphic novel like *Maus* (Spiegelman, 1997). At higher levels of organization in literary texts, it is these patterns that please us and give the work its longevity in our imaginations.

However, whether we start from literary theory (narratology) or from linguistics, walking this interface is the major task of this chapter. In this enterprise, we attempt to understand and render visible the craft in choices made by a composer. Whether consciously or not, a storyteller always chooses whether to tell a tale from the point of view of a narrator who is either outside or inside the world of the story, whether the narrator is to be part of the action or observing from a distance in time, and whether she or he is reliable or unreliable, emotionally aware of the implications of what happens or not. There are decisions to be made about whose consciousness will refract experience for readers, how dialogue will be managed and with what degree of mutual understanding. All these choices will influence our responses to a work and will 'infuse' the language of the text. And our lenses on meaning should enable us to see these more clearly.

In this and the next chapter, we invite readers to put on the metafunctional lenses to explore key aspects of narrative technique such as these. We show how an ideational lens reveals interesting aspects of setting, characterization and plotting. And we survey grammatical features of narration, focalization and voicing through our interpersonal lens. Finally, and all too briefly, we look at signposting and layout through the textual lens. The test of our disciplinary excursions is whether such connections yield fruitful insights into literary meaning and the wordings (and images) that produce this. They should enable learners to better understand 'how language does it', how images do it and how, in multimodal texts, these work together to produce higher order meanings that are more than the sum of the parts. Some might argue that this unnecessarily complicates the engagement of a reader (or viewer) with a work of art and that the best place for a grammatics when it comes to literary appreciation is 'out the back'. In our experience, this is a flawed approach to close study of any text. Without access to a toolkit that brings aesthetic patterning in the construction of a text into view, we are more likely to resort to vague (even idiosyncratic) responses to texts. Such responses may be sufficient for book clubs and bedtime reading, but they will not serve in the specialised study of literary texts that students undertake in subject English, especially in later years of schooling. As sensitive readers, we may have strong intuitions about characterization, point of view or theme but lack a grammatical (or semiotic) basis for explaining these.

If we are to understand what turns a text into 'verbal art', we need to attend to both artistic and linguistic levels of communication. This is a two-level process as Ruquaiya Hasan has emphasised:

> There exist two levels of semiosis: one that is the product of natural language, itself a semiotic system; and the other which is the product of the artistic system through foregrounding and repatternings of the first order meanings. This is why paraphrase is never sufficient to describe the meanings of a

literature text. The art of verbal art consists of the use of language in such a way that this second order semiosis becomes possible.

(Hasan, 1985, p. 98)

In other words, attention to grammar (patterns of choice in language) and artistic technique (the shaping strategies of a composer) are both important in disciplinary practices focussed on literature. And the grammatics must serve both, with first order analysis informing second-order interpretation. For example, once we can recognize quoted thought and speech in a stretch of text (first order), we are in a much stronger position to describe and explain how dialogue aligns us with (or alienates us from) particular characters or viewpoints in the work (second order interpretation). Once we can identify lexical choices that encode affect, judgement and appreciation in stretches of text (first order analysis) (Martin & White, 2005), we can use this to augment our interpretation of evaluation in narrative (second order). This approach to analysis of interpersonal meanings has been employed productively in educational linguistics (Macken-Horarik & Isaac, 2014; Martin & Rose, 2008; Rothery & Stenglin, 2000). It informs the work we have done in The Grammatics Project.

The same two-level process of analysis applies to images in multimodal literature. The verbal narrative in the picture book *Rosie's Walk* by Pat Hutchins (1968) consists of one simple sentence and a string of prepositional phrases of place. The visual narrative, however, depicts a desperate fox attempting to catch Rose the hen as she walks to different places. A first order analysis would identify the contrast between the circumstantial meanings in the verbiage and the rich visual background revealing the true challenge facing Rosie on her walk. A second order interpretation would show how the contrast produces humour through the two narrative lines. Attention to circumstantiation is also important in a different picture book, *Luke's Way of Looking* written by Nadia Wheatley and illustrated by Matt Ottley (1999). This narrative contrasts the sepia tones of the drab world of Luke's school with splashes of colour representing his inner world. A first order analysis of colour would identify the colour palette used in key sections of the text and changes in these. A second order analysis would then link these changes in palette to the symbolic transformation of Luke's experience (and that of the school master) in the final image of the book. A similar approach could be applied to analysis of other picture books like *Granpa* (Burningham, 1984) in which image and verbiage counterpoint one another to generate a rich and poignant perspective on a relationship between a child and grandparent. Literary picture books offer powerful opportunities to begin work of symbolic interpretation with students. But exploration of the interplay of modes should begin with close attention to verbal and visual choices on each page.

The Lost Thing by Australian author Shaun Tan (2000) is about a boy who discovers a bizarre-looking creature while out collecting bottle-tops at the beach. Having guessed that it is lost, he tries to find out where it belongs, but meets only indifference by everyone. Strangers and even parents are unwilling to entertain this uninvited interruption to day-to-day life. Even his friend is unable to help, despite brief interest. The boy shows concern for this hapless creature, and attempts to feed it where he has hidden it in the back shed. Figure 2.1 presents the stage of the narrative where the boy feeds the lost thing.

The creature is tilted towards the boy standing on the top of a ladder as he takes Christmas decorations from a box and throws them into the open lid of the lost thing. The globe held by one of its tentacles throws a light onto the boy, the yellow star and the red baubles he gives to the creature with its organic and mechanical innards. In spite of its strangeness, there is a playful relatedness between the two characters as they lean towards each other, the boy with his open hand and outstretched arm, the thing with its waving tentacles. The whole scene suggests intimacy in stark contrast to the interactions between the boy and others inhabiting this alienating world. As viewers, we are positioned at a distance from the interaction and the two characters gaze at one another rather than at us. The image invites contemplation rather than involvement. Furthermore, the warmth of their

FIGURE 2.1 A page from *The Lost Thing* by Shaun Tan.

encounter contrasts with the emotionally neutral and diffident first-person account of the boy's verbal narrative. The image appears to 'say' far more than the language and their interplay generates awareness of the emotional and even symbolic importance of the encounter, especially for the boy.

Literary study is increasingly attentive to the symbolic, especially as students move into later years of study in English. But careful observation and description of choices whether grammatical or visual is a crucial first step as Abousnnouga and Machin argue: "What is important is that we do not overlook the actual act of description which is so undervalued, in our eagerness to show what something means" (Abousnnouga and Machin, 2010, p. 136). Drawing on Hasan's distinction between first and second order semiosis, this means taking adequate account of what is selected, how it is arranged and what is given salience in a work (see Bezemer & Kress, 2010 for discussion of such processes in analysis of multimodal texts).

Grammatics and genre

Perhaps because it is so culturally salient, the notion of genre has had remarkable traction with teachers in literacy education (Rose & Martin, 2012). 'Sydney School' linguists propose that texts vary in their overall shape (or gestalt) because of the purposes they have evolved to serve in the culture. Getting things done in the culture is achieved through genres that Jim Martin defines as "staged, goal-oriented, social processes" (Martin, 1985, 1992; Rothery, 1989). In this formulation, *generic structure* is used to describe the sequence of communicative acts in a text (e.g. explaining, describing, evaluating) which together contribute to larger scale communicative purposes such as telling a story, providing instruction for a task, arguing a case and so on. However, as van Leeuwen points out, "the concept of genre is a multimodal concept" (van Leeuwen, 2005, p. 129). Telling a story can be realized linguistically or in combination with visual and other modes such as layout, colour and typography. This is not to claim that modes in which narrative is created are equivalent, only that genre is a "common semiotic principle" (van Leeuwen, 2005, p. 14) for exploring text structure and relating this to its social purposes.

Western cultures tend to see narratives as texts about an encounter with a disruption to the status quo calling for the action of an individual to resolve the disruption. This social function shapes the structure of narrative and primes expectations in an audience about how a text will unfold. A culturally salient narrative features an *Orientation* stage, establishing the situation of characters – their location in time and space, a *Complication* (or problem) characters must attempt to resolve and a *Resolution,* providing closure of some kind – perhaps a solution to the problem, perhaps a larger order revealed in a failure to resolve it. Sprinkled throughout events of a narrative are *Evaluations* that highlight the significance of what happens, often sourced to the thinking, feeling, saying or seeing of characters in a narrative. The *Evaluation* is a vital aspect of any narrative. It fends off the 'so what?' question that threatens the validity of the tale and its teller (Labov, 1972).

Linking the social purpose of a genre like narrative ("to entertain and inform readers") to its unfolding pattern of stages makes intuitive sense to teachers (Martin, 1993; Rothery, 1989, 1994). If all texts innovate on the possibilities of genre, they nevertheless 'trade' on its predictable patterns of structure. Table 2.1 displays teachers' notes about the social function and stages of narrative as developed to account for verbal texts (see Macken-Horarik & Adoniou, 2008; Macken-Horarik et al., 1989; Rothery, 1994;).

More recently, the framework has been adapted to techniques of 3D multimodal authoring (e.g. O'Brien, Chandler & Unsworth, 2010; Unsworth & Thomas, 2014). It should be noted that whilst all narratives deal with a problem in experience (with the Complication an obligatory stage of the genre), they innovate on structure to some extent. Some fiction begins with the Complication (like a murder) and novels introduce Complications over several phases with temporary Resolutions leading to further challenges for characters. Television serials tend to conclude with a cliffhanger that leaves the Complication unresolved (till next episode perhaps). In our experience, early scaffolding into a genre as a sequence of stages can be useful for introducing children to narrative structure. However, it needs to be superseded in later study as the category of genre comes to include understandings of more delicate moves within a generic stage; what is called 'phases', following Malcolm (2010). This enables us to track subtle shifts in patterns of meaning in narrative – often revelatory of character as well as plot.

For example, in the relatively accessible narrative like Roald Dahl's *Fantastic Mr Fox* (1970), the Orientation stage includes two settings: the world occupied by

TABLE 2.1 Teachers' notes on narrative (Macken-Horarik & Adoniou, 2008)

Narrative as genre	Notes for teachers on purposes and stages
Social function (purpose)	Narratives 'project' a possible world in which unexpected things happen to individual characters and problems that they need to confront and resolve. Narratives explore human experience in order to entertain, move and instruct their readers/viewers.
Overall pattern of stages of genre	**(Western) narratives innovate on these stages:** **Orientation:** Setting up the 'possible world' of the characters and their situation; **Complication(s):** Introducing problem(s) to be resolved by (one or more) character(s); this can be internal or external problem for the characters; **Evaluation(s):** Pointing up the significance of what happens in the narrative by narrator or characters, often realized prosodically throughout alternating phases of a text; **Resolution(s):** Providing some closure on the events for characters – resolving problems, posing new questions. **Coda:** (optional stage) Bridging between events of the story and the present, often pointing out moral of the story.

the protagonist, Mr Fox and his family, and that of his antagonists, the evil farmers, Boggis, Bunce and Bean. While these farmers live "down in the valley", the foxes live "on a hill above the valley" "under a huge tree". The Orientation occurs over two chapters and each phase brings readers increasingly close not just to the different sets of characters, but to their habitual ways of interacting with one another. In the following extract, we experience a typical interaction between Mr Fox and his wife as they prepare for dinner:

> Every evening as soon as it got dark, Mr Fox would say to Mrs Fox, "Well my darling, what shall it be this time? A plump chicken from Boggis? A duck or a goose from Bunce? Or a nice turkey from Bean?" And when Mrs. Fox had told him what she wanted, Mr Fox would creep down into the valley in the darkness of the night and help himself.
>
> *(Dahl, 1974, p.16)*

This phase within the larger Orientation stage of the novel achieves several things simultaneously: it establishes the 'possible world' of the two sets of characters and the reasons for their antagonism; it foreshadows the Complication soon to intrude on the foxes' regular routines; and it aligns (compliant) readers with the viewpoint of Mr Fox, primarily through the intimacy of husband and wife (which contrasts so markedly with that of the violent language of the aggrieved farmers). Like most engaging narratives, this Orientation is multifunctional. It creates two experiential worlds, contributes to characterization and aligns us with one set of characters whilst dis-aligning us from another set.

Like other successful authors, Roald Dahl exploits the culturally salient patterns of the genre. As readers, we delight in Mr Fox's daring attempts to outwit his opponents and in his resourceful overcoming of the many complications posed by the rapacious farmers – his lost tail, the destruction of his home under the tree and the starvation and thirst they impose on the family as they wait for the foxes' surrender. The delayed Resolution of the Complication only increases our desire that Mr Fox will outwit the farmers – which he eventually does with the help of 29 woodland animals. Table 2.2 attempts to bring out the pattern of alternating Complications, Evaluations and (temporary) Resolutions that move the narrative towards the climax of the novel and lead to Mr Fox's ingenious plan to feed his family (and friends) and outwit the farmers.

The short story too is a site for genre knowledge. It is particularly useful for classroom work on narrative structure, if only because it is a relatively compressed form that operates in texts that rarely exceed 2000 words (Bulman, 2007). *The Weapon,* by Fred Brown (1951/69), is a short story that explores the ethical dilemmas facing scientists who design technologies like the atomic bomb that wreaked such havoc on cities like Hiroshima at the end of World War II. The action of this narrative centres on a confrontation between two men with radically different ideologies about the value of such work. The Orientation stage of the narrative situates us in the domestic world of Dr James Graham, a key scientist working on a 'very important project' who is sitting alone in an unlighted room of his house thinking

TABLE 2.2 Stages of the narrative in the first half of *Fantastic Mr Fox*

Stages of text	Events that mark each stage of the narrative
Orientation	The characters and their situation (the nature of their conflict) are introduced. We meet the farmers – Boggis, Bunce and Bean and the family of foxes – and where they live. Dahl recounts a typical routine in which Mr Fox steals a duck or other creature from one of the farmers' houses for dinner.
Complication 1	The farmers decide to get rid of Mr Fox once and for all. They wait outside his hole with guns trained on the entrance. They shoot at Mr Fox who loses his tail but escapes to fight again.
Evaluation	Mrs Fox is terrified for her children and the foxes wonder what to do. Mr Fox decides that they have to dig deeper so they can escape the farmers.
Temporary Resolution	The foxes dig down deeper to escape the "terrible shovels" of the furious famers who are now determined to destroy Mr Fox and his family.
Complication 2	The farmers bring in mechanical shovels to ensure that the foxes cannot dig down faster than the tractors can excavate.
Temporary Resolution	The foxes manage to escape the tractors.
Two different evaluations	The foxes celebrate as they appear to have won out but the farmers decide to camp outside the fox hole and starve them out.

about his project and his mentally arrested son in the next room. A stranger called Niemand knocks at the door and asks to speak to him. Grateful for the interruption to his anguished thoughts about his son, Graham invites his visitor inside and they sit to talk. Niemand attempts to confront Graham with the graveness of his work on a 'weapon' but the scientist parries his intrusion, assuming Niemand is a 'crackpot' – one he must eject as soon as possible. Their encounter is interrupted by the sudden presence of Graham's son, Harry, who wants his father to read him the story of Chicken Little. Following a pleasant interchange with Niemand, he is sent back to his room and Niemand and Graham complete their discussion of the significance of Graham's work on the weapon. Graham rationalises that his work on a "rather ultimate weapon" is justified because it is "advancing science" and Niemand poses the question on which the narrative turns: "Is humanity ready for an ultimate weapon?"

Changing his mind about having a drink, Niemand goes into Harry's room and explains as Graham returns that he has taken the liberty of bringing a small gift for his son. Enigmatically, Niemand asks for Graham's forgiveness for this seemingly innocuous act of kindness to the son. Graham thanks him and Niemand leaves. Graham returns to read the story of Chicken Little to his son and realizes with a sudden sweat that Niemand has given his son a loaded revolver. He manages to get it back from Harry but his last thought reveals the profound lack of insight into the significance of Niemand's 'gift' to his mentally retarded son:

He thought, only a madman would give a loaded revolver to an idiot.

Although it is shorter than the novel, *Fantastic Mr Fox*, this narrative is more complex in its interweaving of two viewpoints on the nature of Dr Graham's work. It embodies what Mary Louise Pratt (1994, p. 99) calls a "moment of truth" structure. These are moments of crisis in a central character's life that change the course of events and lead to new perspectives on life. The first half of the narrative is presented from Graham's perspective, but as it unfolds and we learn just how problematic his 'creative thinking' really is, we begin to see things through Niemand's viewpoint, which is not accessible to us through internal processes (focalization) but through external ones (voicing). It is possible to represent the generic structure of this tale in two ways. In the table below, we draw on an earlier study by Martin (1996), focussing on evaluated disruptions in *The Weapon*.

Table 2.3 presents the two perspectives and the way in which they invite readers to construe story structure firstly from Graham's perspective and then to reconstrue it from the point of view of Niemand's verbalised perspective.

The construct of genre is necessary for exploring the contribution of grammatical choices and arrangements to the purposeful direction of the text as a whole. In some ways, it gives grammar its socially inflected telos or end-point. If *Fantastic Mr Fox* has a serial structure, in its economy of means, *The Weapon* offers a "concentration of the imagination rather than an expansion" (Oates, 1998, p. 47).

Their innovation on structural possibilities of narrative differs, but accounting for the distinctive use of a predictable cultural construct like genre is a key task in our analysis of narrative semiosis. It applies to multimodal narratives such as *The Lost Thing*, a page of which we presented above. We are really at the beginnings of such work in school English and this brief discussion here represents a step towards a fuller analysis of texts in which visual and verbal meanings "cooperate, bi-modally, in the instantiation of a genre" (Martin, 2008, p. 136).

In the original picture book of *The Lost Thing*, the story opens with a conversational response to an implied request from the reader for a story – "So you want to hear a story?" This engages readers directly and leads us into the strange tale of the boy's discovery of the creature on a beach and his attempt to find a home for it. We can map the stages of the narrative relatively easily, though with several attempted Resolutions to the Complication presented by the lost thing. It is possible to do this but in so many ways, the category of genre developed to account for structure

TABLE 2.3 Two perspectives on stages of one narrative (based on Martin, 1996, p. 161)

	CONSTRUE (story structure from Graham's perspective)	*RECONSTRUE* (story structure from Niemand's perspective)
Orientation	sitting at home	[before setting off …]
Complication	visitor arrives and challenges research	getting gun to boy in bedroom
Evaluation	research rationalised	[… reaction in bedroom …]
Resolution	drinks and leave-taking	drinks and leave-taking
Coda	"Only a madman would give …"	"I hope you'll forgive me"

of texts, fails us when we apply it to here. The second order semiosis is created through a synergy of choices such as the arresting combination of text books in faded newsprint that provide the background to each page of the book. It is unclear where these mathematical equations and figures and their strange snippets of texts come from. However, if we use the information from the letter to Pete from Shaun on the back page of the book, it appears that they could be extracts from textbooks on Applied Industrial Algebra. The background appears to confirm the impression of industrial decay yet it is lightened by the whimsical clouds that appear above alienating cityscapes on most pages. Then there is the sheer sweetness of the creature with its organic/mechanical body and the intimacy in the farewell between the thing and the boy communicated in part through the lifted arms of the boy and the equivalent gesture of thanks in the vast claws of the thing, with their red bells shaking goodbye. In order to catch something of the poetry in this multimodal text, we need to engage with the subtle implicature of such choices. This means close attention to what is selected, careful description of these and (perhaps only then), consideration of the symbolic meanings generated by multimodal artistry in this book. We return to this issue in Chapter 8 as we deal more fulsomely with multimodality.

To sum up, genre provides a culturally significant schema for exploring semiotic (including grammatical) choices in texts. In fact, recognizing and describing choices by means of a functional grammatics has been crucial to a meaningful analysis of genre structure. As Rose and Martin have observed, "(G)enre pedagogy was only possible because it could build on the functional approach to language that Halliday designed" (Rose & Martin, 2012, p. 23). A crucial tool for looking more closely at these choices has been the principle of *metafunctions* introduced in the first chapter. It is powerful because it theorises meanings as multiple and can be extended productively to multimodal analysis.

Grammatics, meaning and metafunctions

There is no special 'content' specific to narrative. Any topic can become the subject matter of storytelling but there is something distinctive about the approach to subject matter in narrative. The task of composers is to create a plausible 'possible world' peopled by characters and their attempts to solve problems at the heart of human experience. They do this through exploiting interpersonal resources that prompt interest, empathy, awe, suspense and ethical discernment in an audience. And the composition is managed through creation of a text that 'hangs together', most often through textual resources known collectively as **Cohesion** (see Macken-Horarik & Adoniou, 2008 for earlier application of the idea of lenses on meaning). Whether the composer is creating a verbal, visual or multimodal text, the concept of metafunctions applies to the three tasks above as follows:

1. *Ideational* – text as 'representation' of experience;
2. *Interpersonal* – text as 'exchange' between interactants;
3. *Textual* – text as 'composition'.

Each dimension of meaning is simultaneously present in acts of meaning but is realized in a different kind of structure. This makes the analysis (and perhaps the grammatics) more demanding but more relevant to the subtle workings of narrative. In exploring metafunctions, Halliday has often remarked on the fact that grammatical descriptions emphasise the segmental organization of the clause, identifying clear boundaries between grammatical elements, while interpersonal and textual dimensions of clause meaning are realized in different ways. Because they are less obvious to many grammarians, they are easier to miss in grammatical analysis.

> In its status as an exchange, the clause depends on prosodic features – continuous forms of expression, often with indeterminate boundaries; while in its status as message, it tends to favour culminative patterns – peaks of prominence located at beginnings and endings. It is not yet clear how far English is typical in these particular respects; but it is certainly true that the kinds of structure found in language are rather varied, and different kinds of meaning tend to be realized in systematically differing ways.
>
> *(Halliday, 1994, p. 35)*

How does the notion of different types of structure work when it comes to narrative? Let's consider some examples from *Fantastic Mr Fox* by Roald Dahl and *Blueback* by Tim Winton, beginning with the interpersonal metafunction.

Interpersonal meanings are subtle and sinuous – distributed opportunistically over the whole of an utterance. Consider the cumulative impact of attitudinal in the introductory description of the farmer known as Boggis:

> Boggis was a chicken farmer. He kept *thousands* of chickens. He was *enormously* fat. This was because he ate *three* boiled chickens *smothered* with dumplings *every* day for *breakfast, lunch and supper*.

Evaluative meanings such as those in italics above infuse the 'content' meaning of a phase of text, lending it a distinctive tone or feeling. But they work through prosodic rather than discrete forms of expression. What Martin and White call **Inscribed Appraisal** captures the direct expression of attitude, whilst indirect (more subtle forms) are referred to as **Invoked Appraisal** (Martin & White, 2005, pp. 66–67). The latter forms are typically realized prosodically, often through wordings that imply attitude and generate connotations through their association with other choices in a stream of wordings. The same phenomenon appears to be present in choices such as colour in images in picture books like *Luke's Way of Looking*, discussed above (Painter Martin & Unsworth, 2013). We return to this point in later chapters.

In the following two paragraphs from a novel for older students, *Blueback*, the author, Tim Winton evokes the underwater experience of the young protagonist, Abel, through a careful interweaving of Invoked Appraisal (communicated through figurative language and vivid verbs) and Inscribed Appraisal (through explicit naming of feelings). We attempt to show this interplay using *italics* for Invoked Appraisal and underlining for Inscribed Appraisal.

> *Great*, round boulders and *dark* cracks *loomed* below. *Tiny* silver fish *hung in nervous schools*. Seaweed *trembled* in the *gentle* current. *Orange* starfish and *yellow* plates of coral *glowed* from the *deepest* slopes where his mother was already *gliding like a bird*.
> Abel <u>loved</u> being underwater. He was ten years old and *could never remember a time when he could not dive*. His mother said he was a diver before he was born; he *floated and* swam in the warm ocean inside her for nine months, so maybe it came *naturally*. He <u>liked</u> to watch his mother *cruise down into the deep* in her *patchy old* wetsuit. She looked *like a scarred old seal* in that suit. She was <u>a beautiful swimmer, relaxed and strong</u>. Everything he knew on land or under the sea he learned from her.
>
> (Winton, 1997, p. 13)

While analysis of Invoked Appraisal is typically more subjective than that of Inscribed Appraisal, if only because what appears connotative for one can seem neutral for another, teachers involved in The Grammatics Project were struck by the power of this approach, especially as they began to explore evocative verbs in passages like this. Many acknowledged that they had previously taught students that adjectives were the key to a good description. Now, however, they began to look closely at how authors use verbs to arouse feelings of different kinds in readers (Macken-Horarik, Sandiford, Love & Unsworth, 2015).

Experiential meanings work differently from interpersonal ones. In contrast to the sinuous realization of evaluation we encountered in the text above, a principle of discreteness operates in the representation of experience. (Halliday & Matthiessen, 2004, p. 61). The clause, "Boggis kept thousands of chickens", for example, can be segmented into three constituents: the **Participant** (Boggis), **the Process** (kept) and the second Participant (thousands of chickens). We can bring out the function of each constituent through probe questions that enable us to chunk the components. It is a productive 'way in' to functional analysis and teachers find it very helpful when working with functional grammatics (Humphrey, Droga & Feez, 2012). We include relevant probe questions underneath the examples in italics below:

Participant	*Process*	*Participant*
Boggis	kept	thousands of chickens
Who or what?	*What did he do?*	*What did he keep?*

As we noted in the introduction, Material Processes are realized by what are often called 'doing verbs', as in the example above. Relational Processes are realized by 'being verbs', which relate entities, as in the example below:

Participant	Process	Participant
Boggis	was	a chicken farmer
Who or what?	*What relates these?*	*What was he?*

When we chunk clauses into Participants, Processes and Circumstances in analysis of TRANSITIVITY, we acknowledge the segmental nature of grammar in its representation of experience. An experiential lens highlights the components of experience and TRANSITIVITY analysis allows us to capture their contribution to the meaning of the whole clause. As we will see, this operates in a similar way in visual representation in multimodal narratives.

Although they are part of the ideational metafunction, *logical meanings* work differently from the experiential ones. They are iterative rather than discrete in realization and they chain clauses in a series, either independently (as in parataxis) or dependently (as in hypotaxis). Contrary to commonsense 'wisdom' that assumes speech is simpler than written language, it is now clear that unselfconscious spoken grammar is full of choreographic complexity. As Halliday has observed, "The complexity of the written language is static and dense. That of spoken language is dynamic and intricate" (Halliday, 1985, p. 87). Although we deal only with written language here, we can bring out the serial nature of clause complexing through the system of EXPANSION. These resources are outlined in detail in Halliday and Matthiessen (2004), but we illustrate their rhetorical possibilities briefly here. There are three types of EXPANSION: **Extension**, which adds meaning to a clause as indicated in the numerical symbol for addition (+); **Enhancement**, which embellishes meaning through circumstantial meanings such as time, space, cause and consequence as indicated through the mathematical symbol for multiplication (X); and **Elaboration**, which reformulates or exemplifies meanings that have already been made in the prior clause. This is indicated through the mathematical symbol for equation (=). As will be seen this resource is crucial to the development of ideas in sentences.

Independent clauses	*Dependent clause*	*Type of relation*
1. He was ten years old	*and* could never remember a time [[when he could not dive]]	Extending (+)
2. he floated || and swam in the warm ocean inside her for nine months,	*so* maybe it came naturally	Enhancing (x)
3. She was a beautiful swimmer = relaxed and strong. = [[Everything he knew on land or under the sea]] he learned from her.		Elaborating (=)

The above examples from *Blueback* reveal the different logic–semantic relations that can occur in complex sentences. While embedded clauses (marked with double square brackets) are not part of the serial structure of logico-semantic meaning (because down-ranked), they are included here as they contribute to the experiential richness of narratives. Like other kinds of Expansion, Elaboration occurs both within and across sentences. Where conjunctions mark the boundaries, these are indicated in italics:

Textual meanings are different again. They are realized in wave-like structures that distribute information in clauses. Halliday draws attention to two message lines in the distribution of information and the ways in which these complement one another:

> In English, the clause is organized textually into two simultaneous message lines, one of Theme + Rheme, and one of Given + New. The former presents the information from the speaker's angle: the Theme is 'what I am starting out from'. The latter presents the information from the listener's angle – still, of course, as constructed for human by the speaker: the New is 'what you are to attend to'. The two prominent functions, Theme and New, are realized in quite distinct ways: the Theme segmentally, by first position in the clause, the New prosodically, by greatest pitch movement in the tone group.
>
> *(Halliday, in Halliday & Martin, 1993, p. 90)*

The system of THEME is "the element which serves as the point of departure for the message" (Halliday & Matthiessen, 2004, p. 64). By means of first position, we signal what we are 'on about' in a message. This is not to be confused with literary theme and many educational linguists prefer to refer to this resource as 'grammatical theme' (e.g. Humphrey, Love & Droga, 2011, p. 113). When we look through a textual lens, we don't focus on discrete aspects of experience or prosodies of evaluation but on beginnings and endings and special points of emphasis. We deal first with beginnings, crucial to method of development in texts.

In *Fantastic Mr Fox*, the first sentence begins "*Down in the valley* there were three farmers". Because the prepositional phrase comes first and is not subject of the clause, it is called a **marked Theme**. This is a motivated choice as it provides a geographical contrast with the home of the foxes. Both locations are highly significant to the unfolding drama of the struggle between the two groups and the reader needs to be able to see where things occur in order to track events accurately. First position is important to the distribution of information in a clause. In fact, the thematic principle extends beyond the clause to operate within sentences. For example, where a dependent clause precedes the main clause, it can be interpreted as having thematic status for the sentence as a whole, as in "Every evening as soon as it got dark, Mr Fox would ask Mrs Fox what she wanted for dinner". In this example, the whole clause becomes marked because it precedes the subject of the main clause. Drawing on Martin's notion of periodicity, it is now possible to explore this principle for the organization of larger units like the paragraph and the text:

> In a similar way, the initial clause complex of a paragraph may be seen as functioning as a kind of 'paragraph Theme' (the Topic Sentence of traditional

accounts), while the introductory paragraph itself has a thematic status vis-à-vis the text as a whole.

(Martin, Matthiessen & Painter, 2010, p. 28)

But what we put last is also crucial and tends to coincide with the resting point of an argument, the coda in a narrative or the evaluative significance of a statement. The following paragraph from *Fantastic Mr Fox* begins with a helicopter view of the valley, then the wood and zooms in to pick out the tree and the hole where the foxes live. By the end of this paragraph, we come to the new information that becomes culminative by being placed at the end of this stretch of wordings.

> *On a hill above the valley* there was a wood. *In the wood* there was a huge tree. *Under the tree* there was a hole. *In the hole* lived <u>Mr and Mrs Fox and their four Small Foxes</u>.

The textual lens highlights waves of information in unfolding clauses. As Halliday observed above, the movement is from the writer's angle ('where I am starting out from') to what the reader needs to know ('what you should attend to'). In narratives, authors often place orienting information early in the text and load evaluative material later in the text. In the example above we begin with an orientation to the story world (in this case, <u>where</u> a new set of characters live) and end with new information (in this case, <u>who</u> live there – the family of foxes). It is clear that there is a parallel between micro-choices at clause level and macro-choices at text level. The ending of a sentence often carries evaluative punch, just as the ending of a story carries the twist or coda.

What does the metaphor of the lenses offer English teachers? In the first place, it allows us to focus on one kind of meaning at a time. And secondly, it enables us to see more clearly how each kind of meaning is expressed through different kinds of structure. When we 'put on' our ideational 'glasses', we perceive 'what is going on', who or what is taking part and in what circumstances (experiential); and experience is developed through different logico-semantic relations. When a friend asks us what a novel we are reading is about, they are probing experiential meaning. And our reply to their question will typically be some kind of summary or synopsis of the story line, major characters and their situation. The interpersonal glasses, on the other hand, highlight matters of stance and evaluation – whether a text engages us emotionally, aesthetically or ethically. It is what comes into focus when the same friend asks us whether we liked the novel, whether it hooked us in, was 'a page turner' or a bore. The textual glasses focus our attention on matters of composition, texture, balance and organization. It orients us to page layout, method of development and paragraph organization, the pattern of verse and chorus in a song, the metre in a poem or dialogue in a play. It is what we talk about when our friend asks us about aspects of composition or structure. It has special importance in aesthetic appreciation of literature.

Of course, while we are explaining the metafunctions separately, they operate simultaneously: we make sense of narrative 'content' as we respond to the stance of an implied author while we process the unfolding clauses and the patterns they form in texts. And yet, once we begin to look at particular domains of textual practice, some texts seem to privilege one kind of meaning over others. Like other forms of persuasion, advertising works 'the interpersonal' angle very consciously, while scientific writing tends to emphasize the experiential (content) aspects of meaning and to neutralize or flatten the interpersonal. Some might argue that poetry 'plays with' the possibilities of composition, thus privileging textual patterns rather than inviting us to 'see through' the poem into its 'content' meaning. Roman Jakobson and his colleagues were among the first to see how some genres and modes made some functions 'dominant', pressed them upon our attention (Jakobson, 1987).

In the remaining part of this chapter, we explore the potential of one metafunctional lens – the ideational – for illuminating study of language and image in narrative. Later chapters deal with textual and interpersonal lenses on meaning, linking these to tools in grammatics. Our focus here is on how grammatics serves in key tasks of the discipline, in this case, narrativity. We begin with literary craft and with choices narrators must make as they endeavour to create a plausible 'possible world' of experience for readers. In this way, we aim to explore 'resonances' between clause and text (Martin, 1995) and between verbiage and image (Kress & van Leeuwen, 2006; Painter *et al.*, 2013) in narratives students encounter in English.

Applying an ideational lens to narrative

We begin at the interface, adopting the point of view of the composer and consider some grammatical and visual consequences of choices made by composers as they shape a literary artefact. In this perspective, grammatical choices are interpreted as motivated by 'designs' of the author and affordances of available resources. Let's begin with the ideational lens on meaning – what happens to whom, where, when and why.

Setting and Circumstantiation

Whether they work with verbal, visual or multimodal resources, storytellers need to situate their tale in a given time and place. These settings can be general or particular; real or imagined; highly elaborated or relatively simple; but circumstantial meanings will always be present to some extent and in some way. We have already touched on Dahl's use of circumstantiation in *Fantastic Mr Fox* to create setting. The author of the short story, *The Weapon*, Fred Brown, adopts a different strategy. He locates the reader in a nondescript room in the house of a famous scientist as he tries to work in the room near his 'mentally arrested son'. The narrative opens with the following sentence: "The room was quiet <u>in the dimness of early evening</u>". We are invited in to share the uneasy peace of Dr Graham's reflections before the disruption created by Niemand and his call for an end to Graham's scientific work.

While language can indicate **Circumstances of Location** in **Time or Place**, **Manner, Cause, Condition, Extent, Role and Matter** (Halliday & Matthiessen, 2004, p. 262), the visual depiction of circumstance reveals the nature and location of the physical environment in which characters act. It can do this through images of clocks, the sun or moon and various lighting effects which can indicate location in time (Painter *et al.*, 2013, p. 78). These depictions of spatial location however, are rarely inert in relation to realizing higher order thematic concerns of the narrative. For example, in Shaun Tan's story of *The Lost Thing* (Tan, 2000), the ubiquitous, mechanical structures dominating the images of the beach and city environments, both completely devoid of vegetation, while never mentioned in the language of the story, are highly suggestive of an over-industrialised society resulting in individuals living self-absorbed, isolated, 'lost' lives within a crowded metropolis. In the image that comes before the page we presented earlier, visual circumstantiation contributes to a growing sense of alienation when the boy takes the lost thing home. The image shows the boy and his parents sitting in their lounge room with the lost thing, whose height reaches the ceiling of the lounge room and its width more than three lounge chairs. In spite of its visual dominance however, the creature is not noticed by his parents and he must point it out to them. In the story *Way Home* (Hathorn & Rogers, 1994), at the concluding stage, Shane tells the kitten that he has rescued that they are heading home while the image depicts the lights of nearby houses in the night. However, as Shane says "Here we are. We're home!" The reader is completely unprepared for the final page showing the image of the boy crawling into a pathetic windowless shelter, which is his 'squat'. The divergence between the language and the visual circumstantiation are significant in highlighting the theme of the importance for everyone of 'belonging' somewhere (Painter *et al.*, 2013, pp. 152–153).

Sometimes what is significant to thematic interpretation is the change in circumstantiation from one image to the next. In the book *The Great Bear*, written by Libby Gleeson and illustrated by Armin Greder (1995), images of wheeling stars in the cosmos begin to appear well before their full significance becomes apparent. This story is about a dancing bear who spends her days in a cage and her nights performing for a circus crowd in one of the many villages visited by the circus troupe. The crowd often taunts her as she dances, poking her with sticks and throwing stones. On one fateful night, after another harrowing episode of human cruelty, the bear decides to stand up for herself. But we get a hint of what is to come for her in the circumstantial detail of the sky in Figure 2.2.[1]

Characterisation and participant depiction

Stories are typically about people – or at least about the human or quasi-human characters that 'people' the numberless narratives of our world. The characters of *Fantastic Mr Fox* are either human beings (farmers) or anthropomorphized animals (foxes, badgers, etc). The characters represented in *The Weapon* are human as are those in the image above. Grammatically speaking, however, they all serve as Participants

FIGURE 2.2 Circumstantiation as foreshadowing in *The Great Bear*.

involved in the Processes expressed in each clause. Participants can be depicted minimally in simple nominal (or noun) groups such as proper nouns 'Mr Fox', 'Mrs Fox', 'Boggis', 'Bunce' or 'Bean' and subsequently by means of pronouns that refer to these, like 'he' 'him', her', 'they'. They can be depicted by means of nominal groups containing **Classifiers**, as in "Boggis was a chicken farmer" or "Bunce was a duck-and-goose farmer". And they can be evaluated via **Attitudinal Epithets** as in "They were also nasty men" and these attitudes can be further amplified through clauses like, "All three of them were about as nasty and mean as any men you could meet". The negative qualities of characters like the three farmers are underscored through comparison with positive qualities of heroic characters like "fantastic Mr Fox" and his "finest tail for miles around". In these ways, authors like Dahl exploit the potential of the nominal group for depicting and evaluating characters.

But characterization also occurs through coupling of Participants with Processes representing the actions of participants. For example, Boggis is described as "enormously fat" and the causes of his obesity are explained in the following sentence: "This was because he ate three boiled chickens smothered with dumplings". Representation of the role, appearance and behaviour of the farmers evoke revulsion in readers and contribute in no small measure to our delight in the victories of "fantastic Mr Fox" and his resourceful family and woodland friends.

Some stories like *The Weapon* involve minimal depiction. We are introduced to Dr James Graham early in the narrative as "key scientist in a very important project" whilst Niemand (which is German for "no one") is simply 'a stranger'. In this text, however, representation of Niemand's identity is filtered through the (increasingly unreliable) viewpoint of Dr Graham. Even so, by comparison with participant depiction in *Fantastic Mr Fox*, the characters in *The Weapon* are not individualised. They are stock figures and the Classifiers in the nominal groups that identify these as: 'important scientist', 'mentally-arrested son' and 'unwelcome stranger'. The individual identities of each character are less important than their role as ethical points of reference – amoral intellectual power (the scientist), vulnerable humanity (his son) and radical social activism (the stranger). Naturalistic representation would be out of place in a short story that explores a moral dilemma in a pithy way as some science fiction short stories do.

However, if the detail of character depiction is left understandably generic in this text, what *is* interesting is the way this changes throughout this narrative. Niemand goes from being identified as 'a stranger' and described through Graham's view as "a small man, nondescript, obviously harmless", to "a crackpot" and finally "a madman". Characterisation of Graham goes the other way, initially depicting his work as "creative" via narrator's voice to "destructive" in Niemand's voice. The final words of the coda invite us to turn Graham's critique of Niemand onto his own actions in 'creation' of a weapon of mass destruction without attending to ethical problems of a flawed and vulnerable humanity. The two contrasting views of Dr Graham and his work can be related to key stages of the unfolding narrative. Table 2.4 presents each opposing view, underlining the nominal groups that construe the characters through deployment of nominal groups.

This short story can be seen as an allegory and the characters are depicted in light of higher order questions they embody. Minimal characterization serves the moral purposes of the author but the changes in character put Graham's view of his work increasingly 'at risk'. This strategy of representation invites readers to ask the same question as Niemand does: Is humanity ready for an ultimate weapon?

Analogous strategies can be explored in analysis of characterization in images, within limits of course. The only explicit knowledge we can gain about characters from their depiction in images is their physical appearance and what the images show them as doing. How much and what kind of knowledge we can glean about

TABLE 2.4 Two perspectives on Graham and his work

	Dr Graham and his work	*Niemand's views*
Orientation	Dr James Graham, key scientist of a very important project; "his best work, his most creative thinking"	
Complication		He said "You are the man whose scientific work is more likely than that of any other man to end the human race's chance for survival".
Evaluation	"I am a scientist and only a scientist"	But Dr Graham, is humanity ready for an ultimate weapon?
Resolution		
Coda		"Only a madman would give …"

a character's appearance depends on the depiction style. This may be located along a cline from 'minimalist' to 'generic' and ranging to 'naturalistic' (Painter et al., 2013). The minimalist style for a human character is one that uses circles or ovals for people's heads, with dots or small circles for eyes, and does not need to maintain accurate facial or body proportions. The generic drawing style is more realistic than the minimalist but not as naturalistic as a colour photograph. Images from the generic to the naturalistic end of the cline may allow fairly firm inferences about characters regarding factors such as age, class, ethnicity and role, whereas the very minimalist approach such as that of Oliver Jeffers in his picture book *Stuck* (2011), for example, using little more than lines, circles and dots, places limits on inferences of this kind. But even minimalist depictions enable explicit facial, gestural and postural expression of affect, which can significantly influence how the reader/viewer interprets the disposition and behaviour of the character – and changes in the visual portrayal of the pattern of affect are a means of showing changes in characterization, which are significant in relation to the narrative theme.

Other visual attributes of participant images, such as clothing, may also be significant in conveying what the character is like. In the beginning pages of Browne's book, *The Tunnel*, the soft, muted colour of the jumper Rose is wearing contrasts with the bold, vibrant colours and striking design of Jack's jumper. The difference in their characters is also shown in frequent depictions of each child with objects of attachment. In the following figure, we can see each child leaving behind the object in entering the tunnel. Figure 2.3[2] shows Jack disappearing into the tunnel, leaving behind his soccer ball.

In the second-to-next image (Figure 2.4),[3] Rose is depicted with her book of fairy tales left open showing a picture of the wicked witch, perhaps symbolizing her fears.

A grade four student observed that the abandoned book and the soccer ball represent the characters' leaving behind of previous identities. Interpreting Participant attributes in this way, she is clearly moving towards symbolic reading that a careful scrutiny of visual choices and a relating of these to the larger narrative makes possible.

Looking at characterization through the lens of ideational meaning draws attention to the depiction of participants and the processes, most commonly actions, they are shown to be involved in. But the interpersonal or interactive meanings constructed in images – the pseudo interpersonal relationship constructed between the reader/viewer and the characters through choices of focalization, social distance and vertical and horizontal angles from which characters are depicted – can significantly influence the ways readers/viewers interpret characters and the extent to which they align with some characters rather than others. We will discuss this further in Chapter 3.

Depiction of actions is not only crucial to characterization but to creation of the 'possible world' in which they act (and react) In this aspect of a functional grammatics, we focus on the grammatical role of Processes in creation of experiential worlds and the larger logic that governs relationships between one process and another in narrative. Some call this the plot and others, as we shall show, call it the situation.

FIGURE 2.3 Jack leaves his soccer ball behind as he enters the tunnel.

FIGURE 2.4 Rose leaves her book of fairy tales behind as she enters the tunnel.

Plotting and Processes

The storyteller has a tale to tell and it centres on events involving characters and situated in time and space. But if story consists of events to be depicted, "plot is the chain of causation which dictates that these events are somehow linked and that they are to be depicted in relation to each other" (Cobley, 2001, p. 5). In a narrative, events are related through chronology – often termed 'diegesis' (Genette, 1980) – which is the fictional world in which narrated events occur. But it is plot that turns events into narrative – related through causation rather than just chronology. Many years ago, the novelist E. M. Forster provided a simple and useful example of what plot adds to story:

> Let us define a plot. We have defined a story as a narrative of events arranged in their time-sequence. A plot is also a narrative of events, the emphasis falling on causality. 'The king died and then the queen died' is a story. 'The king died and then the queen died of grief' is a plot. The time-sequence is preserved, but the sense of causality overshadows it.
>
> *(Forster, 1963, p. 42)*

Plotting generates a sequence of events governed by causality, as Forster explains. Of course, as many authors report, the creation of a narrative world striated by (a particular kind of difficulty) is not straightforward or even necessarily rational. In fact, some authors work with looser notions of 'what is to happen' than others and the notion of plotting is too mechanistic for some. In Stephen King's account of his composing process, the more intuitive notion of 'situation' is more helpful than plot.

> The situation comes first. The characters – always flat and unfeatured, to begin with – come next. Once these things are fixed in my mind, I begin to narrate. I often have an idea of what the outcome may be, but I have never demanded of a set of characters that they do things my way. On the contrary, I want them to do things their way. In some instances, the outcome is what I visualized. In most, however, it's something I never expected. For a suspense novelist, this is a great thing. I am, after all, not just the novel's creator but its first reader. And if I am not able to guess with any accuracy how the damn thing is going to turn out, even with my inside knowledge of coming events, I can be pretty sure of keeping the reader in a state of page-turning anxiety.
>
> *(King, 2000, p. 190)*

Producing a text that keeps a reader in a state of page-turning anxiety must be a powerful incentive whether one starts with plot or situation. It draws our attention to the choices an author or artist needs to make in creating his or her imaginary world. These choices are the result of the composer's response to questions such as the following: how much detail to include in representing an action or event, pacing (fast or slow), whether to create events that unfold successively (the norm) or simultaneously (the marked option), whether to highlight causal links between events or to leave these implicit. A grammatics of the interface needs to face towards questions of literary technique and to the resources by which techniques are turned into wordings or image relations.

In above sections, we explored the role of Participant depiction in characterization and of Circumstances in creation of setting. Here, we focus on the system of TRANSITIVITY – which sorts the world of experience into a manageable set of Process types (Halliday & Matthiessen, 2004, p.106). As we indicated in Chapter 1, the Process is the obligatory element in every clause. The clause, 'Run' for example, consists only of a Process but the message is clear and the relevant Participant (you) is understood. A Process is realized through a verbal group. This may be one verb (e.g. crept) or a combination of a lexical verb and auxiliary or helping verbs (e.g. would creep or 'shall have to find'). The most familiar kind of process is captured by the traditional notion of verb as 'doing word'. This is a good starting point when we examine 'what happens' in a narrative. What Halliday calls Material Processes represent actions on which creation of a situation or plot depends. For example, "Mr Fox crept down into the valley and helped himself" or "Dr Graham sat in his favourite chair". Furthermore, Material Processes are the crucial resource in sequences of actions linked by temporal conjunctions like 'and', 'when' or 'then' or causal conjunctions like 'so' or 'because'. In *The Weapon*, Graham sits in his favourite chair and *when* the doorbell rings, he rises, turns on the light, *then* goes through the hallway to the door *and* opens it. If writers are to represent activity sequences (Martin, 1992) such as welcoming a visitor, they typically use Material Processes (doing words) to do this.

But there is more to this approach to transitivity and processes than an additional layer of functional labels like Participant, Process and Circumstance. Transitivity is a theory of experience and the kinds of verbs selected to represent goings on and our responses to these reflect (and indeed create) the worlds imagined by writers and artists (to name only those who interest us here). If Material Processes are crucial to depiction of actions or events, they are not always dominant, especially in passages of description, internal monologue or dialogue. Creation of these imagined realities require different kinds of verb. The first paragraphs of *Fantastic Mr Fox*, for example, introduce us to the characters of Boggis, Bunce and Bean and uses what Halliday calls **Relational Processes** (sometimes called 'being and having' verbs) to assign attributes to these Participants. With respect to the three farmers, we learn that "They were rich men. They were also nasty men. All three of them were about as nasty and mean as any men you could meet." In a similar way, the author of *The Weapon* uses the same processes to situate us in the room of the scientist: "The room was quiet in the dimness of early evening" … and … "It was so still …" Of course, even when a sequence of events is the dominant consideration for a composer, there are still choices to be made about detail, sequence, pacing and logical connections. This last is crucial because readers need to understand what is happening and why characters do what they do and say what they say.

In *The Weapon*, for example, the events leading to Graham's first meeting with Niemand are not simply recounted in a blow-by-blow fashion but rationalised.

In the following extract, we highlight the relation between processes of action (Material processes) and processes of reflection (whether cognitive, perceptive or behavioural). Material processes are highlighted in underlined and processes that intertwine these (Mental, Verbal, Behavioural or Relational) are in italics.

> The doorbell <u>rang</u>.
> Graham <u>rose</u> and <u>turned on</u> lights in the almost-dark room before he <u>went</u> through the hallway to the door. He *was not annoyed*; tonight, at this moment, almost any interruption to his thoughts *was* welcome. He <u>opened</u> the door. A stranger <u>stood</u> there: he *said*, 'Dr Graham? My name *is* Niemand; I'd *like to talk* to you. <u>May</u> I <u>come in</u> for a moment?'
> Graham *looked at* him. He *was* a small man, nondescript, obviously harmless – possibly a reporter or an insurance agent.
> But it *didn't matter* what he was. Graham *found* himself *saying*, 'Of course. <u>Come in,</u> Mr Niemand.' A few moments of conversation, he *justified* himself by *thinking, might divert* his thoughts and *clear* his mind.
> '<u>Sit down</u>,' he *said*, in the living room. '*Care* for a drink?

It is clear this passage contains not only Graham's actions but the reasons behind these. Brown represents Niemand's visit in this way because he needs to produce a plausible event sequence. As readers, we need to understand why a scientist so absorbed by his work would welcome a visit by a stranger like Niemand. Brown explains this using Mental Processes such as "was not *annoyed*" or "*justified* himself by *thinking*") or Relational Processes like "any interruption to his thoughts *was* welcome". As readers, we understand better his reasons for inviting Niemand inside because of the supply of reasons – the need for an interruption to his sadness and ennui, his need for a mental diversion and the seemingly harmless nature of the stranger. As we discover, Niemand is far from 'harmless' and is about to disrupt Graham's work in ways he cannot predict. Because we 'see with' Dr Graham, we are subject to his ways of representing what is happening, at least prior to Niemand's challenge. If the expected sequence of events is mediated by Graham, counter-expectancy is delivered by the world beyond his preoccupations. The alternating play of expected and unexpected actions is part of the plotting of this story and inflects choices for process type. If Graham is a man of thought with a habit of rationalisation, Niemand is a man of speech and (later) action. Transitivity choices and links between clauses gives us access in microcosmic ways to the pattern of action, reaction, challenge, defence and epiphany that are central to the second-order patterning of this short story.

Whether we consider the action of a narrative in terms of plot or 'situation', close attention to their process and sequence illuminates literary craft. Within an unfolding sequence of events, actions can be rendered minimally or more fully. In *Fantastic Mr Fox*, for example, the first 'raid' Mr Fox makes on the animals owned by the farmers is indicated minimally. Following the 'order' placed by his wife, 'Mr Fox "<u>would creep</u> down into the valley and <u>help</u> himself". However, the second foray is represented in a much fuller way and we can seek the reasons for this in Dahl's literary technique. By the time the two sets of antagonists are introduced, we know that things are moving to 'all out war'. By Chapter 3, Mr Fox has been emboldened by ease of access to the chickens, ducks, geese or turkeys owned by the farmers. However, they have decided to wait outside his hole and to shoot Mr Fox when he comes out the following night. Having established just how high the stakes are, Dahl now takes us down into the hole that Mr Fox is about to leave and recreates the sequence of events occurring simultaneously with the action outside the hole. The effect is suspenseful.

The Process types in the extract below are highlighted as we did above for *The Weapon*. Material processes are underlined with the others that intertwine these in italics. We should note just how important **Behavioural Processes** are in this sequence. The keen senses of a fox require representation that enables us to experience the world as an animal like this would do so, primarily through smell. But because this is an anthropomorphic account, we also get access to the reasons for his behaviour.

> Mr Fox <u>crept</u> up the dark tunnel to the mouth of his hole. He *poked* his long handsome face out into the night air and *sniffed* once.
>
> He <u>moved</u> an inch or two forward and <u>stopped</u>.
>
> He *sniffed* again. He *was* always especially careful when <u>coming</u> out from his hole.
>
> He *inched* forward a little more. The front half of his body *was* now in the open.
>
> His black nose *twitched* from side to side, *sniffing* and *sniffing* for the scent of danger. He <u>found</u> none, and he *was* just about *to go trotting* forward into the wood when he *heard* or *thought he heard* a tiny noise, a soft rustling sound, as though someone <u>had moved</u> a foot ever so gently through a patch of dry leaves.
>
> Mr Fox *flattened* his body against the ground and *lay* very still, his ears *pricked*. He <u>waited</u> a long time, but he *heard* nothing more.
>
> 'It *must have been* a field-mouse,' he *told* himself, 'or some other small animal.'
>
> He <u>crept</u> a little further out of the hole … then further still. He *was* almost right out in the open now. He <u>took</u> a last careful look around. The wood *was* murky and very still. Somewhere in the sky the moon <u>was shining</u>.
>
> Just then, his sharp night-eyes *caught* a glint of something bright behind a tree not far away. It *was* a small silver speck of moonlight <u>shining</u> on a polished surface. Mr Fox lay still, *watching* it. What on earth *was* it? Now it <u>was moving</u>. It <u>was coming</u> up and up … *Great heavens! It was the barrel of a gun!*

As with other extracts, this one centres on action and precedes the first Complication of the narrative – Mr Fox's lost tail. One could ask why on this occasion Roald Dahl provides such a detailed account of Mr Fox's actions. The answer lies at least in part in the need to create not only an interior sense of solidarity with the protagonist (we 'see with' Mr Fox) but a shared sense of the drama that is about to unfold as the three farmers attempt to destroy him. The full account of this action is powerful because as readers we already know that the farmers are waiting outside the hole whilst Mr Fox does not. Dahl plays with this awareness, rendering the fox's movement towards the opening of his hole as precisely as possible. This is achieved through vivid Behavioural Processes like poking, sniffing, twitching, trotting and pricking. These are a powerful resource for representing processes of consciousness as forms of behaviour (Halliday & Matthiessen, 2004, pp. 248–250).

The fox's growing awareness that the moonlight shining on the polished surface is light on the barrel of a gun and that his life is in danger is portrayed as if in slow motion. This single action is slowed down, in process of what Genette (1980) calls 'deceleration' so that as readers we experience it as Mr Fox does. The links between the actions are made, as in *The Weapon*, through additive and temporal conjunctions. But in both texts, the logic operates as much between sentences as within them. This also applies to relations between images in picture books as we show later. And the internal processes of the fox – evaluative moments – are created through the interplay between doing (Material Processes) and responding (Verbal or Relational Processes). In this way, Dahl moves the plot to a new level of intensity shifting our attention between two simultaneous sets of actions – those of the farmers and those of Mr Fox. The resulting action of the farmers proves painful if not fatal to Mr Fox and the battle lines are drawn. This activity sequence marks a pivot point in the narrative. Understanding the artistry in the author's choices and the ways in which grammar makes these possible (realizes them) are key to enhanced appreciation of the novel.

Artists make related choices in their representation of visual processes. Kress and van Leeuwen distinguish Actional, Reactional, Mental and Verbal processes (Kress & van Leeuwen, 2006, p. 63). Actional Processes (equivalent to Material Processes in clauses) are realized by what they call Vectors and what Nodleman (1988, p.160) discusses as 'action lines'. These include choices like the angle of a raised arm as if a snapshot was taken in the process of throwing something or a line formed by an outstretched leg, as if the represented participant were about the take a step forward. Action lines can also appear separately to represented participants such as a series of close parallel lines each side of a pole to show that it is vibrating or blurring of images to suggest speed of movement. Vectors also realize Reactional meanings in which the eye line of a Participant is directed toward something in the image, or may be directed outside of the image, where whatever the participant is reacting to is not visible. Mental Processes are often realized by 'thought clouds' above or beside a character's head, which may contain a verbal or visual expression of his or her thoughts. Verbal processes are indicated by 'speech balloons' in which are located the words spoken by the participant. The latter two resources are a feature of comics and graphic novels.

Of course, in texts that unfold through sequences of pages such as picture books, illustrated stories and graphic novels, readers need to interpret not only the actions depicted in a single image but the way one event relates to another in successive images. As we noted earlier, in language, activity sequences are realized by Material Processes and these can be linked temporally or causally using conjunctions, such as 'then', 'when', 'so' and 'because'. But to track activity sequences in visual narratives, readers need to compare adjacent or successive images and infer temporal or causal relations from the similarity or variation between the images. Research on picture books has provided a detailed account of how relations between adjacent and successive images indicate simultaneous or progressive unfolding of narrative events within an activity sequence or between activity sequences (Painter *et al.*, 2013). For example, successive images in the first three pages of *The Lost Thing* (Tan, 2000) depict events within the activity sequence of the boy's meeting and playing with the lost thing on the beach. The relations between the images indicate temporal unfolding. As the boy searches for a place where the lost thing might belong, one image shows his hand about to press a button on a wall and the following image shows an open door and a utopian scene inhabited by other bizarre creatures. As well as temporal unfolding, the images suggest causal relations between depicted events; pressing the buzzer leads to accessing the world of other lost things. The last three pages in the book involve two activity sequences – that of the boy and the lost thing saying goodbye; and an activity sequence involving the boy on a train sometime later reflecting on his encounter with the lost thing.

As well as temporal succession, the relation between two images can be that of simultaneity. In this case, the actions of different characters are seen at the same time in two separate panels on a single page or in two separate images on facing pages. While a simultaneous view of the same character across two images implies temporal succession, a simultaneous view of different characters implies temporal simultaneity. We have noted Mental Processes within an image, where the activity of a character is related to the activity that character is thinking of, perhaps projected as an image in a thought cloud. Mental projection can also occur between successive images, where one image shows a character thinking, and the second image shows the content of what the character is thinking (for a discussion of examples of this kind of projection in the picture book, *Granpa* (Burningham, 1984) and in *Hyram and B* (Caswell & Ottley, 2003), see Painter *et al.*, 2013). Understanding the implied logic of different kinds of sequencing is important if readers are to make appropriate inferences about 'the why' beneath 'the what' of narrative choices.

It is now possible to summarise the relationship we have been exploring between questions of literary craft related to creation of 'plausible possible worlds' – setting, characterization and plotting and ideational tools in systemic functional grammatics. Table 2.5 provides an overview of kinds of questions we ask about the creation of plausible possible worlds and how these relate to the ideational lens on meaning. The questions for each aspect of narrative craft are formulated so that they can be used with students (for example, through direct and second person forms of address).

Although we have only looked carefully through the ideational lens highlighting connections between choice and craft, between grammar as the ground of

62 Investigating a grammatics for narrative

TABLE 2.5 Probe questions related to an ideational lens on narrative craft

Ideational lens – building a plausible 'possible world' of experience	*Overarching Question*: How does the text create a plausible 'possible world' so we understand what happens, how and why?
	Setting and Circumstantiation When and where is the story set? How are Circumstances (e.g. of time and place) created in verbal narratives? How are they generated (if they are) visually in multimodal narratives? Does circumstantiation change over the course of the narrative? How do you know? What do you notice about these changes?
	Characterisation and participant depiction Who or what is depicted? Are characters represented minimally, generically or naturalistically? Do you notice differences between visual and verbal depiction of characters in a multimodal narrative? What changes in character representation do you notice (if any)? What is the effect of this for characterization?
	Plotting and Processes What happens in the story? How are the actions or events sequenced? Do the characters face one or more problems in this narrative? If so, how do we learn about the challenges they face? Are their problems resolved? How do you know?

(a linguistically informed) study of narrative, the others are very important too. Other chapters deal with the interpersonal and textual aspects of meaning in greater detail.

Conclusion

We began at the interface, with an inquiry about how a functional approach to grammar (a grammatics) might inform narrative interpretation, providing a metalanguage that works for verbal and visual aspects and adds depth to analysis of literary craft. In this task, any metalanguage we develop must serve the ends of literary appreciation, with grammatics in a helping role. It cannot do all the work, nor should it. In this service role, grammatical labels need to be bought into dialogue with narratology (as one approach to narrative theory) and associated notions like plotting, focalization, characterization and setting. Our view is that with a grammatics that aims to be relevant to this task, teachers can both assist students to identify particular choices like Participants, Processes and Circumstances, drawing on formal, functional and systemic knowledge, via what Halliday calls a trinocular view of grammar. It can also help them to describe the role such constituents play in clauses (at least in their experiential nature). Observing patterns of choice in transitivity, it is then possible to observe patterns of contrast (action and reaction for example, or agentive and passive approaches to experience) in texts and to track changes in such choices over the course of a text (perhaps how a character takes on an increasingly agentive role in the actions that occur in a story). If a functional grammatics is part of the shared knowledge of a class, it enables all students involved to be 'on the same page' in their reading of narrative: they are aware of 'what' is being referred to in a sequence of wordings (clause, sentence, phase), 'how' this is working as it does and then (hopefully) 'why' it is working as it does given the direction of the genre itself. In this way, the grammatics 'opens out' to literary study and supports it, without attempting to be 'the whole story'. If the task is to explore what Hasan calls "second order semiosis", students cannot get to this if they don't have access to first order understanding.

It will be clear now that we are attempting a more ambitious task through image grammatics. A Participant can be depicted in a verbal narrative quite minimally, as in 'Mr Fox' or 'Dr Graham'; or it can be depicted more extravagantly as in 'Fantastic Mr Fox' or 'Dr James Graham, key scientist on a very important project'. But it can also be depicted visually – through a simple line drawing of minimal features on a face – or naturalistically through detailed representation of the shape of the face, hair, skin colour and even texture. An understanding of styles of depiction – whether in verbal or visual choices – can have profound advantages for narrative interpretation. Some genres – like scientific short stories – tend to use minimalist depiction of characters – especially if they are moral tales. Others pursue more detailed even complex forms of depiction – especially if they involve psychological studies of character and motive. The key is to have access to a common terminology for identifying these things – Participants and Processes amongst other units of meaning – and for describing their function and rhetorical effects.

The educational value of a narrative grammatics is that it gives students (grammatically principled) tools for the tasks of interpretation. When we ask learners to analyse the strategies used by authors and artists in their works, we need to give them tools for doing so. A grammatics can help in this task if it is (i) oriented to meanings of different kinds, (ii) principled in its account of resources for meaning and their deployment in texts and (iii) portable for analysis of different modes through common terminology. The longer-term goal in this domain is to deepen appreciation of literary meaning and to offer students 'ways in' to this that are within the purview of all learners and adequate to literary texts of many kinds.

Notes

1 Text © 1995 Libby Gleeson. Illustrations © 2010 Armin Greder.From THE GREAT BEAR by Libby Gleeson, illustrated by Armin Greder. Reproduced by permission of Walker Books Ltd, London SE11 5HJ: www.walker.co.uk.
2 *The Tunnel* © by Anthony Browne (1989). From THE TUNNEL by Anthony Browne. Reproduced by permission of Walker Books Ltd, London SE11 5HJ: www.walker.co.uk.
3 *The Tunnel* © by Anthony Browne (1989). From THE TUNNEL by Anthony Browne. Reproduced by permission of Walker Books Ltd, London SE11 5HJ: www.walker.co.uk.

References

Abousnnouga, G. & Machin, D. (2010). Analysing the language of war monuments. *Visual Communication*, 9(2), 131–149.
Bal, M. (1985). *Narratology: Introduction to the theory of narrative*. Toronto: University of Toronto.
Barry, P. (1995). *Beginning theory: An introduction to literary and cultural theory*. Oxford & New York: Manchester University Press.
Barthes, R. (1977). *Introduction to the structural analysis of narratives*. Image, music, text (S. Heath, Trans., pp. 79–124). New York: The Noonday Press.
Bezemer, J. & Kress, G. (2010). Writing in multimodal texts: A social semiotic account of designs for learning. *Written Communication*, 25(2), 166–195.
Browne, A. (1989). *The tunnel*. London: Julia McRae Books.
Brown, F. (1951/1969). The weapon. In J. Sallis (Ed.), *The war book*. London: Rupert Hart-Davis.
Bulman, C. (2007). *Creative writing: A guide and glossary to fiction writing*. Cambridge: Polity.
Burningham, J. (1984). *Granpa*. New York: Crown,
Burton, D. (1982). Through glass darkly: Through dark glasses. In R. Carter (Ed.), *Language and literature* (pp. 195–214). London: Allen & Unwin.
Butt, D. (1983). Semantic 'drift' in verbal art. *Australian Review of Applied Linguistics*, 6(1), 38–48.
Carter, R. (2004). *Language and creativity: The art of common talk*. London & New York: Routledge.
Caswell, B. & Ottley, M. (2003). *Hyram and B*. Sydney: Hodder Headline.
Cobley, P. (Ed) (2001). *The Routledge companion to semiotics and linguistics*. London: Routledge.
Cox, A. (2011). *Teaching the short story*. Hampshire (UK) & New York: Palgrave Macmillan.
Dahl, R. (1974). *Fantastic Mr Fox*. London: Puffin Books.
Doecke, B., Howie, M. & Sawyer, W. (2006). Starting Points. In B. Doecke, M. Howie & W. Sawyer (Eds.), *Only connect: English teaching, schooling and community* (pp. 4–24). South Australia: Wakefield Press.
Eagleton, T. (1983). *Literary theory: An introduction*. Oxford, UK: Blackwell.
Fearn, L. & Farnan, N. (2007). When is a verb? Using functional grammar to teach writing. *Journal of Basic Writing*, 26(1), 63–87.
Forster, E. M. (1963). *Aspects of the novel*. England: Penguin.
Genette, G. (1980). *Narrative discourse* (J. Lewin, Trans.) Ithaca, NY: Cornell University Press.
Gleeson, L. & Greder, A. (1995). *The great bear*. Sydney: Scholastic.
Halliday, M.A.K. (1964/2002). The linguistic study of literary texts. In J.J. Webster (Ed.), *The collected works of M.A.K. Halliday: Language studies of text and discourse (Vol 2)* (pp. 5–22). London & New York: Continuum.
Halliday, M.A.K. (1971/2002). Linguistic function and literary style: An inquiry into the language of William Golding's 'The Inheritors'. In J.J. Webster (Ed.), *The collected works of M.A.K. Halliday: Language studies of text and discourse (Vol. 2)* (pp. 88–125). London & New York: Continuum.
Halliday, M.A.K. (1985). *Spoken and written language*. Geelong, Victoria: Deakin University Press.
Halliday, M.A.K. (1994) *Introduction to functional grammar* (2nd edition). London: Edward Arnold.
Halliday, M.A.K. & Martin, J.R. (1993). *Writing science: Literacy and discursive power*. London: The Falmer Press.
Halliday, M.A.K. & Matthiessen, C. (2004). *An introduction to functional grammar* (3rd edition). London: Arnold.

Hasan, R. (1985). *Linguistics, language and verbal art*. Geelong, Victoria: Deakin University Press.

Hathorn, L. & Rogers, G. (1994). *Way home*. London: Andersen Press.

Humphrey, S., Love, K. & Droga, L. (2011). *Working grammar: An introduction for secondary English teachers*. Port Melbourne, Victoria: Pearson.

Humphrey, S, Droga, L. & Feez, S. (2012). *Grammar and meaning*. Newtown, NSW: Primary English Teaching Association Australia.

Hutchins, P. (1968). *Rosie's walk*. London: Bodley Head.

Jakobson, R. (1987). The dominant. In K. Pomorska & S. Rudy (Eds.), *Roman Jakobson: Language in literature* (pp. 41–46). Cambridge, MA & London: Harvard University Press.

Jeffers, O. (2011). *Stuck*. London: Harper Collins.

King, S. (2000). *On writing: A memoir of the craft*. New York: Scribner.

Knolwes, M. & Malmkjaer, K. (1996). *Language and control in children's literature*. London: Routledge.

Kress, G., & van Leeuwen, T. (2006). *Multimodal discourse*. London, UK: Arnold.

Labov, W. (1972). *Language in the inner city*. Philadelphia, PA: University of Pennsylvania Press

van Leeuwen, T. (2005). *Introducing social semiotics*. London & New York: Routledge.

Macken-Horarik, M. & Adoniou, M. (2008). Genre and register in multiliteracies. In B. Spolsky & F. Hult (Eds.), *Handbook of educational linguistics* (pp. 367–382). Cambridge, MA: Blackwell.

Macken-Horarik, M. & Morgan, W. (2011). Towards a metalanguage adequate to linguistic achievement in post-structuralism and English: Reflections on voicing in the writing of secondary students, *Linguistics and Education*. 22(2), 133–149.

Macken-Horarik, M. & Isaac, A. (2014). Appraising appraisal. In G. Thompson & L. Alba-Juez (Eds.) (pp. 67–92). *Evaluation in context*. Amsterdam: John Benjamins.

Macken-Horarik, M., Martin, J. R., Kress, G., Kalantzis, M., Rothery, J. & Cope, W. (1989). *An approach to writing K-12: Vol. 1–4*. Sydney: Literacy and Education Research Network and Directorate of Studies, NSW, Department of Education.

Macken-Horarik, M., Sandiford, C., Love, K. & Unsworth, L. (2015). New ways of working 'with grammar in mind' in School English: Insights from systemic functional grammatics. *Linguistics and Education*, 31, 145–158.

Macken-Horarik, M. & Sandiford, C. (2016). Diagnosing development: A grammatics for tracking student progress in narrative composition. *International Journal of Language Studies*, 10(3), 61–94.

Malcolm, K. (2010). *Phasal analysis: Analysing discourse through communication linguistics*. London & New York: Continuum.

Martin, J. R. (1985). *Factual writing: Exploring and challenging social reality*. Geelong, Victoria: Deakin University Press.

Martin, J. R. (1992). *English text: System and structure*. Amsterdam: Benjamins.

Martin, J R (1993). Genre and literacy – modelling context in educational linguistics. *ARAL*, 13, 141–172.

Martin, J. R. (1995). Text and clause: Fractal resonance. *Text*, 15 (1), 5–42.

Martin, J. R. (1996). Evaluating disruption: Symbolising theme in junior secondary narrative. In R. Hasan & G. Williams (Eds.), *Literacy in society* (pp. 124–171). London & New York: Longman,

Martin, J. R. (2008). Intermodal reconciliation: Mates in arms. In L. Unsworth (Ed.), *New literacies and the English curriculum* (pp. 112–148). London & New York: Continuum.

Martin, J. R. & White, P. (2005). *The language of evaluation: Appraisal in English*. New York: Palgrave Macmillan.

Martin, J. R. & Rose, D. (2008). *Genre relations: Mapping culture*. London & Oakville: Equinox.

Martin, J. R. Matthiessen, C. & Painter, C. (2010). *Deploying functional grammar*. Beijing: The Commercial Press.

Nodelman, P. (1988). *Words about pictures: The narrative art of children's picture books*. Athens, GA: University of Georgia Press.

O'Brien, A., Chandler, P. & Unsworth, L. (2010). 3D multi-modal authoring in the middle years: A research project. *Synergy*, 8(1), 1–5.

Oates, J. C. (1998). The origins and the art of the short story. In B. Lounsberry, S. Lohafer, M. Rohrberger, S. Pett & R. C. Feddersen (Eds.), *The tales we tell* (pp. 47–52). Westport: Greenwood Press.

Painter, C., Martin, J. R. & Unsworth, L. (2013). *Reading visual narratives: Image analysis of children's picture books*. London: Equinox.

Pratt. M. L. (1994). The Short Story: The long and the short of it. In C. E. May (Ed.), *The new short story theories* (pp. 91–113). Athens, OH: Ohio University Press.

Prince, G. (1982). *Narratology: The form and function of narrative*. The Hague: Mouton.

Rose, D. & Martin, J. R. (2012). *Learning to write, reading to learn: Genre, knowledge and pedagogy in the Sydney School*. London: Equinox.

Rothery, J. (1989). Learning about language. In R. Hasan & J. R. Martin (Eds.), *Language development: Learning language, learning culture* (pp. 199–256). Norwood, NJ: Ablex.

Rothery, J. (1994). *Exploring literacy in school English (Write it right resources for literacy and learning)*. Sydney: Metropolitan East Disadvantaged Schools Program.

Rothery, J. & Stenglin, M. (2000). Interpreting Literature: The role of appraisal. In L. Unsworth (Ed.), *Researching language in schools and communities: Functional Linguistics approaches* (pp. 222–244). London: Cassell.

Scholes, R. (1985). *Textual power*. New Haven, CT: Yale University Press.

Simpson, P. (1993). *Language, ideology and point of view*. London & New York: Routledge

Simpson, P. (2004). *Stylistics: A resource book for students*. London & New York: Routledge.

Spiegelman, A. (1997). *Maus: A survivor's tale*. New York: Pantheon.

Stephens, J. (1992). *Language and ideology in children's fiction*. London & New York: Longman.

Tan, S. (2000). *The lost thing*. Sydney, NSW: Lothian.

Toolan, M. (1988). *Narrative: A critical linguistic introduction*. London & New York: Routledge.

Trimarco, P. (2011) Short shorts: Exploring the relevance and filling in narratives. In A. Cox (Ed.), *Teaching the short story* (pp. 13–27). Hampshire (UK) & New York: Palgrave Macmillan.

Unsworth, L. & Macken-Horarik, M. (2014). Interpretive responses to images in picture books by primary and secondary school students: Exploring curriculum expectations of a 'visual grammatics'. *English in Education*, 49(1), 56–79.

Unsworth, L. & Thomas, A. (Eds.) (2014). *English teaching and new literacies pedagogy: Interpreting and authoring digital multimedia narratives*. New York: Peter Lang Publishing.

Wheatley, N. & Ottley, M. (1999). *Luke's way of looking*. Rydalmere, NSW: Hodder Headline Australia

Winton, T. (1997). *Blueback*. London: Picador.

3
'THE WILD WEST'
Understanding resources for meaning in narrative

Moving into the sometimes forbidding territory of language and image

In Chapter 2, we proposed that a grammatics adequate to disciplinary practices in English should deepen students' intuitions about how narrative works and support reasoning about why it works this way. We assumed that an understanding of the grammar-genre connection was a good starting point if we want to relate grammatical choices to the design of texts. We considered the principle of metafunctions as 'lenses on meaning', considering their association with different kinds of grammatical structure. Then we applied this principle to narratives like *Fantastic Mr Fox* and *The Weapon* and to images in picture books like *The Great Bear* and *The Lost Thing*. Finally, we looked closely at Ideational meaning and how the system of TRANSITIVITY helps us understand the 'building blocks' of characterization, plotting and setting in narratives.

It will be clear by now that what Hasan (1985, p. 98) calls 'second order semiosis' is not restricted to verbal art. It is just as relevant to images in multimodal texts. Because the theory of grammar is based on meaning, we can deploy analogous resources within TRANSITIVITY to explore visual representation. This is not to suggest that words and pictures mirror each other; they do different kinds of work and operate differently in different contexts. Semiotic modes are shaped "both by the intrinsic characteristics and potentialities of the medium and by the requirements, histories and values of societies" as Kress and van Leeuwen (1996, p. 34) point out. But a functional grammatics enables us to investigate commonalities, counterpoints and differences between 'what is going on' visually and verbally. As with verbal transitivity, analysis of images is not intended to suggest that simply identifying components like Participants, Processes and Circumstances gives us privileged access to narrative artistry in relation to 'world building'. Rather it is to suggest that a grammatics can (and should) ground insights into this through analysis of choices for language and image in multimodal texts.

When we look more closely at semiotic resources in their own right, we shift our gaze away from the 'true north' of disciplinary practices and consider verbal and visual systems and the levels at which they work. For many teachers of Language Arts and English, this is an invitation to enter the dark woods or, to shift metaphors, the open spaces of the 'wild west'. As we acknowledged in Chapter 1, this is often forbidding territory for teachers, especially those without a strong grounding in linguistics. It has both theoretical and practical implications too, because teachers firstly have to understand how grammar works before they can apply this effectively in teaching and assessment. Furthermore, this is territory where a native-like grasp of 'what works' in communication is insufficient. Teachers need a specialised metalanguage for explaining the workings of grammar to students, beyond folk terminology used in everyday metalanguages. In this chapter, we turn our attention to how grammar figures in the larger territory of language and SF principles of organization can be adapted to exploration of non-verbal semiotic resources like images.

Trekking into unfamiliar territory requires a good map and navigational tools for finding our bearings. Maps provide a holistic view of the larger territory and its parts. They are variable in scale and do well with large delineable patterns. As Halliday maintains, maps vary significantly: "We can have interpersonal maps (the coloured ones showing political boundaries), ideational maps (physical or 'bathyorographical' ones) and even textual maps (maps of railway systems, power lines, dialects and the like)" (Halliday, 2008, p. 73). For those making forays into the wild(er) territory of grammar and the even less well-mapped grammar of visual communication, maps need to be accurate enough to guide the passage of walkers and runners who are keen to explore the territory and make it to home base in good time. This is the approach we offer in our guide to the internal organization of language: we attempt to be faithful to some of the complexity of verbal and visual systems and to highlight their relevance to tasks of subject English.

In this chapter, we look more closely at systemic functional principles of **system** and **stratification**, focussing on how these work in narratives produced for and by students. We focus first on the interpersonal metafunction, dealing with interactive resources of MOOD, POLARITY and TAGGING and then turn to APPRAISAL to consider how narratives position readers through direct and indirect forms of evaluation. This is such a rich area of exploration that we give this chapter over to resources associated with interpersonal meaning, leaving textual meaning to exploration of persuasion in later chapters. This chapter introduces additional narratives – a story by Paul Jennings called *Unhappily Ever After* (1999) and student texts. As with earlier chapters, first mention of a technical term is indicated with initial capitals and highlighting and the names of systems like MOOD with small capitals. Where possible, we explain choices in systems using examples from familiar texts. Occasionally, we need to confect examples that highlight relevant contrasts in choices.

Exploring interactive systems of choice in verbal texts

It is common to think of choice as an individual matter, in the case of composers, as a matter of specialised (often inspired) artistry. An author or artist chooses from a range of options to shape a 'possible world' of experience, engage readers subjectively and shape his or her composition in particular ways. We can use metafunctional lenses on this process, focussing on decisions made in composing a text: Who will narrate the story? Who will speak and to whom? What about? From whose point of view will events be presented? How will they be evaluated? And so on. All storytellers must find their own answers to such questions, even if they aren't conscious of doing so. If our 'optic' is attuned to questions of narrative craft, it is easier to predict the consequences of a composer's decisions.

A subjective narrative is likely to result in use of **First Person,** evaluative language and limited omniscience in the narrator. Semantically kindred choices occur in visual interaction. Within the system of SUBJECTIVITY for example, we consider how involved or detached viewers are from represented participants and how much visual power we are 'given' in our view of them. A more 'objective' narrative will lead to different choices – perhaps **Third Person** narration, external focalization (limitation of point of view to what can be observed only) and restrained levels of evaluation. Within the contrasting visual system of OBJECTIVITY, we are more likely to experience a knowledge-oriented view of what is happening, perhaps a top-down, more distanced view of things in the image. As we read the texts, we interpret choices as motivated by higher order concerns and here we are once again in the domain of second order semiosis. Having access to a multilevel model of text can support this kind of work, enabling us to shift upwards from forms of expression to their function in stretches of text to their thematic significance in the work as a whole.

In Chapter 2, we used the Ideational lens to probe the grammar of setting character and plot. The same approach is relevant to interpersonal meaning which engages us with the overarching question of how a text positions readers to adopt a given point of view on experience. With this lens, we consider different questions related to narration, focalization, dialogue and evaluation. Table 3.1 highlights the relationship between each aspect of narrative composition.

Let's look at an early interaction between two characters in *Fantastic Mr Fox* and how the grammar of this exchange communicates the quality of their relationship.

> Every evening as soon as it got dark, Mr Fox would say to Mrs Fox, 'Well, my darling, what shall it be this time? A plump chicken from Boggis? A duck or a goose from Bunce? Or a nice turkey from Bean?' And when Mrs Fox had told him what she wanted, Mr Fox would creep down into the valley in the darkness of the night and help himself.

This exchange, in microcosm, exemplifies the intimacy of this couple's connection. But we only know this because the grammar of the interaction can enact it

TABLE 3.1 Probe questions related to interpersonal aspects of narrative craft

Interpersonal Lens – interacting with and positioning readers & viewers	*Overarching Question:* What is the point of view from which you are being positioned to experience the text? *Narration:* (Who tells the story?) – a narrator or character? Is this 'person' internal or external to events in the story? First/third person? How reliable is their knowledge of what happens? *Focalization* (Who sees?): Through whose eyes are events presented? How is this viewpoint mediated verbally? Visually? *Dialogue or voicing* (Who speaks?): How do characters address one another? Do they use endearments, intimate language or formal language or the language of antagonists? Does the dialogue reveal character? How does it do this? How is dialogue represented in images if at all? *Evaluation* (What attitudes are expressed?): Systems within ATTITUDE include the following three sub-systems within APPRAISAL: AFFECT: How are characters' feelings of un/happiness, in/security and dis/satisfaction portrayed? Do you empathize with them or feel distanced? JUDGEMENT: How are personal traits (capacity, normality, tenacity) of the characters portrayed? How are evaluations of truth or moral and ethical issues conveyed? Do these invited social and ethical judgements align you or distance you from the characters? APPRECIATION: How is a particular atmosphere or ambience conveyed? *Intensity* (How loud or soft is Evaluation?): Consider GRADUATION – use exclamatives, intensifiers or repetition in language and strong colours and contrasts in the images? Where do such choices occur? Why here?

so vividly. Mr Fox's use of the **Vocative** – 'my darling' – signifies his love for his wife. The offer, carried through the **Interrogative Question** – 'What shall it be this time?' – leaves the decision to Mrs Fox (you decide!). A **Wh-interrogative** (often called 'content interrogative') has a distinctive structure: the Wh-element (in this case, 'What') is followed by a **Finite** verb (shall) and this comes before the **Subject** (it) and the **Predicator** (be tonight). A third aspect of the grammar of this exchange is Fox's use of **Ellipsis**. When something is ellipsed, it is left out of a wording but taken for granted as understood by one's interlocutor. The first move in the exchange is a full one ('Well my darling, what shall it be tonight?') with Subject and Finite verb supplied. But the following question takes the Subject and Finite verb for granted and identifies only the meal options available to Mrs Fox and their 'suppliers'. We can supply this in brackets '(Shall it be) a plump chicken from Boggis? A duck or a goose from Bunce?' Taken together, these choices for Vocative, Wh-Interrogative and Ellipsis provide a snapshot of the interpersonal milieu of the foxes, its warmth and courtesy. The grammatical choices align us with the two characters and advance the plot through making their needs and intentions clear. It is the co-patterning of choices for MOOD, VOCATION and ELLIPSIS that generates this higher order intersubjectivity but we need to understand the role of grammar in this process. For many students in mainstream classrooms, these choices and their arrangements are a taken-for-granted feature of English in this interactive context (though not for those learning English as an additional language). The grammatics makes them visible and nameable and available for conscious uptake by students in all classrooms.

It can be fascinating to apply an understanding of interpersonal grammar to exchanges in different narratives. The first interaction in *The Weapon* works differently from that in *Fantastic Mr Fox*, through counter-expectancy rather than expectancy (Martin, 1996). This is in keeping with the goal of stories like this that overturn common-sense. The opening dialogue in *The Weapon*, challenges the assumption that science is beyond moral dilemmas. The stranger, Niemand, who is a seemingly 'harmless' man, knocks on the scientist's door and introduces himself:

> Dr Graham? My name is Niemand. I'd like to talk to you. May I come in for a moment?

When Graham assesses his visitor as inoffensive, he offers him a drink. As in the interaction between Mr Fox and his wife, this offer is managed grammatically through polite Ellipsis '(Would you) Care for a drink?' Following a series of polite speech acts, Niemand asserts:

> You are the man whose scientific work is more likely than that of any other man to end the human race's chance for survival.

This highly amplified declaration disrupts the expected direction of the exchange, shifting it from a relatively banal service encounter to an ideological battle about the global impact of Graham's work. Again, it is the grammatical resources – in this case, **Declarative Mood** – that enact the exchange. Understanding how the grammar 'does this' is essential groundwork.

This is not to suggest that in a literary text like this, it is just local exchanges between characters that carry the interpersonal meaning of the text as a whole. As readers, we often know more than the characters themselves and see more in dialogues than they do. For example, we are aware of Mr Fox's imminent danger when he leaves the fox-hole and this lends pathos to his expressions of confidence in his earlier conversation with Mrs Fox. By the end of *The Weapon*, we know just how destructive Graham's work is and perceive the irony in his final reflections on Niemand's actions:

> He thought, only a madman would give a loaded revolver to an idiot.

The narrative as a whole invites certain kinds of responsiveness on the part of (implied) readers. Because the larger interaction is between author and reader, we re-read dialogues in light of this second order semiosis: the narrative mediates our evaluations of the characters' words and actions (see Macken-Horarik, 2003 for further discussion of this point). And what is the role for the grammatics here? It enables us to analyse the local context of interactions between characters like Mr and Mrs Fox or Niemand and Graham and specific ways in which Vocatives, Mood and Ellipsis (amongst other features) work. More globally, it enables us to explore the combined effect of choices positioning readers in particular ways. It is the simultaneous work of these choices that shape our viewpoints on a character like Niemand or (at the other extreme) Mr Fox. Seeing how grammatical choices pattern and co-pattern gives us privileged access to the power of narrative to align, entertain and challenge us to new ways of thinking, whether about foxes, farmers or nuclear science.

It is clear that the notion of choice is vital to an understanding of narrative craft. But how does the grammatics incorporate the principle of choice in its internal 'architecture'? Let's consider this question through a close look at the system of MOOD, which is the resource at clause rank that enables us to interact with others. As Matthiessen and Halliday explain:

> In interacting with one another, we enter into a range of interpersonal relationships, choosing among semantic strategies such as cajoling, persuading, enticing, requesting, ordering, suggesting, asserting, insisting, doubting and so on. The grammar provides us with the basic resource for expressing these speech functions in the form of a highly generalised set of clause systems referred to as Mood.
>
> *(Matthiessen & Halliday, 2009, p. 3)*

What kinds of choices are available to us within the system of MOOD? The most general distinction in English (and Chinese and Japanese) is between **Indicative** and **Imperative**. An Indicative clause is used to exchange information while an Imperative is used to direct action. An Indicative clause can offer information through a **Declarative** or demand it through an **Interrogative**. An Interrogative can be a **Polar Interrogative** (often called a yes–no question) or a **Content Interrogative** (often called a 'Wh-question). In Table 3.2 the first example in each

TABLE 3.2 Examples of Mood choices and their structural forms

Example	Mood Type
Mr Fox crept up the dark tunnel.	Indicative: Declarative
Did Mr Fox creep up the tunnel?	Indicative: Polar Interrogative
Where did Mr Fox creep?	Indicative: Content Interrogative
Creep up the tunnel.	Imperative
He opened the door.	Indicative: Declarative
Did he open the door?	Indicative: Polar Interrogative
What did he open?	Indicative: Content Interrogative
Open the door	Imperative

set is taken from *Fantastic Mr Fox* and *The Weapon* and this is indicated through italics. The other three examples are created to bring out contrasts in Mood that make a difference to the exchange.

Choices within Mood are meaningful because they contrast with other choices available in a given grammatical environment. A quick look at each of these examples reveals structural differences (e.g. in what is put first) and similarities (e.g. the fact that all contain a verb) and we need to understand both. Structurally, the two basic MOOD types of Indicative and Imperative have features in common: they are ranking clauses (because they all include a verb) and they predicate (or assert) something about the **Subject**. But they differ in crucial ways and here we need to recognize formal differences between types of verb. Grammatically speaking, Indicative clauses have a **Finite** verb (e.g. open<u>ed</u>, <u>did</u> open), whereas Imperatives do not. A verb is finite if it is marked for **Tense** – past or present; and this form relates the verb to the Subject in person and or number. A **Non-Finite** verb can take two major forms: an infinitive (to-form as in 'to open') or a participle. A present participle adds -ing to a verb base as in 'an open<u>ing</u> door' while a past participle adds – ed to a verb base, as in 'an open<u>ed</u> door').

What about the other functional component of the Mood – the Subject? Classically defined, the **Subject** is 'that noun or pronoun that is in Person and Number concord with the verb'. In English, a third Person singular Subject occurs with a singular verb and a plural Subject occurs with a plural verb, as in 'He walks' versus 'They walk'. Of course, much of this information is available in traditional school grammatics too. Here we are attempting to show how particular choices for one option in an exchange affect others and how they function in an exchange.

For example, Indicative clauses take a Subject (e.g. Mr Fox, He) whereas Imperatives do not. More precisely, the Subject is 'understood' or supplied only in highly marked (emphatic) contexts, as in '<u>You</u> open the door! Many teachers we have worked with used a notional understanding of the Subject as 'what the sentence is about'. This is adequate as a starting point but will not help with recognizing more complex Subjects – whole clauses in nominalized forms of English for example. The Subject can be recognized as 'that element in a declarative clause that is picked up in the tag (Halliday & Matthiessen, 2004, p. 112). Teachers in The Grammatics Project found tag questions useful in identifying the Subject in sentences like 'What the fox stole was a plump chicken' where the Subject is 'What the fox stole'. Table 3.3 brings out the connection between Subject and Finite and the **Tagfinite** and **Tagsubject**. It also includes the remainder **(**called **Residue** in SF grammatics).

TABLE 3.3 A paradigm relating Subjects to Tags

Subject	Finite	Residue	Tagfinite	Tagsubject
The fox	stole	a plump chicken	didn't	he?
He	stole	a plump chicken	didn't	he?
What the fox stole	was	a plump chicken	wasn't	it?
Subject	**Finite**	**Residue**	**Tagfinite**	**Tagsubject**
				Tag

In Chapter 1, we briefly introduced the notion of the 'trinocular' view and the importance of this for a rich interpretation of grammar (Halliday, 2008). Preeminent within functional grammatics is the view 'from above', the view that highlights the function of choices in context. Viewed from this 'meta' vantage point, Mood types do different semantic work. Indicative Mood is essential to negotiation of propositions (giving or demanding information); Imperative Mood, on the other hand, is used to negotiate proposals (specifically demanding goods or services). There are more polite ways of getting services rendered than through the bald imperative of course. But Imperative Mood is the most direct (and congruent) way for commanding others (as any tired or stressed parent or teacher would attest). We will not focus on indirect forms of exchange in our current overview of interactive systems, only with most general and direct forms (see Halliday & Matthiessen, 2004 or Martin, Matthiessen & Painter, 2010 for full accounts).

The view 'from above' is central to the work of English and likely to be most familiar to teachers. But it is also necessary to understand the view from 'from below' which means from the point of view of grammatical form. However, as we acknowledged in Chapter 1, this can cause problems for teachers with a weak linguistic knowledge. It can lead to problems with 'functional shift' in which words change their word class depending on their function in a clause. If teachers rely too much on notional or semantic understandings of word classes (the view from above), they cannot see how they function differently in different roles. They may be able to classify 'ran' as a verb when it clearly functions as a 'doing word', but have trouble identifying its form when it is used as a Classifier in a nominal group in '<u>running</u> shoe' or as Thing in 'going for a <u>run</u>'. As we indicated in Chapter 1, functional shift presents difficulties for many teachers of English in Australia (Jones & Chen, 2012) and in the United Kingdom (Cajkler & Hislam, 2002; Myhill, 2000; Myhill, Jones & Watson, 2013). Being able to adopt the view 'from below' is necessary to address this kind of weakness. It supports confident recognition of the structure or form of grammatical choices and their structural consequences.

Each semantic choice in an exchange has structural consequences. If we ask a yes/no question, we put the Finite verb before the Subject and if we ask a Content or Wh-question, we put the Wh element first (e.g. What, Where, Who). In this 'orienteering' task, a knowledge of traditional school grammar can be helpful. We must be able to recognize a Subject, Finite verb or Wh-element if we are to experiment with speech functions in our interactions with others. And we must repair this when we experience problems with these, not so much for the sake of grammatical 'correctness' for its own sake as for the sake of successful interactions. Students learning English as an additional language have a keener awareness of this than those who have learned grammar through immersion in English but understanding how 'grammar does it' is essential knowledge for all students.

However, it must also be said that an understanding of formal differences between one MOOD choice and another is insufficient. A second, more grammatically specialised, knowledge base is available through what Halliday (2002, 2008) calls the view 'from around'. Once we are in a particular grammatical 'environment', such as the clause, we can explore the mutual interplay of one system and another within the same region of meaning. Some systems are closely related to others. Mood type is connected to the system of **POLARITY** (with features of Positive or Negative). Grammarians can make the relationships between choices more visible using paradigms like the following in Table 3.4 below.

So far, the systems we have introduced for managing interactions with others have been relatively simple. But a grammatics adequate to more complex interactions must account for the full range of available options. For example, the **Tagged Declarative** is a specific kind of Declarative as in 'They were rich men' versus 'They were rich men, weren't they?' and a **Polar (yes/no) Interrogative** is a kind of Interrogative that is structured differently from the Wh- (content) interrogative, as in 'Do you want a plump chicken from Boggis?' versus 'What shall it be tonight?' The general options within Mood become the environment for more delicate (fine-grained) ones that 'inherit' more general properties on the left. In this way, we can see how specific options are related to general systems (see Matthiessen & Halliday, 2009 for further explanation).

Figure 3.1 arrays choices within MOOD to bring out the structural consequences for two types of Interrogative and Tagged Declaratives within Indicative Mood.

The view 'from around' a system like MOOD often involves linguistic arguments about which differences 'make a difference' in grammar. They are less likely to feature in a grammatics for school English, which privileges the view 'from above'. This latter perspective invites questions like 'what does this mean?' and considers grammatical choices as motivated by higher order purposes. For instance, in the exchange between Mr and Mrs Fox, we considered the combined effect of the intimate Vocative ('my darling'), the Ellipsis typical of casual conversation and Mr Fox's use of a Wh-Interrogative to ask Mrs Fox what she wants for dinner. Taken together, these grammatical selections index the intimacy of their relationship and the graciousness of his query. But we need to understand how resources like MOOD and associated systems work if we are to interpret the role of grammar in communicating this intimacy.

As we move into more delicate regions of the lexicogrammatical network, we move towards lexis as 'most delicate grammar' (Hasan, 1987). While general choices for interaction can be accommodated through MOOD, more specific attitudinal features are better explored within lexis and we pick up on this later in the chapter when we outline aspects of the system of APPRAISAL (Martin & White, 2005). But it

TABLE 3.4 A paradigm relating Mood Type to Polarity

		Mood Type	
		Indicative	*Imperative*
Polarity:	Positive	Adam opened the door	Open the door
	Negative	Adam didn't open the door	Don't open the door

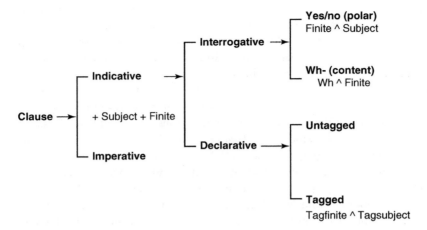

FIGURE 3.1 Options for meaning in Mood and their structural consequences.

is possible to shift from interaction in language to the virtual interaction suggested by images using the system network as a 'way in' to visual choices.

Exploring interactive systems of choice in images

Analogous choices for interpersonal meaning can be discerned in systems within visual communication. Theorists of picture books like Perry Nodelman (1988) anticipated the contribution to interpretation afforded by what we refer to as a 'grammatics of images'. Nodelman was anticipating:

> the possibility of a system underlying visual communication that is something like a grammar – something like the system of relationships and contexts that makes verbal communication possible.
>
> *(Nodelman, 1988, p. ix)*

System networks like the one for MOOD display options for meaning in a given semiotic environment with an entry condition on the left hand of the network and more delicate choices on the right. A curly brace indicates that all systems contained within this are freely combinable. Each system within represents contrasts in meaning: to choose one option is to exclude others. Many teachers report that children find it easier to identify contrasting options when beginning to analyse images. They learn to recognize a form (e.g. a Figure directing the gaze outwards to viewers) and to label its function (e.g. **Demand**). Figure 3.2 identifies the systems of SOCIAL DISTANCE, SUBJECTIVITY and OBJECTIVITY (Kress & van Leeuwen, 2006). It includes probe questions developed in The Grammatics Project to make identification of features easier for students. We explore our adaptation of what Kress & van Leeuwen call CONTACT for visual FOCALIZATION later in the chapter.

'The Wild West': resources (narrative) 77

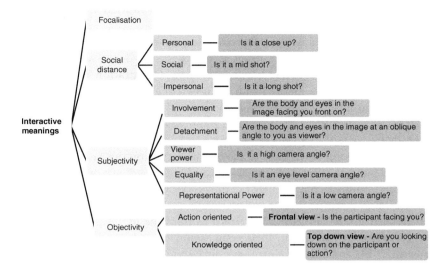

FIGURE 3.2 Three major systems for interactive meaning in images.

The system of SOCIAL DISTANCE (Kress & van Leeuwen, 2006) is realized by 'size of frame'. For example, if represented participants appear as head and shoulders only, they are up close to viewers. If the entire body of the participant is visible, the character appears more distant; and if the participant's whole body is depicted in the background, the character appears more remote. These extremes are commonly referred to in film metalanguage as a **Close-Up**, **Mid Shot** and **Long Shot** respectively. Greater social distance is associated with appreciative engagement and close-up images with empathic engagement.

The system of SUBJECTIVITY includes options of **Involvement** or **Detachment** in viewer relations with depicted characters. Involvement positions viewers to feel more closeness to participants. This is influenced by the horizontal angle (Kress & van Leeuwen, 2006, p. 133). If the depicted participants are presented facing the viewer 'front on', there is a maximum involvement with them. On the other hand, if the participants are depicted at an oblique angle, this positions the viewer as more detached from depicted participants. The greater the oblique angle the more detached is the viewer. Also included in this system are options relating to the relative power accorded to the viewer or the depicted participants and these are realized by the vertical angle of the image. If participants are seen from a **High Angle**, with the viewer looking down on them, then they are depicted as if the viewer has power over them. If the participants are seen at **Eye Level** there is a sense of equality between them and the viewer. When the viewer is positioned at a **Low Angle** – below depicted participants – they are represented as having power *over* the viewer. *The Great Bear* (Gleeson & Greder, 1999), which we introduced in Chapter 2, is a story about an ill-treated dancing bear in a circus who eventually rebels and escapes her bonds. The high angle view of the villagers in the image presented in Figure

78 'The Wild West': resources (narrative)

2.2 depicts the potentially powerful position of the bear in relation to the crowds who are tormenting her.

In another of the visual systems related to interpersonal meaning, of OBJECTIVITY refers to whether the view of an image is 'frontal' or top-down. Most images in narratives are frontal images and adopt an **Action Orientation** to represented events. Top-down views associated with a **Knowledge Orientation** are rare, but when top-down images do occur their narrative effect is very pronounced. One such image occurs in *The Lost Thing* (Tan, 2000) when the boy and the lost thing are outside the Federal Department of Odds and Ends – "a tall grey building with no windows". The top down view of the two characters on the pavement outside this very tall building emphasises the de-personalized experience of their encounter with this institution. Interestingly, the movie version of the story includes more subjective images, thus inviting a more empathic relationship with central characters (Ruhemann & Tan, 2010). We return to this issue in Chapter 8 where we consider uptake by students in their composition of multimodal texts (and see Unsworth, 2014a and 2014b for extensive discussion of this issue).

Figure 3.3[1] presents an image from *The Tunnel* (Browne, 1989) in which a young girl called Rose stands outside a dark tunnel waiting for her brother to re-emerge. The composer has chosen to represent Rose's frontal plane parallel with the frontal plane of the viewer. This combined with the relatively close 'shot' and eye-level view generates a high degree of emotional involvement between Rose and viewer.

The principle of system is a useful resource for exploring verbal and visual choices, though it represents a synoptic rather than dynamic approach to this. An artist chooses to depict a character in a particular way and this is an unfolding process. A system network is a heuristic that attempts to capture available choices within the vast meaning potential from which we select when we produce a message. As we indicated earlier, systems are multiple and, within each metafunction, mutually sensitive. Grammatical systems like POLARITY, MODALITY and MOOD are all 'in play' in

FIGURE 3.3 An image from The Tunnel depicting Rose.

a dialogue, along with attitudinal meanings to which we turn shortly. When it comes to images, interactive systems such as SOCIAL DISTANCE, SUBJECTIVITY and OBJECTIVITY collectively shape our response to depicted figures like Rose above. Having a view of the potential of image or verbiage can support students' work on texts – giving them a powerful purchase on the features in a text and how to talk about them insightfully.

Managing interaction in narrative composition

As we indicated earlier, the text is a kind of macro-exchange with the reader, or at least the 'implied reader' (Toolan, 1988, pp. 78–80). Within the 'possible world' generated by the narrative, dialogue can reveal character, establish motivations and advance a plot. But learning to manage the structural demands of MOOD, MODALITY and POLARITY can be a trial, especially if writers' dialogues are to function effectively. Text 3.1 is called *The Door*. It was produced by a Year 7 student prior to work with The Grammatics Project and represents starkly the difficulty many writers have with dialogue, even with its layout. The text (Text 3.1) is reproduced in publisher's typeface for ease of reading.

> "Dinner time" Mum said, "coming" Jim said, "same" bob said, dinner was roast lamb and mash. "dinner is nice mum" said bob, "may I be excused from the Table" Jim said. Jim walked to the bin to put his food in it. bob did the same and they both went outside to play.

TEXT 3.1 *The Door* - transcribed text by Year 7 student.

Text 3.2 is both more successful and more ambitious:

> "Why would you do something like that James." Mum yelled.
> Your proubley wondering how i got to be in this problem.
> Well if all started when we moved to Summer Hight a pretty little town.
> But my new school was quite the opasort.
> I had no friends at all.
> Until John hardley walked up to me and offered to be apart of his gang.

TEXT 3.2 Dialogue by Daki.

Daki has produced a dramatic snatch of dialogue in her opening sentence but she struggles to use this to introduce the situation facing the protagonist and to manage the shift between the 'you' of the character yelled at by her mother and the 'you' of the implied reader. Learning to manage dialogue is far more than a task of indicating what one character says to another, separating the words used by different characters and making decisions about alternatives to 'said', something often taught in writing classes. It involves managing the to and fro of exchanges between characters (shifts of MOOD, MODALITY and POLARITY) whilst simultaneously advancing the larger exchange with readers. Daki is struggling to integrate her strategy of beginning 'in media res' – plunging readers into the middle of the action – with her need to orient readers successfully to the characters' situation.

As we discovered in The Grammatics Project, incorporating such strategies can disturb the relatively settled repertoires of writers with their standard approaches to the Orientation stage of a narrative. The problem Daki faces is how to establish the situation facing the protagonist (in this case his move to a new town and a difficult school and the need to find a friendship group) whilst using dialogue to do so. The response of the character's mother to what we later discover is a theft by the protagonist of an engagement ring as part of a dare by 'John Hardley' is an early experiment with foreshadowing. It is not an easy feat to manage the larger interaction created by the text with its implied (hopefully ideal) reader whilst establishing the interpersonal realities of characters within the worlds generated by narratives.

Text 3.3 comes from a young adult novel about a girl who discovers a body at the funeral home where she works and must piece together the mystery after her boss goes missing under a cloud of suspicion. In this extract, the nineteen-year old author – Janicka – deploys dialogue to advance the plot, reveal character *and* express humour:

"Hello?"
"I've got news for you," my grandma said.
"What is it? I have to get back to work."
"You mean you still have a job?"
"Of course, I do!"
"But your boss … he's a murderer."
"No. He isn't."
"Well," she purred, "*I* heard from a woman at the Salon – who's sleeping with a cop from Duri – but you didn't hear it from me – that the woman they found *didn't* die of natural causes."
My body wilted in the chair, the phone almost sliding out of my hand.

TEXT 3.3 Janicka's dialogic Orientation to her narrative.

In this short stretch of dialogue, the author communicates important news in the exchange but does so in a way that illuminates character. It is clear for example that the grandma in this story is a gossip. The verb 'purred' and the aside – 'but you didn't hear it from me' – confirms an impression of her salacious interest in affairs of people at the Salon. Learning to generate interpersonal meaning through creative use of interactive resources is a hard-won achievement. Knowledge of the systems that make it possible and how to use them in writing is a crucial part of the process.

Exploring stratification in language and image

We turn our attention now to the principle of stratification and the viewpoints on grammar that different strata (or 'landing places') afford. Most people who study language recognize that it is a multilevel phenomenon. As Halliday explains this:

> We are accustomed to talking about language under different headings. School grammar books used to have chapters on pronunciation, orthography, morphology (earlier 'accidence') and syntax, with a vocabulary added at the end. This acknowledged the fact that a language is a complex semiotic system, having various levels, or **strata**.
>
> *(Halliday & Matthiessen, 2004, p. 24, highlighting in original)*

As we explained in our Chapter 1, systemic functional theory stratifies language into different levels of organization (semantics, lexicogrammar and phonology or graphology). However, shifting in informed ways between these levels of organization requires a theory of language that will support this kind of work and takes us beyond rule of thumb expressions such as 'text, sentence and word levels of language'. It requires a theory of language that enables teachers not simply to be able to recognize which level they are on but to understand the kind of work they can do at each level. We have spent some time earlier in this chapter on the importance of recognizing grammatical forms and being able to label and describe their function in syntagms (clauses, for example). We have also explored the ways in which choices for meaning and form are motivated by higher order themes or preoccupations of the author or artist. These are shaped by the social context in which texts are produced and read.

If we work from the level of context 'downward', contexts are 'realized' or expressed through clusters of choices for meaning (often called registers integrated into genres). For example, narrative genres 'package' experience in particular ways, invite certain kinds of interaction with readers and tend to have a predictable, often temporal, organization. At the level of what Martin (1992) calls 'discourse semantics', we find predictable (and sometimes surprising) patterns of IDEATION, CONJUNCTION and APPRAISAL in texts. At the level of lexicogrammar, we find meanings turned into wordings and, at the level of phonology, wordings are realized in patterns of sound or in the case of graphology in visible marks on a page or screen. More recent research in multimodality has extended the stratified model of language to images, typography, displayed art and film. Early extensions of the theory into analysis of artworks such as that by O'Toole (1994) explored the relevance of a stratified model of communication for non-linguistic communication. While some multimodal theorists (e.g. Kress & van Leeuwen, 2006) have little use for this principle, others exploit it productively to explain the workings of complex semiotic forms such as film narratives (Bateman, 2013).

Stratification may appear complex but it is a linguistic interpretation of an educational commonplace. Teachers decode the grammatical choices in students' writing, inferring meanings made through their wordings. Where handwriting is poor, they comment on the difficulty this material form of expression poses for decoding and thus understanding meaning. This is one version of Halliday's claim that we need a 'trinocular' view of grammar – a view 'from above' with an emphasis on 'function in context'; 'from below', with an emphasis on grammatical form; and 'from around', with an emphasis on relevant systems. At discourse semantics level, we consider patterns of meaning in texts; at the grammatical level, we explore wordings and their function; at the level of output, we work with formal arrangements. Each level is a kind of 'landing place' and we do different kinds of work and adopt different viewpoints depending on which level we are standing on at the time. Several studies have confirmed the importance of attention to word, sentence and text levels of language (Christie, 2002; Christie & Derewianka, 2008; Rose & Martin, 2012; Wray, Medwell, Fox & Poulson, 2000). We are only just beginning to understand the implications of this insight and the importance of different viewpoints available at each level.

Formalist and traditional approaches put the view 'from below' at the centre of their descriptions and give less attention (if any) to the function of structures (the meanings they make). Traditional grammatics, for example, emphasises the need for subject-verb agreement in sentences. But it mostly ignores 'the why' beneath the rule. By contrast, a functional grammatics is interested in why subject-verb agreement is important. If the connection of Subject and Finite verb is crucial to interaction, it is because it enables us to predict and respond to moves in an exchange – ask and (perhaps) answer a question, give information, offer something, command someone to do something and so on. In an exchange about the truth or falsity of a claim, it is the Mood element that is central to the argument, and is in italics in the following exchange:

> *This is* a real worry,
> *No, it's not* (a real worry'),
> *Yes, it is* (a real worry') ... and so on.

The Subject and Finite verb are held constant, while Polarity (yes and no) varies and the exchange hinges on the shift between yes and no. But if we consider the territory between 'yes and no', we move into a different region in the same interpersonal territory – **Modality**. Modality is the region between yes and no in which degrees of probability (from 'may be' or 'could be' to 'must be') and assessments of truth are discussed and typically it is realized grammatically by modal verbs (e.g. could or might), adverbs (e.g. definitely or probably) and even nouns (e.g. the possibility, the probability).

> This is a real worry,
> Well, it *could* be (a real worry'),
> It is *definitely* a worry.

Of course, if we are to understand the grammar of interaction, both function and form (and hence views 'from above' and 'from below') are important. As we explained earlier, students need to be able to identify the Subject and Finite verb in a clause, along with other constituents. But they also need to be able to gloss or describe the contribution each makes, to success (or otherwise) of a speech act. And this is where it all gets so interesting. In a functional perspective, we investigate how systems like MOOD, MODALITY and POLARITY contribute to dialogue in narrative, to rhetorical tropes in persuasion and to political and indeed all kinds of arguments.

Like language, visual communication cannot be tackled on one level of description. Whether in static bimodal texts like picture books or dynamic multimodal texts like films, this notion enables us to distribute the work of analysis across different levels. Whilst all choices are open to interpretation, a stratified analysis allows us to "determine just which material distinctions are to be considered 'semiotically charged' and which not" (Bateman, 2013, p. 56). In analysing images, for example, teachers may begin at the material level of form, identifying, for example, whether a character's gaze is direct or averted, whether viewers are positioned above, at eye level or below depicted Figures. They then discuss the significance of these 'charged' options, drawing on a visual metalanguage. If they are analysing colour, students might identify the colour palette on pages of a picture book and features they notice. They might investigate contrasts between features and whether these change in the course of the text. In this way, they shift upwards the levels of organization in multimodal texts, moving from form to function to consider the contribution of charged options to the interpersonal meaning of the whole. The same principle works for point of view, or what is called visual FOCALIZATION (Painter *et al.*, 2013).

Within this system, students investigate gaze. A direct gaze on the part of a represented Figure makes **Contact** with the viewer, whereas a Figure that does not gaze at the viewer calls forth contemplation in what is called an **Observe** image (Painter *et al.*, 2013, p. 30). We can find differentiation within Contact: it can be **Direct** (via a frontal gaze) or **Invited** (with the eyes/ head of the character turned towards the viewer from the side). Focalization can also insinuate the viewer into the world represented by the image. If the viewer is positioned either 'along with' or 'as' a character this is regarded as **Inscribed Mediation.** It contrasts with **Inferred Mediation**, which is managed through relations between one image, one page or one shot and another. In **Unmediated Focalization,** a character makes 'contact' or is observed without any intervening relation to other features of the image (such as occurs through extended hands or a shadow produced by a character standing outside an image (see Painter *et al.*, 2013 for discussion of these). Figure 3.4[2] presents the major options within the visual system of Focalization, building on the work of Painter *et al.*, 2013.

Once students can identify formal choices like gaze and describe their function using a semiotic metalanguage, they can more easily relate individual features to larger clusters or 'syndromes' of meaning in the text. Figure 3.3 above shows Rose waiting for her brother outside the tunnel. In terms of the system of FOCALIZATION, her gaze invites Direct Contact with the viewer. Combined with other interactive choices within SOCIAL DISTANCE (close up), SUBJECTIVITY (frontal orientation and eye level angle) this aligns us with Rose. However, once she has

'The Wild West': resources (narrative)

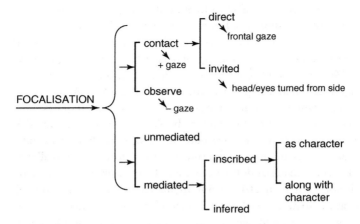

FIGURE 3.4 Options within visual Focalization.

confronted her fears and entered the tunnel, travelling through the dark forest to rescue her petrified brother and they are reconciled, Brown's representation of gaze changes correspondingly.

Figure 3.5 below reveals the combination of an 'over the shoulder' view of her brother in close-up, the hint of a smile on his face and overlapping backgrounds (which were previously quite distinct) all highlight a change in their relationship.

This image embodies in their mutual regard the change in the relationship between Rose and her brother. The images exist in a complementary relationship to the words in this literary work, generating by their synergy the larger themes of sibling rivalry and the creation of sibling solidarity that these two characters find at the end of their adventure.

The principle of stratification allows teachers to address and transcend challenges often issued by those with an investment in grammatical form. We can 'land on' analysis of formal units like word classes, but not be limited to exercises of parsing. Teachers do need to help students learn to identify a constituent (e.g. verb group, with verb as head) but also to describe the work (or function) of that constituent in clauses (e.g. sensing, doing, saying, relating). At higher landing places, they need to help students interpret clusters of choices in 'syndromes' of meanings – whether generated visually or verbally. Traditional school grammatics offers tools for identifying the formal structure of grammatical syntagms but does not 'reach into' higher levels of organization. This limits its value to study of narrative, rhetoric or other domains of inquiry.

How does this work in relation to literary texts that are more complex in their structure and thus in the syndromes of meaning they deploy? At this point we return to a short novel introduced earlier. *Blueback* by Tim Winton (1997) deals with the adventures of a boy who lives with his mother on the edge of a marine park. It is a powerful coming of age story and raises important issues of environmental protection. Its subtitle – 'A Contemporary Fable' – suggests its instructional

FIGURE 3.5 Final page of *The Tunnel*.

purpose. But its power to teach lies in large part through its ability to engage readers with the interior world of Abel, the central character, as he moves towards awareness of the need to fight for the protection of fragile aquatic environments and vulnerable species. Abel's encounter with the groper in Chapter 1 sets the scene for this ongoing transformation. A key resource for inviting identification with Abel is strategic use of Focalization. It is on display in the first two paragraphs of the novel:

> Just as the sun came up, Abel pulled on his wetsuit and ran down the jetty. Already his mother was in the dinghy with the outboard motor running. It was cold this morning and Abel was still half asleep. He got down into the boat, untied the bowline and pushed them clear. With a purr of the outboard they surged away.
>
> In the bow, he looked around, slowly waking up in the cold rush of air. Sunlight caught the windows of the shack above the beach so that every pane of glass looked like a little fire. He watched his mother's hair blow back off her shoulders. She squinted a little. Her skin was tanned and wrinkled from the sun. He felt the sea pulsing under him as the little boat skimmed across the bay.

In the first paragraph, we move the external perspective on two characters' morning fishing trip to an internally focalised account in the second paragraph. We see what Abel sees, communicated primarily through Mental Processes like 'looked', 'watched' and 'felt'. But what Abel sees is communicated through other Process types, metaphoric Material ones like 'caught' and 'skimmed', Behavioural Processes like 'squinted' and Relational ones like 'was'. The grammar does the work here, shifting us between the world of Abel's consciousness and the external world of air, sunlight, his mother's hair and skin. This back and forth movement is akin to the 'point of view' shot in films that moves between the focalising character's face and the world he or she sees. This strategy is a mainstay in cinematic storytelling and aids in generating identification between viewer and character (Bordwell, 1985).

If we can ensure that students are secure on each landing place – recognition of forms, description of their function (e.g. through functional labelling) and interpretation of their larger significance for the text – then we are well on the way to meeting curriculum requirements to 'learn about connections' between levels of organization in language (ACARA, 2012). Recent research on how visual and verbal choices 'couple' in multimodal texts can be followed up in Bednarak and Martin (2010), whilst the importance of undertaking this work is underscored in Unsworth (2006). For our purposes, the key is to have access to a framework that supports the intuitions of teachers and students as they make forays into literary interpretation. However, a full understanding of how texts position us cannot be achieved without a closer look at more subtle dimensions of interpersonal meaning in narrative which Martin and White (2005) capture under the rubric of APPRAISAL.

A step into more delicate regions of the interpersonal territory – APPRAISAL

So far, we have looked closely at two principles of organization in language (system and stratification), focussing on interpersonal meaning in verbal and visual communication. If the system of MOOD is crucial to the grammar of exchange, it is only one (admittedly crucial) factor in the negotiation of an exchange (see Martin, 2000 for a seminal paper on this issue). There are also evaluatively charged resources at more delicate ends of the lexicogrammatical spectrum that express the 'personal' within interpersonal meaning. These are delicate choices in vocabulary that colour the 'mood' or ambience of a text and position us to see, feel, judge and appreciate things in particular ways. Furthermore, as we indicated earlier, they are typically prosodic in realization – dispersed across stretches of text rather than discrete. If we return to the analogy of the map, these features are part of a closer reading of the semiotic terrain, subtler gradations in topology or environment of a text.

Moving into this ineffable region has been both challenging and crucial to the engagement of school English with systemic functional theory. As Martin explains:

> Our work on secondary school and workplace discourse in the 1990s (e.g. Christie & Martin, 1997; Martin & Veel, 1998) convinced us that this

essentially grammatical perspective on interactivity needs to be complemented with a more lexically based focus on 'personal' meanings. So, alongside NEGOTIATION, we tried to develop systems for evaluative meaning, which we referred to as APPRAISAL (Martin, 2000).

(Martin, 2004/2010, p. 343)

As Martin would be keen to point out, there is far more to interactions like those between Mr Fox and his wife or Dr Graham and Niemand than the exchange of either goods or services or information. If we are to explore the attitudes at play in such dialogues and the way they co-pattern in larger phases of text, we need a more nuanced account of interpersonal meaning that takes us beyond grammar into 'discourse semantics' (Martin, 1992; Martin & Rose, 2003). It necessarily involves a focus on lexis too, since evaluation is expressed in open class lexical items – verbs, adjectives, adverbs and nouns – which often carry evaluation in very subtle ways in concert with other items. Whilst it is beyond the scope of this chapter to introduce the full system of APPRAISAL, we touch briefly on major systems of ATTITUDE and GRADUATION, exemplifying choices from these in extracts from our narratives.

At the heart of APPRAISAL theory is the system of ATTITUDE which incorporates three domains of feeling: AFFECT (the domain of emotion), JUDGEMENT (the domain of ethics) and APPRECIATION (the domain of aesthetics). The ATTITUDE system has some defining features: explicit attitudinal wordings are inherently gradable (they can be intensified and compared); they are biased in their LOADING, being primarily either positive or negative; and forms of expression of attitudinal meaning tend to sprawl, especially in the case of INVOKED ATTITUDE. Easiest to recognize in evaluation is INSCRIBED ATTITUDE, which is explicitly realized in attitudinal lexis. From the outset, the farmers in *Fantastic Mr Fox* are described as 'mean and nasty' men. The LOADING is consistently negative when it comes to these three characters and Dahl is adept at upscaling the evaluations of their defects, as in the following example about the typical eating habits of Boggis: 'He was *enormously* fat. This was because he ate *three* boiled chickens *smothered* with dumplings *every day* for *breakfast, lunch and dinner*.' However, if we are to come to terms with the highly amplified nature of Dahl's evaluative style, we need access to a precise metalanguage for capturing the intensity of his evaluations.

Martin and White (2005) coined the term GRADUATION to describe the use of resources to up or down scale the intensity of attitudes and the degree of precision in their rendering. In *Fantastic Mr Fox*, Dahl's use of intensifiers (what Martin & White, 2005 call FORCE) is a consistent feature of his exaggerated style and a large part of what children love about his narratives. The baddies are always <u>terribly</u> bad and goodies, well, they are consistently interesting and resourceful and brave if not always 'good' in the traditional sense. In the above example, attitudinal choices carry judgement to do with SOCIAL ESTEEM (how greedy Boggis is). Later, when the farmers decide to destroy the fox's home under the tree, the lexical choices communicate judgement to do with SOCIAL SANCTION (the destructive actions of the farmers). The antinomies in this story are clear, even extreme. While we loathe

the farmers and their rapacious greed, we increasingly admire the foxes and their allies as they struggle to escape the farmers' violent actions. The emotional and ethical lines are clearly drawn from the outset and INSCRIBED ATTITUDE is central to this process.

It can be helpful to see how evaluation is realized in a range of examples from mentor texts such as those in use here. Teachers in The Grammatics Project used the material in Table 3.5 in their work with students as they highlighted examples of Appraisal in class narratives. The examples are taken from texts used in this and Chapter 2.

We know that images also convey ATTITUDE, most obviously, AFFECT. In this and Chapter 2, we referred to images of Rose and her brother Jack in Anthony Browne's book, *The Tunnel*. The close-up image of Rose waiting outside the tunnel for her brother portrays an attitude of anxiety. Later after Rose has rescued her brother and the siblings are reconciled the close-up image shows the hint of a smile on her face. While facial expression can convey a range of affective responses, AFFECT can also be expressed through gesture and bodily posture. We see gestures of puzzlement and curiosity in the depiction of the boy in *The Lost Thing* (Tan, 2000) with his thumb and forefinger to his chin. In Anthony Browne's book, *Zoo* (1994), the description of the orang-utan as a 'miserable thing' is complemented by the rear-view image of the orang-utan slumped in the corner of the enclosure.

Images can also convey judgement of SOCIAL ESTEEM and SOCIAL SANCTION. However, while AFFECT is mostly inscribed through facial expression, judgements are more frequently invoked from the portrayal of experiential meaning in images. In *Zoo* for example, the illustration of the family looking at the gorillas, shows the father beating his chest and a speech balloon showing his grunting "Uh-Uh-Uh-Uh!", invoking a judgement of SOCIAL ESTEEM – how boorish the father is. Judgement of SOCIAL SANCTION may also be invoked. In *The Tunnel* (Browne, 1989), the image of Jack, wearing a wolf mask and creeping into his sister's room while she is asleep, may invoke a judgement of inappropriate behaviour. Some readers may come to such judgements and some may not, so the judgement is simply 'afforded' by the experiential meaning. In other cases however, the invocation to judgement may be stronger. In another of Anthony Browne's books, *Voices in the Park* (Browne, 1998), young Charles, is very much constrained by his domineering mother, and in one image depicting Charles alone observing the dogs having fun in the park, he is shown standing in the shadow of his mother, although she is not actually in the image. This image seems to symbolize the domination of Charles and so 'flags' judgement of the mother.

An even stronger evocation of judgement of SOCIAL SANCTION occurs in *Zoo*, in the image depicting only the mother's horizontally extended forearm and hand in the upper left corner pointing as the children with their backs to her hand are shown walking, heads down, away from her. The strength of this evocation may be said to 'provoke' judgement of SOCIAL SANCTION in relation to the children's inappropriate behaviour. In some cases, images may be considered to inscribe judgement. This seems to be the case when widely recognized symbols for visual

TABLE 3.5 Evaluation – key resources, realizations and examples

Resources	Grammatical realizations	Examples from our texts
FOCALIZATION (internal) – Resources that take us inside the consciousness of a character or cue us via bodily reactions VOICING (dialogue) – Resources that attribute or source evaluations to one or more speakers	• Use of Mental and Behavioural Processes to highlight interior processes of perception and bodily reaction. • Use of Verbal Processes represented through conventions like speech tags or via conventions like indentation or dashes. • Use of Projection to quote speech in dialogue.	*Mental* – felt, looked, thought, knew, heard, saw, noticed, realized, frowned. *Behavioural* – sniffed, wept, stared, howled, snorted *Verbal* – said, replied, yelled, cried, told, added, spoke, responded *Projection in dialogue* – He rose, in dismissal. He said 'I fear you're wasting your time and mine Mr Niemand …' 'But Dr Graham, is humanity ready for an ultimate weapon?' Graham frowned, 'I have told you my point of view, Mr Niemand …'
ATTITUDE (evaluative words) – Resources for expressing feelings, judgements & appreciation of people, places and things. ATTITUDE can be overt (INSCRIBED) or covert (INVOKED).	• Evaluative nominal groups to reveal attitude – feeling, judgement or appreciation (often include adjectives and embedded material). • Evaluative verbal groups to render experience precisely and vividly. • Evaluative adjectives – to describe people, places and things. • Comment Adverbials – to evaluate actions or events explicitly • Figurative language – to compare one thing to another through similes or metaphors. This often provokes evaluation in the reader.	*Evaluative nominal groups* – those goons, nasty men, a disgusting paste, a crackpot, bitter anguish, key scientist of a very important project, an embarrassing interview, the sweet laugh of a child of four, a beastly temper. *Evaluative verbal groups* – loved, hated, disliked, shrieked, towered, whimpering, screamed, loomed, frowned, skipped, trembled. *Evaluative adjectives*: happy, wild, free, rude, disgusting, mindless; *Comment adverbials* – excitedly, bitterly, bashfully, truthfully, enormously *Simile* – he was <u>as thin as a pencil</u>; his mother was already gliding <u>like a bird</u>. *Metaphor* e.g. he <u>rained</u> blow after blow on the helpless, shaking child; seaweed trembled; coral glowed.

TABLE 3.5 Continued

Resources	Grammatical realizations	Examples from our texts
GRADUATION – Resources for adjusting the force of an utterance – in narrative especially for upscaling attitude	• Intensifiers – various resources for amplifying the force of a description or experience. This can be done through comparatives, intensified verbs, nouns or exclamatives and repetition.	*Comparative* – 's<u>o</u> cold', '<u>colder than</u> …' or *superlative* – col<u>dest</u>'; cleverest of them all, 'about as nasty and mean as any men you could meet'. *Intensified verbs* e.g. released, smothered, mashed, stuffed, shattered, skipped, brainwashed. *Intensified nominal groups* e.g. thousands of chickens, a beastly temper; *Exclamative* – 'It deserved to die!' 'How simple it all was!' *Repetition of negation* – 'In their place, <u>nothing</u>. An expanse of <u>nothingness</u> met my eyes, <u>no</u> colour, <u>no</u> heat.'
	• Elaboration – reformulating a message through restatement, exemplification, precise rendering	*Elaboration* – 'Graham did his best work = his most creative thinking …'. He was a small man = nondescript = obviously harmless'; 'Yes, it is public knowledge I am working on a weapon = a rather ultimate one.'
	• Phasing in verbal groups • Use of graphology – underlining or Capital letters.	*Phasing in verbal groups* – started to swirl, began to pound, tried to budge, began to appear, managed to focus.

metaphors are included in images (Unsworth, 2015; White, 2014). In *Zoo*, an image of 'Dad' responding to the boys' request for chocolate brought by Mum to the zoo, is an extreme low-angle, close-up frontal view of a very large Dad looking down with annoyance, presumably at one or both of his sons. The aggressive representation of Dad is emphasised by the cloud formation in the sky, which appears to attach clouds in the shape of bull's horns to the sides of Dad's head (the image may be viewed in an illustrated reading of *Zoo* on YouTube, www.youtube.com/watch?v=-7OMD5I-cNU, uploaded by ferniekat on 21 November 2010). These horns may have different symbolic meanings in different cultures but in an Anglo culture they are associated with devilish and/or bullying behaviour. It would be difficult to view the image without seeing it as a judgement of SOCIAL SANCTION about the father. We return to this issue in Chapters 5 and 6 in relation to persuasion.

The source of attitude can be an omniscient narrator, as in *Fantastic Mr Fox*, with the narrator shaping our reactions through his all-knowing account of what happens and what it means. Or it can be restricted in some way, with the knowledge of the narrator limited in some way. Authors often experiment with point of view and with the attitudes expressed by Figures within the diegesis. It is a crucial aspect of narrative craft that shapes readers' attitudes without our being conscious of it, as we shall show. In the following student narrative, we can see the experiment with the possibilities of Invoked Attitude and Graduation at full stretch. Text 3.4 presents the opening paragraph of a longer text, produced by a Year 10 student following an introduction by her teacher to narrative grammatics.

The Shadow and the Beast

The fear in the boys eyes grew as he stayed at it. His stomach churned and there was a slight shake present in his right knee. Death and Life were hand in hand at the present time.

The shadow lurked above him, rising higher and consuming the light as he went. The shadow was hungry, ready to make his attack at will. But he wouldn't budge, not even a single shake of an unsteady finger was being made, for the shadow was waiting. Waiting for the boy to make the first move.

His name is Tom. The boys name is Tom. Did he want to die? No. Was it the inevitable? Very much so. For the shadow knew much about Tom, and Tom knew much about he.

Text 3.4 Opening paragraph of a text produced by a Year 10 student.

In our work with grammatics, we discovered that students enjoyed constructing narrative beginnings that 'hook the reader in' and 'make us care' as one put it so succinctly. The student who produced Text 3.4 (Cate) has applied well what her teacher called 'strong verbs' and the logico-semantic resource of Elaboration. These strategies are in evidence in sentences like: "The shadow lurked above him, (=) rising higher and consuming the light as he went" and "The shadow was hungry, (=) ready to make his attack at will". Cate is learning to manage second order semiosis through close study of narratives introduced by her teacher and also through analysis of resources like APPRAISAL (especially the intensifying potential of GRADUATION). In this classroom, students were encouraged not only to explore patterns of choice in class narratives, but to use these in their own compositions.

One narrative we used in The Grammatics Project was a story called 'Unhappily Ever After' by Paul Jennings, which is from a selection of tales with the playful title, *Quirky Tails* (Jennings, 1999). It is an interesting (if syntactically simple) narrative that experiments with alternative points of view on the same event. Early in the text we meet Albert Jenkins (a child) and Mr (Bald Head) Brown (the boarding school principal):

> Albert pulled up his socks and wiped his sweaty hands on the seat of his pants. He did up the top button of his shirt and adjusted his school tie. Then he trudged slowly up the stairs.
> He was going to get the strap.
> He knew it, he just knew it. He couldn't think of one thing he had done wrong but he knew Mr Brown was going to give him the strap anyway. He would find some excuse to whack Albert – he always did.
> Albert's stomach leapt up and down as if it was filled with jumping frogs. Something in his throat stopped him from swallowing properly. He didn't want to go. He wished he could faint or be terribly sick so he would have to be rushed to hospital in an ambulance.
> But nothing happened. He felt his own feet taking him up to his doom.
> He stood outside the big brown door and trembled. He was afraid but he made his usual resolution. He would not cry. He would not ask for mercy. He would not even wince.
> There was no way he was going to give Mr Brown that pleasure.
> He took a deep breath and knocked softly.
> Inside the room, Brown heard a knock. He said nothing. Let the little beggar suffer. Let the little smart alec think he was in luck. Let him think no one was in.
> Brown heard Albert's soft footsteps going away from the door. 'Come in Jenkins,' he boomed.

This extract is interesting for several reasons. But here we focus on the author's alternation between two contrasting points of view on the same event (punishment of Albert by Brown for an assumed insult). The evaluation is refracted first through the eyes and feelings of young Albert and later through those of the principal, Mr Brown. The contrast is stark and it is achieved through Mental Processes communicating Albert's s high levels of anxiety – just the kind of galloping panic any young person would experience in the face of this fate: 'he *knew* it, he just *knew* it. He *couldn't think* of one thing he had done wrong but he *knew* Mr Brown was going to give him the strap anyway.' The evaluation is not overt (INSCRIBED ATTITUDE); there are no strictly attitudinal words. Even so, the emotion is palpable because it is rendered in the voice and the idiom of the child. It features what we described above as GRADUATION and works through repetition (e.g. 'knew' three times) and Elaboration (e.g. not being able to swallow, longing for a fainting fit, trembling). Coupled with metaphors that evoke the boy's anxiety (e.g. 'Albert's stomach leapt up and down as if it was filled with jumping frogs'), the choices (literally) embody the feelings of the young boy Albert. They are a grammatical expression of a 'show rather than tell' strategy.

But this story is even more interesting because of a shift in point of view that occurs as we move 'inside' Brown's head. As the principal listens for the boy's knock, there is a shift to pleasurable anticipation on the part of the tormentor:

> Inside the room, Brown *heard* a knock. He said nothing. Let the little beggar suffer. Let the little smart alec think he was in luck. Let him think no one was in. Brown *heard* Albert's soft footsteps going away from the door. 'Come in Jenkins,' he *boomed*.

Brown's viewpoint is mediated in a similar way through verbs like 'heard' and his external voice through Verbal Process verbs like 'said', or in this case, 'boomed'. Unlike the attitude projected by the boy, Brown's is that of a brutal authority Figure filled with a denigratory lexis like 'smart alec' and 'little beggar'. Point of view is a fascinating region to explore in the territory of interpersonal meaning, especially in narrative. Grammatically speaking, it is rendered primarily through – direct or indirect speech or thought – what Halliday and Matthiessen (2004) call **Projection**. **Ideas** are projected through Mental Process clauses as in the following sentence: Brown *heard* Albert's soft footsteps [[going away from the door]]. **Locutions** are projected through Verbal Process clauses and the wordings can be quoted or reported. In the following sentence, we have a quoted locution coming first in the sentence: Come in Jenkins,' he *boomed*. The grammatical basis of sensing and speaking is often very clear and parallels the distinction between **Focalization** (Who sees?) and **Narration** (who speaks?) that we presented earlier in this chapter. Literary theorists such as Mieke Bal (1985) emphasise the need to 'make explicit the distinction between the vision through which the elements are presented and the identity of the voice that is verbalising that vision: i.e. those who 'see' and those who 'speak'" (Bal, 1985, p.101).

But even point of view can get complex. Although projection is the primary grammatical resource for both internal Focalization (ideas) and Voicing (locutions), there are intermediate forms that allow an author to fudge the source of an evaluation. The grammatical resource here is **Free Indirect Discourse** which blurs the distinction between narrator (even author) and character. Halliday describes this as a kind of anomalous 'projection space' which combines features of both quoted and reported speech or thought (Halliday & Matthiessen, 2004, p. 465). In its speech form, it retains the independence of quoted speech while remaining free of a projecting clause. It retains the tense and deixis of the narrative while inserting the speech and the idiom of the character whose voice is reported. The same applies to free indirect discourse in thought form. For example, in the extract above from *Unhappily Ever After*, readers would probably interpret expressions like 'little beggar' and 'little smart alec' as coming from the character, Brown, rather than from the narrator. But actually, there is no explicit projecting clause (tag) like 'He thought' that links the evaluation to Brown.

Free indirect discourse evaluates <u>indirectly</u> and is used often to simultaneously tell a story and evaluate its significance (Toolan, 1988). In this sense, the grammar of free indirect discourse is important to our analysis of reader positioning. In *The Weapon*, for example, our first source of insight about Dr Graham's world is Dr Graham himself. He focalises experience for us and aligns us with his viewpoint until this is challenged by an external voice (and a new source of evaluation), Niemand. Consider how the author takes us inside the scientist's mind, rendering his evaluations in the idiom typical of a man like this:

> Mostly he thought about his mentally arrested son – his only son – in the next room. The thoughts were loving thoughts, not the bitter anguish he had felt years ago when he had first learned of the boy's condition. The boy was happy; wasn't that the main thing? And to how many men is given a child who will always be a child, who will not grow up to leave him? Certainly that was a rationalization, but what is wrong with rationalization when it. ... The doorbell rang.

Again, what is striking here is how seamlessly the author shifts from narration into internal focalization and from there into free indirect discourse. If we ask, 'Who is speaking when Graham asks himself questions about his son? Who says, 'Wasn't that the main thing?' the answer of course is that it is <u>both</u> narrator and character. Initially, readers have access only to Graham's view of his reality and this is achieved primarily through the grammar of free indirect discourse. Once Niemand arrives of course, it is verbal discourse that opens up a very different point of view on Graham's work (and the reality as perceived by a peace activist). This takes us into the region of literary craft and to deeper questions of narrative instructiveness (Macken-Horarik, 2003).

As Figure 3.4 reveals, an image may construct different points of view on characters and events. Furthermore, shifts in point of view can have a significant impact on the interpretive possibilities of a story. We see this very clearly in comparing the same episodes in the picture book and movie versions of Shaun Tan's story *The Lost Thing*. The image from the picture book presented earlier in Figure 2.1 shows the boy feeding the lost thing while it is hidden in his parents' back shed. The distant, 'Observe' view of their interaction on this page contributes to the distance between the reader and the characters. The vertical angle is at eye level and the horizontal angle is somewhat oblique so that we observe the scene with the boy almost in profile. According to Kress and van Leeuwen (2006), when the horizontal angle is such that the frontal plane of the represented participants is parallel to the frontal plane of the viewer, this generates maximum involvement of the viewer with represented participants. An oblique horizontal angle however, constructs the relationship between the viewer and the represented participants as detached and the participants as somewhat 'other'. Notwithstanding the first Person narration of the verbal text, the image constructs an external, unmediated point of view, positioning the viewer as remote from the world of the character.

In the movie version of this incident, there is much more variation in point of view and the shifts in Focalization are crucial to the alignment of viewers with the boy and the lost thing (Ruhemann & Tan, 2010). As this episode opens, the rear view of the boy shifts our point of view from external to mediated. Initially, inside the shed, we experience a rear view of the boy and a front view of the lost thing facing each other as the lost thing searches along the shelves on the shed wall. This changes to show the full body of the boy and part of the lost thing in profile as the lost thing manipulates the box of coloured items into the boy's arms and then gestures with its tentacle for the boy to follow it. The view then changes to a rear view of the boy in front of the lost thing as they face each other. Now, rather than being a detached observer, the viewer is positioned to see 'along with' the boy and this viewpoint is maintained as the lost thing opens its top lid. The perspective then shifts to a very high angle, looking down on a front view of the boy holding his box below. To the left and right of the screen in partial view are the very large pincers of the lost thing, with the right one beginning to move a ladder (Figure 3.6).

As viewers, we are now positioned to share the point of view of the lost thing. This is confirmed by our view of the top of the ladder as it responds to the push from the pincer to fall and lean up against the side of the lost thing, and our high angle view down on the boy as he begins to climb the ladder towards our gaze. The next shift is an extreme low angle view from the left of the bottom of the ladder depicting the soles of the boy's shoes in a close up and a rear view of him as he climbs up the ladder. While our point of view is not that of the boy, we view the climb up the ladder in a similar way that he would. Our next view is from across the top of the brightly lit opening at the top of the lost thing at the face of the boy looking straight at us. Since the depicted character's gaze is directly toward the viewer, it is as if a pseudo interpersonal contact is being made. The next shift is to an eye-level profile view of the boy atop the ladder feeding the lost thing from his box. This is quite similar to the corresponding image in the book shown

FIGURE 3.6 Point of view of the lost thing (Ruhemann & Tan, 2010).

in Figure 2.1 in our previous chapter. In the movie, however, a warm yellow light seems to emanate from inside the lost thing, whereas in the book the light is much dimmer and emanates from a single bulb being held aloft by one of the tentacles inside the top of the lost thing. These differences in the deployment of point of view in the book and movie reflect a thematic interpretive difference between the two versions of the story. In the movie, the relationship between the boy and the lost thing is developed as one of collaborative companionship, whereas in the book the boy's quest on behalf of the lost thing is dutiful but more detached, and the lost thing seems more of a passive recipient.

The integral contribution of images to the narrative art of picture books and illustrated stories has long been appreciated (Nodelman, 1988; Lewis, 2001) and the significance of images to interpretation of media texts and texts of popular culture has also been well established. What is proposed here is that the grammatics of language as an analytical tool is complemented by the kind of image grammatics we have outlined to provide a means of articulating the multimodal narrative art of picture books and illustrated stories, which is available as a pedagogic resource to enhance students' interpretive capacities in responding to literary texts. Common semiotic terms like Focalization, Attitude and Graduation enable us to explore the distinctive contribution of visual and verbal choices and to inter-relate them in principled ways to higher order meanings.

Concluding remarks

In this chapter, we have taken a foray into the more complex regions of grammatical study, investigating aspects of 'how language is organized to mean', as Halliday often puts it. We considered the internal organization of language and image, with a special focus on interpersonal meanings. It is one thing to claim that language is a resource for making meanings and quite another to show how this notion is embodied in the grammatics. Of special interest here has been the principle of system that we argue is a way of building choice into the architecture of language. In interacting with others, we make choices from within the system of MOOD (Declarative mood for statements, Interrogative for questions) and other systems such as POLARITY (positive or negative) and MODALITY (degrees of certainty) come into play too, along with TAGGING if we want to check the status of an exchange with others. Although representing choice in this way may seem complex, if the grammar of a language is to be meaningful and comprehensive, we need to understand how these choices are organized in exchanges with others. Similar choices for visual interaction were introduced, using the heuristic of the system network and we exemplified these with images from picture books such as *The Tunnel* and *The Lost Thing*.

Beyond the grammar of exchanges, English deploys more subtle resources for evaluating experience and positioning readers. We considered the lexical end of the system through attitudinal meanings commonly gathered under the heading of APPRAISAL, focussing particularly on ATTITUDE and GRADUATION. Of particular interest for English is an understanding of how INVOKED APPRAISAL is used in connotative stretches of language that are prosodic (dispersed) in realization. Research into development of this in students' writing is at an early stage (see Macken-Horarik & Sandiford, 2016 for one foray into this field). It is clear that one hallmark for development in students like Cate (who wrote *The Shadow and the Beast*) is a growing capacity to deploy metaphor, Elaboration and other resources associated with Invoked Appraisal. Hence understanding these is crucial for teachers if they want to foster this kind of growth in writing.

Although we have presented only typological systems here which present options for meaning as discrete and opposed, it is increasingly clear that we need to capture prosodic forms of realization as well. Recent work on parametric systems shows promise for representing choice in less discrete (either-or) ways and this will be important for future analysis of evaluative splashes of meaning in texts, whether verbal or multimodal (see Bednarek & Martin, 2010; Painter, 2007; Painter *et al.*, 2013; van Leeuwen, 2009).

In addition to the principle of system, we considered that of stratification, which enables us to distribute the work of analysis across the larger canvas of a text, the contributing parts of a text and the forms of expression by which meanings are manifested. We considered how focalization works from the point of view of the creation of identification with a character, like Abel in *Blueback* through whose eyes (and heart) we see and experience the world of early morning fishing trips with his mother and like Albert and (Bald Head) Brown in the story 'Unhappily Ever After'. If we adopt a stratified perspective on strategies like focalization (amongst others relevant to narrative craft identified in Table 3.1), we need to see how they work across phases of narrative, the grammatical features that embody these (e.g. Mental Processes for internal focalization) and the grammatical forms that realize these (e.g. verbal groups). In this way, we shunt from one level or stratum of organization to another, keeping our feet on the grammatical ground (form and function) and reaching into literary interpretation (patterns of meaning in texts). We do different kinds of analytical work on each level (or landing place) and it is useful to be clear about 'where we are' and what kinds of metalanguage we need to employ on each level. Teachers use the principle of stratification in analysis of images. As we showed in our exploration of the two versions of *The Lost Thing*, the same incident in a story can be treated differently, constellating a different relation between characters and viewers in each case.

In Australia, the motivation for English teachers to expand grammatical expertise has been sharpened by the introduction of the Australian Curriculum: English (AC:E) with its requirement that they teach 'the structures and functions of word and sentence-level grammar and text patterns and the connections between them' (ACARA, 2009, p.7). Gaining a purchase on resources for meaning and how they are structured and deployed in texts is a key aspect of interpretation. The principle of stratification makes space for all aspects.

Of course, it is all very well to claim that these principles make teachers' work with grammatics accessible and productive; it is quite another to show how it works in practice. In our next chapter, we move into classrooms and show how this kind of knowledge can be applied to the teaching of narrative in primary and secondary classrooms.

Notes

1 *The Tunnel* © by Anthony Browne (1989). From THE TUNNEL by Anthony Browne. Reproduced by permission of Walker Books Ltd, London SE11 5HJ, www.walker.co.uk.
2 *The Tunnel* © by Anthony Browne (1989). From THE TUNNEL by Anthony Browne. Reproduced by permission of Walker Books Ltd, London SE11 5HJ, www.walker.co.uk.

References

Australian Curriculum, Assessment and Reporting Authority (ACARA, formerly National Curriculum Board) (2009). *The shape of the Australian curriculum: English*. Sydney: ACARA. Retrieved from www.acara.edu.au.
Australian Curriculum Assessment and Reporting Authority (ACARA) (2012). *Australian curriculum: English*. Version 3.0. Sydney: ACARA. Retrieved from www.australiancurriculum.edu.au/English/Curriculum/F-10
Bal, M. (1985). *Narratology: Introduction to the theory of narrative*. Toronto: University of Toronto Press.
Bateman, J. (2013). Multimodal analysis of film within the GEM framework. *Ilha Do Desterro: A Journal of English Language, Literatures in English and Cultural Studies*, 64, 48–84.
Bednarak, M. & Martin, J. R. (Eds.) (2010). *New discourse on language: Functional perspectives on multimodality, identity and affiliation*. London & New York: Continuum.
Bordwell, D. (1985). *Narration in the fiction film*. New York: Columbia University Press.
Browne, A. (1989). *The tunnel*. London: Julia McRae Books.
Browne, A. (1994). *Zoo*. London: Random House.
Browne, A. (1998). *Voices in the park*. London: Doubleday.
Cajkler, W. & Hislam, J. (2002). Trainee teachers' grammatical knowledge: The tension between public expectations and individual competence. *Language Awareness*, 11(3), 161–177.
Christie, F. (2002). *Classroom discourse analysis*. London: Continuum.
Christie, F. & Derewianka, B. (2008). *School discourse: Learning to write across the years of schooling*. London: Continuum.
Christie, F. & Martin, J. R. (Eds.) (1997): *Knowledge Structure: Functional linguistic and sociological perspectives*. London: Continuum.
Gleeson, L. & Greder, A. (1999). *The great bear*. Sydney: Scholastic.
Halliday, M. A. K. (1991/2007). The notion of 'context' in language education. In J. Webster (Ed.), *The collected works of M. A. K. Halliday: Language and education (Vol 9)* (pp. 269–290). London & New York: Continuum.
Halliday, M.A.K. (2002). On grammar and grammatics. In J. Webster (Ed.), *The collected works of M. A. K. Halliday: On language and linguistics (Vol. 3)* (pp. 384–417). London: Continuum.
Halliday, M.A.K. (2008). *Complementarities in language*. Beijing: The Commercial Press.
Halliday, M.A.K. & Matthiessen, C. (2004). *An introduction to functional grammar* (3rd edition). London: Arnold.
Hasan, R. (1985). *Linguistics, language and verbal art*. Geelong, Victoria: Deakin University Press.

Hasan, R. (1987). The grammarian's dream: Lexis as most delicate grammar. In M. A. K. Halliday & R. P. Fawcett, (Eds.), *New developments in systemic linguistics: Theory and description* (pp. 184–211). London: Pinter.

Hasan, R. (1995). The conception of context in text. In P. H. Fries & M. Gregory (Eds.), *Discourse in society: Systemic functional perspectives* (pp. 183–283). Norwood, NJ: Ablex.

Jennings, P. (1999). *Quirky tails*. Ringwood, Victoria: Penguin Books.

Jones, P. & Chen, H. (2012). Teachers' knowledge about language: Issues of pedagogy and expertise. *Australian Journal of Language and Literacy*, 35(2), 149–174.

Kress, G. & van Leeuwen, T. (1996). *Reading images: A grammar of visual design* (1st edition). London & New York: Routledge.

Kress, G. & van Leeuwen, T. (2006). *Reading images: A grammar of visual design* (2nd edition). London & New York: Routledge.

Lewis, D. (2001). *Reading contemporary picture books: Picturing text*. London & New York: Routledge Falmer.

Macken-Horarik, M. (2003). Appraisal and the special instructiveness of narrative. In M. Macken-Horarik & J. R. Martin, (Eds.), *TEXT*, 23(2), 285–312.

Macken-Horarik, M., Sandiford, C., Love, K. & Unsworth, L. (2015). New ways of working 'with grammar in mind' in school English: Insights from systemic functional grammatics. *Linguistics and Education*, 31, 145–158.

Martin, J. R. (1992). *English text: System and structure*. Amsterdam: Benjamins.

Martin, J. R. (1996). Evaluating disruption: Symbolising theme in junior secondary narrative. In R. Hasan & G. Williams (Eds.), *Literacy in society* (pp. 124–171). London & New York: Longman.

Martin, J. R. (2000). Beyond Exchange: Appraisal systems in English. In S. Hunston & G. Thompson (Eds.), *Evaluation in text: Authorial stance and the construction of discourse* (pp. 142–175). Oxford: Oxford University Press.

Martin, J. R. (2004/2010): Sense and sensibility: Texturing evaluation. In W. Zhenhua (Ed.), in *The collected works of J. R. Martin: Discourse semantics (Vol. 2)* (pp. 341–375). Shanghai: Jiao Tong University Press.

Martin, J. R. & Veel, R. (1998). *Reading science: Critical and functional perspectives on the discourses of science*. London: Routledge.

Martin, J. R. & Rose, D. (2003). *Working with discourse: Meaning beyond the clause*. London: Continuum.

Martin, J. R. & White, P. (2005). *The language of evaluation: Appraisal in English*. New York: Palgrave Macmillan.

Martin, J. R., Matthiessen, C. & Painter, C. (2010). *Deploying functional grammar*. Beijing: The Commercial Press.

Matthiessen, C. & Halliday, M. A. K. (2009). *Systemic functional grammar: A first step into the theory*. Beijing: Higher Education Press.

Myhill, D. (2000). Misconceptions and difficulties in the acquisition of metalinguistic knowledge. *Language and Education*, 14(3), 151–163.

Myhill, D., Jones, S. & Watson, A. (2013). Grammar matters: How teachers' grammatical knowledge impacts on the teaching of writing. *Teaching and Teacher Education*, 36, 77–91.

Nodelman, P. (1988). *Words about pictures: The narrative art of children's picture books*. Athens, GA: University of Georgia Press.

O'Toole, M. (1994). *The language of displayed art*. London: Leicester University Press.

Painter, C. (2007). Children's picture book narratives: reading sequences of images. In A. S M. O'Donnell & R. S (Eds.), *Advances in language and education* (pp. 40–57). London: Continuum.

Painter, C., Martin, J. R. & Unsworth, L. (2013). *Reading visual narratives: Image analysis of children's picture books*. London: Equinox.
Rose, D. & Martin, J. R. (2012). *Learning to write, reading to learn: Genre, knowledge and pedagogy in the Sydney School*. London: Equinox.
Ruhemann, A., & Tan, S. (Writers) (2010). *The lost thing* [DVD/PAL]. Australia: Madman Entertainment.
Tan, S. (2000). *The lost thing*. Sydney, NSW: Lothian.
Toolan, M. (1988). *Narrative: A critical linguistic introduction*. London & New York: Routledge.
Unsworth, L. (2006). *E-literature for children: Enhancing digital literacy learning*. London and New York: Routledge/Falmer.
Unsworth, L. (2014a). Point of view in picture books and animated film adaptations: Informing critical multimodal comprehension and composition pedagogy. In E. Djonov & S. Zhao (Eds.), *Critical multimodal studies of popular culture* (pp. 201–216). London: Routledge.
Unsworth, L. (2014b). Multimodal reading comprehension: Curriculum expectations and large-scale literacy testing practices, *Pedagogies: An International Journal*, 9(1), 26–44.
Unsworth, L. (2015). Persuasive narratives: Evaluative images in picture books and animated movies. *Visual Communication*, 1(1), 73–96.
van Leeuwen, T. (2009). Parametric systems: The case of voice quality. In C. Jewitt (Ed.), *The Routledge handbook of multimodal analysis* (pp. 68–77). London & New York: Routledge.
White, P. R. R. (2014). The attitudinal work of news journalism images – a search for visual and verbal analogues. *Quaderni del CeSLiC Occasional Papers del CeSLiC*, 6–42.
Winton, T. (1997). *Blueback*. New York: Scribner.
Wray, D., Medwell, J., Fox, R. & Poulson, L. (2000). The teaching practices of effective teachers of literacy. *Educational Review*, 52(1), 75–84.

4
MOVING SOUTH

Teaching narrative in classrooms

Introduction to the teachers and the teaching and learning cycle

The previous chapters have outlined the grammatics of narrative, the ways in which grammatical choices enable composers to build plausible 'possible worlds', engage readers with characters intersubjectively and organize the narrative in coherent ways. Chapter 2 explored the possibilities of grammatics for illuminating narrative craft. It focussed on the interface of the grammatics with disciplinary practices in school English. Chapter 3 examined ways in which an understanding of the internal 'architecture' of language sheds light on interpersonal meanings in narrative. For example, we examined how Focalization serves to align readers with the viewpoint of the protagonist, Abel, in Tim Winton's *Blueback* (1997) or how Roald Dahl's description of the farmers in *Fantastic Mr Fox* (1974) relies on highly amplified, mostly overt evaluative choices through Inscribed Attitude. We probed more subtle choices for Invoked Appraisal and looked at Free Indirect Discourse in Fred Brown's story, 'The Weapon' (1951/1969). Then, because the metalanguage of functional grammatics has been extended to visual communication, we considered interactive choices in images from Anthony Browne's picture book, *The Tunnel* (1989) and Shaun Tan's *The Lost Thing* (2000). We were able to show how some students struggled with dialogue in their narrative compositions and how they were learning to manage exchanges between characters as part of the larger interaction of narratives with readers. These examples illustrate just some of the possibilities of a functional grammatics for teaching about language and image in narrative.

But of course, teachers need to operationalise these understandings in classrooms. And guidance from others who have actually done this in practical circumstances of teaching with different students can be particularly helpful in this task. To adapt our exploration metaphor somewhat, this is 'where the rubber hits the road' for any teacher making a foray into functional grammatics.

In Chapter 1, we introduced the south point of the compass as one of enhancing students' repertoires. It directs attention to teaching practices that assist students to understand and work with narrative grammatics. In this chapter, we explore some ways that teachers have used grammatics to enrich their teaching of narrative in primary and secondary Language Arts and English. To make this relevant, we provide scenarios which draw directly on our research with Australian teachers from 2011–2014 in the project we introduced in Chapter 1. Because these teachers were in the process of implementing a new curriculum (ACARA, 2009), they were necessarily working with the content for learning expected at their year level and with the metalanguage contained in the curriculum. This is heavily influenced by the systemic functional model of language with its emphasis on text in context, on genre-based approaches to text structure and on the different 'threads of meaning' that Halliday's theory of metafunctions illuminates. In two of our earlier papers, we explored the challenges of implementing this new curriculum with its increased role for grammar and the requirement that grammatical knowledge be related to literary study (Love, Sandiford, Macken-Horarik & Unsworth, 2014; Macken-Horarik, Love & Unsworth, 2011). In drawing on the work of teachers implementing this curriculum, we need not only to refer to learning goals articulated in their planning and their source in the Australian Curriculum for English (AC:E) (ACARA, 2012), but to the metalanguage employed by teachers. In this chapter, it means shunting between terminology of functional grammatics (e.g. Mental Processes) and that used by teachers (e.g. sensing verbs). In scenarios presented in this chapter, we draw on their application of functional grammatics as they taught students in Years 4, 7 and 10. All teachers whose work is featured here adapted the toolkit to the circumstances, timetabling arrangements and context of their particular schools.[1]

In the workshops teachers attended over the course of three years, we drew primarily on the scaffolding pedagogy outlined in Chapter 1. What has become known more widely as the teaching-learning cycle (TLC) is based on the principle of 'guidance through interaction in the context of shared experience' (Gray, 2007; Humphrey, 2017; Martin, 1999; Painter, 1986). The approach built on earlier research into genre pedagogy in primary schools (Martin, 2009; Rose & Martin, 2012) and later extensions of this (incorporating register) for secondary school learning in the Disadvantaged Schools Program in New South Wales (Christie & Martin, 1997; Rothery, 1994). The approach has been productive and has informed several offshoots like 'Accelerated Literacy' (Cowey, 2005; Gray, 2007; Rose, Gray & Cowey, 1999) and 'Reading to Learn' (Rose, 2006, 2011). These closely related pedagogies have expanded professional knowledge of crucial links between teacher knowledge, explicit pedagogy and improved student literacy outcomes. The grammatics workshops incorporated the TLC into guidance of teachers as they planned units of work based on what they had learned. Each stage of the TLC supports students as they learn to analyse the grammatical and text features of key genres via different kinds of social interaction (Butt, Fahey, Feez & Spinks, 2012; Humphrey & Feez, 2016). Our hope was that the framework would scaffold students as they learned 'how to mean' in English (Halliday, 1993). The four stages of the TLC include:

Building the context for work on narrative

Narratives play a crucial role in the culture and students need to understand their sociocultural function – not just how they work but why they work as they do. In building the context for work on narrative, teachers often explore 'big questions' in opening the field and these foreshadow the kinds of activities to come in the upcoming unit of work. The questions can be general: Which stories have you read that mean most to you? What makes them compelling? Were these stories turned into movies? What changes did you notice? Did they work as well? Why? Opening talk need not just focus on written texts. Many students prefer to 'read' narratives in graphic novels, picture books, movies and even games. The questions can be specific to aspects of narrative craft: How do authors create 'possible worlds' so that we can place ourselves in the environment in which events occur? How do we know when something awful or momentous is about to happen in a story? How do authors make us love or hate some characters? And so on. The crucial task is to open up the field of knowledge in such a way as to pique students' curiosity and engage their interest in crucial questions of narrativity, especially those that the unit of work itself addresses.

Modelling the structure and features of narrative

A key feature of the TLC is its text-based focus (de Silva Joyce & Feez, 2012; Humphrey, 2017). In preparation for modelling, teachers select mentor texts that are likely to reward close reading and then identify extracts from these for special focus in classrooms. In scaffolding pedagogy, it is common to choose segments that will serve as models for student writing (powerful beginnings, great descriptive passages, good dialogues, action-reaction phases, moments of crisis, or, as one teacher in The Grammatics Project put it, 'really meaty bits'). This stage of the TLC is often called 'deconstruction' because it involves 'breaking open' the text. It can involve work on the stages of a narrative, annotation of texts, discussion of the stages and features of a narrative; 'detailed reading' of selected extracts focussing on Circumstantiation, Focalization, dialogues and APPRAISAL (see Axford, Harders & Wise, 2009; Gibbons, 2015; Gray 2003; Rose, 2006 for more on strategies of this kind). The purpose here is that students get to know how texts work and can identify, describe and interpret their features.

Guided practice – Joint construction of a new text

Following analysis of texts, students prepare for joint creation of a new text in the genre which is based on the model text(s). The term, 'guided practice' refers to a whole set of learning activities that give students a greater share of responsibility for production of texts under the guidance of an expert 'other'. The preparation activity should enable students to share writing of a whole or part of a narrative. This might be writing of an effective Orientation stage, a dialogue that pushes the action forward, a vivid character description, a suspenseful build-up to a crisis, resolving of a Complication and so on. Collaboration with partners in producing plot outlines, character descriptions, narrative arcs and so on should enable students to contribute confidently to the class text so that the exchange between teacher (or other expert) is as equal as possible. The teacher acts as a guide and scribes for students as they help to jointly construct a text (or extract) in the focus genre. Features given special attention during modelling stages of the TLC can be further explored and explained as the group text is composed. Joint construction of a whole text can be difficult in the secondary English classroom. In our experience, secondary school timetables do not allow for joint composition of a whole narrative. We use the term 'Guided Practice' for this stage of the pedagogy in order to make space for 'short writes', work on parts of texts (beginnings perhaps) or for closely supported tasks like 'joint reconstructed writing' (see Axford *et al.*, 2009 and Gray, 2003 for details about such strategies).

Independent composition of narratives and reflection on outcomes of learning

When they are ready to work alone, students begin to compose their own narrative, drawing on grammatical patterns explored in earlier stages of learning (in the model and jointly constructed texts). They may decide to innovate on genre structure, to experiment with point of view in images, to explore alternative views of characters. Students innovate on the possibilities of the genre. Many students who find narrative difficult find that patterning their writing on mentor narratives allows them to produce texts that they could not otherwise produce but which expand their repertoires in pleasing ways. In our approach, we assume that independent work on a text has a creative aspect (where students try new things, experiment with possibilities of genre and grammar) and a control aspect (where students learn how to make sense, compose coherent texts, edit for flow and correct faulty sentences).

As Figure 4.1 illustrates, each stage of the pedagogy aims to build discipline knowledge and to develop the literacies that provide access to this in English.

The three scenarios introduced below combine resources and strategies used by several teachers, often with stunning results. We introduce each teacher and their learning goals before providing a detailed account of how they implemented grammatics in their units.

Three scenarios in teaching a grammatics for narrative

Meet primary school teacher Alex, currently working in a Year 3 /4 classroom, Blair a Year 10 English teacher in a secondary school and Liam, a teacher of a class of Year 7 students in a large urban-rural fringe secondary school. All teachers are working

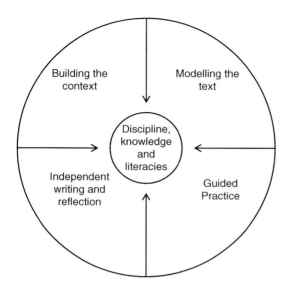

FIGURE 4.1 A text-based teaching learning cycle (adapted from Humphrey & Feez, 2016 and Humphrey, 2017).

to build their students' understandings of narrative through challenging mentor texts that are suitable for their students and will support them in realizing their learning goals for this unit. But their goals are different. Alex is interested in helping her students to produce engaging Orientations, capturing the reader's interest from the outset. She also wants her students to understand and deploy dialogue and point of view effectively (called Focalization here).

Blair also intends to work on Focalization, but at a more sophisticated level. As students are beginning to read texts that encourage ethical reflection on matters of human survival, they need to understand more of the instructiveness of narrative semiosis. Early in his unit, he intends to consolidate students' understanding of Narration, Focalization and Evaluation. The class need to understand how narratives move readers between internal and external worlds before moving on to consider the strategy of Free Indirect Discourse – which blurs the distinction between the narrator and character and between internal and external worlds. 'The Weapon' (Brown, 1951/1969) is a good mentor text not only because it raises ethical issues related to science but also because it displays telling examples of Free Indirect Discourse.

Liam is interested in visual narration and so are his students. Liam wants to capitalise on his students' preoccupation with social media and video games to help them understand better how language and image work to shape their viewpoints and experiences of issues. In particular, he intends that they will explore interactive meanings through analysis of systems of Focalization, Social Distance and Subjectivity in multimodal texts. His mentor text is an adolescent picture book called *Grandad's Gifts*, written by Paul Jennings and illustrated by Peter Gouldthorpe (1992).

In preparing for work on narrative, each teacher has established some 'big questions' to inform initial and ongoing talk about the craft of narrative ('the why beneath the what' as one teacher put it). They have selected mentor texts to use in modelling the structure and features of narratives. They are examples of what Gray (2007) calls 'literate discourse' and display effective use of features that are in focus. Depending on the length of the narrative, teachers might read the whole text to/with the students or read up to the extract(s) selected for special focus. As will be seen, Alex has read *Fantastic Mr Fox* to her Year 3/4 group, while Blair has read the first of his exemplars, *Unhappily Ever After* (Jennings, 1999) with his Year 10 group prior to work on point of view. Liam plans to study *Grandad's Gifts*, drawing students' attention to the contribution of images and language to creation of suspense. Each text will be used as resources for analysis and as models for writing.

Scenario 1 – teaching narrative in a primary classroom

Alex plans to use *Fantastic Mr Fox* with her Year 3/4 composite class of students, focussing her teaching on specific grammatical choices which support the interpretation and composition of narratives. This also allows for flexibility to exploit the teaching possibilities of different texts. Alex has already collected samples of her students' narrative writing and, through her analysis, noted that the Orientation stage of the narratives need to be stronger to 'hook the reader in', provide more details of the setting and to introduce readers to the characters in ways that will create an interest in them and what happens to them. Like other Australian teachers, Alex uses the Australian Curriculum for English (AC:E) to guide planning (ACARA, 2012). The content relevant to study of literature in Year 4 recommends that students "discuss how authors and illustrators make stories exciting, moving and absorbing and hold readers' interest by using various techniques like character development and plot tension" (ACELT 1605).[2] For Alex, the first step will be to teach students the rudiments of circumstantiation in creating setting. A key aspect of this work will involve understanding "how adverb groups/phrases and prepositional phrases work in different ways to provide circumstantial details about any activity" (ACELA 1495). A further step will involve discussion about why Roald Dahl (1970) is so precise about where the two sets of characters live and how this impacts on our understanding of the world created in the text.

Alex has also noted that much of the dialogue in her students' texts is just talk and not revealing of relationships between characters. For the most part, her students rely on description of physical features for characterization. Instead, she would like her students to appreciate that the words that characters speak, and how they relate to each other through dialogue, contribute to the reader's sense of character development. The children have enjoyed listening to other narratives by Roald Dahl (*The Twits* is a favourite, for example). Alex now wants them to experiment with dialogue in the same way in their own writing, learning how it can generate

TABLE 4.1 Alex's planning for work on the grammatics with *Fantastic Mr Fox*

Guiding Question: How do authors create 'possible worlds' so we can 'see' <u>where</u> we are and know <u>when</u> something is happening in a narrative?

Narrative focus: Experiential Lens	Grammatics focus
How details of setting can be built through locating in place and time	Prepositional phrases of place and time (ACELA 1495).

Guiding Question: How do authors make us like or dislike certain characters?

Narrative focus: Interpersonal Lens	Grammatics focus
How the words that characters say are introduced and represented How attitudes of characters are revealed through their dialogue	Verbs of saying (different choices) Dialogue – direct speech (ACELA 1494). Words spoken by a character which reflect attitude usually through evaluative noun groups and adjectives; Vocatives – e.g. endearing names

a sense of character, even revolting characters like those that feature in many of Dahl's narratives. One aspect of this work will involve investigating "how quoted (direct) and reported (indirect) speech work in different types of text" (ACELA 1494). In this task, Alex is planning to make use of what she learned in grammatics workshops about Projection and the literary technique of Focalization. Table 4.1 illustrates Alex's planning, beginning with the question guiding this part of her work. It relates the grammatics to relevant metafunctional lenses and required learning content in the AC:E.

These goals will see Alex and her students looking at narrative through an Experiential lens as they examine how to exploit the power of generic structure to invite readers into the narrative in crafted orientations. They will also use an Interpersonal lens to consider how readers are invited to understand the words of the characters and what they reveal, and how readers feel for, judge and appreciate what happens to characters in particular ways. Because of her need to implement the metalanguage of the AC:E, Alex necessarily uses its grammatical terminology, but as will be seen, she is pushing it in imaginative directions.

Building the context for work on narrative

Because she has already read the novel to the children during afternoons prior to this unit of work, Alex considers how she will introduce it in a 'literary' way to the students and which extracts of the text will be best for close examination. She selects three or four extracts from the text which will allow her to model effective interpretation in the first instance, and which will be used to model for writing later in the teaching and learning cycle. The opening chapters are crucial for work on Orientation, the first conversation between Mr and Mrs Fox and the first major

TABLE 4.2 A framework for donning an experiential lens on what happens in a narrative

Experiential lens – building a plausible 'possible world' of experience for readers

Setting: Where and when does it take place?
Characterisation: Who or what is involved in the story? How are they depicted – through description, dialogue, thought, action – all of these?
Plotting: What problem (Complication) faces the characters? How is this established? What verbs tell you about the character's actions? Do you know what is going on in the character's mind? How?
Struggle: (Attempt at resolution): How do characters attempt to resolve the problem? Is there an internal or external struggle?
Crisis: Is there a moment of high tension, a decisive moment in the action?
Resolution: Is the problem resolved? How? Does it work out well for some characters and not well others?
Theme: What is the story about? Is there a theme (a big idea)?

'stoush' between the farmers when they fail to kill Mr Fox are two obvious extracts for work on dialogue. While she believes that her students have a rudimentary understanding of the different stages of narrative (e.g. Orientation, Complication and Resolution), she wants them to appreciate how phases that involve external events (action) and internal responses (reaction) contribute to the reader's response of the unfolding narrative. Mr Fox's careful movement up the tunnel before being shot by the farmers is a good example of this action-reaction patterning.

Alex begins by asking children if they can remember what the characters are called, where they live and what happens in the first part of *Fantastic Mr Fox*. As part of this process of remembering the setting, she asks a few who can remember to come up to the board and draw a small map of the locations of the characters' homes. Following this, so all can share in the talk that follows, she re-reads the first two chapters of the novel to the class and they check (and if necessary, amend) the class map as they listen. Then she asks, 'Why is it important that we know where the characters live? Is it important to what happens next?' Following this she tells the children that they are going to learn more about setting and how authors let readers 'see' <u>where</u> they are and know <u>when</u> something is happening.

Before beginning her work, Alex has been reading several narratives to her students, including picture books and short novels as models of narratives. In this unit, she is going to use probe questions such as those introduced in Chapter 2 for experiential meaning. These will guide her students' attention to key stages of the narrative and provide the context for literary craft (focussing particularly on setting and characterization in this unit). Table 4.2 presents the general framework Alex has used in planning work on *Fantastic Mr Fox*.

Modelling features of narrative (setting and dialogue)

Alex has already read *Fantastic Mr Fox* to her students for enjoyment, stopping at points to ensure comprehension of what is going on in this episodic narrative. In this way, she knows that students have at least a vague idea of what happens in the story (plot) and will be ready to talk about why the author chooses particular phrasing at key stages of its unfolding. In short, the students move from appreciation to analysis as Alex begins to use the text for explicit teaching purposes. To implement her plan to explore setting, Alex familiarises the students with the first part of *Fantastic Mr Fox* through a strategy called 'Text Orientation'. As she moves into closer study, she zooms in on the extract selected for focus on setting and circumstantiation. This can be called 'Language Orientation' and it invites students to look closely at grammatical choices and patterns (Axford, Harders &, Wise, 2009). Alex has already determined that the Orientation is established through prepositional phrases of place and time and that understanding of character relationships through dialogue will be the focus of her teaching. With these in mind, her orientation to this chapter proceeds with a brief reminder about the question she asked the class earlier – Is it important that we know where these characters live? Why might this be so?

For many students, how to begin a narrative can be quite a daunting task. Guidance on the structure of narratives as well as careful modelling of grammatical features that introduce and build setting, describe characters and make us aware of their situation as Stephen King (2000) has pointed out in his book *On Writing*. Having a clear purpose, as well as grammatical knowledge to draw upon, supports students in their interpretation and composition of narratives. In this stage of the TLC, the emphasis turns to specific language choices and their impacts. The first purpose of modelling here is to foreground the use of prepositional phrases of place and time (Circumstances of Location) in establishing the setting and to distinguish between when the author is speaking and when the characters are speaking. These guides support the comprehension of the text, ensuring that students are aware of what is at stake in the story – who the characters are and what their situation is. The second purpose is to look at the grammar of conversations between characters that tell us a lot about the kind of 'people' they are.

Exploring the grammar of setting

Alex selects a short extract of the second phase of the Orientation in Chapter 2 of the narrative for closer study of the setting. Using this extract, she focusses on how prepositional phrases of place work experientially to locate the family of foxes in the physical world:

> **On a hill above the valley** there was a wood. **In the wood** there was a huge tree. **Under the tree** there was a hole. **In the hole** lived Mr and Mrs Fox and their four Small Foxes.

> Alex: *Yesterday we talked about where the characters live. We are introduced in the first chapter to three farmers. Can anyone remember their names and where they live?*

> In Chapter 2, we are introduced to the hero of the story, Mr Fox, and his family. We find out that Mr Fox lives with Mrs Fox and four little Foxes. We also find out where they live. Who can remember where the foxes live? You can use the little map we made on the board if you have forgotten.
>
> Well we know that the first stage of a narrative is often called the Orientation. Now the Orientation of Fantastic Mr Fox sets out two different settings. In Chapter 1 we are told that the farmers live 'Down in a valley' and in this chapter we find out where the Fox family lives in a similar way. It begins with 'On a hill above the valley' and zooms in to the exact place where they live, 'in the hole'. Can anyone tell me why Roald Dahl wants us to know exactly where the characters live?

Following this orienting discussion, Alex selects students to come up to the whiteboard and highlight the words that tell where the wood was, where the huge tree was and where the hole was. In order to emphasise the importance of Circumstantial meanings, she asks students to read the first sentence aloud, leaving them out. She asks whether the sentence makes sense (yes) and what is missing if these words are left out (details of where they live). She then explains that words which signal where people live or where actions happen are often called prepositional phrases. These are noun groups fronted by a preposition like 'on', 'above', 'in' and 'under'. In this extract, the prepositional phrases are used to signal <u>where</u> something happens. But they can tell <u>when</u> something happens, as in later examples – 'The next day', or 'Every evening' or 'At six o'clock' and so on. Alex now guides the students to appreciate how the Circumstances of place help us to 'zoom in' on the exact place where the Foxes live. The examples in the extract are compared with similar ones that tell us where the farmers live in Chapter 1: '<u>Down in the valley</u> there were three farms.' In this way, Alex is enabling her students to identify the wordings formally (as prepositional phrases), label them functionally (as Circumstances of place) and interpret their larger role is specifying the setting and establishing the location of the later series of Complications. Alex asks her students to find other examples of prepositional phrases of place in the narrative, guiding groups of students to locate these at different points in the narrative. They write them on strips of paper or cardboard that Alex collates as a display for them to return later in the teaching and learning cycle.

Exploring the grammar of dialogue and characterization

Returning to the Orientation in Chapter 2 of the novel, Alex continues her modelling of narrative worlds, this time focussing on Mr Fox, the hero of story. Here, the students' attention is drawn to resources that build character and dialogue. Dialogue is one way in which authors attach evaluations to characters, not only through the choices of saying verbs ascribed to the character, but in the evaluative words spoken by the characters. Students are already quite familiar with this first part of the novel, so will be able to work with a sense of the meaning of the whole text, just focussing on a new aspect of the grammatics. She asks students whether they like Mr Fox or the farmers better? Then she asks how authors like Roald Dahl make us like or dislike the characters? The dialogue might begin this way:

Alex: *In Australia, many farmers hate foxes for the damage they do to lambs and chickens. In narratives, foxes are usually portrayed negatively, as characters who cannot be trusted, as sneaky even. Roald Dahl wants us to think differently about the foxes in his story. Sometimes we hear his voice as he tells us about the farmers and the Fox family. Other times, we hear the voices of Mr and Mrs Fox through the words they use when they talk to each other. These dialogues help us to understand the characters, how Mr and Mrs Fox relate to each other, and what they think of the farmers. But the characters speak very differently to one another don't they? Let's have a close look at the first conversation between Mr and Mrs Fox:*

> Every evening as soon as it got dark, Mr Fox would say to Mrs Fox, "Well *my darling*, what shall it be this time? A plump chicken from *Boggis*? A duck or a goose from *Bunce*? Or a nice turkey from *Bean*?" And when Mrs Fox had told him what she wanted, Mr Fox would creep down into the valley in the darkness of the night and help himself.

The exchange between the Foxes is a regular one, signalled in the first instance through the adverbial clause 'Every evening as soon as it got dark'. Alex asks students which words tell us that Mr Fox collected dinner regularly from Boggis, Bunce or Bean. She explains that these words come first in the sentence because they are important. They signpost the time that something happens, rather like prepositional phrases that they looked at earlier but in this case they are part of a noun group. If the class has done something on signposting earlier, she can draw attention to this, even highlighting marked Themes (as we discussed in Chapter 2). Here the focus is on the way that dialogue reveals character. Alex reminds her students that when a character speaks in a casual conversation, they often leave words out like the Subject and verb, as in "(Do you want) a plump chicken from Boggis?" (Do you want) a duck or goose from Bunce?" She names this strategy of leaving words out we take for granted Ellipsis. She tells students that we put quotation marks around what is said so that readers know that these words belong to the character and not the narrator. She asks students to point to these marks.

Alex may go on to ask students which of the words in the exchange indicate that Mr Fox loves Mrs Fox. To make the language more visible, she could ask some children to role play this exchange to bring out the warmth of their relationship. Following this, she might ask the questions like:

> *How do Mr and Mrs Fox address one another? What does this tell you about how they feel about each other?*
>
> *Which words tell you that Mr and Mrs Fox have this conversation regularly? What does their dialogue reveal about them as characters?*
>
> *How do Mr and Mrs Fox speak about the farmers? What does their dialogue reveal about their attitude to the farmers? How does it do this?*

TABLE 4.3 A Table for comparing the grammar of two dialogues

What do Mr & Mrs Fox say to each other?	How does this dialogue make us feel about Mr & Mrs Fox?	What do the farmers say?	How does this dialogue make us feel about the farmers?

Moving between identification of wordings, description of their function and (later) interpretation of the patterns, Alex guides students to discuss how Dahl lets us know that Mr and Mrs Fox love each other. She points to endearments like 'my darling' and the contrast between the blunt use of surnames for the farmers. She asks students to find words that suggest rudeness on the part of the farmers (expressions like 'Dang and blast' from Boggis) and contempt for each other in dialogues. Like the exchange between Mr and Mrs Fox, this too could be role-played to bring out the unpleasantness in their way of talking to each other.

As a way of consolidating work on the dialogues and how they build character, students are asked to compare the language used in each one. This could be set out in a comparative table such as Table 4.3.

With each step building upon the other, the TLC sequence enables Alex to show children how to analyse the grammatical choices and then how to reason about the effects of these. Because the narrative is familiar, it becomes a resource for work on grammar and offers students an opportunity to deepen their appreciation of Dahl's craft as an author. Alex is able to build her students' metalanguage and to recycle and reinforce this in later stages of teaching and learning. Of course, the grammatical focus of the three steps of identification, description and interpretation/explanation would be different for different texts, and would take place at different points in the text. For example, Alex might also select an extract which reveals attitude in implicit or explicit ways, noting whether there is a negative or positive loading over a series of choices (as in the 'baddies' versus goodies' characters in *Fantastic Mr Fox*). In this way, she turns linguistic understanding of APPRAISAL (particularly INSCRIBED and INVOKED ATTITUDE and GRADUATION to practical use in her classroom.

Guided practice – joint construction of a new narrative

Alex wants her students to not only be able to interpret how Roald Dahl's language choices in this example build setting, but also to be able to 'think like writers' (Gray, 2003, cited in Axford, Harder & Wise, 2009, p. 84) as they compose texts. At this point, she decides to capitalise on her teaching about narrative, and move from interpretation to composition of text through a joint construction of a text. Returning to the narrative, she draws their attention to their responses to the experiential probe questions displayed in the classroom. They are there to prompt students to generate a list of alternative settings for a narrative – a place in the city,

TABLE 4.4 Probe questions to support planning for a jointly constructed narrative

Experiential lens – building a plausible 'possible world' of experience for readers

Setting: Where and when does it take place?
Characterization: Who or what is involved in the story?
Plotting: What is the problem facing one or more of the characters?
Struggle (Attempt at resolution): How might characters attempt to resolve the problem? Is there an internal or external struggle?
Crisis: Will there be a moment of high tension, a crisis?
Resolution: How will the complication be resolved? Will it work out well for some characters and not well for others?

a school in suburbs, a housing estate, etc. Alex sets up groups of four to make notes on ideas for a narrative, based on the probe questions in Table 4.4. Although the class text will not be completed in one session, she wants students to think about development of the whole narrative as this composition will have to be directed in purposeful ways from the outset.

The children come to the joint construction session armed with notes made earlier and offer ideas about what the narrative situation should be. Some propose they produce a story in which foxes are represented as pests disturbing the peaceful life of farmers and their sheep. Others suggest that it take place in the inner city where possums keep a family awake with their nocturnal escapades around their house. They select one of the options, and begin work on an Orientation that establishes the setting and introduces characters using the probe questions to guide them. Alex encourages the students to choose wordings that make readers want to read on. As they jointly construct the Orientation stage, Alex uses the metalanguage she has been establishing and scribes for the students. As she does so, she asks guiding questions to develop the two connected settings, as in *Fantastic Mr Fox* – one where the Owl Family lives, and the other where the Possum Family lives. For example:

> *In a run-down house near a large park in the city lived the Owl Family. In the garden of the run-down house there were many delicious fruit trees.*
>
> *In a quiet street near the run-down house there was a park. In the park there was a huge tree. High up in the tree there was a hollow. In the hollow lived Mr and Mrs Possum and their two Small Possums.*

Having written the Orientation as a group, the students read it over and review it. Then they go on to decide on the characters. As in *Fantastic Mr Fox*, the class narrative will include 'good' and 'bad' characters. Alex asks her students to think about which characters will be included and reminds students that they need to think about the problem that the characters will have (with one another). Table 4.5 includes class notes made about the characters.

TABLE 4.5 Collated notes about characters and dialogues in the class narrative

The Owls	*The Possum Family*
Who are the characters? Mum, dad and three kids who take no notice of the fruit that grows on their apple trees and pear trees except to throw it at each other or passers-by, and are always fighting with each other.	*Who are the characters?* Mum (Jill), dad (Jack) and two small possums who look after each other and love fruit.
What are they like? Beady eyes, small mouths, short and plump, stumpy fingers, down turned eyebrows which make them always look angry, selfish, mean, lazy.	*What are they like?* Soft and furry, agile, quick and nimble, clever, alert, caring
How do they speak to each other? "Give me that bike!" "Get out of my way!" "Ha ha! I just hit that man with an apple!"	*How do they speak to each other?* "I would love to eat some apples tonight darling Jack. Do you think you could try to find some for us without being hurt by the Owls?" said Jill Possum. "Of course, my dear. Whatever you want."

Reviewing the class plan, Alex asks the children if the language they have used will make readers like one family and dislike the other. It is clear that the group have decided that the Possum Family will be the heroes of the story, so together they suggest ways to portray the Possum Family positively, and the Owls negatively. Next, they need to decide on what will happen to bring the two families into conflict (what the major Complication will be) and how the characters might try to resolve it. In doing so, Alex guides the students to generate a text, mindful of development across the Orientation, Complication and Resolution stages.

Once the plan has been agreed upon and the Orientation completed, Alex may decide to jointly construct the remaining narrative with students or she may ask the groups to work on this together. In class groups consisting of students with very different literacy abilities, it can be helpful to work with students who are likely to struggle and to leave others to collaborate in small groups. The resulting narratives can be read aloud if students are happy to do this and decisions made about language choices and effectiveness of the texts.

Independent composition of narratives

Once students have completed the class text, it is likely they will be confident to begin their own writing. In this Year 4 classroom, Alex provides children with a choice of ideas from the plans mapped out during Guided Practice or to develop their own ideas if they have some good ones. As Alex likes her students to plan their writing, she once again draws their attention to the experiential probe questions to guide their thoughts. They begin writing.

Extension work – other possibilities for work with functional grammatics

There are possibilities for close attention to the language of narrative that Alex might use to extend students. Depending on the direction of class work, they could:

- Examine wordings that reveal attitude and intensify attitude about the farmers, such as '<u>enormously</u> fat', 'these <u>horrible</u> crooks', 'Bunce <u>reeks</u>' and so on These choices can be discussed highlighting how the descriptions of the farmers make us dislike them even more. Some teachers have referred to this as 'Bumping up or turning down the volume'.
- Explore action/reaction sequences throughout the narrative which give the reader insight into Mr Fox's external and internal worlds. For example, in Chapter 3 as Mr Fox creeps down towards the farm, we are told of his reaction to his surroundings (e.g. 'his black nose twitched', 'he heard or thought he heard a tiny noise', 'his ears pricked').
- Investigate instances of Focalization where events are projected through Mr Fox's thinking, for example where we see the farmers from the point of view of Mr Fox as he makes his way out of the hole. ('But Mr Fox would not have been quite so cocky had he <u>known</u> exactly where the farmers were waiting at that moment'.).
- Compare choices that alienate from characters in Fantastic Mr Fox with others in stories like *The Twits* (which this class already knows and likes). To do this, students can read the description of Mrs Twit and highlight choices that present her in a negative light. They can then rewrite the description to include positive choices such as, 'Mrs Twit, she was the most beautiful woman ever. Her eyes were as sparkly and blue as the ocean itself' or 'Mrs Twit had a huge smile and large blue eyes which makes everyone want to love her.' They reflect on and discuss the impact these have on our feelings for the character.

In one discussion around negative attitudinal resources used to describe the farmers in *Fantastic Mr Fox*, Alex's students debate whether choices like 'reek' can ever be positive. They create sentences to put a positive spin on the word choice, such as "Sammy, you reek beautifully today". One student responds: "Yeah, but the word 'reek' still sounds bad. I don't want to be told I <u>reek</u>!" What this conversation illustrates is how insights into grammatical choices, however small, provide a launching pad for exploration of possibilities, and how writers can learn to control the impression they want to make through grammar.

Scenario 2 – teaching narrative in a secondary classroom

Blair has planned a unit of work on science fiction and is keen to explore the question of how narratives with an ethical agenda manage to both entertain and instruct readers. Some of his students have done work on dialogue and point of view in earlier units but those new to his class have not. He decides to consolidate understandings of the class about how narrator voice is established, how interior worlds are explored and how characters' feelings and reactions are revealed. The curriculum content he plans to cover in this unit relates to narrative viewpoint (ACARA, 2012). His students will learn to "identify, explain and discuss how narrative viewpoint, structure and characterization (amongst other techniques) shape different interpretations and responses to text" (ACELT 1642). In this respect, he aims to shift them towards an understanding of higher orders of 'interpersonality' – ways in which the text itself shapes readers' viewpoints so that they 'transcend' those of the characters who inhabit the 'possible world' of the text. The question of 'second order semiosis' was the subject of Chapter 2 and in this scenario we show something of how a teacher can orient students to the larger interaction between implied author and ideal reader. It is through this relationship that the narrative 'teaches'. The mentor text selected for investigation of this question – how do narratives teach when they aren't explicitly didactic? – is ideal for Blair's purposes because it features an unreliable focaliser, whose viewpoint is later shown as inadequate by another voice – that of Niemand's. Our discussion of this issue and the ways in which Brown's story *The Weapon* uses Free Indirect Discourse occurred in Chapters 2 and 3. Investigation of 'voicing' in this short story will contribute to the larger purpose of the unit of work on science fiction to assist students to "evaluate the social, moral and ethical positions represented in texts" (ACELT 1812).

Reviewing and consolidating students' understandings of narrative viewpoint

Prior to his work on *The Weapon*, however, Blair needs to ensure that the students, especially those new to his class, understand the more rudimentary features of narrative point of view. Prior to this, his students have read the short story by Paul Jennings called 'Unhappily Ever After'. They need to be able to "identify, explain and discuss how narrative viewpoint, structure and characterization (amongst other techniques) shape different interpretations and responses to text" (ACELT 1642). He uses the following Table to guide his modelling of choices related to viewpoint. Note that terms in Table 4.6 like 'sensing and behavioural verbs' are related to curriculum metalanguage (ACARA, 2012) rather than functional grammatics.

TABLE 4.6 Blair's review of interpersonal meanings in 'Unhappily Ever After'

Narrative focus: Interpersonal Lens	Grammatics focus
How narrator voice is established	First or third Person
How interior worlds of characters are made visible	Sensing and behavioural verbs
How character feelings and reactions are revealed	Evaluative wordings intensified through GRADUATION

Focalization and narrator voice

Blair re-reads the extract (see below) from 'Unhappily Ever After' and says to students: 'As I read to you, I want you to think about the following questions: *Who is telling the story? Is it a character or someone outside the events? Whose eyes do we see through? Which words tell you this?*' After the shared reading, Blair checks responses to these questions. The class discuss which choices indicate whether the narrator is omniscient (all knowing) or limited to the viewpoint of one character (restricted)? Is it narrated by someone who has experienced events (First Person)? or by someone 'outside' the action (Third Person)? They decide that this is a third Person narrative and highlight words that indicate this (e.g. 'Albert', 'he', 'his'). He highlights these words on a copy of the extract as they identify these, drawing attention to how pronouns such as 'he' and 'his' help us to keep track of what is happening to Albert (the boy) and to Brown (the principal).

Blair then raises the question about whose 'eyes' we see through in the story. He asks students to focus on verbs that let us know what Albert is thinking or feeling. He highlights these as students identify them. He points out that verbs such as 'knew', 'wished' and 'felt' invite us into Albert's interior world so that we can 'feel with' and identify with him.

Character and Attitude

Using the same extract, Blair now focuses on choices that communicate Albert's attitude to his situation. In this extract, Blair notes that evaluative words are mostly inscribed or explicit: they leave us in no doubt about Albert's emotional state. Here, rather than sensing verbs, the author uses behavioural verbs to 'show rather than tell' (e.g. 'He <u>did up</u> the top button of his shirt and <u>adjusted</u> his school tie'). He asks students to find other examples of Albert's discomfort through bodily behaviours. These are highlighted on the class copy below, with sensing verbs indicated in italics and behavioural verbs underlined below:

> Albert <u>pulled up</u> his socks and <u>wiped</u> his sweaty hands on the seat of his pants. He <u>did up</u> the top button of his shirt and <u>adjusted</u> his school tie. Then he <u>trudged</u> slowly up the stairs.
>   He was going to get the strap.
>   He *knew* it, he just *knew* it. He couldn't *think* of one thing he had done wrong but he *knew* Mr Brown was going to give him the strap anyway. He would find some excuse to whack Albert – he always did.
>   Albert's stomach <u>leapt up and down</u> as if it was filled with jumping frogs. Something in his throat <u>stopped</u> him from <u>swallowing</u> properly. He didn't *want* to go. He *wished* he <u>could faint</u> or be terribly sick so he would have to be rushed to hospital in an ambulance.

But nothing happened. He *felt* his own feet taking him up to his doom.

He stood outside the big brown door and <u>trembled</u>. He was afraid but he made his usual resolution. He <u>would not cry</u>. He would not ask for mercy. He would <u>not even wince</u>.

There was no way he was going to give Mr Brown that pleasure.

He took a deep breath and knocked softly.

Blair closes the review by showing that it is relatively easy to distinguish between the inner and outer worlds of experience in this and other texts. Figure 4.2 (produced by one teacher working on focalization) depicts and defines these vividly.

Building the context for work on narrative

Having taught students to identify grammatical choices that enable them to distinguish inner and outer worlds, Blair now problematises this somewhat. He tells students that the stories they will read in this unit aim to teach as well as entertain. Science fiction often challenges our perspectives. An author may structure the narrative to let us 'see with' a character and then distance us from his or her viewpoint. This often occurs through the intervention of another character. In science fiction, this is achieved through the words or actions of a stranger (an alien) with a fresh viewpoint. Blair asks students to think about the big question that is to be explored in this unit: How does science fiction instruct as well as entertain us? He asks them to think about how a narrator 'gets inside' a reader's head. The questions the class will explore in next lessons are: *Who is telling the story? Is this person internal/external*

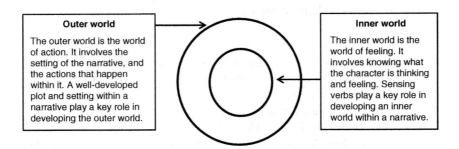

FIGURE 4.2 Inner and outer worlds of experience.

TABLE 4.7 Blair's planning framework for a grammatics of *The Weapon*

Guiding Question: How does science fiction instruct as well as entertain us?	
Narrative focus: Interpersonal Lens	**Grammatics focus**
How are differing views introduced into a narrative?	Verbs of sensing and saying
How do fresh viewpoints interrupt and challenge the reader's alignment with a character?	Evaluative noun groups and adjectives
How does Free Indirect Discourse work to blur the distinction between character & narrator?	Thoughts or expressions which are typical of a character's voice but appear to emanate from the narrator.

to events in the story? Whose point of view is represented? How do we know? Table 4.7 presents the questions he will use to guide his work on *The Weapon*.

Modelling the text

Blair orients students to the narrative as follows:

> Blair: *In the Orientation, we are introduced to Dr Graham and learn that he is a scientist working on an important project. We also learn that he has a 'mentally arrested son'. See if you can hear as I read it to you that the narrator is at times external to the events, but there are points where we hear the voice of Dr Graham although there is no explicit use of projected thoughts or dialogue.*
>
> *The Complication is precipitated by the arrival of Niemand. He is 'a stranger' and Dr Graham sees him as 'a small man, nondescript, obviously harmless'. As Niemand begins to explain his reason for his visit, Graham's appraisal of him shifts suddenly. He decides Niemand is 'a crackpot'. Their conversation is interrupted by the appearance of Graham son. We are told that Niemand appears to be aware of the existence of the boy Harry. But again, we learn this through Graham's point of view. Niemand's challenge alerts us to a more sinister problem with Dr Graham's work as a scientist. He asks, 'But, Dr Graham, is humanity ready for an ultimate weapon?'*
>
> *Dr Graham's rejects this view and yet, we have become aware by now that he has an amoral stance towards scientific research: he doesn't care that it could have destructive consequences for humanity.*
>
> *The Resolution sees Niemand departing after accepting Graham's offer of a drink, after giving Graham's son 'a gift' while Graham prepares the drinks. In the coda, Graham's lack of awareness of the significance of the 'gift' to his son is revealed through a final comment: 'He thought, only a madman would give a loaded revolver to an idiot'.*

He now works with students to identify shifts in point of view across the text. Using the text on the whiteboard or project, he asks students to identify grammatical choices that indicate these shifts between Dr Graham's internal point of view

TABLE 4.8 Working through the grammar of point of view in *The Weapon*

	Dr. Graham's viewpoint	Niemand's viewpoint
Orientation	The room was quiet in the dimness of early evening. Dr James Graham, key scientist of a very important project, sat in his favourite chair, *thinking*. It was so still that he *could hear* the turning of pages in the next room as his son leafed through a picture book Often Graham did his best work, his most creative thinking, under these circumstances, sitting alone in an unlighted room in his own apartment after the day's regular work. But tonight his mind would not work constructively. Mostly he *thought* about his mentally arrested son – his only son – in the next room. The thoughts were loving thoughts, not the bitter anguish he had felt years ago when he had first learned of the boy's condition. *The boy was happy; wasn't that the main thing? And to how many men is given a child who will always be a child, who will not grow up to leave him? Certainly, that was a rationalization, but what is wrong with rationalization when it …*	
Complication	The doorbell rang. Graham rose and turned on the lights … *He was not annoyed; tonight, at this moment, almost any interruption to his thoughts was welcome.* He opened the door. *A stranger* stood there … Graham *looked at* him. He was *a small man, nondescript, obviously harmless – possibly a reporter or an insurance agent.* But it didn't matter what he was. Graham *found himself saying*, 'Of course. Come in, Mr. Niemand.' A few moments of conversation, *he justified himself by thinking*, might divert his thoughts and clear his mind. 'Sit down,' he **said**, in the living room. 'Care for a drink?' *A crackpot*, Graham *thought*.	Niemand **said** 'No, thank you.' He sat in the chair; Graham sat on the sofa. The small man interlocked his fingers; he leaned forward. He **said**, 'Dr. Graham, you are the man whose scientific work is more likely than that of any other man to end the human race's chance for survival.'

TABLE 4.8 Continued

	Dr. Graham's viewpoint	Niemand's viewpoint
Evaluation	Graham suddenly *had liked* Niemand when Niemand had shown liking for the boy. Now he *remembered* that he must close the interview quickly. He rose, in dismissal. He **said**, 'I fear you're wasting your time and mine Mr. Niemand. I know all the arguments, everything you can say I've heard a thousand times. Possibly there is truth in what you believe, but it *does not concern* me. I'm a scientist and only a scientist. Yes, it is public knowledge that I am working on a weapon, a rather ultimate one. But, for me personally, that is only a by-product of the fact that I am advancing science. I have *thought* it through, and I have found that that is my only concern.'	'But, Dr Graham, is humanity ready for an ultimate weapon?'
Resolution	[...] (Section of narrative omitted)	Niemand **said**, 'I took the liberty of bringing a small gift to your son, doctor. I gave it to him while you were getting drinks for us. I hope you'll forgive me.'
Coda	'Of course. Thank you. Good night.' There was a sudden sweat on his forehead, but he forced his face and voice to be calm as he stepped to the side of the bed. 'May I see that, Harry?' When he had it safely in his grasp, his hands shook as he examined it. He *thought*, only a madman would give a loaded revolver to an idiot.	

and those of Niemand which trigger a different perspective. Blair stops as he reads through phases where it is unclear who is speaking and asks students to decide whose voice is heard. While Blair will not use the term, Free Indirect Discourse, with his students, he intends to make them aware of how we are moved into Dr Graham's psyche through internal musings not signalled through a projected clause (direct speech or thought). Table 4.8 highlights choices students should find as they work through the model. Verbs of sensing are in italics, verbs of saying are in bold italics and expressions that indicate psychological responses are underlined. Phases of Free Indirect Discourse are in underlined italics. A portion of the story has been left out.

122 Moving South: teaching narrative

Blair's next task is to draw students' attention to phases in the Orientation where the distinction between narrator and Graham is blurred. He asks students, *'Who is speaking when Graham asks himself questions about his son? Who says, 'Wasn't that the main thing?'* He uses this point to demonstrate how the reader aligns with the scientist, understands his world because the character and narrator are as one; we can identify with his distress over the sad circumstances of his disabled son because we are 'thinking along' with him.

Now he asks the students to highlight grammatical features for Niemand. Once these have been identified, Blair asks the class to focus on Dr Graham's changing view of Niemand:

a stranger – a small man, nondescript, obviously harmless – a crackpot – a madman

Blair asks students to pinpoint where the shifts in Dr Graham's perception of Niemand take place. He asks students to represent shifts through a diagram like the one in Figure 4.3.

Through the rather extensive examination of the short story, and the diagrammatic representation of the alternating points of view, Blair has given his students an intelligible means of interpreting the unfolding narrative as well as opened up 'repertoires of possibility' for their own writing. Through mapping out the different viewpoints, the students can see how they are at first invited to view the world

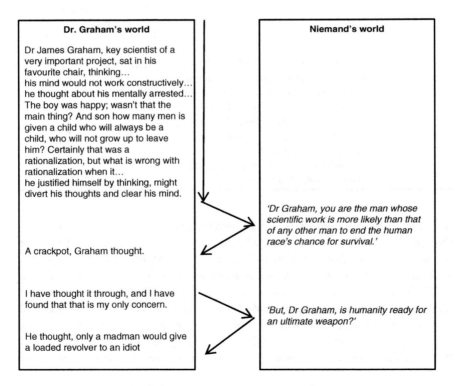

FIGURE 4.3 Tracking the shifts in narrative viewpoint in *The Weapon*.

along with Dr Graham, and later to have this viewpoint questioned through the Niemand's dialogue. In this way, they move towards a greater understanding of how this narrative like many others in the literary canon establishes a virtual relationship with its readers that transcends the relationships (and viewpoints) expressed by the characters who interact within it.

Guided practice

To support the students to include a similar model of shifting viewpoints in their own writing, Blair decides to innovate on *The Weapon* by providing an alternative scenario which allows for two contrasting points of view to be presented. He asks the students to make suggestions about the possible scenarios such as:

- a scientist who has developed a means of mind control
- a stranger arrives in a community, isolated except for a connection with one member
- a computer wizard who develops a game which fuses reality with virtual worlds.

Selecting one of the scenarios, Blair works with students to plan a joint text using questions like the following:

> *Who are the two characters to be introduced?*
> *What is the issue for the two opposing characters?*
> *With whom are we going to identify (i.e. whose internal world will be represented?)*
> *How will the encounter be set up?*
> *Is there a vulnerable third person needed (e.g. like the disabled son)? How might the hidden cost of the new invention be related to this character?*

There are extensive opportunities for talk, as the students make suggestions about the possible scenarios and characters. Writing an extended text with the whole class can not only be quite time consuming, but also difficult to engage all students in the collaboration. For a jointly constructed text with a peer, the teacher can still provide guidance as the students compose their texts. For example, Blair reminds students about the importance of exploring ethical issues in their narrative and giving two characters different views on one of these. At key points throughout the process of composition, Blair stops the class and asks different pairs to share part of their texts, providing feedback and seeking it from students.

Once the jointly composed narratives are completed, Blair asks students to review their drafts, highlighting language choices on which they had focussed earlier (e.g. verbs of sensing, saying, Free Indirect Discourse). This grammatically focussed review alerts the students to ways in which they can position readers so as to adopt a given viewpoint. Where appropriate, students edit texts based on feedback from other groups working on narrative.

Independent writing and reflection

Following Joint Construction work, Blair asks students to select another scenario from their list of possibilities to write about independently. When completed, he asks students to select parts of their narrative which illustrate competing viewpoints on the issue explored in their narrative and to articulate the language choices which they feel bring these out. Blair wants his students to not only be cognisant of the choices that are evident in their writing, but to be able to explain the impact these choices have (the why beneath the what). Allowing time for them to talk about what they write is important in building their capacity to do so. It also affords Blair another opportunity to model language choices at work and to assess which of these his students have been able to appropriate in their writing. Following this work, the students move on to consider another narrative from the corpus of science fiction narrative selected by Blair for this unit.

Scenario 3 – multimodal narrative interpretation and text creation with Year 7

Liam teaches a class of Year 7 students in a large urban-rural fringe high school. He plans to capitalise on their interest in Facebook, Instagram and video game narratives and to show them how to analyse language and image in multimodal texts. He wants to inform their enthusiastic participation in the world of social media with knowledge of how images and language work to position viewers. In other words, he hopes to make them more critical consumers of multimedia narratives. This goal is supported by the AC:E curriculum content for Year 7 (ACARA, 2012) which recommends that students learn to "Compare the ways that language and images are used to create character and to influence emotions and opinions in different types of text" (ACELT 1620). But his students are also enthusiastic storytellers. Beyond analysis of image and verbiage in multimodal texts, however, Liam is keen to give them the opportunity to compose multimodal narratives and to deploy images to position viewers more knowledgeably. In this aspect of their work, they will "Experiment with text structures and language features and other effects in creating literary texts like layout, gaze, navigation and colour" (ACELT 1805).

Liam has drawn on aspects of literature for children that are popular with his pre- and early adolescent students such as supernatural or 'other worldly' experience, negotiating parental and peer relationships, and the ever-popular motif of the fox. The fox has been a prominent motif in many works of children's literature including Roald Dahl's *Fantastic Mr Fox* (Dahl, 1974), which we discussed in Chapters 2 and 3, the realist fiction of Betsy Byars' *The Midnight Fox* (Byars, 1968), and the multiple award-winning picture book, *The Fox* (Wild & Brooks, 2000). For this classroom work Liam has chosen two books for young readers set in contemporary Australia that centre on the association of the fox with the supernatural and other worlds. One of these is the illustrated story, *Grandad's Gifts* by the popular Australian writer Paul Jennings and illustrator, Peter Gouldthorpe (Jennings & Gouldthorpe, 1992).

The story appeared earlier as an unillustrated version by Paul Jennings published in the volume *Unbearable* (Jennings, 1994). In this story pre-adolescent Shane and his family move into his Grandfather's old house in the country. Shane's bedroom, formerly his father's room, contains a wardrobe, which the late Grandfather has warned should never be opened. Mysterious guidance leads Shane to discover a fox skin fur wrap inside. Further mysterious influences result in Shane's transporting lemons from the trees under which the remains of the fox and his Grandfather were buried, to the fox in the wardrobe. Ultimately, one night the family discovers the forbidden wardrobe door open and observes a blue-eyed fox at the edge of the garden.

The second book is the novel for young adolescents, *Foxspell* (Rubinstein, 1994), which negotiates the delicate transitions between fantasy and reality and between human, spirit and animal worlds, as the main character, Tod experiences events beyond his control dragging him into adolescence. His fascination with foxes, which inhabit the quarry near his grandmother's house leads him into a world whose simplicity seems to offer relief from his everyday life of complexity and compromise, until one day he finds he has to choose between two very different worlds.

Foxspell will be read alongside *Grandad's Gifts*. Following their analysis of ATTITUDE in the images used in *Grandad's Gifts*, students will jointly compose a multimodal narrative based on *Foxspell*. The goal will be to bring out attitudinal meanings made only implicitly through images, thus opening up the interpretive possibilities of the text.

Planning for teaching

The initial unillustrated and subsequent illustrated versions of *Grandad's Gifts* afford an opportunity to examine how the interaction of images and language influence various aspects of literary narrative technique. Using an Experiential lens, one such issue is 'foreshadowing' – how the author/illustrator gradually suggests the emergence of the supernatural before it actually emerges. In fact, with respect to composition, this has a textual aspect too in that it previews what is to come later in the narrative. In the picture book, the fox is not mentioned in the text until the third double page spread, however on the first opening of the book in the first image the wood grain pattern of the wardrobe door un-mistakenly represents the head of a fox, and there are other subtle intimations of the supernatural in the language such as:

> Something inside seemed to call to me.
> It was almost as if a gentle voice was stirring the shadows of years gone by. The stillness seemed to echo my name, "Shane, Shane, Shane …"

Further exploration of the joint role of images and language in foreshadowing in *Grandad's Gifts* offers an opportunity for highly engaging classroom work (Unsworth, 2001), but Liam wants to focus on how evaluative resources of language construct the character's attitudinal responses to events and how images portray the character's inner experience.

Liam sets out his goals for the sequence of lessons, drawing upon evaluative resources in language in the Appraisal Framework as discussed in Chapter 3 (see Table 4.9).

In preparation for class analysis of the images and how they work in tandem with the wordings, Liam has examined how attitude through image-language interaction in the first four double page spreads of *Grandad's Gifts* is communicated.

A strong indication of Shane's affective response is provided in the image that fills the right-hand side of the first double page spread (Figure 4.4).[3]

At this point we do not know about the fox, but our view of Shane through the keyhole not only confirms something unknown is watching him, but this together with the 'contact' image gazing straight at the viewer (and the keyhole) and the raised eyebrows and wide-open eyes, clearly portrays Shane's feeling of disquiet.

After this, Shane notices two lemon trees in the garden, one shrivelled and one growing very well. Apparently, Shane's grandfather shot a fox and buried it under the second tree. This adds a new dimension to Shane's feeling of disquiet:

> *I gave a shiver. I knew that I would never peel one of those lemons. Or eat one.*

This does not directly state how Shane is feeling, but the bodily response of 'shiver' invokes a feeling of disquiet.

In the account of that night for Shane, the language further intimates the supernatural and invokes feelings of increasing disquiet:

> *I turned my back on the secret cupboard and tried not to listen to the gentle voice lapping like waves in my head. "Shane, Shane, Shane ..."*

TABLE 4.9 Liam's plan for work on multimodal narrative

Big Question: How do multimodal texts position us to feel, see and judge?	
Interpersonal Lens	**Grammatics focus**
How attitudes and feelings of characters are revealed through language choices	Evaluative nouns groups which reflect character: Focus on both Inscribed (explicit) and Invoked (implicit) AFFECT (e.g. un/happiness, in/security, dis/satisfaction).
How attitudes and feelings of characters can be discerned in images	Realisation of AFFECT in images through facial expression, body posture and gesture.
How attitudes and feelings of characters can be graduated	Intensification of core vocabulary and the prosodic impact of AFFECT in language.
How images position the viewer interpersonally in relation to the story characters	Choices of interactive meanings and Focalization in particular.
How language and images work together to portray attitudes and feelings of characters in a multimodal narrative	Convergence and divergence of Affect in the language and images and influence on reading position.

FIGURE 4.4 Looking at Shane from inside the cupboard.

When peering into the keyhole, Shane thinks he sees two points of light twinkle in the darkness, and then he says:

> *I shivered. This was creepy. I didn't really want to live in this room.*

The bodily function of shivering again invokes AFFECT in terms of somewhat fearful uneasiness. Then 'creepy' inscribes APPRECIATION of the room as sinister, and the last sentence elaborates on the fear. So, what we have is a prosodic building up or graduating of the feelings of fearfulness. But the image on the right-hand side of this double page (Figure 4.5) accentuates this growing apprehension.

The verbal text says:

> *That night I couldn't sleep. Every time I opened my eyes I saw the cupboard door.*

In Figure 4.5[4] the moonlight shining into the bedroom highlights the wood grain image of the fox on the wardrobe. The vectors of the bars on the windows reinforce

128 Moving South: teaching narrative

FIGURE 4.5 Shane gazes fearfully at the light in the darkness.

the gaze of Shane towards the wardrobe (and the highlighted fox image). His raised eyebrows, right hand held up to his mouth, and left hand clenching the sheet clearly convey the feeling of uneasiness.

Having prepared for the work on *Grandad's Gifts*, Liam is ready to orient students to the text.

Building the context for work on multimodal narrative

Liam begins by reminding his students about other stories by Paul Jennings that they have read and invites brief sharing of recollections of favourites. They discuss other texts that students found either frightening or mysterious and Liam asks them to think about what made them scary. He wants students to consider how narratives influence the emotions of readers and thus prepare the way for exploration of the combined effect of words and pictures in the class narratives.

He then introduces *Grandad's Gifts* as a different kind of story and one that has been published in unillustrated and illustrated versions. He reads the story aloud to the class and they discuss the mystery of the fox and why it continues to trouble the house. They talk about why Shane seems so sensitive to the mystery of the fox and the lemon tree. Then Liam invites the students to consider how the images contribute to creating a sense of fear in readers. At this point, students will understand the bare bones of the action but have questions about why things happen as they do. Their work on the images will only heighten the sense of mystery.

Liam asks the students to re-read the narrative in groups of three or four, providing them with a copy of the illustrated version. This time they are to examine the images in more detail, musing over the images and commenting on features or perceptions. They come back to the larger group and share their responses to images as they re-read the story. Liam asks the students to consider what kinds of attitudes the images are primarily showing. They talk about the kinds of attitudes – feelings, judgements and appreciation – that the images seem concerned with. As the students respond, Liam makes a note of words for emotions that they suggest in discussion of the attitudes expressed by the images. He puts these on a large piece of paper or on a whiteboard and tells them they will return to these as they continue to study the illustrator's choices and compare these to those of the author, Paul Jennings. Liam indicates that follow-up work for the week will be to investigate how the images and the language separately and in combination function to communicate ATTITUDE. He tells the class that the big question they are exploring in this work is: How do multimodal texts position us to feel, see and judge? Their next activity will be to look closely at some of the images and consider how they work together with the language to generate a sense of mystery.

Modelling the text – from teacher to small groups

Liam reviews the first four double page spreads with the class. Then he models an examination of two images and corresponding text segments to show how AFFECT is conveyed in both the images and in the language. Later they will engage in a joint analysis of a third image and related text segment based on what he does now. Liam has arranged for the first two double page spreads of the book to be displayed so that all students can see them. He provides a copy of the book for small groups to share as he guides them through the analysis.

Liam begins by displaying and reading the first two double page spreads of the book. He establishes with the students that the language does not include any expression of Shane's feelings, although there may be some hint of uneasiness in his appearing to perceive a voice calling his name. Following this, students are shown image two (Figure 4.4) and asked to respond to the following questions:

- How does this image indicate that someone is watching Shane?
- You can see Shane though a keyhole, so where are you as a viewer?
- Do Shane's eyes appear to be looking straight at you? (So, this is a Contact image with the participant in the image making direct eye contact with the viewer).

- What do you notice about Shane's eyes and eyebrows?
- What is indicated by the position of Shane's arms and hands and the position of his head in relation to his body?
- What does the image indicate Shane is feeling?

These questions should help to establish that the image has the major role in communicating AFFECT here. Students can be encouraged to look again at the words Liam has listed on the board and to add to these as they talk about the feelings that Shane (the character) seems to be feeling and those that the image evokes in them (the readers). He explains that just as words can invoke as well as inscribe attitudes, so too can images. He reminds the class of the meaning of inscribe and invoke, building on earlier work on denotation and connotation. INSCRIBED APPRAISAL is explicit, coded directly through vocabulary or facial expressions. INVOKED APPRAISAL is implicit, suggested indirectly through combinations of choices.

Liam then displays and reads the third double page spread and draws attention to the last three sentences in paragraph two beginning with 'I shivered'. He asks what feelings are indicated by the word 'shivered' and establishes that this might indicate being frightened but it does not say this directly, so 'shivered' invokes feeling frightened rather than inscribing or saying directly that he was frightened.

- In a similar way, the last sentence invokes insecurity rather than inscribing it directly.
- The students are asked to suggest what 'creepy' implies. Liam points out that this refers to the phenomena occurring in the room and not to a person so this is not AFFECT but is called APPRECIATION as it applies to an evaluation of something inanimate.

A similar procedure is followed as Liam examines the image and evaluative language on the fourth double page spread exploring their construction of AFFECT as outlined in the background discussion above. At the end of this session, Liam and the students consolidate what they have learned and Liam explains that in the next lesson the students will conduct similar examinations of different images in small working groups and that this will prepare them for their composition of a multimodal narrative following the analysis. It is crucial that students have the opportunity to practice analysis of the kind Liam is modelling so that they can internalise the strategies and undertake the careful work of description that is so important in multimodal analysis.

For the next task, students will work in small groups of three, each of which is allocated one of double page spreads seven, twelve or fourteen. Their task is to investigate how the images and the evaluative language in their story segments construct AFFECT following the approach demonstrated in the previous lesson. Liam has examined each of these double page spreads making notes about what he might draw the students' attention to as they work (see outline of segments below). He encourages the students to consult the class whiteboard as they analyse their double

Moving South: teaching narrative **131**

page spread, noting first impressions of each page and then finding evidence of choices in their segment that confirms, challenges or adds to these impressions. The students work together on each double page spread. Following this, they will join an expert group to present their group findings on one of these.

As the students work in small groups, Liam provides support and prompts to guide them to note the realizations of AFFECT in words and pictures. For example, the first segment for analysis occurs after Shane has decided to move the bed. In doing so, he discovers the key to the wardrobe but must work all day helping his father in the garden before he has a chance to try the key. After he successfully unlocks the wardrobe door he 'swung open the door', and on the left-hand side of the following page we see the image shown in Figure 4.6.[5]

The point of view is from inside the cupboard and from this position the viewer observes the frightened look on Shane's face. Liam draws students' attention to the raised eyebrows, wide opened eyes and open mouth, as well as the left hand extended in self-protection. As readers, we remain unaware of what Shane has seen

FIGURE 4.6 Shane discovers what is inside the cupboard.

until we read on the next page: 'The fox didn't move.' Then after a brief description of the dead fox, we read:

> Suddenly the fox moved. Its mouth opened a fraction. My brain froze. The world seemed to spin. I was filled with terror. I gave a scream and slammed the door shut. Then I ran downstairs.

The words – 'My brain froze' – invoke Insecurity because the author has used a metaphor to communicate this. But in the next sentence the fear is inscribed, with 'terror' intensifying the feeling followed by a surge of emotion in 'scream'. Liam encourages students to note this prosodic build-up of emotion in the wordings here. He asks students to discuss whether the words confirm the meanings of the image or not. In this case there is a definite convergence of highly graduated fear in the portrayal in both image and language.

The second story segment allocated for student group examination occurs after Shane has discovered that if he puts lemons in the mouth of the fox they disappear overnight and rejuvenate part of the fox's body. Eventually only the eyes remain to be rejuvenated and that morning Shane looks out of the window to see that his father is mulching the last of the lemon tree – and the last of the lemons. His reaction is depicted in Figure 4.7.[6]

The text segment corresponding to Figure 4.7 reads:

> 'No,' I yelled. 'No.' I ran to the window. 'Stop', I screamed. 'Stop'.

Liam prompts students working on this segment to consider what AFFECT is invoked in this text. Students might give suggestions like 'frustration', 'anxiety' and these are all related to a larger feeling of Dissatisfaction. However, the unhappiness inscribed in the surge of feeling in the text is not depicted visually and this divergence can be explored further:

> Tears ran down my face. I thought of the blind fox, still hanging in the blackness of the cupboard that had for so long been its coffin. I stood there and sobbed.

The last story segment for group work occurs after Shane's father (still unaware of the fox and thinking Shane was upset about the lemons) indicates that the second shrivelled lemon tree has two lemons. Shane tries putting these in the fox's mouth but since they did not come from the tree under which the fox was buried, Shane believes he failed the fox. However, the next morning the family hears a noise and when they go to investigate they discover the wardrobe door open and Shane sees that the fox is gone, but Shane picks up two glass eyes from the floor. This is depicted in Figure 4.8.

Although Shane has been exposed disobeying his father in opening the door, he says:

I didn't care what he said or what he did. I was happy in a way I had never been happy before. I picked up the two glass eyes that lay rejected on the floor.

The image of course, does not show happiness at all, but is rather a look of sadness, or perhaps remorse or even foreboding. So here we have a case of divergence between the AFFECT shown in the image and that conveyed in the language.

In the next lesson, the re-constituted groups consist of at least one student who worked on each of the different text segments outlined above. This strategy for sharing and consolidating learning is often called 'jigsaw' group work. As spokespersons sharing the collaborative work with their colleague in the former groupings, each student is able to take an authoritative role in articulating the understandings of the image-language relations they derived. The teacher prompts these new discussion groups to note issues such as the principal role of the images in conveying Affect, and to consider for further exploration in the next lesson, the shifts in AFFECT patterns as the story develops, and patterns of convergence and divergence in the nature of the AFFECT communicated through language and images.

FIGURE 4.7 Shane looks out the window.

FIGURE 4.8 Shane picks up the glass eyes.

Following this analytical work, Liam and the class review the whole story, applying the approaches they have learned to use earlier and noticing important aspects of AFFECT in the story that are not associated with images. An example of this occurs in the eleventh double page spread where Shane places his hand on the fox's chest:

> I can't describe the thrill that ran up my arm. The fox's heart was beating. It was alive but not alive. It still dangled from the peg. But its nose was wet and warm. A red tongue trembled between its teeth.

As they read, Liam asks the students to point to wordings that show how intensely Shane is feeling the thrill of realizing the fox is alive. This can be explored nontechnically at first but later incorporated into technical analysis of Appraisal systems like AFFECT (including sub-systems like Un/happiness, Dis/satisfaction and In/security). It is important that students begin to become aware of the ways in which these feelings are Inscribed (expressed explicitly as in 'thrill') or invoked (expressed implicitly as in 'trembled'). It can be fascinating to explore parallel patterns in the images too. The students should simultaneously develop an enjoyable appreciation of this literary narrative and explicit knowledge of systems of choices drawn upon to create its interpretive possibilities.

Guided practice – applying the tools to composition of a multimodal narrative

The class work on the novel *Foxspell* enables the students to apply and extend their understanding about how language and image can be deployed to construct Affect as part of the portrayal of characters in literary texts. In this program of work, a similar approach of modelling, joint teacher-student analysis and peer collaborative work leading to independent individual student response is implemented. Through devising an approach to producing an illustrated version of *Foxspell* consistent with the increasing emergence of such illustrated versions of popular and classic novels such as *The Da Vinci Code* (Brown, 2003).

After introducing and reading the entire novel with the class, Liam identifies several key incidents in the book as potential arenas for including illustrations. One of these is developed by Liam in discussion with the class to provide a model of what needs to be considered and what illustrative strategies are possible in appropriately augmenting the story through illustration to enhance the portrayal of characters in relation to the key themes of the narrative. Liam selects Tod's first direct encounter with the fox (Rubinstein, 1994, p.71):

> He didn't have to call the fox. It was already there, waiting for him. He saw it beyond the olive bushes, watching him, motionless. Their eyes met briefly. The fox turned. He caught a glimpse of the white-tipped brush as he dived into the thicket of branches to follow it.

Liam has worked with multimodal texts and encouraged students to find model images in other units of work. He knows that a very expeditious approach to obtaining illustrations is to search the internet for images meeting the design criteria. He points out that in the quotation above there is no direct expression of Tod's Affect, hence the inclusion of images would be a way of augmenting this aspect of the story. The questions to ask here would be what kinds of feeling would be apposite to this incident. For example, students would be asked: What kinds of images would be consistent with 'He saw it ... watching him' and 'Their eyes met briefly'?

Addressing these issues in class discussion would orient students to appropriate images from their internet searches. Liam guides his students to find images that portray Tod's first spotting of the fox 'watching him'. Websites such as www.boredpanda.com/beautiful-fox-pictures/ provide access to a number of suitable images. Although they undertake internet searches often, in this activity, these are purposeful, guided by the need to find images that support, challenge or counterpoint in interesting ways, the wordings of the text. Alternatively, students can draw their own images and this may be an activity to be done in co-ordination with Visual Arts classes. Students have choices here to portray a different affective responses when 'Their eyes met briefly'. For example, one image of Tod might be Contact: Invited, showing Tod looking directly towards the viewer from the corner of his eye, and that of the fox Contact: Observe. Another combination might be Contact: Direct with images of both Tod looking directly at the viewer in a front on (Action oriented) position. Consult Figure 3.2 for further options in a selection of images to go with the narrative.

As Liam supports the students to work in groups to explore images in other text segments allocated to each group, issues such as consistency of character representation are raised. This happens as students notice that they cannot find sufficient images of the same boy showing different AFFECT. The concept of 'work around' is explored. Work around can entail taking close-up photos of class members in character roles and using long shots from the internet of boys of the same age to indicate the context such as Tod and Adrian fighting (p. 89), with the close-up shots of each character depicting Affect before and/or after the fighting. Other options might include searching the internet for multiple photos of child movie stars depicting different feelings. A similar class grouping and re-grouping approach is used in the same manner as was implemented in the *Grandad's Gifts* lessons and, following sharing of work through re-grouping, new student groups sought to identify their own segments of the story to illustrate. Each group's work could then be analysed by a different group to discuss convergence and divergence of Affect depiction in language and image and how the construction of characters' feelings related to the development of the story and the ideas being proposed for debate.

Independent composition of multimodal narratives

The final stage of this unit of work could take different forms. In our pedagogic imaginations, we suggest that it could lead to the composition of original illustrated narratives to be authored by the students and informed by explicit semiotic knowledge of how images and language work independently and in combination contribute to characterization and to the exploration of mysterious themes such as those in our two class texts. Follow up discussion of the effect of choices would consider the degree of convergence or divergence of words and pictures. In our experience, teachers and students enjoy this kind of work and talk about the different meaning potentials of each choice and their interplay can be a powerful 'way in' to multimodal interpretation (Painter et al., 2013). This issue will be taken up when we investigate the relational aspect of a grammatics in service to multimodal composition in Chapter 8.

Conclusion

Through the teaching scenarios presented in this chapter, various opportunities for grammatically informed teaching about writing have been examined. The teachers have learnt about the principles and resources of functional grammatics and integrated them into the teaching of narrative. Alex has introduced her Year 4 students to resources for building plausible possible worlds of experience, showing students how Roald Dahl does this in creating a setting that is vital to the situation that the foxes and farmers struggle to resolve. She has looked at the role of dialogue in establishing characters and drawn students' attention to the resources of Mood, Ellipsis and evaluative language in this process. All her work has been oriented to deepening children's appreciation of narrative craft and their joint and later independent compositions draw on this earlier work. Many of the primary teachers who worked with *Fantastic Mr Fox* or other Dahl novellas like The *Twits* found that children delighted in discovering more of how language works in these texts and how they too could appropriate strong contrasts between goodies and baddies and intensify their descriptions in their own writing. The grammatics was a source of pleasure in this work – something that as we explained in Chapter 1 is rarely associated with work on grammar.

Blair was appropriately ambitious in his teaching Focalization, Voicing and Evaluation, building strongly on early work on a text featuring two points of view – 'Unhappily Ever After' – and then moving to consider the subtler impact of Free Indirect Discourse in *The Weapon*. We continue to learn that teachers should never underestimate the capacity of students to engage with challenging material, even complex canonical works of literature. The key to their engagement is to introduce the material in as explicit a way as possible. Liam used his knowledge of functional grammatics to shed light on shifts between inner and outer experience in short stories and encouraged his students to explore higher orders of interaction that they establish with readers. Work on Narration, Focalization and Voicing could begin with questions about how narrative positions readers powerfully without being overtly didactic.

As noted by Myhill, Jones, Lines and Watson (2012), when teachers do not make a connection between grammatical choices and impact, students often think that they simply need to 'put the item in', resulting in lessons which have limited impact. However, when students are guided through carefully sequenced and scaffolded teaching, where language choices are identified, described and explained, they are more likely to use their knowledge about language and how it works to craft meaning as they write.

Liam too was ambitious in his work on multimodal narrative, especially the combined effects of images and language in Grandad's Gifts. Given how enthusiastically his Year 7 students were about multimedia communication, he could capitalise on this to push them to look at the way images both invoke and inscribe affect. He worked with his students to examine APPRAISAL choices in images and the interplay between verbal and visual choices. Teaching about language and image in explicit, meaningful ways is a supportive approach for both primary and secondary learners and allows teachers to provide clear guidance and feedback to their students. Discussions that examine semiotic choices in verbal and visual texts, and which invite the use of a shared metalanguage understood by both teacher and student, open up access to repertoires of possibility in both interpretation and composition.

In the next section of the book, we turn to a different domain of practice in English, but one that is equally central to its disciplinary practices – the domain of persuasion.

Notes

1 We take the opportunity here to thank the 29 teachers who participated in workshops on narrative and who shared their own work and that of their students so generously in the course of the large Australian Research Council project (DP110104309).
2 In the AC:E, (ACARA, 2012) curriculum content related to literature is ACELT while the number following it indicates specific focus of learning (e.g. ACELT 1605). The acronym for Language is ACELA with special focus number following this (e.g. ACELA 1494 and ACELA 1495).
3 From *Grandad's Gifts* by Paul Jennings and Peter Gouldthorpe Copyright © Paul Jennings and Peter Gouldthorpe, 1992. Reprinted by permission of Penguin Random House Australia Pty Ltd.
4 From *Grandad's Gifts* by Paul Jennings and Peter Gouldthorpe Copyright © Paul Jennings and Peter Gouldthorpe, 1992. Reprinted by permission of Penguin Random House Australia Pty Ltd.
5 From *Grandad's Gifts* by Paul Jennings and Peter Gouldthorpe Copyright © Paul Jennings and Peter Gouldthorpe, 1992. Reprinted by permission of Penguin Random House Australia Pty Ltd.
6 From *Grandad's Gifts* by Paul Jennings and Peter Gouldthorpe Copyright © Paul Jennings and Peter Gouldthorpe, 1992. Reprinted by permission of Penguin Random House Australia Pty Ltd.

References

Australian Curriculum, Assessment and Reporting Authority (ACARA, formerly National Curriculum Board) (2009). *The shape of the Australian curriculum: English.* Sydney: ACARA. Retrieved from www.acara.edu.au.

Australian Curriculum Assessment and Reporting Authority (ACARA) (2012). *Australian curriculum: English.* Version 3.0. Sydney: ACARA. Retrieved from www.australiancurriculum.edu.au/copyright.

Axford, B., Harders, P. & Wise, F. (2009). *Scaffolding literacy: An integrated and sequential approach to teaching reading, spelling and writing.* Camberwell, Victoria: ACER Press.

Brown, F. (1951/1969). The weapon. In J. Sallis (Ed.), *The war book.* London: Rupert Hart-Davis.

Brown, D. (2003). *The Da Vinci code.* New York: Doubleday.

Butt, D., Fahey, R., Feez, S & Spinks, S. (2012). *Using functional grammar: An explorer's guide* (3rd edition). South Yarra, Victoria: Macmillan Education Australia.

Byars, B. (1968). *Midnight fox.* New York: Viking Press.

Christie, F. & Martin, J. R. (Eds.) (1997). *Genre and institutions: Social processes in the workplace and school.* London: Cassell.

Cowey, W. (2005). A brief description of the National Accelerated Literacy Program. *TESOL in Context*, 15(2), 3–14.

Dahl, R. (1974). *Fantastic Mr Fox.* London: Puffin Books.

Dahl, R. (1980). *The twits*. London: Jonathan Cape.
Gibbons, P. (2015). *Scaffolding language, Scaffolding learning: Teaching English language learners in the mainstream classroom* (2nd edition). Portsmouth, NH: Heinemann.
Gray, B. (2003). *Key elements of scaffolding literacy: Pedagogy and teacher support*. Schools and Community Centre, University of Canberra, published electronically: www.canberra.edu.au/centres/schools-community/literacy-research.
Gray, B. (2007). *Accelerating the literacy development of Indigenous students*. Darwin: CDU Press.
Halliday, M. A. K. (1993). Towards a language-based theory of learning. *Linguistics and Education*, 5(2), 93–116.
Humphrey, S. (2017). *Academic literacies in the middle years: A framework for enhancing teacher knowledge and student achievement*. New York and London: Routledge.
Humphrey, S. & Feez, S. (2016). Direct instruction fit for purpose: Applying a metalinguistic toolkit to enhance creative writing in the early secondary years. *Australian Journal of Language and Literacy*, 39(3), 207–219.
Jennings, P. (1994). *Unbearable*. Melbourne: Penguin.
Jennings, P. (1999). *Quirky tails*. Ringwood, Victoria: Penguin Books.
Jennings, P. & Gouldthorpe, P. (1992). *Grandad's gifts*. Ringwood, Victoria: Puffin Books.
King, S. (2000). *On writing: A memoir of the craft*. New York: Scribner.
Love, K., Sandiford, C., Macken-Horarik, M. & Unsworth, L. (2014). From 'bored witless' to 'rhetorical nous': Teacher orientation to knowledge about language and strengthening student persuasive writing. *English in Australia,* 49(3), 43–56.
Macken-Horarik, M., Love, K. & Unsworth, L. (2011). A grammatics 'good enough' for school English in the 21st century: Four challenges in realizing the potential. *Australian Journal of Language and Literacy*, 34(1), 9–21.
Martin, J. R. (1999). Mentoring semogenesis: 'Genre-based' literacy pedagogy. In F. Christie (Ed.), *Pedagogy and the shaping of consciousness: Linguistic and social processes* (pp. 123–155). London: Continuum.
Martin, J. R. (2009). Genres and language learning: A social semiotic perspective. *Linguistics and Education*, 20, 10–21.
Myhill, D., Jones, S., Lines, H. & Watson, F. (2012). Re-thinking grammar: The impact of embedded grammar teaching on students' writing and students' metalinguistic understanding. *Research Papers in Education,* 27(20), 139–166.
Painter, C. (1986). *The role of interaction in learning to speak and learning to write*. In C. Painter & J. R. Martin (Eds.), *Writing to mean: Teaching genres across the curriculum* (pp. 62–97). Applied Linguistics Association of Australia (Occasional Papers 9).
Painter, C., Martin, J. R. & Unsworth, L. (2013). *Reading visual narratives: Image analysis of children's picture books*. London: Equinox.
Rose, D. (2006). Reading genre: A new wave of analysis. *Linguistics and the Human Sciences*, 2(2), 185–204.
Rose, D. (2011). *Reading to learn: Accelerating learning and closing the gap*. Sydney: Reading to Learn. Retrieved from www.readingtolearn.com.au.
Rose, D. & Martin, J. R. (2012). *Learning to write, reading to learn: Genre, knowledge and pedagogy in the Sydney School*. London: Equinox.
Rose, D., Gray, B. & Cowey, W. (1999). Scaffolding reading and writing for Indigenous children in school. In P. Wignell (Ed.), *Double power: English literacy and indigenous education* (pp. 23–58). Melbourne: Language Australia.
Rothery, J. (1994). *Exploring literacy in school English (Write it right resources for literacy and learning)*. Sydney: Metropolitan East Disadvantaged Schools Program.
Rubinstein, G. (1994). *Foxspell*. Melbourne: Hyland.

de Silva Joyce, H. & Feez, S. (2012). *Text-based language and literacy education: Programming and methodology.* Sydney, Australia: Phoenix Education.

Tan, S. (2000). *The lost thing.* Sydney, NSW: Lothian.

Unsworth, L. (2001). *Teaching multiliteracies across the curriculum: Changing contexts of text and image in classroom practice.* Buckingham, UK: Open University Press.

Wild, M., & Brooks, R. (2000). *Fox.* Sydney: Allen and Unwin.

Winton, T. (1997). *Blueback.* London: Picador.

5
TRUE NORTH

Investigating a grammatics for persuasion

Exploring the interface of grammatics and persuasion

Just as narrative is at the heart of children's lives and cultures, so too is persuasion. From their earliest years, they are exposed to myriad forms of persuasion, from everyday domestic talk where parents and siblings argue for their point of view – how loud the music should be, what clothes are suitable, what they want to eat – to electronic and social media that seek to persuade them to buy a product, join a group or take action on an issue. As their social awareness grows, young people draw on various persuasive techniques to achieve their own social ends, whether through talk, writing or electronic media. Some participate in rhetorical activities in the civic domain, seeking to convince local councils to provide better recreational facilities or end what they see as a particular injustice. As they approach voting age, many tune in to political rhetoric, critically examining the content and form of arguments put by local, national and international spokespeople seeking to influence voters. Throughout their lives, the forms of persuasion young people are surrounded by in different domains shape not just their habits but their very identities.

In the digital literacies context, young people use social media platforms such as Blogs, Facebook and Instagram on a daily basis to share information about their lives. But they are also the target of increasingly sophisticated market forces seeking their purchase of products or services. Most online persuasion includes images or videos, giving their appeals a salience that goes beyond what can be achieved by words alone. Persuasion is crucial to the marketplace. In a digital age, almost every interaction is 'interested' in something, agenda-driven. Whether we are considering the roles of individuals seeking to influence others or larger groups soliciting business, we need to adopt what Kress calls 'a rhetorical approach to communication'.

> The rhetor, as maker of a message now makes an assessment of all aspects of the communicational situation: of her or his interest; of the characteristics of the audience; the semiotic requirements of the issue at stake and the resources available for making an apt representation; together with establishing the best means for its dissemination.
>
> *(Kress, 2010, p. 26)*

Young people are also becoming agentive in their use of digital media and their interests are not simply local and personal. In the civic sphere, for example, many use online means to share views on social issues about which they seek to shape public opinion. We only need to visit a site such as PETA (People for the Ethical Treatment of Animals: peta.org.au) to view these expressions of concern for, and engagement with, campaigns against animal cruelty for example. Here the persuasive power is carried in verbal expressions of concern about abuse of animals, strategically combined with emotionally charged images of vulnerable animals. Selections of video clips heighten the persuasive force of the message, either through appeals to emotion (as in close-ups of vulnerable animals), appeals to viewers' sense of ethics and logic (as in sequences of facts and figures reported by the author; see for example www.peta.org.au/news/deakin-university-dissection-protest-peta/). Focussing briefly on multimodal forms of persuasion in students' civic life, we can illustrate a little of the complex interrelationship of modes at play with reference to one poster brought out by Zoos Victoria presented as Figure 5.1 (www.zoo.org.au/callingonyou). This was produced to galvanise the public to re-cycle old mobile phones and thus reduce the illegal mining of coltan which has devastated gorilla habitats in the Congo.

The poster is headed by a salient claim which metaphorically links the 'call' commonly associated with phones to a call for help addressed to us by endangered gorillas. Perhaps because the appeal depends on an active response, the gorilla's gaze 'invites' us to get involved rather than demanding action (Painter, Martin & Unsworth, 2013, p. 20). A persuasive text composed entirely of commands in Imperative MOOD is likely to alienate, rather than engage viewers. So, the designer of this text selects interpersonal choices to galvanise readers. The very first sentence, for example, ('They're calling on you') is in Declarative MOOD and addresses readers directly through the second Person pronoun 'you'. This combination of direct address and information in a statement provides the appeal on which the subsequent command is based, and its salience is further enhanced by the size and colour of the font — white against a striking green background (with all the connotations of an environmentalist discourse). Following the appeal in largest typeface, there are two commands — '*Recycle* your old mobile phones and *help* save wild gorillas'. These are followed by a short but authoritative rationale in Declarative MOOD that supplies information about Coltan and its effect on gorilla habitat (e.g. 'Coltan *is used* in many mobile phones'). Significantly, these unmodulated Declaratives are combined with a modulated form of the verb in proposals ('You *can* help ...' and 'You'*ll* help reduce ...'). These suggest strong capacity in the reader (directly addressed as 'you')

FIGURE 5.1 Multimodal appeal in a persuasive poster.

to make an impact through recycling. In Chapter 3 we presented Modal verbs on a continuum to reveal different degrees of obligation and probability in the territory between yes and no. In terms of second order semiosis, it is through this patterning of Declarative and Imperative MOOD and MODALITY choices that the verbal text works. And because it is a multimodal text, the coupling of image and verbiage in this poster enhances the impact of the call to action by the gorillas of the Congo.

Young people's lives are crowded with persuasive texts such as these, which strategically combine verbal and other modes of meaning to position their viewers towards various forms of action. They can occur in civic domains (as with the poster above), or in their domestic, social, academic or purchasing lives (Humphrey, 2017). What is very much at stake is young people's capacity to identify semiotic resources that are deployed in such texts, to evaluate these critically and design texts that draw on the affordances of different modes to influence viewers. In our earlier chapters, we introduced resources for meaning organized by metafunction. In Chapter 2 we focussed on the role of Ideational resources such as TRANSITIVITY in creating plausible 'possible worlds' in narrative. Then in Chapter 3, we considered Interpersonal resources such as MOOD, MODALITY and APPRAISAL in engaging readers interactively and positioning them attitudinally. When it comes to rhetorical perspectives on multimodal texts such as Figure 5.1 or political speeches introduced later in this chapter, we need a third lens if we are to capture the dynamic shaping of texts to particular 'ends'. The textual lens sheds light on 'text as composition' – on the shaping of individual messages and the phases and stages in which these are embedded and the ways in which all are directed to particular communicative purposes.

If we study composition within a textual orientation, we can look at a text displayed on a page or on a screen (completed) or we can consider it in the process of 'logogenesis' or unfolding meaning. Halliday and Matthiessen explain this as follows:

> As the text unfolds, patterns emerge, some of which acquire added value through resonating with other patterns in the text or in the context of situation. The text itself is an instance; the resonance is possible because behind it lies the potential that informs every choice made by the speaker or writer, and in terms of which these choices are interpreted by listeners and readers. We refer to this ongoing creation of meaning in the unfolding of text as logogenesis.
>
> *(Halliday & Mathiessen, 2004, p. 43)*

In tracking meaning in a text, we pick up on waves of information that begin locally as moves from a speaker's starting point (angle on a topic) to something newsworthy about the topic. As we indicated in Chapter 1, every language signposts Theme in some way or another. In Japanese, it is identified through the 'wa' particle. In English, it is realized in what comes first in a message. We can identify THEME as the first constituent within a ranking clause. In the unmarked case, this is the Subject of the clause. However, if the first constituent in the clause is not the Subject, this is regarded as non-typical or marked. Selecting a non-Subject Theme gives a constituent local significance; it says, 'I am putting this first in order to mark it as my starting point'. But if it becomes part of a pattern of choice, it takes on more global significance as we shall see in the two speeches explored in this chapter. Unlike the first sentence in *Fantastic Mr Fox*, which begins with a marked Theme 'Down in the valley there were three farmers', Severn Suzuki begins her address to the United Nations with a first-Person Declarative: 'Hello, I am Severn Suzuki, speaking for E.C.O. – the Environmental Children's Organisation.' The second speech, the apology to the stolen generations by then Australian Prime Minister Kevin Rudd, also begins in First person ('I') but moves quickly in the second clause to mark the time of the act (today) and to move to the more inclusive 'we' of citizens: 'I move that today we honour the indigenous peoples of this land.' First position is important not just to the distribution of information in clauses but to signposting of developments in the logogenesis of a text.

But what we put last is also crucial and tends to coincide with the resting point of an argument, the coda in a narrative or the evaluative significance of an utterance. In the sentences above, each rhetor moves from an angle on the topic (where the story is set or who is speaking) to what they see as newsworthy: In Severn's case, it is the organization on whose behalf she speaks – 'the Environmental Children's Organisation'; in Rudd's case, it is 'the indigenous peoples of this land'. In the case of the opening sentence in *Fantastic Mr Fox,* it is 'three farmers.' More generally, what we put last in a clause, at the end of a paragraph or even the text as a whole is what we want our reader to attend to as news (the point). In fact, although we map it onto written language, the New is a feature of INFORMATION STRUCTURE that creates emphasis through the tonic in the intonation contour. In writing, we assume that the New comes at the end of a clause, at least in its unmarked form. If we want to emphasise some other part of a message, we underline, halo or bold it. While Theme indicates a rhetor's angle on the topic, New is what we indicate a reader should attend to in the message. It typically comes after THEME (though not always as Halliday & Matthiessen, 2004, pp. 91–98 remind us).

As we revealed in Chapter 1, the wave-like pattern that we see in microcosm in clauses and on a larger scale in the organization of texts is what Martin 1992 calls 'periodicity'. It has proved invaluable in teaching writing, especially in disadvantaged schools (Christie & Martin, 1997; Martin & Rose, 2007; Rose & Martin, 2012). In working with the concept to teach disciplinary literacies, Humphrey introduces the notion of periodicity through the metaphor of 'waves of information':

> A useful way of talking about the way information flows across a well written text is to talk about packaged 'waves of information' – discrete parcels of information that help the reader to more easily digest the flow of information. Like waves in the surf, there are larger waves and small waves, and each wave has peaks and a trough. In written texts, 'peaks' are the parts of the text that the reader tends to notice first – either because they are marked out as headings, or because they are in first or last position in the text paragraph or sentence.
>
> *(Humphrey, 2017, p. 146)*

In this chapter, we focus on first position in terms of **Signposting**. The New, on the other hand, is a resource for creating **Salience**, whether through end-weight or other means such as underlining. Visually, we assign emphasis to parts of an image through strong or contrastive colours, special highlighting or size. The poster in Figure 5.1 is a good example of these choices.

There are other resources that give coherence to texts. Beyond resources of Theme and New, texts are knitted together through cohesive resources of different kinds. For example, in written texts, we use **Connectives** to add information, give examples, sequence ideas in a temporal or logical order and show cause and effect. We keep track of participants introduced into a text through pronoun **Reference**. We use repeated, synonymous and contrasting lexical choices to give unity to a text through **Lexical Cohesion**. Wordings can be related to images through various kinds of connections (see Bateman, 2014 for an overview of these).

Table 5.1 presents probe questions related to features made visible with a textual lens on meaning that we draw on in our work in this and the next chapter.

The study of persuasion dates back to classical antiquity. In Ancient Greece, oratory was central to political survival in classical antiquity, where Roman senators for example studied various codified rhetorical strategies rigorously before applying them in the high stakes persuasive environment of the Roman senate. Learning to deploy these strategies was regarded as crucial to effective oratory. Students would study suitable topics for argument, learn the varieties of evidence or proof in support of a claim, become familiar with ways of appealing to an audience and practice techniques in moving an audience to take a particular view or action.

Most significant of these codified rhetorical strategies were the appeals to ethos, pathos and logos, as originally documented by the Greek philosopher, Aristotle. *Ethos* is based on building both trust in the moral integrity of the rhetor and a sense of collective endeavour or rapport; *Logos*, on rationality, on consideration of

TABLE 5.1 Probe questions related to textual lens on craft of persuasion

Textual lens – Producing a coherent text	*Overarching Question*: How is the text organized?
	Staging / Phasing: Is the text partitioned into major sections or stages? (e.g. in an argument, there is a Thesis or Issue followed by Arguments and Evidence and then a Conclusion or Recommendation).
	Layout/organization: How is the text organized? What do you notice about layout, paragraphing, quotes, etc? If the text is a written argument, is the line of argumentation clear from the text opener (Macro Theme), the paragraph openers or topic sentences (Hyper Theme), and the Sentence opener (Sentence Theme)? If multimodal, are visual elements bound or separated into units by frames, margins or page edges? What is the nature of the image-language placement within the layout? What is the significance of these arrangements?
	Signposting and Salience: What is given prominence in the text? In writing, this may be achieved through placement of clauses and end-position. In an image, this may be achieved through positioning on the page, through highlighting or size of an object.
	Cohesive Devices: Are Connectives used between clauses to add information, show cause and effect, give an example, sequence ideas?
	• Does pronoun reference (and other lexical items) enable us to keep track of who or what is being written about?
	• Are there repeated words, phrases or sentences? Are they used for rhetorical effect?
	• For multimodal texts, how do patterns of word, sentence and paragraph choices relate to meanings made in other modes? Do they complement, strengthen or contradict these?

objective data and on dispassionate observation; and *Pathos*, on explicitly emotional appeals (Kennedy, 2007, p.21). Along with other rhetorical strategies, these were codified by Roman rhetoricians and philosophers who rehearsed them for their use in oratory in the civic action. In documenting such strategies, the Roman philosopher and political theorist, Cicero, described rhetoric as "artificial eloquence … a political science which is made up of many and important particulars" (Cicero, n.d.).

While the particulars of classical rhetoric revolved largely around the spoken word, contemporary forms of rhetoric draw analogously on more or less codified 'particulars' related to visual and other modes of persuasion (Kalantzis & Cope, 2012). Who can forget the compelling graphs and flow charts that provided visual evidence of the effects of global warming in Al Gore's 'slide show' filmed as *An Inconvenient Truth: A Global Warning* (Gore & Guggenheim, 2006). Closer to home for the authors, we salute Jim Martin's analysis of the combined effect of image and verbiage in the moving report of the stolen generations, the subject of Rudd's apology to which we turn shortly (Martin, 2004/2010). When it comes to the rhetorical design of multimodal persuasion, we live in exciting times. Recent research in this arena is proving catalytic for many educators working within and beyond systemic functional theory (e.g. Archer & Newfield, 2014; Bateman, 2014; Bednarak & Martin, 2010; Kress, 2010). The emphasis on multimodal design complements a resurgence of interest by educators in the power of rhetoric to unify the disparate concerns of school English (Andrews, 2005, 2010; Humphrey, 2013; Green, 2009, 2017; Moon, 2012).

In exploring the interface between grammatics and rhetoric in this chapter, we aim to contribute to the dialogue with colleagues working in this area. It is our view that a functional grammatics offers a powerful means of identifying the choices that rhetors make from various semiotic systems, as they shape appeals to Ethos, Logos and Pathos towards particular persuasive ends. The capacity to harness these rhetorical 'particulars' is just as important in civic life in the twenty-first century as it was in the Ancient Roman senate, and possibly more so, given the broadening of our democratic base and educational aspirations towards a critically active, well-informed citizenry. Access to these rhetorical strategies, and their linguistic and multimodal underpinnings, can powerfully shape young people's sense of agency as they structure their own persuasive texts to achieve their personal, social and ideological ends.

To this end, in the remainder of this chapter we explore how grammatics can be deployed to deepen comprehension, critical awareness and production of persuasion in verbal and visual modes and across civic and promotional domains of semiosis. We start first with oral forms of persuasion in the civic domain and with critical appreciation of the rhetoric of orators responsible for bringing about significant social change in contemporary western institutions. Our brief foray into visual persuasion takes in images created in civic and promotional domains. In Chapter 6 we sharpen our focus on the composition of written exposition as a privileged form of persuasion in the academic domain, while making brief excursions into analogous/ accompanying multimodal forms of persuasion. Then in Chapter 7, we outline a pedagogy for teaching Expositions, drawing on the metalanguage deployed in The Grammatics Project.

Rhetoric and grammatics: the case of one young orator

Severn Cullis-Suzuki can be considered as a modern-day orator, who, in her role as a young environmental activist, sought to influence international policy about the need for urgent action on issues related to poverty and climate change. As a 12-year-old, she assumed the voice of the Environmental Children's Organization (ECO) as she addressed a Plenary Session of the UN's Earth Summit in Rio de Janeiro in 1992 with a short speech where she pleaded with world leaders to "act as one single world towards one single goal" in addressing poverty, environmental damage and warfare. She received a standing ovation for the speech, which went viral on You Tube, where it is called "The Speech that Silenced the World for Five Minutes" (https://www.youtube.com/watch?v=TQmz6Rbpnu0). A transcript of this speech is produced below, with paragraphs numbered for ease of reference.

1. Hello, I am Severn Suzuki speaking for E.C.O. – the Environmental Children's Organization. We are a group of 12- and 13-year-olds trying to make a difference, Vanessa Suttie, Morgan Geisler, Michelle Quigg and me. We've raised all the money to come here ourselves, to come 5,000 miles to tell you adults you must change your ways. Coming up here today, I have no hidden agenda. I am fighting for my future. Losing my future is not like losing an election, or a few points on the stock market.

2. I am here to speak for all generations to come. I am here to speak on behalf of the starving children around the world whose cries go unheard. I am here to speak for the countless animals dying across this planet, because they have nowhere left to go. I am afraid to go out in the sun now, because of the holes in our ozone. I am afraid to breathe the air, because I don't know what chemicals are in it. I used to go fishing in Vancouver, my home, with my Dad until, just a few years ago, we found a fish full of cancers. And now we hear of animals and plants going extinct every day, vanishing forever. In my life, I have dreamt of seeing the great herds of wild animals, jungles and rainforests full of birds and butterflies, but now I wonder if they will even exist for my children to see.

3. Did you have to worry of these things when you were my age? All this is happening before our eyes and yet we act as if we have all the time we want and all the solutions. I'm only a child and I don't have all the solutions, but I want you to realize, neither do you. You don't know how to fix the holes in our ozone layer. You don't know how to bring the salmon back up a dead stream. You don't know how to bring back an animal now extinct. And you can't bring back the forest that once grew where there is now a desert. If you don't know how to fix it, please stop breaking it.

4. Here you may be delegates of your governments, business people, organisers, reporters or politicians. But, really, your mothers and fathers, sisters and brothers, aunts and uncles and all of you are someone's child. I'm only a child, yet I know we are all part of a family, 5 billion strong, in fact 30 million species strong. And borders and governments will never change that. I'm only a child, yet I know we are all in this together and should act as one single world towards one single goal.

5. In my anger, I am not blind, and in my fear, I am not afraid of telling the world how I feel. In my country, we make so much waste, we buy and throw away, buy and throw away, buy and throw away and yet Northern countries will not share with the needy. Even when we have more than enough, we are afraid to share, we are afraid to let go of some of our wealth. In Canada, we live the privileged life. We've plenty of food, water and shelter. We have watches, bicycles, computers and television sets. The list could go on for two days. Two days ago, here in Brazil, we were shocked when we spent time with some children living on the streets. This is what one child told us, 'I wish I was rich and if I were, I would give all the street children food, clothes, medicines, shelter and love and affection'. If a child on the street who has nothing is willing to share, why are we who have everything still so greedy? I can't stop thinking that these are children my own age, that it makes a tremendous difference where you are born. And that I could be one of those children living in the favelas of Rio. I could be a child starving in Somalia, or a victim of war in the Middle East or a beggar in India. I am only a child, yet I know if all the money spent on war was spent on finding environmental answers ending poverty and in finding treaties, what a wonderful place this earth would be.

6. At school, even in kindergarten, you teach us how to behave in the world. You teach us to not to fight with others, to work things out, to respect others and to clean up our mess, not to hurt other creatures, to share, not be greedy. Then, why do you go out and do the things you tell us not to do? Do not forget why you are attending these conferences, who you are doing this for. We are your own children. You are deciding what kind of a world we are growing up in. Parents should be able to comfort their children by saying 'Everything is going to be all right, it's not the end of the world, and we are doing the best we can'. But I don't think you can say that to us anymore. Are we even on your list of priorities? My dad always says, 'You are what you do, not what you say'. Well, what you do makes me cry at night. You grown-ups say you love us. But I challenge you, please, make your actions reflect your words. Thank you.

Severn's appeals to ethos, pathos and logos connect this speech in the 1992 United Nation's Earth Summit to those of Ancient Rome's senate. Our metafunctional and stratified view of language allows us to explore Severn's rhetorical strategies, noting which syndromes of grammatical choices realize (or express) her various appeals and how these collectively contribute to the rhetorical impact of the speech as a whole.

Ethos

A strong appeal to ethos opens Severn's speech (see paragraph 1 above). Through this appeal, she seeks to build her audience's trust in her moral integrity, build a sense of collective endeavour and establish her authority to speak on behalf of all young people who are "trying to make a difference". The grammatical resources that Severn draws on to enact this appeal are many, but, using the interpersonal toolkit introduced in Chapter 3, we can note firstly that her choice of Mood has immediate impact. She selects unmodulated Declarative and positive Polarity to identify herself and her group ('I am', 'We are', 'We've raised') and in combination with active Voice, she construes the Environmental Children's Organization as a 'can do' group of young people. The only Declarative that selects negative Polarity ("Losing my future *is not* like losing an election.") relates to an abstraction over which she has no control. This adds further poignancy to her position. The only Modulation ("to tell you adults you *must change* your ways") strongly amplifies the sense of obligation on her audience to act immediately and in unison, further increasing the authoritativeness of her opening stance.

In paragraphs 2 and 3, Severn subsequently strengthens this appeal to ethos by building a sense of shared enterprise and empathy. This is realized grammatically in patterned combinations of Declarative and Interrogative Mood, amongst other features. In paragraph 2, her series of Declarative offerings about her personal environmental anxieties ("I am afraid to go out in the sun now, because of the holes in our ozone. I am afraid to breathe the air") is followed by her selection of Interrogative Mood ("Did you have to worry of these things when you were my age?") that Severn addresses directly to her audience. Such Interrogative Mood choices, in which there is no real answer option, are often referred to broadly as rhetorical questions, and their local role in directly engaging audiences and building shared ethos is well understood. What is less well understood is how the interactive force of such questions is enhanced through their juxtaposition with other choices, as with Severn's juxtaposition of declarative and interrogative Mood choices, as above.

At two key points (in paragraphs 3 and 6 above), Severn builds interpersonally on direct engagement generated through this prior combination of personalised statements and rhetorical questions to direct an authoritative command at the same audience. These commands, realized grammatically in Imperative Mood ('Stop breaking it' and 'Make your actions reflect your words'), construe the authority the rhetor has accumulated so far and builds the sense of shared enterprise developed in earlier phases of her speech. In terms of second order semiosis, we can see that through this strategic patterning of Declarative, Interrogative and Imperative Mood resources, Severn's appeal to ethos gains strength. Furthermore, it is not just in one grammatical choice or another that we discern second order patterning, but in the syndrome of choices, that taken together, create this striking appeal to ethos.

We could further explore how other interpersonal resources, such as her use of modality and personal pronouns co-pattern with such Mood choices to further build an ethos of shared responsibility. For example, Severn uses Modality largely to strengthen, rather than dampen the impact of her assertions, choosing high obligation ("parents *should* …") and probability ("you *can't* bring back") throughout her speech as she builds a categorical stance on the issues. The few usages of low Modality occur when she is voicing other, more vulnerable children ("I *would* give …"; "I *could* be a starving child"). Such modality choices align rhetorically with her patterned use of personal pronouns, as she selects pronominal references to herself as a representative of young people ('I') distinct from the references to her particular audience ('you') as world leaders. In so doing, she construes a distinction between 'agentful' adults and relatively agentless children. One exception to this is in paragraph 5, where she uses the pronoun 'we' to include herself as a member of the wasteful "Northern countries". Through this strategic inclusion of herself, she builds a sense of shared responsibility, though in subsequent paragraphs resumes the pronominal opposition. In so doing, she lays the groundwork for her final ethical challenge – "I challenge you, please, make your actions reflect your words."

One final set of interpersonal resources that Severn exploits as she builds her appeal to ethos are lexical choices that infuse her speech with moral positions related to her cause. Recall from Chapter 3 that APPRAISAL offers a systematic set of resources for exploring more delicate choices in vocabulary that colour the atmosphere or tone of a text and position us to see, feel, judge and appreciate things in particular ways. Where the system of MOOD is crucial to negotiation of exchanges, APPRAISAL functions at more delicate ends of the lexicogrammatical spectrum to express the 'personal' within interpersonal meaning. In Chapter 3, we identified three domains within the system of ATTITUDE, itself a key component of the APPRAISAL SYSTEM: AFFECT (the domain of emotion), JUDGEMENT (the domain of ethics) and APPRECIATION (the domain of aesthetics). Explicit attitudinal wordings (Inscribed ATTITUDE) can be intensified or weakened on clines of strong/weak and loaded on clines of positive/negative. The same gradation occurs with implicit attitudinal wordings (Invoked ATTITUDE) and we explore the visual analogue of these later in this chapter.

Choices of JUDGEMENT relate most closely to the creation of appeals to ethos. Yet explicit encodings of critique of the behaviours of the Summit attendees are relatively rare across Severn's speech. They are restricted to criticism of their lack of capacity to stem the environmental effects of globalization ("You *don't know* how to fix the holes in our ozone layer. You *don't know* how to bring the salmon back up a dead stream. You *don't know* how to bring back an animal now extinct. And you *can't bring back* the forest that once grew where there is now a desert"). This Inscribed JUDGEMENT challenges, rather than alienates, her audience, as she seeks to enlist them in her shared enterprise. Some additional JUDGEMENT of delegates' lack of action and insight is implied, rather than made explicit through the Mood and pronoun choices described above, and most saliently in her choice of interrogatives at key stages of her speech.

In relation to ethos, the grammatics has shed light on first order semiosis – enabling us to identify choices within systems of MOOD, MODALITY, PERSON and APPRAISAL across Severn's speech. It has helped us explain second order semiosis – how such patterning helps simultaneously build her moral integrity as young rhetor and a sense of urgency for collective endeavour. Accompanying this cumulative appeal to ethos is an equally powerful rhetorical appeal to pathos. Again, our access to functionally motivated systems of lexicogrammar provides us with deepened insights into how such appeals achieve their rhetorical force.

Pathos

The system of APPRAISAL incorporates and extends the limited focus on features like Attitudinal Epithets or Comment Adjuncts in the lexicogrammar. It is powerful source of insight into the rhetorical strategy of Pathos, as well as Ethos. We illustrate this with reference to that section of Severn's speech in paragraph 2, which occurs shortly after Severn's introduction:

> I am here to speak for all generations to come. I am here to speak on behalf of the *starving children* around the world whose *cries* go unheard. I am here to speak for the *countless animals dying across this planet*, because they have nowhere left to go.

Severn consolidates her personal integrity and strengthens the need for collective endeavour through her appeal to pathos. If ethos appeals to the need for justice, for legitimate authority and for action to protect our natural environment, pathos appeals to the heart, calling for empathy for those affected by environmental degradation. This appeal is inscribed through Severn's selection of highly negatively charged emotional vocabulary, what is captured within AFFECT within ATTITUDE (Martin & White, 2005). Here, as in every stage of her speech, negative or positive LOADING of AFFECT relates to certain participants: happiness relates to those who are victims (starving children) along with positive Loading; happiness relates to those living in the so-called 'first world' ("In Canada, we live the *privileged* life"). The ease of life for those in western countries is contrasted strongly with the difficulties of life in poorer countries. The antinomies are simple and the lines drawn strongly.

There is much more that could be said about how the appeal to Pathos is realized through Severn's choices – for example, where AFFECT is scaled up ('starving children') or down ('makes me cry'); and where GRADUATION shifts at different phases of the speech. In Chapter 6, we explore further how the system of APPRAISAL with its more delicate sub-systems provides a metalanguage for describing and interpreting the rhetorical impact of appeals to Pathos. Recent work on APPRAISAL in middle years education is supporting teachers as they seek to study evaluation in a range of texts necessary in disciplinary literacies of English and other subjects (Humphrey, Love & Droga, 2011; Humphrey, Droga & Feez, 2012; Humphrey, 2017).

Logos

The grammatics also offers systems for exploring appeals to reason, or Logos. In this kind of appeal, rhetors rely on reasoning from evidence and build warrants through what are presented as uncontested facts. As we argue later in this chapter, the capacity to marshal detached and well-sourced bodies of evidence in support of a thesis has long been a central component of argumentation (Toulmin, 1958). It is a process much valued in school and academic writing (Andrews, 2005, 2010; Hillocks, 2010; Hood, 2010). For 12-year-old Severn, these bodies of evidence are related to what is personally salient for her, and early in her speech, she builds a representation of a world with references to "holes in our ozone", "fish full of cancers" and "animals and plants going extinct every day" (Paragraph 2). Grammatically speaking, these non-human Participants have no agency, as is evident in them being objects rather than subjects of action in the clauses. In the same way, children are also construed grammatically as agentless objects to which, as with other victims of environmental neglect, the negative AFFECT discussed above is attached (starving *children*, countless *animals*). Severn contrasts these with conference attendees, whose agency as "delegates of your governments, business people, organisers, reporters or politicians" is expressed grammatically by Subject position (e.g. '*You* are deciding what kind of a world we are growing up in'). As she builds evidence about the limitations of adult agency, the impression of their negative capacity, 'not knowing' or 'not being able to bring back' is increasingly foregrounded.

> You *don't know how to fix* the holes in our ozone layer. You *don't know* how to bring the salmon back up a dead stream. You *don't know* how to bring back an animal now extinct. And you *can't bring back* the forest that once grew where there is now a desert.

Through such choices, Severn represents two contrasting types of Participants in her world: one of 'agentful' and authoritative adults, the other agentless children and vulnerable animals. In a further strategic move, in paragraph 4, she subsequently attempts to combine these two sets of participants into one 'family' as she introduces supposedly factual quantitative evidence in a lengthy nominal group that links the human participants as mutually responsible. "'I'm only a child, yet I know we are *all part of a family, 5 billion strong, in fact 30 million species strong*." The use of the Relational Process here (we are) is central as she builds this further warrant for her central argument about the urgent need for action. But note here too her clever use of the logical-semantic resource of Elaboration, introduced in Chapter 2 in our discussion of narrative. If we adopt once again the formalism of the mathematical equals sign to represent this expanding family of members, we get: 'We are *all part of a family,* = *5 billion strong,* = *in fact 30 million species strong*'. In this way, Severn moves from one representation of an admittedly big Participant to one that includes the whole of humanity and beyond this but equally importantly incorporates all the species on earth. The arrangement of the appeal to logos is managed adroitly and the grammatics helps us see how the strategy of syntactic Elaboration is deployed to powerful effect as one aspect of Severn's 'dispositio' – arrangement of her unfolding argument (Cicero, n.d.).

She develops this point about shared responsibility in paragraph five using the inclusive first Person, 'we' ("W*e make* so much waste, *we buy* and *throw* away").

In this way, she holds all human agents accountable for those material processes that contribute to the vulnerability of the other species. Through her choice of Participants and their differing agency in knowing, relating and action processes, Severn builds a 'factual' evidence base which underpins her appeal to Logos. Simultaneously her use of interpersonal resources such as the inclusive personal pronoun 'we' feeds into her appeal to a shared ethos, while choice of affective lexis (e.g. 'dead stream') feeds into her appeal to pathos.

Severn weaves the various propositions together into a text which, though short, has integrity and power. To explore the compositional aspect of her rhetoric, we take up our textual lens. This shows how resources like Theme and New bring Severn's angle on the issue into relationship with the point of her mission. The flow of starting and resting point in her speech is evident in the opening paragraph. Severn begins with herself and her group (Theme) and moves to the point in words about change, her agenda and her future (New). Table 5.2 presents Theme and New in paragraph 1 of Severn's speech.

The rhythmic shift from Theme to New in and across clauses is one aspect of a well-known rhetorical strategy for organizing persuasive texts – the tricolon. This too has its origins in Cicero's 'Di Inventione' and is referred to in some contemporary English/Language Arts curricula as 'the rule of three' or 'parallelism'. Severn draws on this rhetorical strategy at many points in her speech, its first instance being in the opening of her speech examined earlier:

> I am here to speak for all generations to come. I am here to speak on behalf of the starving children around the world whose cries go unheard. I am here to speak for the countless animals dying across this planet, because they have nowhere left to go.

In broadly rhetorical terms, we can readily identify Severn's repetition of 'I am here' in each of three sentences and note that this strategy adds emphasis to her utterance.

TABLE 5.2 Patterns of Theme and New in Severn's opening paragraph

Theme (point of departure)	New (point of arrival)
Hello, I	Severn Suzuki
	for E.C.O. – the Environmental Children's Organization
We	a group of 12- and 13-year-olds, trying to make a difference
	Vanessa Suttie, Morgan Geisler, Michelle Quig and me
We've	ourselves
	5000 miles
	change your ways
Coming up here today, I	no hidden agenda
I	for my future
Losing my future	losing an election, or a few points on the stock market

Drawing on a grammatically informed analysis of this tricolon provides us with a much richer illumination of its effect than does this simple noting of repetition as a strategy of persuasive reinforcement. In functional linguistic terms, we can identify for example that 'I am here' is the point of departure for each sentence, thus making salient or thematising Severn's presence and agency. A striking feature of her use of this strategy is the fact that each of her three sentences increases in length, from the first single clause sentence; to the second sentence with its two clauses to the third sentence with its three clauses. We can thus identify how, as each sentence in this tricolon accumulates proportionately in length and complexity, a distinctive prosody is mapped grammatically. The principle of end-weight too ensures that the most important material occurs later in this phase of text. Drawing on textual systems such as Theme and New, this grammatical mapping allows us to describe the prosodic patterning of effective persuasive texts and explain how their rhetorical purposes are achieved not just in isolated extracts, but as they accumulate over the course of the unfolding text.

In concluding this brief exploration of Severn's speech, we summarise just some of those grammatical resources she has harnessed as she draws on rhetorical strategies that connect her back to the powerful oral cultures of the Ancient Greeks and Romans. Her patterned choices of MOOD, MODALITY, APPRAISAL and PERSON have contributed to her convincing appeal to *Ethos*, building trust in her moral integrity and a sense of collective endeavour. APPRAISAL resources carry her appeal to *Pathos*, as she builds explicitly emotional evaluations of environmental causes and effects. TRANSITIVITY works alongside these interpersonal resources to build the 'objective' evidence for her argument, based as this is on a distinction between adult human Participants with agency and non-human Participants (and children) who are the 'acted on'. These resources contribute to her appeal to *Logos*. Finally, her use of textual resources such as Theme and New contribute to a distinctive prosody that is both memorable and powerful. It is Severn's unique harnessing of these and other grammatical resources that underpin the rhetorical 'particulars' that have contributed to the enduring power of her speech.

Rhetoric and logogenesis: the case of a political orator

The above description of Severn's speech illustrates some of the ways in which tools of functional grammatics and discourse semantics allow us to examine how co-occurring language choices "pick out" or "manner one another" (Hasan 1988, p. 62) in distinctive ways. In this illustration, we touched on how textual, experiential and interpersonal meanings unfold through logogenesis (Halliday, 1993; Klein & Unsworth, 2014; Martin, 1999). We now explore resources used by other rhetors in high-stakes contemporary speechmaking. In doing so, we illustrate the further contribution of grammatics to the study of rhetorical strategies.

One high-stakes speech often referred to in Australian schools is that of that country's then Prime Minister, Kevin Rudd who in 2008 made an inaugural parliamentary speech that was a landmark moment for relations with Indigenous

Australians. It sought to have parliament endorse a formal public apology for past wrongs inflicted on Australia's first peoples. The speech, since titled "The Apology to the Stolen Generations of Australia" (Rudd, 2008), sought to unify sharply divided social groups through a reasoned and empathic set of strategies. In doing so, it made distinctive appeals to logos, ethos and pathos, and, like Severn's, drew on a range of other rhetorical strategies. The resounding importance of Rudd's apology grows cumulatively throughout his speech, as he draws on resources that co-pattern to achieve his persuasive purpose. Rudd's unifying purpose contrasts with the confrontational intent of Severn's speech to the United Nations and we see this inflected in the strategies and the grammar of his apology.[1]

In earlier work, we dealt extensively with the logogenesis of argument in this text (Love & Macken-Horarik, 2009). Here we focus on a selection of four of ten distinct phases in the Apology. The notion of **phase** as a unit of meaning intermediate between stage and clause has proved useful in analysis. Phases are identifiable stretches of meaning within larger stages of a text. Each phase displays a distinctive set of choices for Ideational, Interpersonal and Textual meaning as these are related to the discourse situation (Gregory & Malcolm, 1981; Malcolm, 2010; Martin & Rose, 2008). The action-reaction phases in the Complication stage of narratives such as *Fantastic Mr Fox* or *Blueback* represent one example. Severn's speech too exhibits shifts between phases marked by the personal voice of a young activist and her public critique of the passivity of her adult addressees on environmental matters. In longer texts like those encountered in English, it is helpful to have a fine-grained tool for 'netting in' text structure, especially when we consider prosodies of meaning often found in culturally valued works. In exploring selected phases from Rudd's speech, we focus primarily on interpersonal resources, because these are crucial to alignment of socially diverse audiences with the national apology. Such choices inevitably co-pattern with related ideational and textual resources to reinforce this intersubjective work, and as such, will also be touched on.

On that historic day, Prime Minister Rudd opened with a motion, ostensibly for debate:

> I move that today we honour the indigenous peoples of this land, the oldest continuing cultures in human history. We reflect on their past mistreatment. … We apologise for the laws and policies of successive parliaments and governments that have inflicted profound grief, suffering and loss on these our fellow Australians.

An apology is an illocutionary speech act that enacts the process it names (Searle, 1969). Accordingly, Rudd selects verbs like "reflect" and "honour", thus performing the role to which he has committed his government. Verbs like "move" and "apologise" are interpersonally potent because they join rhetorical with actual power of the sort carried in a Prime Minister's role. These verbs are in the present tense, effecting a process that is taking place now, in the moment of speaking. Rudd's choice of highly charged **Verbal Processes** with strong illocutionary force, perfectly fits, or 'realizes' his immediate purpose of moving a motion for urgent verbal action in this opening phase. This is an unambiguous apology, clearly phrased and immediately accessible by the heterogeneous audiences he addresses, from educated urbanites to outback children. Rudd takes considerable care throughout his speech to address both Indigenous and non-Indigenous Australians groups and their respective communities as inclusively as possible, enacting a range of speech roles to set up nuanced relationships and accumulate solidarity with his listeners. How does he manage the complex tenor demands of this address across the phases of his speech?

Phase 1

Rudd starts by foregrounding his authority in this opening phase. This authoritativeness in his relationship with his presumed audience here is evident in his choice of Declarative MOOD, i.e. selecting statements, rather than questions or commands, as he unflinchingly represents and acknowledges the pain of the stolen children generation. These statements are completely unqualified and unambiguous, with no use of Modal verbs such as 'might' or Modal Adjuncts such as 'probably' that could reduce the impact of his assertions (as he addresses the non-indigenous community) or the veracity of his apology (as he addresses the indigenous community). Accompanying the MOOD choice in this opening phase is Rudd's choice of PERSON, which indicates saliently who is speaking and on whose behalf. While it is Rudd as Prime Minister who moves the motion, using the First-Person Singular 'I', all the active Subjects in sentences after this first line are expressed in the First-Person Plural 'we'. So, it is 'we' who are honouring, reflecting, apologising. The 'we' is explicitly associated with the Parliament of Australia towards the end of this phase (sentence 11), but is also implicitly associated with 'the nation' earlier in the phase. Given the vastness of the overhearing audience, there is no doubt that the watching nation is included in this first person plural pronoun. Significantly, as the whole speech progresses, Rudd's patterning gradually shifts from the singular pronoun (I) to the inclusive plural (we) and finally to the more formal (Let us), reflecting in language his intention to reconcile disparate communities towards future action. The co-patterning of personal pronoun selections with Declarative MOOD and illocutionary verbs in this opening phase simultaneously enacts a new era for relationships between Aboriginal and non-Aboriginal Australia.

Along with these choices for interaction, Rudd invites his listeners to share in his feelings and judgements in order to share his actions, i.e. the act of apologizing. How does he align diverse groups of Australians in this opening to his speech? Here, the system of APPRAISAL provides important insights (Martin & White, 2005). We illustrate with the three sentences below from the end of Phase 1.

> For the pain, suffering and hurt of these stolen generations, their descendants and for their families left behind, we say sorry. To the mothers and the fathers, the brothers and the sisters, for the breaking up of families and communities,

> we say sorry. And for the indignity and degradation thus inflicted on a proud people and a proud culture, we say sorry.

Rudd's appeal to pathos here is explicitly inscribed in his choice of highly emotive yet abstract nouns such as 'pain', 'suffering', 'degradation' which seek to build a strong empathy about the plight of Indigenous Australians. His evaluations of human behaviour are likewise explicit, inscribed in his choice of highly judgemental adjectives, positive for those associated with the Aboriginal peoples e.g. 'proud' and negative for those associated with the colonizers e.g. 'blemished'; and in his choice of strongly negative verbs such as 'inflicted', the agents or perpetrators typically being past generations of white Australians. Such appraisals are not graduated, but operate at full amplification, with a force appropriate to a sincere apology. Rudd is both expressing his own feelings about these shameful events in Australia's past, and acknowledging the feelings of members of the stolen generations in an act of imaginative projection. The effect of this strong appeal to ethos is to bind all Australians to the apology.

The evaluative force of this opening phase is realized not just by individual words but also by combinations of often long noun groups, verb groups and prepositional phrases, which cohere into two basic oppositions between the ethical worlds of Aboriginal and non-Aboriginal people. Appraisal choices for the history of Aboriginal cultures are positively loaded: 'oldest continuing cultures in human history' and 'a proud people'. These are counterposed to negatively loaded oppositions for European dispossessors, with their 'blemished' history – laws and practices that 'inflicted profound grief, suffering and loss on these our fellow Australians'. Through these grammatical choices Rudd takes for granted the ethical position of his listeners, fellow Australians deeply implicated in the mistreatment of the stolen generations. Rudd's act of apologising in this opening phase is achieved most tellingly in his interpersonal language choices, realizing as they do the intensity of his feeling, his acknowledgement of the feelings of the stolen generation, his unequivocal judgements of past policies and the extent to which the overhearing audience is implicated in these policies.

This interpersonal work is accompanied by equally strong organizational work, as Rudd textures the flow of information as a speech delivered for maximum impact to a wide listenership through diverse channels. Most notable here is Rudd's use of the tricolon as a rhetorical and organizational strategy, operating at word, sentence and phase level throughout this opening phase. These tricolon structures do so much more than simply re-iterate his point. Within each sentence, consecutive repeated words or phrases are embedded (as in 'pain, suffering and hurt'; 'these stolen generations, their descendants and their families left behind'). At times, this embedded tricolon is replaced by an embedded pairing, as in 'families and communities'; 'the indignity and degradation', a strategy which avoids listener ennui by varying the poetic rhythm. This textual effect is enhanced by use of repeated interpersonal choices, such as the attitudinal Epithet 'proud' within the pairing "a *proud* people and a *proud* culture". As we saw earlier, such choices contribute to the building of a shared ethos on the matter of Aboriginal identity, while their repetition simultaneously contributes to the building of the speech's coherence.

The texture of this opening phase and its structure in the unfolding speech, is woven in even more complex ways. Rather than structuring each sentence in the more prosaic Subject, Verb, Object sequence, Rudd fronts circumstantial meanings at the beginning of each sentence, thereby drawing particular attention to the conditions framing his apology. As we indicated above, the primary resource for signposting information in a clause or sentence is Theme and the unmarked or typical constituent to select as Theme is the Subject. When Rudd chooses non-Subject Themes, he gives these items special prominence. In the tricolon above, he signposts wordings to do with the suffering of the Aboriginal people: ('For the pain …'; 'To the mothers …' and 'For the indignity …'). These phrases signpost the conditions or circumstances of the speech act of apology. Importantly, the act of apology is carried in the independent clause and occurs in New at the end of each sentence. Thus 'we say sorry' takes on additional salience both through end-weight and through repetition. This pattern most closely relates to the rhetorical strategy documented by Cicero as epiphora, the repetition of a phrase at the end of a sentence.

Rudd draws on constellations of many other aspects of grammatical choices which co-pattern, or 'manner' each other throughout his speech. For example, while creating the almost liturgical prosody described above, he simultaneously builds imaginatively the world and experiences of key participants. His experiential choices contribute to building the individual identities of the members of this 'people and culture' as '*the* mothers and *the* fathers', '*the* brothers and *the* sisters'. The marked repetition of the non-essential Definite article is not accidental. It functions grammatically to individualise members of the Stolen generation, whose experiences have been historically collectivised. Brief though our exploration of these experiential resources has been, it illustrates how Rudd's selection of a feature as small as article choice co-patterns with (or manners) his choices of interpersonal resources (MOOD, MODALITY, PERSON and APPRAISAL) as he builds complex forms of intersubjectivity; and with his textual choices as he builds a cohesive and memorable opening to his speech. Our exploration of how these metafunctional resources 'manner each other' is not restricted to what happens within phases of a persuasive text; a functional grammatics allows us to open out to consider the rhetorical unfolding of this momentous apology. We illustrate something of this logogenesis by exploring how Rudd deploys metafunctional resources in Phase 3 that manner those of Phase 1.

Phase 3

In Phase 3 Rudd's purpose shifts distinctively from the illocutionary act of putting the Apology as a parliamentary motion, to recounting the life story of one Indigenous Australian, Nanna Nungala Fejo, who was physically present in the Parliament during the delivery of this speech. Here, he assumes an intimate relationship with this one person and it is through his recount of the problems and resolutions of her long life that outsiders to her community are given a chance to acknowledge similarities and differences to their own experiences. This occurs by 'getting inside' the mind, heart and body of individuals to whom Rudd is apologising and in so doing, draws on different patterns of lexical, clausal and text choices. A short extract is presented here:

> Let me begin to answer by telling the parliament just a little of one person's story – an elegant, eloquent and wonderful woman in her 80s, full of life, full of funny stories, despite what has happened in her life's journey … Nanna Nungala Fejo, as she prefers to be called, was born in the late 1920s. She remembers her earliest childhood days living with her family and her community in a bush camp just outside Tennant Creek. She remembers the love and the warmth and the kinship of those days long ago, including traditional dancing around the camp fire at night. She loved the dancing. She remembers once getting into strife when, as a four-year-old girl, she insisted on dancing with the male tribal elders rather than just sitting and watching the men, as the girls were supposed to do. But then, sometime around 1932, when she was about four, she remembers the coming of the welfare men. Her family had feared that day and had dug holes in the creek bank where the children could run and hide. What they had not expected was that the white welfare men did not come alone. They brought a truck, two white men and an Aboriginal stockman on horseback cracking his stockwhip. The kids were found; they ran for their mothers, screaming, but they could not get away. They were herded and piled onto the back of the truck. Tears flowing, her mum tried clinging to the sides of the truck as her children were taken away to the Bungalow in Alice, all in the name of protection. A few years later, government policy changed. … After she left the mission, her brother let her know that her mum had died years before, a broken woman fretting for the children that had literally been ripped away from her.

The individuality of Nanna's experiences is strikingly foregrounded in this biographical recount, and follows Rudd's choice in phase one of the Definite article to individuate those who would otherwise be collectivised. As a biographical recount phase in a persuasive text, Nana's story is told through a distinctive perspective and in a different voice to that used in Rudd's opening phase. This is strikingly marked by less formal interpersonal language choices. This is one person's story told to Rudd by Nanna, and Rudd suggests initially in his choice of verbs that he is merely her mouthpiece. This rhetorical decision is most evident in the opening four sentences of his recount, when Rudd uses the verb 'remembers', with Nanna as the active Participant, to indicate that he is simply reporting what she recalls. Remembering is a Mental Process that typically projects (and frames) the phenomenon that is remembered. In this sense, he borrows the grammar of interiority to project the positive experiences of Nanna's early life e.g. 'her family', engaged in community building activity, dancing outside Tenant Creek in the late 1920s.

The disruptions to the equanimity of this recalled early childhood world are small, and realized in colloquial terms ('getting into strife') that capture experiences common to both black and white children, but also suggest a culture comfortable with in its own order. Rudd strategically deploys such colloquial lexis at other key phases throughout his speech, as he draws for example on colloquialisms such as 'fair go for all' and 'pretty basic Aussie belief' to create a sense of common humanity within a national context.

After these opening sentences of Phase 3, however, Rudd reverts to direct reporting of the action in Nanna's life, dropping the projecting Mental Process and presuming that the listener now understands that the rest is Nanna's projection. In this way, Rudd and his listeners become increasingly aligned with Nanna and her experiential world. This world is appraised positively as an idyllic early childhood, full of activities such as 'camp fire dancing' and marked by the 'love and the warmth and the kinship of those days'. The disruption to her world is signalled by the marked use of a contrastive Conjunction 'But' which inaugurates an opposing world of separation from loved ones. Here the APPRAISAL choices shift dramatically, and the volume or force of the feelings carried is amplified in an attempt to help non-Indigenous Australians, especially the doubters, to identify and stand with Indigenous people. This combined appeal to ethos and pathos instructs and moves us to stand with Nanna and her kin through evocation of the anguish of the separation from mother (see Macken-Horarik, 2003, for further exploration of the instructiveness of this kind of identification). These evaluative choices co-occur with a change from Active to Passive VOICE. Nanna and her family are no longer agents of their own actions but instead are acted upon: they were herded and piled', 'handed over', 'told', 'sent', 'allowed' and 'broken up'. The appraisal choices ensure we see things as Nanna and her family experience them and the Voice ensures that we understand they have become the objects or goals of other people's actions or decisions, both linguistically (in the use of the Passive VOICE) and in real life. These wordings enable Rudd to simultaneously represent the horror and grief experienced by Nanna's family and to avoid naming perpetrators of these actions, a move that would disrupt the social inclusiveness he is trying to create in this speech.

From a textual perspective, we see little of the marked frontloading, or thematising of suffering of Phase 1. Most of the sentences here are structured in the more typical Subject, Verb, Object pattern. The ordering in the clause mirrors the ordering of experience. However, when he does position temporal markers such as 'But then', 'A few years later, now' or a dependent clause like 'After she left the mission' at the beginning of a sentence, this draws attention to the progression of time, an important organizational feature of well-structured recounts. While deliberately not as poetic as the anaphoric, epiphoric and tricolon structures used in Phase 1, temporal markers signpost the unfolding of narrative sequencing. The subsequent News deals primarily with Nana's experience such as 'dancing around the campfire at night' and 'the coming of the welfare men'. It is possible to summarise patterns of text organization as follows: time is where Rudd jumps off from in the clause; lived experience is where he asks us to land.

Through these and other constellations of interpersonal, experiential and textual choices, Rudd builds a sense of his authoritative role as recounter of and empathiser with Nanna's story and calls for his listeners' emotional alignment with this individual. In this way, Rudd builds on the strong ethical imperative that characterized his opening. Having personalied his proposal for change through his strategically designed recount, he now extrapolates from it in later phases.

Phase 4

In the immediately subsequent phase (Phase 4), for example, Rudd is freed up to concentrate a strong appeal to Logos, having built this ethical and emotional alignment. Here, he selects different constellations of language choices again, as the argumentative import of this recount is generalized beyond one woman's story, as we can see in the extract below.

> But should there still be doubts as to why we must now act, let the Parliament reflect for a moment on the following facts: that, between 1910 and 1970, between 10 and 30% of indigenous children were forcibly taken from their mothers and fathers; that, as a result, up to 50,000 children were forcibly taken from their families; that this was the product of the deliberate, calculated policies of the state as reflected in the explicit powers given to them under statute; and that this policy was taken to such extremes by some in administrative authority that the forced extractions of children of so-called mixed lineage were seen as part of a broader policy of dealing with the problem of the Aboriginal population.

Interpersonally, a more formal relationship with a named audience (The Parliament) is once again assumed as Rudd commands them, albeit through the formal MOOD choice ('Let us reflect') to consider Nanna's story in light of undeniable broader facts. The argumentative point here is more explicit, general and abstract than in Phase 3 and draws on empirical rather than personal warrants to substantiate it. The appeal to Logos is most evident experientially in the choice of abstract nouns to describe phenomena in a highly conceptual way (e.g. explicit powers), general nouns that refer to groups of people symbolically rather than as individuals (e.g. the state, administrative authority) and nominalizations of phenomena (e.g. 'the forced extractions'). The generality, abstraction and technicality of Rudd's choice of Participants here construe a more detached, even 'scientific' field of warrants in support of his claim that the proposal is needed. These choices contrast markedly with the specific, concrete and everyday participants at the basis of his personal warrants in the previous recount phase. Yet the generality, abstraction and technicality only achieve the rhetorical force because of its relationship with the concrete, specific and everyday world produced so powerfully in Phase 3. It is through the juxtaposition of these two worlds and the evaluative colouring with which they are represented, that the argument for the apology is most potently progressed.

Phase 7

By mid-way through his speech (Phase 7), where Rudd again puts the formal motion for the parliamentary apology, the cumulative effect of these combined rhetorical strategies becomes unassailable. In terms of textual strategies, the rhetorical point has been made and Rudd no longer needs to deploy the end focus he used in Phase 1. Instead, he returns to a congruent Subject, Verb, Object structure, incorporating the material introduced earlier into the embedded portions of each clause (which we indicate below in double square brackets):

> We apologise for the hurt, the pain and suffering [[that we, the parliament, have caused you by the laws that previous parliaments have enacted]]. We apologise for the indignity, the degradation and the humiliation [[these laws embodied]]. We offer this apology to the mothers, the fathers, the brothers, the sisters, the families and the communities [[whose lives were ripped apart by the actions of successive governments under successive parliaments]].

Rudd now repeats 'we apologise' at the beginning of each of these three sentences, drawing on the rhetorical strategy of 'anaphora'. It is now members of the parliament (we) foregrounded in Subject position who are responsible for righting the historical wrongs that have been so graphically illustrated in the recount of Nanna's life, rather than the conditions under which such wrongs were conducted. As further grammatical evidence of logogenetic development, Rudd's repetitions in Phase 7 mirror the structures with which he opened his speech, but with the burden of meaning that has accumulated in the intervening phases now contained in the embedded clauses at the end of each sentence. Experientially, these embedded clauses carry a condensed version of his prior warrants for the apology (with their distinctive appeal to logos) and make explicit the agency of previous parliaments and their laws ('suffering [[that *we, the parliament,* have caused you by the laws that *previous parliaments* have enacted]]'). Interpersonally, these embedded clauses also carry a condensed version of the accumulated valuation of the impact of these laws on 'communities [[whose lives *were ripped apart* by the actions of successive governments under successive parliaments]]'. Here, the highly amplified negative affect attached to processes such as 'ripped apart' signal further escalation of the strategies of ethos and pathos drawn on in the intervening phases.

In its capacity to describe such meaning escalations, our grammatics has allowed us to go beyond the simplistic use of isolated rhetorical labels such as 'tricolon' or 'anaphora' to a richer examination of how repeated patterns build a cumulative impact and weave the complex texture of Rudd's speech as a whole. At our second level of semiosis, we have seen how, from a textual perspective, choices such as those for Theme and for New and rhythmic repetition of wordings create a memorable rhetoric, a prosody of meanings around the act of the apology which forms a trope that is returned to at critical points of the speech. Such mnemonic and poetic devices simultaneously reduce the cognitive load on listeners of a long speech by making salient important elements of the spoken message. They work in conjunction with unfolding patterns of interpersonal resources such as APPRAISAL, MOOD and PERSON to cumulatively bind listeners to the speaker, to engage them in the act of the apology, and to develop sympathy and responsibility towards aboriginal peoples. And they work with unfolding constellations of experiential resources to build imaginative insights into the past and present worlds of Indigenous peoples, juxtaposed with bodies of detached evidence about their past lives that constitute compelling appeals to reasoned redress through Logos.

Grammatics and rhetoric in the broader civic domain

In exploring the logogenetic unfolding of one high stakes speech, we have touched on a small range of resources from our grammatical toolkit. Yet even this range allows us to compare the logogenesis of one persuasive text with that of others. For example, in the same year that Rudd gave his Apology to the Stolen Generations the US President, Barak Obama gave his Victory speech (Obama, 2008). Like Rudd's Apology, Obama's Victory speech occurred at a pivotal moment in his nation's history, and was a deeply symbolic opportunity for him to unite disparate community groups, engage all citizens in difficult political decisions, maintain a sense of optimism and agency during troubled times and establish a strong identity for his new government. As with Rudd, Obama's capacity to draw convincingly on a range of rhetorical strategies was central to his skill as an orator and thus to his victory. Obama's speech too contained an embedded biographical recount of an elderly woman of colour (Anne Nixon Cooper) and drew strategically on this across subsequent phases, to build a shared sense of enterprise through empathy. Yet because of the distinctive context of culture and situation, Obama's rhetoric draws on somewhat different constellations of interpersonal resources to Rudd's as he builds unique forms of solidarity, establishes his particular authority as the first US president of colour and reassures the potentially disaffected. For example, he has no need in a Victory speech for the explicit appraisal that Rudd needs to imaginatively align his non-Indigenous audience emotionally and morally, with the experiences of the stolen generations. The distinctiveness of the political and cultural contexts drives the distinctive patterning of interpersonal, experiential and textual resources and their distinctive logogenesis in these two speeches (see Love & Macken-Horarik, 2009 for further details).

Likewise, revealing comparisons can be made with other iconic speeches. For example, through a detailed linguistic analysis of Nelson Mandela's speech at the end of his book 'Long Walk to Freedom', Martin brilliantly illustrates the power of a logogenetic analysis. He deploys tools in systemic functional linguistics to analyse how "the story of Mandela's day-to-day experience as he moves through space and time unfolds alongside the story of his political development as his understanding of freedom transforms" (Martin, 1999, p. 38). By exploring constellations of interpersonal, textual and experiential features Martin reveals Mandela's journey as "a spiritual quest towards enlightenment" (Martin, 1999, p. 38), as far more than a simple autobiographical recount. In a complete analysis of the rhetorical power of persuasion, we would draw on systems related to each of the metafunctions. However, even focussing on one linguistic feature logogenetically can be instructive. For example, we might examine how patterns of tense unfold across Kevin Rudd's Apology speech as he reconstructs a version of the past (Phase 3), acknowledges present responsibilities (Phases 4–6), proposes immediate actions (Phases 7–8), and envisages a new future (Phases 9–10). But this opportunity must wait for another time.

Our functional grammatics has allowed us to reveal how meaning unfolds across one iconic speech, as we illustrated how selections from various systems are deployed in service of high stakes persuasion. In terms of first order semiosis, we have identified interpersonal, experiential and textual choices most at stake in spoken rhetoric. We have further described how these choices co-pattern within and across phases of varying length. Finally, at a second order of semiosis, we have endeavoured to explain how such patternings achieve rhetorical impact in the context of this speech. Such a toolkit offers powerful resources for young people as they learn to appreciate, critique and compose oral and written forms of persuasion in their own civic lives.

Multimodal forms of persuasion

The persuasive power of the speeches we have studied above is no doubt due, at least in part, to the fact that they had been crafted, perhaps in writing, and rehearsed. In addition, they are often accompanied by other significant modes of meaning. To take the case of Rudd, his speech was delivered in the physical context of the Australian Parliament, and broadcast electronically through television and various forms of social media. An image of him directly facing Nanna Fejo, whose gestures and eye contact reciprocated his, reinforced his verbal and written message of solidarity. Indeed, the deeply intertextual basis on which this solidarity is based was evident in the words Nanna wore on her black tee shirt that day ('Thanks') which were themselves a response to the apology in Rudd's speech, but more broadly to the words 'We say sorry' which appeared on black tee shirts around the country in the lead up to Rudd's speech. The evolution of a range of multimodal semiotic resources has opened up significant persuasive potential for contemporary rhetors, including intertextual networks of meaning like those carried on tee shirts.

Earlier in this chapter, we briefly explored the relationship between the wording and image of a Zoos Victoria poster (Figure 5.1) that sought to persuade viewers to recycle their mobile phones. More radically, some picture books are persuasive texts in the form of illustrated narratives, such as Raymond Briggs' (1984) *The Tin Pot Foreign General and the Old Iron Woman,* which was his acerbic response to the Falklands War between the United Kingdom and Argentina in 1982. Likewise, some animated narrative movies are persuasive texts. The powerful example is the animated movie *9-11/9-11* (Chin, 2008), based on the bombing of the Presidential

Palace in Chile in 1973 in a coup against the Allende government, the subsequent installing of the Pinochet dictatorship, and the terrorist attack on the twin towers of the World Trade Center in New York exactly 28 years later, to the day, on the 11th of September. The ways in which the film morphs symbolically and cohesively between events on these two days in September appear to direct viewers to judge the events and the forces that led to such devastating acts of terror (Unsworth, 2015).

Just as syndromes of grammatical choices achieve distinctive rhetorical effects in spoken oratory, analogous resources can be identified and their contribution to persuasion explained in each of these multimodal forms. We touch briefly here on those grammatical systems for examining persuasive meaning in visual texts. Here again, the persuasive role of images in a range of different types of texts reflects Aristotle's rhetorical strategies of Logos, Ethos and Pathos through their appeal to rationality, ethics and emotion. One aspect of the appeal of images to Logos or rationality is the unwarranted but widespread belief that what images communicate must be true and hence constitute unassailable evidence of claims based on them. Of course, we know that naturalistic images can be manipulated to support a particular interpretation of reality, and from a functional linguistic perspective images are constructed – made. Their iconic function as representations of the 'real' is a necessary fiction. Governments rely on the 'truth value' of photographs in order to achieve political or military ends that have only the faintest connection to the evidence deployed to support these ends. One has only to remember the reliance of the US government on satellite images providing 'empirical evidence' of weapons of mass destruction in Iraq and a rationale for invasion to realize just how important images can be in persuading citizens to adopt or at least accept certain actions.

Closer to home in Australia, the persuasive power of news photographs was underscored when the Coalition government circulated two images to the media (without captions) that purported to show asylum seekers throwing their own children into the water in order to secure rescue by the Australian navy (Macken-Horarik, 2003). This notorious incident which became known as the 'children overboard' affair' revealed something of the duplicity of political forces keen to exploit the unthinking acceptance that photographs contain evidence. The images were only part of a larger campaign to control the borders of Australian territory and prevent boat people seeking rescue. The campaign is ongoing.

Non-pictorial images such as graphs and tables can also be manipulated to portray information such that a particular interpretation appears more likely. This can be for pedagogic purposes and can illuminate realities in ways that cannot be captured adequately in bald tables of figures. A vivid example of this can be seen in the website of the World Wildlife Fund showing the decline in the world's leopard population from 1984–2007 (https://www.wwf.org.uk/). This decline is represented in the figure of a dissolving leopard, itself comprised of smaller leopards whose density diminishes as the timeline moves towards 2007. The image thus combines empirically grounded information about the rate of species decline with a striking visual metaphor symbolizing this. This representation of the dissolving leopard ensures that we read it both literally and symbolically. While there is no explicit judgement of impropriety, it is strongly implied. Images of this kind we might regard as provoking judgement.

While the persuasive strategies of images related to Logos appear to have been addressed quite systematically in accounts of critical literacy pedagogy (Kalantzis & Cope, 2012), somewhat less systematic attention appears to have been given to the significance of strategies related to pathos and ethos in considering the persuasive role of images. These strategies align most closely with semiotic choices related to the interpersonal metafunction within systemic functional linguistics. In Chapter 3 we discussed image resources for constructing the interpersonal relations of interaction between the depicted characters in narrative and the reader/viewer in illustrated narratives, such as SOCIAL DISTANCE, SUBJECTIVITY and OBJECTIVITY. These interactive resources in images reflect the strategy of Pathos, positioning viewers to respond emotionally to, as, or along with, depicted Participants. The persuasive effect is to interactively engage viewers to share the attitude(s) being privileged in what is portrayed in the image. We saw this in Figure 5.1 earlier in this chapter, where the intimate close-up image of the gorilla whose Invited gaze into the eyes of the viewer invoked a solidarity with the reader, persuading them to re-cycle old mobile phones to reduce the illegal mining of coltan in gorilla habitats.

Ethos aligns with semiotic choices for communicating evaluative positions on the basis of ethical judgement. Images can Inscribe JUDGEMENT when they include widely recognized symbols or visual metaphors (Unsworth, 2015; White, 2014). In Chapter 3 we exemplified this with an image of 'Dad' in Anthony Browne's picture book, Zoo (Browne, 1994), where the aggressive image of Dad is emphasised by the cloud formation in the sky, which appears to attach clouds in the shape of bull's horns to the sides of Dad's head. A photograph of the former leader of the Australian Greens Party, Bob Browne, was depicted with an overlay of devil-like horns and tail, clearly inscribing judgement of propriety – aggression specifically (White, 2014, p. 28). An image of a former Australian Prime Minister showed him involved in a card game where the playing card design is the nuclear power warning symbol. The photo-image montage also has the head of the former Prime Minister slightly enlarged, emphasizing his characteristic 'artificial' smile revealing his large teeth, to portray a somewhat mischievous expression. This visual metaphor of 'gambling with nuclear energy' is designed to depict a Prime Minister 'taking risks' or 'playing with danger' with regard to his government's nuclear energy policy (Economou, 2009). It would be very difficult not to regard this image as inscribing ethical judgement. As Unsworth argues:

> In these images, the bringing together of the incongruous elements forces the viewer to construe the visual metaphor. The inclusion of the culturally widely understood symbols (nuclear symbol, playing cards symbolizing chance, and horns symbolizing bovine aggressiveness/cuckoldry) makes it

>impossible to avoid the evaluation normally conveyed by such symbols and hence judgement is entailed in these images.
>
>*(Unsworth, 2015, p. 79)*

Some images "pull or lure readers into the text" positioning them in distinctive ways towards factual content (Economou, 2008). In an image from an information book for children (Barton, 1987, p. 29), it is the combination of two images that strongly suggests a judgement of impropriety in a seal hunt. The baby seal at the bottom of the image stares out at the viewer in a mute appeal and superimposed on this image is another one taken from the cover of a magazine showing a hunter about to batter a baby seal to death. The irony of the headline – The Price of a Seal Skin Coat – is savage.

While this image is an example of a multimodal text that generates judgement, many have a persuasive effect simply through the depiction of their experiential content, which evokes ethical judgement by viewers. The illustrated version of Nelson Mandela's *Long Walk to Freedom* (1996) includes an image of an adolescent African boy carrying the slain 13-year-old Hector Pietersen in the 1976 Soweto uprising. The image strongly contributes to the evoking of the ethical judgement of the immorality of the South African Authorities in their violent and murderous response to the uprising by 15,000 school students at the imposition of the teaching of half of all school subjects in Afrikaans. An image of a black African family in front of their corrugated iron shanty dwelling and behind a barbed wire fence in Apartheid Era South Africa evokes a judgement of the immorality of the ghettoizing of these people (Kress & van Leeuwen, 1990, p. 79). But equally images can evoke positive judgements of propriety, as in the case of a young person helping an elderly person to cross the road, volunteers assisting in disaster relief or children helping their mothers. In such images, there has been no authorial intrusion of judgement into the naturalistic depictions.

The images in Figures 5.2 (reprinted in Mason, 2010, p. 271) and 5.3 (reprinted in Anderson, Low, Keese & Conroy, 2010, p. 300) are from Junior High School history textbooks used in New South Wales in Australia. The images occur in the textbook segments dealing with issues of reconciliation between the indigenous Australian Aboriginal population and the majority non-Aboriginal population. The first image (Figure 5.2) appeared originally in the *Sydney Morning Herald* Newspaper on May 25, 1967, the year of the referendum about including Aboriginal people "to be counted in the reckoning of the population" – as worded on the ballot paper.

The second image (Figure 5.2) is another textbook is simply captioned "Towards reconciliation". It is not referred to in the main text and there is no source or attribution of the image referenced in the textbook. The invitation to celebrate racial harmony and to move towards reconciliation appears to emanate from the represented people and their interaction – in the case of children in friendship, in the case of European baby and traditional Aboriginal elder, sheer mutual interest. The gaze of the depicted people is reserved for each other and we (viewers) look on in appreciation – or at least that is the invitation. It is in this that persuasion lies because reconciliation cannot be coerced.

SOURCE 7.27
Photo from the front page of the *Sydney Morning Herald*, 25 May 1967

FIGURE 5.2 Flagging positive Judgement of inter-racial relations (in Mason, 2010, p. 271).

Towards reconciliation

FIGURE 5.3 Flagging positive Judgement via inter-generational, inter-racial harmony (in Anderson, Low, Keese, & Conroy, 2010, p. 300).

In Chapter 3 we discussed the ways in which the point of view from which narrative is experienced can be manipulated so that viewers can be positioned to regard an image 'as' or 'along with' represented Participants. These Focalization strategies can also be used in persuasive texts to align viewers with the point of view of a depicted participant who is endorsing material depicted. This is most readily observed in advertisements. In mobile phone advertisements for example, the viewer is frequently positioned as the owner of the phone displayed since the phone is portrayed as being held in the palm of the hand from a viewpoint that could only occur if the camera were synonymous with the eyes of the viewer (Figure 5.4).

A similar technique is used in an advertisement for Canadian Mist whisky, which portrays only the legs of a man and a woman extended forward beside each other resting on a couch on a veranda with a male hand holding a glass and in the background a beautiful Canadian mountain scene. The view could only be through the eyes of the man or the woman. Hence the viewer is identified with

FIGURE 5.4 Persuading through focalization as depicted participant.

the participants who have clearly been persuaded about the qualities of the drink and are endorsing the message of the advertisement. The resources of focalization and interactive meanings in images are not only used to persuade viewers to buy products but are widely used in persuasive texts in many social and community campaigns. The websites for organizations such as World Vision and Oxfam, for example, are dominated by images of the recipients of their aid programs that are mostly close-up images with the eyes of the people depicted gazing directly at the viewers. Other such social and community support websites position the viewer to see 'along with' the image of the represented recipient of the aid funds they are trying to persuade the viewer to donate. Decisions about how to position viewers are made with an experienced eye in all campaigns to solicit support. One example is the Hunger Prevention Campaign in the United States (see www.adcouncil.org/Our-Campaigns/Family-Community/Hunger-Prevention). Interpersonal meaning choices within visual systems of FOCALIZATION, SOCIAL DISTANCE, SUBJECTIVITY and OBJECTIVITY relate strongly to a Pathos strategy. They need to be considered alongside those reflecting the Logos and Ethos strategies as powerful persuasive resources.

Our discussion in this section has illustrated just a little of how a functional grammatics can explicate the role images play in persuasive texts. It has not been comprehensive. For further work on the persuasive role of images in newspapers see Bednarek and Caple (2012), Caple (2008a, 2008b, 2010) and Economou (2012, 2013); in advertisements see Feng (2011a, 2011b) and Feng and O'Halloran (2013); and in biography and government reports, see Martin (2002, 2006).

As a fundamental component of school English, students are required to analyse multimodal forms of persuasion, where the images, audio files, animations or hypertext either complement or challenge verbal meaning in appeals to Logos, Pathos or Ethos. Providing analytical tools adequate to this task is crucial to the critical literacy agenda that underpins the current national curricula in the United States, the United Kingdom and Australia (Kalantzis & Cope, 2012). In Australia for example, the national literacy tests require students to interpret persuasive texts such as Figure 5.1, showing the image of the gorilla, which was included in the 2010 NAPLAN reading test (ACARA, 2010). As part of this agenda in our contemporary semiotic landscape, students are also increasingly being asked to compose their own multimodal forms of persuasion, as we shall see in Chapter 7.

More so than ever before, young people and their teachers need a robust metalanguage for exploring how the texts that surround them do their persuasive work, and how they in turn can shape powerful forms of persuasion. Their agency is at the heart of this enterprise, focussing our attention on how young people can work with the rhetorical possibilities of different semiotic resources in producing persuasive texts. But it needs to be a critical as well as 'savvy' agency. If they are armed with a critical awareness of the rhetorical work of design, young people are more likely to become discerning purchasers, intelligent data 'miners' and intellectually probing researchers and advocates. In this sense, school English has a vital role to play in recognizing and building on the fluent use of digital resources through an understanding of how these work and why they work as they do too. However, our research (Love, Macken-Horarik & Horarik, 2015) suggests that teachers still lack a metalanguage for describing intermodal relationships (Painter *et al.*, 2013; Unsworth & Thomas, 2014), even with emerging professional resources to support teachers with this enterprise (e.g. Callow, 2013). We turn to this in our next chapter as we consider a highly privileged form of written persuasion and the potential of a functional grammatics metalanguage for illuminating its workings.

Note

1   The whole of this lengthy speech can be accessed at http://www.smh.com.au/articles/2008/02/13/1202760379056.html

References

Andrews, R. (2005). Knowledge about the teaching of (sentence) grammar: The state of play. *English Teaching: Practice and Critique*, 4(3), 69–76.

Andrews, R. (2010). *Argumentation in higher education: Improving practice through theory and research*. New York: Routledge.

Archer, A. & Newfield, D. (2014) *Multimodal approaches to research and pedagogy: Recognition, resources, and access*. London & New York: Routledge.

Australian Curriculum, Assessment and Reporting Authority (ACARA) (2010). *NAPLAN test papers, 2008–2010*. Retrieved from www.acara.edu.au/assessment/naplan-2008-2011-test-papers.

Anderson, M., Low, A., Keese, I. & Conroy, J. (2010). *Retroactive 2: Stage 5 Australian history* (3rd edition.). Milton, Qld, Australia: Jacaranda.

Barton, M. (1987). *Animal rights*. London: Franklin Watts.

Bednarek, M. & Caple, H. (2012). 'Value added': Language, image and news values. *Discourse, Context & Media*, 1(2), 103–113.

Bateman, J. (2014). *Text and Image: A critical introduction to the visual/verbal divide*. London & New York: Routledge.

Briggs, R. (1984). *The tin-pot foreign general and the old iron woman*. London: Hamish Hamilton.

Browne, A. (1994). *Zoo*. London: Random House.

Callow, J. (2013). *The shape of text to come: How image and text work*. Newtown, Australia: Primary English Teaching Association Australia [PETAA].

Caple, H. (2008a). Intermodal relations in image nuclear news stories. In L. Unsworth (Ed.), *Multimodal semiotics: Functional analyses in contexts of education* (pp. 123–138). London & New York: Continuum.

Caple, H. (2008b). Reconciling the co-articulation of meaning between words and pictures: Exploring instantiation and commitment in image-nuclear news stories. In A. Mahboob & N. Knight (Eds.), *Questioning linguistics* (pp. 77–94). Newcastle, UK: Cambridge Scholars Press.

Caple, H. (2010). Doubling-up: Allusion and bonding in multi-semiotic news stories. In M. Bednarek & J. R. Martin (Eds.), *New discourse on language: Functional perspectives on multimodality, identity, and affiliation* (pp. 111–133). London & New York: Continuum.

Chin, M. (Director). (2008). *9-11/9-11*: indiePix.
Christie, F. & Martin, J. R. (Eds.) (1997) *Genre and institutions: Social processes in the workplace and school*. London: Cassell.
Cicero, (n.d.). *De inventione*, (C.D. Yonge, Trans). Retrieved from http://classicpersuasion.org/pw/cicero/dnv1-1.htm.
Economou, D. (2009). *Photos in the news: Appraisal analysis of visual semiosis and verbal-visual intersemiosis* (Unpublished doctoral thesis). The University of Sydney.
Economou, D. (2012). Standing out on critical issues: Evaluation in large verbal-visual displays in Australian broadsheets. In W. Bowcher (Ed.), *Multimodal texts from around the world: Cultural and linguistic insights* (pp. 246–272). Basingstoke, UK: Palgrave Macmillan.
Economou, D. (2013). Telling a different story. In E. Djonov & S. Zhao (Eds.), *Critical multimodal studies of popular culture* (pp. 181–201). London: Routledge.
Feng, D. (2011a). The construction and categorization of multimodal metaphor: A systemic functional approach. *Foreign Language Research*, 1, 24–29.
Feng, D. (2011b). Visual space and ideology: A critical cognitive analysis of spatial orientations in advertising. In K. O'Halloran & B. Smith (Eds.), *Multimodal studies: Exploring issues and domains* (pp. 55–75). London: Routledge.
Feng, D. & O'Halloran, K. L. (2013). The visual representation of metaphor: A social semiotic approach. *Review of Cognitive Linguistics*, 11(2), 320–335.
Gore, A. & Guggenheim, D. (2006). *An inconvenient truth: A global warning*. Paramount Pictures.
Gregory, M. & Malcolm, K. (1981). *Generic situation and discourse phase: An approach to the analysis of children's talk*. (Mimeo). Toronto: Applied Linguistics Research Working Group, Glendon College of York University.
Green, B. (2009) English, rhetoric, democracy; or renewing English in Australia. *English in Australia*, 43(3), 35–44.
Halliday, M. A. K. (1993) Quantitative studies and probabilities in grammar. In M. Hoey (Ed.), *Data, description, discourse: Papers on English language in honour of John McH. Sinclair (on his sixtieth birthday)* (pp. 1–25). London: HarperCollins.
Halliday, M. A. K. & Matthiessen, C. (2004). *An introduction to functional grammar* (3rd edition). London: Edward Arnold.
Hasan, R. (1988). The analysis of one poem: Theoretical issues in practice. In D. Birch & L. M. O'Toole (Eds.), *Functions of style* (pp. 52–64). London: Pinter.
Hillocks, G. (2010). Teaching argument for critical thinking and writing: An introduction. *English Journal*, 99(6), 24–32.
Hood, S. (2011). Body language in face-to-face teaching: A focus on textual and interpersonal meaning. In S. Dreyfus, S. Hood & M. Stenglin (Eds.), *Semiotic margins: Meaning in multimodalities* (pp. 31–52). London & New York: Continuum.
Humphrey, S. (2013). Empowering adolescents for activist literacies. *Journal of Language and Literacy Education*, 9(1), 114–135.
Humphrey, S. (2017). *Academic literacies in the middle years: A framework for enhancing teacher knowledge and student achievement*. New York & London: Routledge.
Humphrey, S., Love, K. & Droga, L. (2011). *Working grammar: An introduction for secondary teachers*. Melbourne: Pearson.
Humphrey, S, Droga, L. & Feez, S. (2012). *Grammar and meaning*. Newtown, Australia: Primary English Teaching Association Australia.
Kalantizis, M. & Cope, B. (2012). *Literacies*. Port Melbourne, Victoria: Cambridge University Press.
Kennedy, G. (2007). *Aristotle on rhetoric: A theory of civic discourse* (G. Kennedy, Trans.). New York: Oxford University Press.

Klein, P., & Unsworth, L. (2014). The logogenesis of writing to learn: A systemic functional perspective. *Linguistics and Education*, 26, 1–17.

Kress, G. (2010). *Multimodality: A social semiotic approach to contemporary communication*. London: Routledge.

Kress, G. & van Leeuwen, T. (1990). *Reading images*. Geelong: Deakin University Press.

Love, K., & Macken-Horarik, M. (2009). *Obama, Rudd and a grammar for rhetoric in the National English Curriculum*. Paper presented at the Bridging Divides AATE/ALEA Conference, Hobart.

Love, K., Macken-Horarik, M. & Horarik, S. (2015). Grammatical knowledge and its application: A snapshot of Australian teachers' views, *for Australian Journal of Language and Literacy*, 38(3), 171–182.

Macken-Horarik, M. (2003). Working the borders in racist discourse: The challenge of the "Children Overboard Affair" in news media texts. *Social Semiotics*, 13(3), 283–303.

Malcolm, K. (2010). *Phasal analysis: Analysing discourse through communication linguistics*. London & New York: Continuum.

Mandela, N. (1996). *The illustrated long walk to freedom: The autobiography of Nelson Mandela*. London: Little, Brown and Company.

Martin, J. R. (1999). Grace: The logogenesis of freedom. *Discourse Studies*, 1(1), 29–56.

Martin, J. R. (2002). Fair trade: Negotiating meaning in multimodal texts. In P. Coppock (Ed.), *The semiotics of writing: Transdisciplinary perspectives on the technology of writing*. (pp. 311–338). Begijnhof, Belgium: Brepols & Indiana University Press.

Martin, J. R. (2004/2010): Sense and sensibility: Texturing evaluation. In W. Zhenhua (Ed), *Discourse semantics [Vol. 2 of Collected Works of J. R. Martin]*. pp. 341-375. Shanghai: Jiao Tong University Press.

Martin, J. R. (2006). Vernacular deconstruction: Undermining spin. *DELTA (Documentação de Estudos em Linguistica Teorica e Aplicada)*, 22, 173–203.

Martin, J. R. & White, P. (2005). *The language of evaluation: Appraisal in English*. New York: Palgrave Macmillan.

Martin, J. R. & Rose, D. (2007). *Working with discourse: Meaning beyond the clause* (2nd edition). London: Continuum.

Martin, J. R. & Rose, D. (2008). *Genre relations: Mapping culture*. London & Oakville: Equinox.

Mason, K. (2010). *Experience of nationhood: Modern Australia since 1901* (3rd edition). Melbourne, Australia: Nelson Cengage Learning.

Moon, B. (2012). Remembering rhetoric: Recalling a tradition of explicit instruction in writing. *English in Australia*, 47(1), 37–52.

Obama, B. (2008). Acceptance speech in Chicago. *The Baltimore Sun*. Retrieved on 21 February, 2017 from www.baltimoresun.com/news/nation/politics/baltext1105,0,2684817.story?.

Painter, C., Martin, J. R. & Unsworth, L. (2013). *Reading visual narratives: Image analysis of children's picture books*. London: Equinox.

Rose, D. & Martin, J. R. (2012). *Learning to write, reading to learn: Genre, knowledge and pedagogy in the Sydney school*. London: Equinox.

Rudd, K. (2008). *Apology to the Stolen Generations of Australia*. Retrieved from http://www.smh.com.au/articles/2008/02/13/1202760379056.html.

Searle, J. R. (1969). *Speech acts: An essay in the philosophy of language*. London: Cambridge University Press.

Toulmin, S. (1958). *The uses of argument*. Cambridge, UK: Cambridge Unuversity Press.

Unsworth, L. (2015). Persuasive narratives: Evaluative images in picture books and animated movies. *Visual Communication*, 14(1), 73–96.

Unsworth, L., & Thomas, A. (Eds.) (2014). *English teaching and new literacies pedagogy: Interpreting and authoring digital multimedia narratives*. New York: Peter Lang Publishing.

White, P. R. R. (2014). The attitudinal work of news journalism images – a search for visual and verbal analogues. *Quaderni del CeSLiC Occasional Papers del CeSLiC*, 6–42.

6
'THE WILD WEST'
Understanding resources for meaning in persuasion

Moving into the territory of persuasive resources in school English

In Chapter 5, we explored the significant contribution of functional grammatics to study of persuasive strategies used by rhetors in the civic domain, focussing on largely on verbal grammatical systems at stake, but exploring analogous systems for visual and other multimodal texts. We observed how various constellations of experiential, interpersonal and textual resources helped realize rhetorical strategies that dated back to those documented by classical scholars of antiquity. This metafunctional perspective furthermore allowed us to identify how patterns of grammatical choices work in two orders of semiosis across a range of persuasive texts to achieve their rhetorical (and often enduring) power. Recall, for example, how first order analysis allowed us to recognize that Prime Minister Rudd draws on Mood and Modality choices of varying strength across his Apology to the Stolen Generations, while second order analysis allowed us to describe the patterning of such interpersonal choices and explain how these patterns work to oblige listeners to formally approve this Apology in the Australian Parliament. Both of these levels of semiosis are important in disciplinary practices related to persuasion, as teachers shuttle between drawing attention to salient aspects of grammar (e.g. Modality) and to their persuasive effect in shaping listener attitude.

In drawing on these and other analytical systems of our toolkit for both verbal and visual semiotics we can go beyond the listing of rhetorical techniques which has so often characterized curricular advice of the past. We can re-integrate the study of grammar with the study of rhetoric, a connection unfortunately lost through successive generations of curriculum change in the twentieth century (see Christie, 1993). Compatible with the analytical tools referred to by the Ancient Roman Rhetoricians as elements of "artificial eloquence", "the materials of the (persuasive) art" or "the many and important particulars of political science" (Cicero, n.d.), our grammatically informed analytical tools provide powerful insights into how language and image can be crafted to persuade individuals, small groups or whole societies to particular beliefs or courses of action across time and place and how the wordings unfold in particular ways to manage this. In this chapter, we deepen our exploration of those grammatical systems that are most 'at risk' in the construction and analysis of verbal, visual and multimodal forms of persuasion, drawing on the principles and terminology of Metafunction, but also ranging over notions of System, Stratification and Rank as covered in earlier chapters.

Appreciation and critical analysis of high stakes forms of persuasion is a central component of subject English in many Anglophone countries. Students learn to identify the persuasive wordings underpinning the great speeches of our time and cultures, such as Martin Luther King's "I have a dream", Winston Churchill's "We shall fight on the beaches" speech and Kevin Rudd's "Apology to the stolen generations of Australia". Some are explicitly taught how to appreciate the aesthetic and ideological impact of speeches by these and other orators, and to critically evaluate them. Some even learn how to distinguish between various genres of persuasion, such as Analytical and Hortatory Expositions. Increasingly more students are taught to evaluate the multimodal components of public forms of persuasion, as these appear in locations such as newspaper editorials, citizen activist websites and politicians' blogs, where the verbal text is complemented or challenged by accompanying images, audio files, animations or hypertext. Explicit and critical scrutiny of multimodal persuasion is important in a digital world that is all the more coercive when taken for granted. Students need access to well theorised metalanguages if they are to deconstruct the basis of appeals produced in multimodal persuasion.

Study of speeches such as those cited above is rightly a central plank of the English/Language Arts Curriculum, as we can see for example in the supplementary materials that accompany the CCSS in the United States (National Governors' Association 2010a, 2010b). This is especially important as students move into the senior years of schooling and are prepared for civic life (Humphrey, 2010; Macken-Horarik, 1996; McCormack, 2003). Grammatically informed understanding of rhetorical strategies can enhance the work of English/Language Arts teachers who use speeches such as those above for study. Unfortunately, much of the advice that accompanies curriculum documentation across the Anglophone world stops short of explicating the grammatical interface with rhetoric. The advice to teachers accompanying the Australian Curriculum for English (AC:E for short) is a case in point (ACARA, 2012). Here, we can find illustrations from famous speeches of how patterns of three are repeated to achieve effect at three levels of language. However, isolated examples of parallelism offer little insight into how patterns of words, clauses and sentences accumulate and mirror each other as they achieve distinctive rhetorical purposes across a speech, as we have illustrated above. Sally Humphrey crystallises the issue with reference to one specific set of interpersonal resources:

> While many teachers draw on knowledge of rhetorical appeals and isolated realisations such as parallelism and amplification to encourage students to

strengthen their arguments, the function of these devices in expanding or contracting dialogic space and the effect of dynamic interactions between resources across texts is not well understood in educational contexts. Consequently, teachers are often not resourced with a metalanguage to make explicit to their students how the resources function to meet or confound the expectations of the audience.

(Humphrey, 2013, p. 124)

In this climate, there is renewed interest across the Anglophone world in a clearer role for study of rhetoric. Furthermore, many educators are calling for a rhetorically oriented study of language (see for example, Christie, 2004; Green, 2009, 2017; Love & Macken-Horarik, 2009; and Meoon, 2012 in Australia; Hancock & Kolln, 2010; Schleppegrell, 2004 in the US; and Clark, 2010; Myhill, 2009; Myhill, Jones, Watson & Lines, 2013 in the UK). A grammatics of the sort we have illustrated earlier is as essential for students' production of written forms of persuasion as it is for their critical analysis of high stakes oratory or multimodal texts.

Of particular importance to schooling is the expository essay or the written analytical exposition (Martin 1985, p.17). This genre, highly valued in Western education, requires students to structure reasoned, logical arguments, to frontload a Thesis or Position Statement and support this with evidence in subsequent paragraphs backed by a Warrant and citing of appropriate authorities. Expository essays in this form have become the most common mode in high school and college writing instruction (De Stigter, 2015, p. 12). Recall from Chapter 5 that in Western cultures, this form of argumentation is considered a significant marker of the capacity to marshal detached and well-sourced bodies of evidence in support of a position on a social issue or thesis (Andrews, 2005; Hillocks, 2010; Moore & Schleppegrell, 2014; Toulmin, 1958). Written analytical exposition is deeply embedded in curriculum and assessment regimes across many Anglophone contexts (see for example the Common Core Standards in the US; NAPLAN in Australia; and the UK National Curriculum). The Australian curriculum for English has been informed by the school-based research of SFL linguists such as Martin (1985) who made an initial distinction between 'persuading that' (Analytical exposition) and 'persuading to' (Hortatory Exposition). This distinction between Analytical and Hortatory expositions is still relevant in current teacher professional resources (see for example Humphrey, 2017) but can be easily blurred, since hortatory sequences can be embedded in what is considered an Analytical exposition (see for example Christie, 2002). A more helpful distinction for the purposes of school English can be made between Exposition, Discussion and Debate. Exposition concerns the putting of an argument for or against an issue; Debates present two sides of an issue; and Discussions consider a proposition from several different perspectives before arriving at a recommendation (Humphrey, Love & Droga, 2011, p. 15).

Yet, as some educators in the mentioned above have argued, the distinction between formal argumentation of this sort and persuasion more broadly is still poorly understood. Despite earlier claims that grammar is a distraction to the teaching of composition (Hillocks, 1984), Hillocks has more recently turned his attention to the crucial role of rhetoric in a liberal arts education (Hillocks, 2010). He points out the limitations of purely syllogistic reasoning (involving a conclusion derived from a set of premises sharing a common middle term) to logical argumentation in the post-modernist context of the twenty-first century and suggests that appeals to logos can at best be based on probability, rather than undeniable 'truth'. He draws on Aristotle's identification of three kinds of argument: forensic, epideictic and deliberative, representing respectively arguments of fact, judgement or policy (Hillocks, 2010, p. 25) and suggests that it is the forensic form of argumentation that is most highly valued in the academy. Analytical expositions which are geared towards curriculum learning goals have been distinguished by Australian researchers (Humphrey 1996; Martin 1985) as most closely related to the forensic type of argumentation, seeking to persuade audiences that a particular position or point of view is valid and well-reasoned, rather than 'felt' or 'morally obliged'. Here, appeals to logos are of crucial importance, as writers make "a *claim*, based on evidence of some sort, with a *warrant* that explains how the evidence supports the claim, *backing* supporting the warrants, *qualifications and rebuttals* of counterarguments that refute competing claims" (Hillocks, 2010, p. 26). In the academic domain, the genre of Analytical Exposition has become synonymous with the 'essay', where arguments are presented as logical, objective claims, supported by evidence or warrants that typically draw on specialised knowledge, which in turn can be manifest in explanation sequences or other embedded factual genres. Although they vary according to the subject in which they are produced, Expositions have features in common such as an increasing trend towards abstraction and grammatical metaphor as students move into senior years of study (Christie & Derewianka, 2008).

In the US, the importance of this form of argument is underscored in the Common Core State Standards in the NGA Centre (2010b) under the heading "The Special Place for Argument in the Standards". The presumption underpinning this 'special place' is that analytical or forensic forms of Argument "promote clear and critical thinking; that it provides training in the rational deliberation that is essential for a democratic citizenry; and that it imparts to students a form of cultural capital that facilitates their upwards academic and socioeconomic mobility" (De Stigter, 2015, p. 13). Analytical expositions are considered academe's dominant form (De Stigter, 2015, p. 11), distinguished from more passionate forms of "claim and counter claim" by their reasoned analytic processes (Andrews, 2010, p. 10).

This kind of formal argument as "a line of reason that attempts to prove by logic" (Kinneavy, 1993, p. 305), privileges appeals to logos. While the textual lens (introduced in our last chapter) brings out matters of composition, an Ideational lens highlights meanings to do with reasoning. Table 6.1 presents an Ideational lens on persuasion. It parallels the one for narrative, with probe questions oriented to questions of argument as one form of persuasion.

Because our goal is to show how a functional grammatics serves in argument, we link each probe question to relevant rhetorical terms like Thesis, Warrant and

TABLE 6.1 Probe questions related to an Ideational lens on craft of persuasion

Ideational lens – Building a plausible and valid account of an issue	*Overarching Question*: How does the text create a plausible and valid account of an issue? *Thesis*: What is the issue or thesis? How is it established (e.g. through a real-life scenario, rhetorical question, a claim or an abstraction)? *Warrant*: Is the issue based on an appeal to emotion (pathos), morality (ethos) or rational argument (logos)? *Logic*: Does the rhetor expand on points made in topic sentences through reformulation, explanation or examples? How effective are logical links between clauses and between verbiage and image? *Evidence*: What kinds of evidence are used to support the author's position (e.g. real-life examples, research statistics, traditional authorities, common-sense or theories)? How persuasive is the evidence in support of the position? *Citation of authorities*: How are views of authorities cited (e.g. quoted or reported)? Are they credible sources for the purposes of the issue? Are contested claims rebutted? How? How effective is citation? *Overall import*: Is there a call for action? If so, in what way is this done? Is there a rational summary of the argument? If so, is this done through emphatic statements, telling quotations, general, abstract or technical language?

Evidence. We return to the probe questions as we explore development of students in composing written expositions.

Of course, within the English/Language Arts curriculum, forms of written argument are also valued which deliberately design appeals to ethos and pathos, in order to persuade audiences to act on an issue by stirring people's emotions, amongst other strategies. Hortatory Expositions relate to Aristotle's notion of epideictic forms of argumentation. These are used extensively beyond schooling to get things done in the community. Analytical expositions also draw on hortatory resources, as they combine their appeal to logic with various appeals to ethos and pathos, much as we saw Prime Minister Rudd doing in his Apology speech. The attempt to persuade an audience to believe or act in a certain way depends on interactive resources such as MOOD, PERSON and MODALITY. Within the domain of evaluation, writers make choices for APPRAISAL and either intensify or down-tone claims through GRADUATION. Many of these terms will be familiar from our analyses of the speeches of Severn Suzuki and Kevin Rudd. We explore their relevance to teaching of written argument in sections of this chapter to follow. It will be clear that there is an overlap between the semantic orientation of the metafunctions and the application of each one to study of narrative and persuasion. While an Ideational orientation construes 'content' – the world of imaginative experience or rhetorical reasoning – an Interpersonal orientation engages an audience with these – creating intersubjective rapport with or judgement of a character in narrative or development of a stance on an issue in argument. The textual lens introduced in Chapter 5 adopts an aesthetic orientation to the text as composition paying attention to the unfolding text and its patterning and to features like signposting or salience. The same orientations to meaning have been explored in multimodal discourse as we have argued and hopefully demonstrated.

Table 6.2 presents Probe questions for the Interpersonal lens on argument that we developed to assist the teaching of argument in primary and secondary English.

Taken together, the three lenses highlight the nature of achievement (and difficulty) in relation to the craft of persuasion, particularly in the context of argument. The metafunctional lenses bring out the distinctive orientations to content (Ideational), stance (Interpersonal) or composition (Textual). It is our belief that teachers need tools to support their evaluations of students' written arguments (and other texts). Certainly, the teachers involved in The Grammatics Project used the lenses to highlight goals in teaching of genres such as Exposition and Discussion, sharing this metalanguage with students in joint reflections on written texts. Chapter 7 will explore practical matters of pedagogy in primary and secondary English/Language Arts teaching in greater details.

Some might wonder at our focus on Exposition in a field that is characterized by such diverse and changing forms of rhetoric. Expository Essays are used to

TABLE 6.2 Probe questions related to an Interpersonal lens on craft of persuasion

Interpersonal lens – Positioning audiences to understand and adopt a particular stance	*Overarching Question*: How does the text attempt to persuade its audience to believe or act in a particular way? *Stance*: What position does the rhetor take on the issue? Is there a primary appeal – logical, emotional or ethical? Consider MOOD choices – use of Declaratives, Interrogatives, Imperatives and how they contribute to the generation of stance? How definitive or tentative is the stance? Consider Modal verbs, adverbs and nouns. *Evaluation*: What kinds of ATTITUDE are expressed? (Consider AFFECT, JUDGEMENT and APPRECIATION). How directly or indirectly does the rhetor express attitude? Consider Invoked and Inscribed Appraisal choices. If there are images, do they evoke AFFECT, JUDGEMENT and APPRECIATION? *Audience Address*: Does the rhetor use Person in distinctive ways to align the audience? e.g. Is there a shift from personal (I) to inclusive pronouns (we)? Does the author use Second person (you) to address the audience and if so, to what effect? *Graduation*: Does the rhetor amplify evaluation in some places? Why? What about hedges or 'down-toners'? When and why are these used? If the text is multimodal, are there images that intensify a stance or tone it down? *Citation:* Are the views of others, including authorities, quoted or reported to support a claim? At what points of the text? In what role (e.g. as locals affected by an issue, as celebrity endorsers, as experts with authority, as officials, others)? *Interplay*: What do you notice about images in relation to verbiage? Do they confirm, contradict or augment meanings made in verbiage? How?

assess (and indeed to build) learning across a range of subjects. They are often seen as "symbolic of students' success with language at school" (Schleppegrell, 2004, p. 88). For this reason, it is crucial that educators have adequate analytical tools for identifying, describing and explaining the 'semiotically-charged' resources that characterize this valued form of persuasion so they can use these to diagnose and support development across the years. But, as we noted in earlier chapters, it has become clear that many teachers entering the profession are anxious about their ability to teach the grammar of persuasion along with other genres of schooling (Cajkler & Hislam, 2002; Harper & Rennie, 2009; Louden *et al.*, 2005; Sangster *et al.*, 2012). Thinking grammatically about the persuasive practices of writers in The Grammatics Project, we were guided by questions such as: 'What are the most semiotically charged features operating at the interface between rhetoric and grammatics? How do we select from grammatical systems across the metafunctions, across the strata and across the modes to achieve both a first and second order understanding (analysis and interpretation) of persuasive texts?' It is our view that a grammatics apposite to study of the persuasive texts of the twenty-first century needs to be able to answer questions such as these, alongside more specific questions such as: How do rhetors create plausible and valid accounts of issues for readers (or viewers)? Why are we outraged, moved to action, or to question our own beliefs at a particular point in an argument? How does the citing of other authorities alter our beliefs, if at all? How does the amplification of the initial thesis statement in a forceful conclusion leave the reader, emotionally, logically or ethically? How does an image speak to, or against the wording of the text? Our metafunctional lenses gave us some purchase on these questions and a way of making (different kinds of) sense of what persuasion offers and asks of students in English.

Written expositions in schooling: a developmental perspective

We address the questions by simultaneously tracking the development in written expositions of a number of students across the years of schooling. These texts come from the same research project from which the narrative texts in earlier chapters were drawn. As in our narrative chapters, we apply a first and second order analysis to these persuasive texts, identifying their writers' control of generic structure and of various metafunctional resources. We firstly explore Analytical Expositions written by two students in the primary school, one in Middle Primary (Zoe) and one in Upper Primary (Ollie). Our focus in this first part of the chapter will be more sharply on Ollie's texts, using Zoe's largely as a point of comparison. We then examine an Exposition written by a Year 9 student, examining the increased sophistication in her harnessing of experiential, interpersonal and textual resources as she marshals her arguments. Finally, we explore analogous visual resources used by a composer of a multimodal form of Exposition. Our approach firstly is to note distinctive features in each student's text, donning metafunctional lenses to explore general features in their work. Secondly, we look more closely at grammatical choices that contribute to these features. Through this comparative examination, we demonstrate how a grammatics attuned not only to texts, but to the development of resources of argumentation over time can enable teachers to support their students' rhetorical work more effectively. We start by exploring the generic structure of the two primary students' texts.

Written analytical expositions in the primary school: a genre and metafunctional focus

As we saw in Chapter 5, students (in Western cultures at least) learn, more or less explicitly, how to structure reasoned, logical arguments by frontloading a thesis or position statement in some form, supporting this with evidence in subsequent paragraphs, connecting each piece of evidence with others and re-formulating the thesis in a conclusion. Expository essays in this more 'forensic' form have become the most common mode throughout schooling and college writing instruction (De Stigter, 2015, p. 12), seeking to persuade audiences that a particular position or point of view is valid and well-reasoned, rather than 'felt' or 'morally obliged'.

In the Exposition below we see embryonic evidence of this structure. Zoe, a Year 4 (middle primary school) student, was responding in a timed piece of writing to the prompt 'Are video games a good or bad thing?' The five simple paragraphs of Zoe's text follow this prototypical structure of Position or Thesis Statement ^Argument 1^Argument 2^Argument 3^ Position Reinforcement (where the symbol '^' refers to 'followed by'). We italicize the first words in each paragraph in order to draw attention to the signposting strategy Zoe adopts:

I firmly believe that playing computer games is bad for you. Computer games don't help you. Playing computer games aren't (sic) good for you.

Firstly, playing computer games can hurt your eyes. The bright lights can affect your body. People shouldn't be wearing glasses because of playing too much computer games.

Moreover, playing computer games kills your time. People should spend their time learning and playing sport. Playing computer games will affect your learning and communicating skills.

Last but not least, playing computer games makes you forget about everything. Children forget about learning and will always want to play computer games. Playing computer games won't make you better, but worse.

In conclusion, I personally believe that shops should stop selling computer games. I hope that one day people will stop playing computer games and do more sport.

TEXT 6.1 Zoe's Analytical Exposition on the value of computer games

As an apprentice rhetor, Zoe has been supported by her teacher into structuring her argument in this prototypical format, frontloading her position statement and presenting her arguments as claims supported by evidence that draw on common knowledge. Her text is relatively short and within each paragraph, two or three short sentences elaborate on the 'topic sentence' (what we call 'textual Theme') that opens each paragraph. The three sentences of her opening position statement repeat each other without developing the key contention. Signposting is rudimentary and Connectives such as 'firstly', 'moreover' and 'last but not least' suggest an organization based on simple temporal logic and order. Such highly visible manifestations of top-level structure are characteristic of the persuasive writing of younger students as they are apprenticed into the logic of Western forms of argumentation (Thomas & To, 2016). However, while an important component of persuasive meaning, by themselves such textual strategies do not contribute to the 'engaging stance' prized in assessment; their overuse without accompanying interpersonal strategies, can leave teachers "bored witless" (Love & Sandiford, 2016).

In terms of our lenses on meaning, Zoe has produced a coherent written Exposition with visible but routine signposting through Text Connectives at the beginning of each paragraph. Ideationally, the text makes simple claims backed by common sense warrants and minimal logical expansion of her ideas. Interpersonally, the stance is personal (first Person) and directed to a general reader (second Person 'you'). She makes statements that are either categorical or marked by high Modality. It is strong on coherence but weak on nuance, typical of early work by a Year 4 student on the genre of analytical Exposition (Humphrey, Droga & Feez, 2012).

As students move further up the years of subject English, they are sometimes taught how to harness a range of appeals, while maintaining the prototypical structure of arguments. We see this increased range of appeals in the Exposition of Ollie, an Upper Primary school student, also responding in a timed piece of writing to the prompt 'Are video games a good or bad thing?' Ollie's Expository text is reproduced below, with the italicised headings signalling the generic staging as comprised of the prototypical introductory 'Position' or 'Thesis' stage, three distinctive Arguments and a concluding Reinforcement of the position.

Position or Thesis (and background or context)
Lying in bed having a brilliant time. Relaxing in bed playing your favourite video game. Not disturbing anyone in your house. Shouldn't we all get to have a good day like that?

Argument 1
Firstly, video games can help with school work. Video game designers have stated that playing some games can help you with school work. Some video games have strategies which can help improve your brain. Also, there are video games made to help you with school work. You can learn while playing an amazingly fun video game. Don't you want your kids to learn while having fun?

> *Argument 2*
> *In addition to this,* a lot of the video games such as the DS are super lightweight and easy to carry around. Don't you hate when your kids are screaming "Are we there yet?" If they were enjoying a game you would never need to hear it. Even in trains, in long lines and at your mum's house, your kids would annoy you. Don't you want peace and quiet?
>
> *Argument 3*
> *To continue,* your kids would never be bored. When you are not out doing anything, video games are a spectacular pastime for kids. Also video games can bring your family together with some games. Sure, you can play a board game. But do you want to clean up that annoying mess?
>
> *Reinforcement of the position*
> *In conclusion,* don't you want a break from nagging kids, screaming teenagers and crying babies? Well why not get them a video game to stop the noise? Experts suggested tired parents are bad parents. Do you want to be a bad parent?

TEXT 6.2 Ollie's Analytical Exposition on the value of computer games.

From a genre perspective, the five-paragraph structure of Ollie's thesis is almost identical to Zoe's, even though they assume different stances on the value of video games. From a textual perspective, we can likewise identify Ollie's explicit signposting of the logic of his argument, most visible in his use of Text Connectives at the beginning of each of his paragraphs (in italics in the above text). Connectives such as 'firstly', 'in addition', 'to continue' and 'in conclusion' suggest an organization that, like Zoe's, is based on logic and order, at least in the mind of the writer. Ollie's text as a whole is longer than Zoe's and in each paragraph, more work is done to elaborate on the 'topic sentence' or 'textual Theme' which opens each of his paragraphs and which connects back to the contention of Macro-Theme of his opening paragraph.

The most striking difference in their opening theses is that Ollie's position is carried, not in a bald claim, but through the depiction of a vivid scenario, followed by a rhetorical question. As will be explained further in Chapter 7, this deliberately eye-catching way of opening a persuasive text has been scaffolded by his teacher as a 'narrative hook'. Embedding of a narrative-like genre within a persuasive text is an effective rhetorical strategy and signals a developmental progression from Zoe's text. As we shall see below, Ollie has been able to make a further series of interpersonal choices at word, sentence and whole text level to engage his readers intersubjectively, while also signposting the unfolding logic of his argument. One of these interpersonal choices at the level of the sentence is his use of rhetorical questions. Interestingly, his stance is direct (like Zoe's) but addressed to the 'mother' of children who want to play video games and comes across as somewhat 'arch' from someone so young.

From an Ideational perspective, the topic sentences that start each of Ollie's three subsequent paragraphs contain a claim followed by evidence in the form of everyday experience, concluded by a rhetorical question addressed to the mother that appears to seal the argument. This rhetorical pattern is maintained in Ollie's concluding paragraph. Here, rather than synthesising each of his three claims (perhaps as a more mature rhetor would), he summarises the one most salient to his presumed audience (impatient mothers), drawing on the resources of a long nominal group (italicised) within his concluding rhetorical question: "In conclusion, don't you want *a break from nagging kids, screaming teenagers and crying babies*?" Through this repeated paragraph structure, each with a strongly interpersonal orientation, Ollie engages his readers' emotions while rehearsing a text structure that is essentially the same as Zoe's.

Looking at Ollie's and Zoe's texts from both a genre and metafunctional perspective allows us to identify Ollie's relatively sophisticated rhetorical choices. But it is important to understand 'how the grammar does this' and this is a key affordance of functional grammatics. It enables us to be precise about the resources that produce an impression of growing sophistication in writing and pinpoint areas for growth in next steps in writing. We now look at these resources in greater detail, focussing chiefly on Ollie's text but drawing for comparative purposes on Zoe's.

Written expositions in the primary school: a closer look at Ideational meaning

We identified above that Ollie establishes his thesis, not through a bald claim, but rather through a scenario followed by a rhetorical question, and that this forms the launching point for his subsequent paragraphs. This opening scenario is realized in a sequence of non-finite clauses: "Lying in bed having a brilliant time. Relaxing in bed, playing your favourite video game. Not disturbing anyone in your house." Here, the repeated use of the non-finite form of a material process (verb) forms a tricolon of the sort we saw more experienced rhetors use in Chapter 5. Not only is Ollie able to exploit such parallel structures as part of his persuasive toolkit, but he works the repeated non-finite clauses to carry circumstantial meaning, in this case meaning about manner and place. Recall from Chapters 2 and 3 that Circumstances locate narrative processes in time, place and manner, amongst others and that these meanings contextualize experience. The immediacy of Ollie's opening scenario is further carried in his choice of concrete Participants (nominal groups such as 'bed', 'favourite video game', 'your house') and Material Processes (verbal groups such as 'lying', 'relaxing' and 'not disturbing'). Together such grammatical choices construe a world of proximal experience, where events and those responsible for them are close to the daily life-world of the writer and his presumed readers. They create an opening 'narrative' sequence that engages readers in the young writer's life and hooks them into the persuasive issue through his rhetorical question, much as we saw in Chapter 5, with Severn Suzuki's speech.

It is in this rhetorical question that the thesis of the exposition is carried and the remainder of the text offers warrants in support of the implicit claim that video games provide 'good days' for both parents and children alike. Following his opening paragraph, Ollie elaborates on this thesis in three separate Argument paragraphs. As we would anticipate from a young rhetor, many of the warrants on which his claims are built also derive largely from Ollie's immediate personal experience. This is a world of familiar things, realized in concrete Participants such as 'your kids', 'trains', 'board games' and situated in familiar circumstances (as projected of course by Ollie). The experiential world is construed grammatically in congruent representations of Participants and Processes, as illustrated below with reference to one clause:

Participant: Actor	*Process: Material*	*Participant: Goal*
You	can play	a board game

Many of Ollie's clauses take a similar form, where the Actor is followed by a Material Process and then a Goal. However, he demonstrates some capacity to shuttle between concrete and more general Participants as his arguments progress. In his first argument paragraph for example, generalised Participants such as 'school work' and 'video game designers' construe things at one remove from the highly specific ones of his opening scenario:

> Firstly, *video games* can help with *school work*. *Video game designers* have stated that playing some games can help you with school work.

As he moves from the opening narrative hook of his first paragraph into his first claim, we also see a move towards embryonic forms of abstraction. In the first sentence above for example, Ollie has re-packaged the highly personalised nominal group, 'your favourite video game' from his opening paragraph, into the more general 'video games'. Then he re-packages this as 'video game designers', accumulating meaning by choosing a Participant that could be more congruently expressed as 'people who design video games'. Later in the text, he compacts the process into a nominalized clause – 'playing some games'. Table 6.3 shows something of this move in his line of reasoning and the way that Participants in each clause grow in abstraction.

TABLE 6.3 Ollie's Transitivity choices demonstrating an embryonic shift towards abstraction

Video games	*can help with school work*
Video game designers	*have stated that*
[[playing some games]]	*can help you with school work*
Participant	Process and other elements in Transitivity

This grammatical transformation of a verbal into a nominal form represents a shift from a world of proximal experience towards generalised experience. It also represents a capacity to accumulate and compact meaning that has been identified as crucial to the development of written argumentation (Christie & Derewianka, 2008, p. 25). As we shall see later in this chapter, resources such as nominalization are exploited by more mature writers to distil information and organize the argument. While not yet in control of sophisticated or consistent forms abstraction, Ollie demonstrates some of the precursors towards this capacity, and his teachers' ability to recognize and harness this capacity will be crucial to his development as a writer and persuader.

Ollie's choice of different Process types function to achieve these various appeals and establish the warrant or evidence base. In making an appeal to logic in his first Argument paragraph, for example, Ollie selects a Verbal Process (in italics) as he draws on the views of authoritative others as evidence to support his own position. The two clauses are separated by a double vertical line:

> Video game designers *have stated* || that playing some games can help you with school work.

This evidence is 'reported' in a form of pseudo-scientific discourse typical of an apprentice rhetor, not yet in a position to synthesize specific research findings, but signals a further step in Ollie's move towards generalizing beyond his own immediate experience. Note that this move depends on Ollie's ability to exploit the resource of Projection (Halliday & Matthiessen, 2004, pp. 448–452). This capacity to report the views of external authorities in support of a contention was not evident in Zoe's written exposition. Ollie's second and third Argument paragraphs return to a more immediate world of 'being' in Relational Processes (e.g. 'would never *be* bored') and 'action' in Material Processes (e.g. '*doing* anything'). But, in his concluding paragraph, Ollie again choses a Verbal Process to report the views of external authorities to support his (rather overstated) claims:

> Experts suggested || tired parents are bad parents.

In selecting the verb 'suggest' to report evidence that may be less categorical than that construed in his earlier choice of 'stated', Ollie displays a capacity to discriminate between different forms of reporting verbs and signals a move towards the kind of detachment that is valued in argumentative reasoning. As we shall see when we examine an exposition written in the later years of schooling, explicit awareness of the role of saying verbs is crucial to persuasive craft, particularly as students make the leap into using 'quoted' alongside 'reported' warrants.

Projection and Expansion are the resources that enable us to develop and link ideas in clause complexes. As a writer, still early in her rhetorical apprenticeship, Zoe uses many single clause sentences (often called simple sentences) and packs considerably less information into each of these than does Ollie. The sentence below, with the verbal group in italics, is typical.

Computer games *don't help* you.

When Zoe does combine more than one clause in a sentence, this is typically in the form of a compound sentence, where clauses are joined through simple conjunctions such as 'and', underlined in the example below and verbal groups in italics.

Children *forget* about learning <u>and</u> *will* always *want to play* computer games.

The logic of addition represents the clause combining relationship of **Extension**, the easiest form of logic for young writers to grapple with (Christie, 2005, 2010). Clausal relationships of extension also include those of contrast (using for example the conjunction 'but') or simple sequence (using for example the conjunction 'then'), both of which can be over-used (as in students' use of 'and then') as a default means of connecting their ideas.

Ollie's analytical exposition also includes simple sentences (e.g. "Firstly, video games can help with school work"). However, as we saw above, in some of his simple sentences, meaning is compressed into meaty nominal groups or prepositional phrases which construe Participants and Circumstances respectively. This indicates that use of a single-clause sentence in itself doesn't necessarily indicate simplistic thought. In the simple, one clause sentence below for example ("In addition to this, a lot of video games such as the DS *are* super lightweight and easy to carry around"), a great deal of technical meaning is concentrated in both Participant roles.

	Participant	*Process*	*Participant*
In addition to this	a lot of video games such as the DS	are	super lightweight and easy [[to carry around]]
Text Connective	Nominal group	Verbal group	Nominal group

While still drawing on elements of everyday language, Ollie's capacity to compress meaning into nominal groups in ways that Zoe has not yet mastered represents a move towards the more specialised forms of reasoning that are valued in schooling. However, his crafting of a more reflective mode of writing is further indicated in his use of complex sentences and in particular his use of the logic of **Enhancement** (Halliday & Matthiessen, 2004, pp. 376–382). In keeping with his orientation to circumstantiation, his clause complexes expand meanings to do with time, place, manner and condition. The marked frontloading of the dependent clause as the point of departure in the following sentence is the result of deliberate writerly choice:

Dependent clause (Enhancing and thematic)	*Independent clause*
When you are not out doing anything	*video games are a spectacular pastime for kids*

Ollie's capacity to link clauses in a relationship of Enhancement echoes significant research conducted over several decades into children's writing development (e.g. Perera, 1984; Christie & Derewianka, 2008; French, 2012; Klein & Unsworth, 2014). where increasing ability to integrate complex material into the sentence is identified as a key marker of writing success. It is evident too in his choice of conjunctions. If we focus on causal relationships for example, Zoe tends to capture these through explicit use of the Conjunction 'because', as in the example below.

> People shouldn't be wearing glasses *because* of playing too much computer games.

Ollie is able to draw on more nuanced signals of logical relationships, as in the clause complex below, where Causal Conjunctions (including the implied 'then') are indicated in italics:

> *If* they were enjoying a game *(then)* you would never need to hear it.

Ollie's capacity to integrate more complex logical relationships between the clauses of his sentence marks his writing as more developed than Zoe's. Of course, there is more to learn about logical meaning. We shall see later in this chapter how Jenny, a Year 9 student, connects her propositions in more metaphorical ways, using verbs, adverbs and adjectives to carry cause more implicitly within the clause. Control of such implicit use of logical metaphor – sometimes referred to as "cause in the clause" (Martin & Rose, 2007) is a mark of further writing development (Christie & Derewianka, 2008).

Written expositions in the primary school: an interpersonal focus

Whereas the Ideational lenses allowed us to see more clearly how rhetors used experiential resources to build a plausible account of an issue and logical resources to convincingly connect the propositions about that account, our Interpersonal lenses allow us to see how the text engages readers persuasively so they adopt the stance invited by the writer. Our overarching question here is 'How does the text attempt to persuade its audience to believe or act in a particular way?' We again focus on Ollie, observing how he builds appeals to ethos and pathos, through more or less conscious choices from clause level systems such as MOOD and MODALITY, PERSON and PROJECTION and discourse semantic systems such as APPRAISAL.

The most striking interpersonal resource we notice is Ollie's use of rhetorical questions. While Zoe's MOOD choices are all Declarative, Ollie concludes each paragraph with an Interrogative (e.g. "Shouldn't we all get to have a good day like that?"), which explicitly addresses the reader. The reader's degree of freedom to answer questions such as these in the negative is considerably reduced because of the prior highly selective depiction of a scenario. Ollie had been introduced by his teacher to rhetorical questions as a persuasive strategy, and, as is common with young learners, tends to over-use a newly learnt skill as part of his learning strategy. As we shall see later, rhetorical questions can be used in more nuanced ways by mature writers.

Alongside these MOOD choices, we further note that Ollie and Zoe use different selections of MODALITY to vary the degree of obligation on their readers or the degree of probability of an outcome. Overall, Zoe chooses forms of modality that focus on the implied reader's obligation ("People *should* spend their time …"), while Ollie's modality choices further include probability and ability ("You *can* learn …", "Your kids *would* annoy you"). His greater range of modal verbs allows Ollie to assume an interpersonally more nuanced stance than the more didactic stance of Zoe's.

Accompanying these clause level choices, APPRAISAL resources operate in a more diffused way across persuasive texts. We saw above how the immediacy of the scenarios which preceded Ollie's questions was realized through grammatical resources in TRANSITIVITY such as Processes, Participants and Circumstances. Overlain on such selections is an evaluative component. This can be identified most saliently in Ollie's choice of Epithets (e.g. '*brilliant* time', 'a *spectacular* pastime for kids') often intensified with Comment Adjuncts (e.g. '*amazingly fun* video game' and '*super lightweight*'), heightened through accumulation of examples (e.g. 'that annoying mess, nagging kids, screaming teenagers and crying babies'). Each of these lexical items carries significant and explicit evaluative impact and position to reader in interpersonally engaging ways. Typical of a younger rhetor, Zoe's selection of evaluative lexical choices is more limited (e.g. 'I *firmly* believe' and '*kills* your time').

The system of APPRAISAL, introduced in Chapter 3 offers educators a powerful means of tracking the persuasive work of such word choices as they pattern across texts. Within the larger system, the resources of ATTITUDE are used to express emotional reaction (Affect), to evaluate the worth and quality of things and processes (Appreciation) and to judge the behaviour of others (Judgement). In very broad terms, resources from these sub-systems of Appraisal can be seen as roughly relating to appeals to Pathos (Affect), Logos (Appreciation) and Ethos (Judgement). Recall from Chapter 3 that explicit attitudinal wordings are inherently gradable (they can be intensified and compared); they are biased in their LOADING, being primarily either positive or negative; and can realize attitude explicitly in lexis (INSCRIBED ATTITUDE) or implicitly (INVOKED ATTITUDE), especially as realizations 'sprawl' across phases of a text.

Applying these aspects of our interpersonal toolkit to Ollie's text, it is clear that the examples above from his text mostly explicitly inscribe attitude. We can further note that this relates mostly to Affect, which is highly negatively loaded when evaluating experience without video games ('nagging, screaming, crying') and highly positively loaded when evaluating experience with video games ('amazingly fun'). Typical of writers of his stage of development, Ollie bases his opinions on personal preferences and predispositions, privileging resources from Affect in expressing these. With the move to adolescence, there is an expectation that a writer's evaluations will display more awareness of the social values of the community, drawing on a wider range of attitudinal resources from the sub-systems of Judgement and Appreciation to evaluate, critique and challenge in terms of more 'institutionalised' criteria (Christie & Derewianka, 2008, p. 16). Ollie shows some capacity to make these less immediately personal appraisals, as he draws on highly graduated and explicitly inscribed resources of Appreciation to evaluate artefacts such as 'video games' ('super light-weight and easy to carry around'); and on highly graduated inscribed resources of Judgement to praise ('not disturbing anyone') or critique ('bad parent') people's behaviour. Ollie's MOOD and APPRAISAL choices work together across his text to persuade his readers about his stance on video games. His (over)use of rhetorical questions directly address parents as the imagined readers, create a strong inter-subjectivity with them, while his lexical choices create a highly charged appeal to emotions, supported by a more measured appeal to ethos. Through these means, the reader as putative parent is explicitly aligned with the emotional stance of a child video game player.

While not yet able to draw more fully on Appreciation and Judgement resources, nor pattern the modulation of the force, polarity or inscription of his Appraisal resources, Ollie demonstrates control of interpersonal resources that work to position his readers through a strong appeal to emotion. His teachers' knowledge of Appraisal and their capacity to adapt the systems for use by younger learners, give Ollie further access to systems for evaluating the worth and quality of things and processes (through appeals to logic) and for judging behaviour of others (through appeals to ethos), as well as for refining his expression of emotional reaction through more nuanced appeals to pathos.

We saw earlier how Ollie drew on a range of 'saying verbs' to cite the views of external authorities as he builds an evidence base for his arguments. His repertoire for reporting the views of others suggests a broadening of his perspective beyond his immediate world and a capacity to distinguish the argumentative force of a range of positions, as is most evident in his selection of the more emphatic saying verb 'states' at one point of his argument for example and the more modulated 'suggests' at another. As we saw earlier, these are choices from the sub-system of Reporting verbs, where one clause projects the sayings contained in the projected clause. Another sub-system of saying verbs is that of Quoting, where the projected clause is a direct quotation. Direct quoting of researched information requires research skills that Ollie may not yet have mastered. Interestingly, we note that Zoe does not use any form of citation, drawing on neither Reporting nor Quoting verbs.

The PROJECTION, APPRAISAL, MODALITY AND MOOD choices identified above work in conjunction with other grammatical resources to variously align Zoe's and Ollie's readers with their stances.

One final set of interpersonal choices we look at here are from the system of PERSON. In both Zoe's and Ollie's texts, the second Person pronoun 'you' is used to address the readership directly, much as this pronoun was used in the Zoos poster (Figure 5.1) seeking to persuade readers to help reduce the illegal mining of coltan in gorilla habitats. In Zoe's case, the 'you' refers consistently to an implied readership comprised of her peers. Ollie on the other hand seeks to address parents as the implied readership, using the 'you' in a more demanding attempt at solidarity with his maternal readers. Ollie is still learning to harness his choices from various interpersonal systems as he builds a consistent intersubjective stance with his implied audience in this more imaginative act of projection. His referent is not always clear, sometimes relating to the generalized 'one' as in "some games can help *you* with school work"; sometimes referring to the implied reader as in "Don't *you* want your kids to learn while having fun?"; and sometimes referring to a specific young game enthusiast as in "Relaxing in bed playing *your* favourite video game". At times, there is a conflict between the 'you' as putative reader and 'you' as the internalized self, as in "at *your* mum's house". This slippage in the referent associated with personal pronouns is common as young writers juggle their audience awareness with their personal enthusiasm for an issue. Their teachers' awareness of PERSON as an interpersonal system can help considerably in this juggling act.

We have now seen how two young rhetors at different stages of their primary schooling draw on various interpersonal resources to align their implied readers with their argumentative stance. A functional grammatics has allowed us to note how Ollie is able to draw on a wider range of MOOD choices than is Zoe, creating the illusion of negotiating his argumentative propositions with his readership through a series of rhetorical questions which he builds into the structure of his argument. It has allowed us to identify how Ollie's MODALITY choices range across probability and obligation, while Zoe's are more limited to those of obligation. Moving from our first to second order of semiosis has further allowed us to see how Ollie's choices from the APPRAISAL system position his readers through a strong and explicit appeal to emotion, as he makes deliberate appeals to pathos, while Zoe's tend to draw on simple inscribed Appreciation and Judgement resources, as she learns to control her appeals to logos. Typical of writers at this stage of development, the evaluations of both young writers are explicitly inscribed in attitudinal lexis, they tend to be dichotomous in their positive and negative loadings, which are highly graded throughout their texts. While there is no evidence of Zoe's use of Citation resources, Ollie draws on saying verbs to discriminate the argumentative force of various reported authorities. Finally, while noting that both writers use personal pronouns to build intersubjectivity with an implied readership, Ollie's audience is more removed from his personal experience, posing distinctive challenges for him in this imaginative act.

Written analytical expositions in the secondary school

So far in this chapter, we have noted that learning to construct arguments in the primary school involves expanding the learner's semiotic repertoire, or meaning potential (Halliday, 1993). Focussing on two written texts, we have touched on key linguistic indicators of growth in students' capacity to produce written expositions. Recall that in a systemic functional approach to development, students' acts of meaning (their texts in this case) reveal particular kinds of uptake of larger systems of meaning. A key principle here is **Instantiation** – a theory of the relationship between system (resources for meaning) and instance (acts of meaning). This theoretical framework has allowed us to see growth from the point of view of different levels – genre, discourse semantics (text) and lexicogrammar. At the level of genre, we have seen how the wordings selected by student writers are part of, and contribute to, larger patterns of meaning (e.g. a claim followed by evidence). At the level of discourse semantics, we have seen how young rhetors infuse their feelings, judgements and appreciations about aspects of the contentious issue through strategic APPRAISAL choices. At the level of the sentence, we have considered not just control of clause combinations in sentences but message development – a student's growing ability to project and expand messages.

In the Australian curriculum and assessment context (ACARA, 2012), there is an echo of this stratified and metafunctional view of Language that underpins the Australian Curriculum: English (AC:E) which refers to the importance of students learning to describe language as systems of Ideational, Interpersonal and Textual choices, and paying attention to both structure (syntax) and meaning (semantics) at word, sentence and text levels. Such a framework offers educators considerable purchase on different dimensions of development in written expositions, as students across the years of schooling learn how to use the rhetorical tools of the trade to persuade others and to understand how others persuade.

As we have seen in Chapter 5, control of such tools is also fundamental to success in contexts outside of school – in workplaces, social networks, the media and civic life. To be effective in this civic domain, they must learn to marshal not only the appeals to ethos that predominated in Zoe's exposition, and the appeals to pathos that dominated in Ollie's, but also the appeals to logos. In both the civic and academic domains, resources for convincing audiences that a particular position is valid are just as important as those that convince emotionally and ethically.

In the remainder of this chapter we maintain our developmental perspective on written expositions, focussing on those typical of what is valued beyond the years of primary school. Drawing largely on the expository writing of a middle secondary student, Jenny, we will again be guided by the set of questions that structured our exploration of Expositions in the primary school. By the middle years of secondary school, students are expected to be able to marshal logical, objective reasons in support of a contention. The evidence or warrants used in these more sophisticated expositions typically draw on more specialised knowledge bases and can take the form of narrative, explanation or other embedded genres. Jenny's Exposition presented as Text 6.3 below is annotated for its generic structure in order to facilitate our analysis. It seeks to persuade her readership of the potential dangers of mobile phones. Its structure follows that of a well-reasoned written argument as "an artefact or genre characterized by a contested claim, supported by evidence and warrants that adhere to commonly accepted standards of reason" (De Stigter, 2015, p. 13).

Within paragraph two, we have represented in italics aspects of an internal structure and underlined Causal Conjunctions, both of which will be elaborated on further below.

Position or thesis (including Statement of the Issue and Preview of arguments to come)
1. These days many parents are giving their children mobile phones so that they can keep in touch with them and keep them safe. In 2007, a quarter of seven- to 10-year-olds owned a mobile phone, double the numbers from 2001. However, there is evidence that mobile phones themselves can be dangerous. Mobile phones can have a negative impact on children's health and lead to a decrease in the cognitive and communicative skills.

Argument 1
2. The most important danger of mobile phones to children's health concerns the emission of radiation which could lead to cancer (*Point*). Mobile phones transmit high frequency radio and micro waves which can penetrate the body. When this happens, the exposed molecules move around and cause friction and thus, heat. If the radiation is powerful enough, the body tissue will be burned (*Elaboration by way of Explanation*). Recent studies by scientists in Washington show that brain cells are damaged even by tiny doses of radio frequency (*Evidence*), which could lead to memory loss, headaches and possibly cancer (*Link to point*).

Argument 2
3. It is also possible that use of mobile phones could have an effect on children's ability to think and concentrate. While scientists do not fully understand the effects of performing two different types of tasks at the same time, there is evidence that mobile phone use in children was associated with faster and less accurate responses to certain cognitive tasks. Moreover, texting or talking during class or when studying may discourage the focussed and deep thinking necessary for cognitive development.

Argument 3
4. In addition to the effects on cognitive skills, scientists have also raised concerns about the effects of mobile phones on the communication skills of children and teenagers. A new study undertaken by Monash University suggests that many teenagers are losing their spelling skills because of text messaging and over time this has decreased the ability of teenagers to form extensive or coherent sentences. One student recently had her HSC essays rejected because they were all written in the shorthand of text messaging.

Reinforcement of the position
5. Although there is still no conclusive proof that mobile phones are unsafe for children, the evidence above suggests that concerns about the effects on health and cognitive and communicative skills need to be taken seriously.

TEXT 6.3 Jenny's argument against use of mobile phones.

In broad terms, Jenny's text follows the same basic 'Position Statement ^ Arguments ^ Position Reinforcement' structure as Zoe's or Ollie's. It is a clearly signposted argument that manages the textual aspects of composition proficiently. However, this text is much longer, its arguments more elaborated and its generic schema more complex than theirs. Drawing on the concept of phases and embedded genres (Martin & Rose, 2008) allows us to see what Jenny does within each of her paragraphs, signalling as this does her control of an argumentative format that is highly valued in Western cultures. Recall that whereas Zoe's opening paragraph is a bald statement of her position, Ollie's takes the form of a narrative hook. Textually, Jenny's opening paragraph comprises three functionally distinctive phases: it provides background information on the issue (first two sentences), it offers a statement about the issue (third sentence), and it concludes with a preview of arguments to come (fourth sentence). Her three subsequent paragraphs (2–4) provide three distinctive areas of support for her overarching contention, each summarised in the topic sentence that opens the paragraph, and elaborated on in the remainder of each paragraph. In one of her paragraphs (paragraph 2), the argument of her topic sentence about the danger of the emission of radiation is elaborated through the means of an explanation sequence. Here, the three sentences form an embedded Explanation genre, where propositions are related to each other causally ('When this happens …', 'If the radiation is powerful enough …'). Her final paragraph (5) sums up the evidence and reinforces her thesis in a single highly crafted sentence in which considerable meaning is compressed.

The coherence of this overall structure is further supported by the logic that links her propositions within each of her paragraphs. As exemplified in paragraph two, the point or claim of a distinctive argument is contained in an opening topic sentence, is elaborated on and/or exemplified in the remainder of the paragraph and is linked to a prior or subsequent paragraph in a concluding phase. This Point ^ Elaboration ^ Evidence ^ Link structure (sometimes referred to by Australian teachers as the PEEL structure) is a useful heuristic for apprenticing student rhetors into the valued forms of argumentative logic (see Humphrey, 2017 and Weekes, 2014). However, as we shall see below, knowledge of more nuanced grammatical resources for building argumentative logic within and between the clauses of these phases offers teachers and students considerable opportunities for growth in their persuasive writing.

Beyond the issue of genre and phase, we note intuitively that Jenny's is a more formal and detached line of argumentation than is Ollie's, and a more elaborated and reasoned exposition than Zoe's. It follows "a line of reason that attempts to prove by logic" (Kinneavy, 1993, p. 305), rather than predominantly by pathos or ethos. This more elaborated and 'forensic' form of argumentation is, Hillocks (2010, p. 25) suggests, most highly valued in the academy, requiring as it does access to wider bodies of evidence and control of more logical forms of reasoning. It is because of her control of such knowledge and logical forms of reasoning that Jenny's Exposition has earned it a highly graded assessment. Here, she demonstrates control over the key elements of argumentation: "a claim, based on evidence of some sort, with a warrant that explains how the evidence supports the claim, backing supporting the warrants, qualifications and rebuttals of counterarguments that refute competing claims" (Hillocks, 2010, p. 26). As argued in Chapter 5, the logical form of reasoning Jenny demonstrates here is highly valued in schooling (Christie & Derewianka, 2008; National Governors Association Center for Best Practice [NGA Centre], 2010a) and is considered an important foundation on which the further knowledge building of the university sits (Andrews, 2005).

So, what are the key features of the persuasive forms of reasoning that make Jenny's analytical stance so highly valued? How can we identify these rhetorical features grammatically so that, as educators, we can support their development in our students? We now look in more detail at key constellations of linguistic features that demonstrate Jenny's mastery of the reasoning required, focussing particularly on Ideational and Interpersonal metafunctions. These are the meanings most implicated in her deployment of valued analytical forms of reasoning.

Written analytical expositions in the secondary school: an Ideational focus

Exploring those language choices that Jenny uses to build her persuasive world, we focus on how she gives expression to the various entities or Participants in it and the types of Processes they are engaged in. Starting with Participants (realized through nominal groups), we note that Jenny typically uses abstract nouns to describe phenomena in a more conceptual way (e.g. 'danger'), general nouns that refer to groups of people symbolically rather than as individuals (e.g. 'many parents') and technical nouns to describe phenomena (e.g. 'the effects on cognitive skills'). The generality, abstraction and technicality of Jenny's choice of nouns contrasts markedly with the specific, concrete and everyday types of nouns selected by younger rhetors like Ollie, who names most phenomena in his persuasive world through concrete nouns (e.g. 'bed', 'favourite video game'), specifics (e.g. 'your bed') and everyday lexis (e.g. 'house'). Recall that it is through this representation of an immediate and personal world that Ollie seeks to convince his readers through an appeal to pathos. On the other hand, Jenny's capacity to build a larger world of more abstract and general phenomena and marshal technical evidence is crucial to her construction of a more logical form of persuasion.

In this endeavour, her choice of nouns serves in the construction of deeply layered and often technical taxonomies which organize the topics and sub-topics of her arguments. We see an example of this in a key nominal group from the last sentence of the opening paragraph: 'a negative impact on children's health'. Here the pre- and post-modifier classify the phenomenon of 'impact' in ways that lay a foundation for the unfolding of the argument in her subsequent paragraph. In conjunction with the nominal group 'a decrease in the cognitive and communicative skills', Jenny effectively groups the overall topic of 'the effects of mobile phones' into classes (i.e. health, skills) and sub-classes (e.g. cognitive and communication skills) in ways that provide an analytical framework for the remaining arguments to be developed.

A key experiential resource to progress argument is the resource of nominalization. As we saw earlier, this works by turning words that are not normally nouns into nouns, typically creating abstract or technical concepts. Jenny harnesses this resource to build specialised knowledge as evidence within her argument paragraphs. Take the nominal group 'the emission of radiation' in the first sentence of paragraph two. Here, the head noun 'emission' is the nominalized form of something that would more congruently be expressed as 'rays were emitted'. As a key part of the noun group, this nominalization contributes to an even more technical naming of the phenomenon of 'radiation', a phenomenon that is explained in the remainder of the paragraph. Representing such technical phenomena as nouns early in her Exposition, Jenny can further draw upon the resources of the noun to describe and classify them (e.g. 'extensive' radiation), thus packing a great deal of information into the nominal group and providing her with a launching place for further argument building.

These resources work alongside other experiential resources, such as choice of process type, to build ideas and reasoning in persuasive texts. So how is Jenny's choice of Processes different to those of Zoe and Ollie and how do these selections help realize her persuasive intentions? We saw how, through his use of Material Processes, Ollie has built a world in which children play games or annoy parents, paralleled by a world in which game playing is commented on and interpreted. Jenny likewise uses Material Processes at key stages of her exposition, most notably in the background section of her introductory paragraph ('parents *are giving*'). She uses these as a context for her more abstract contentions and in her explanation sequence in her second paragraph ('*transmit* high frequency' and 'the exposed molecules *move around*') as she describes the effects of one phenomenon on another. She also uses Verbal Processes such as 'suggests', much as Ollie does, to report the views of authorities. However, her use of Relational Processes is particularly crucial in her setting up of her Position in her opening paragraph. Here the cause and effect relationships that are crucial to her argument are established through Relational Processes, italicised in the excerpt below:

> However, there *is* evidence that mobile phones themselves *can be* dangerous. Mobile phones *can have* a negative impact on children's health and *lead to* a decrease in the cognitive and communicative skills.

Combining verbs which express cause/effect reasoning (e.g. 'lead to') with nominalization (e.g. 'impact') allows Jenny to expand meanings without creating complexity in the clause. Such expansion of meaning using compressed grammatical structures is highly valued in written forms of persuasion in school English, across the school subjects and in the academy.

What about Jenny's use of logical meaning within the Ideational metafunction? We saw earlier how, at whole text level, Jenny developed her argument logically across her exposition to shape an analytical framework that connected a series of factors, reasons and causes. At paragraph level, we further noted how the point or claim of the topic sentence was elaborated on and/or exemplified and how each paragraph concluded with a link to the subsequent paragraph. In addition to these text and paragraph level structures, we can draw on our stratified model of language to explore how Jenny exploits other grammatical resources that operate between and within clauses to build her argument logogenetically.

Looking firstly at those systems of relationships *between* clauses, we note that Jenny draws on the logical relations of Expansion (including Extension, Elaboration and Enhancement) and Projection (locution and idea) as these operate in clause complexes. Focussing on one section of her exposition, paragraph 2, we have already noted how certain logico-semantic relations work across the phases in a PEEL structure. This second paragraph has been represented below under these phasal headings as a series of clause complexes, with the verbal group in each clause italicised, the notation // signalling clause divisions, and the Conjunctions underlined:

Point
1. The most important danger of mobile phones to children's health *concerns* the emission of radiation // which *could lead* to cancer.

Explanation
2. Mobile phones *transmit* high frequency radio and micro waves // which *can penetrate* the body.
3. When this *happens* //, the exposed molecules *move around* // and *cause* friction and thus, heat.
4. If the radiation *is* powerful enough //, the body tissue *will be burned*.

Evidence
5. Recent studies by scientists in Washington *show* // that brain cells *are damaged* even by tiny doses of radio frequency.

Link to point
6. Which *could lead* to memory loss, headaches and possibly cancer.

We note immediately that considerably more information is packed into the opening sentence above, than in any of Zoe or Ollie's sentences. Starting with the first nominal group ('The most important danger of mobile phones to children's health'), the head noun, 'danger' re-packages the adjectival phrase 'which can be dangerous' from the prior (opening) paragraph into a nominalization. This head noun is expanded by the pre-modifying adjectival group ('the most important') and post-modified by the Qualifier ('of mobile phones to children's health'). Jenny's use of this grammatical metaphor allows her to compress information critical to the development of her argument by presenting contestable processes as uncontested fact. Grammatically, it also frees up the verb ('concerns') to do other work in the sentence, in this case to establish a relationship of identity between the two participants. The combination of nominalization and pre- and post-modification simultaneously compresses the previously referenced information and signals its place in the unfolding logic of the argument.

The second Participant packs in considerable information. It does this through nominalization of the process of emission:

'*the emission* of radiation' (grammatical metaphor in nominal group) =
'radiation *is emitted*' (more congruently expressed in the verbal group 'is emitted')

Through these forms of compression and grammatical transformation, Jenny has been able to package in considerable technical information into one sentence, more so than Ollie or Zoe were able to do in their writing. While compressing information within her clauses (and clause complexes), she has simultaneously linked this information to that expressed more congruently in earlier paragraphs, and laid the foundations of the unfolding argument to come. For example, 'The most important danger' invokes other dangers to be discussed.

Focussing now on her Explanation phase, we note that the clause complexes here act logically to enhance the meanings of her paragraph opening (topic sentence). Jenny links her clauses within these clause complexes through the same logic of Enhancement, connecting these clauses explicitly through Conjunctions of time (when), cause (thus) and condition (if), as the processes in this explanation sequence unfold. Recall that Ollie too drew prominently and explicitly on conjunctions of time, manner and cause to link his clauses as he contextualized his game playing scenarios in an immediate and concrete way. Yet the logic connecting Jenny's clauses is considerably more varied than Ollie's, and the sophistication in her reasoning can be explored in a more nuanced way as we zoom in on logical relations *within* clauses. Her explanation sequence follows on from her opening 'point' of paragraph 2 ("The most important danger of mobile phones to children's health *concerns* the emission of radiation// which *could lead* to cancer") where causal relationships are carried, not visibly in causal conjunctions, but more implicitly through verb groups (e.g. *could lead to*). Likewise, in two subsequent topic sentences, the causal relation is expressed as a noun. We demonstrate this in relation to the opening point for paragraph 4 below, where nominal groups that express cause are underlined and verbal groups are italicised:

In addition to the effects on cognitive skills, scientists *have also raised* concerns about the effects of mobile phones on the communication skills of children and teenagers.

The instantiation of cause in a noun such as 'effects', which is itself part of a complex nominal group, allows Jenny to compress considerable meaning into topic sentences, while progressing her argument. Such a process is grammatically economical, since it requires only one verbal group and therefore one independent clause. Logical relationships such as cause and effect can also be expressed within the clause as verbs, as we see in the bolded verbs of paragraph 2 above ('causes', 'leads to') and phrases ('due to, because of'). This use of verbal and nominal groups to express causal and other logical relationships through grammatical forms other than the more congruent Conjunction is a kind of grammatical metaphor called 'logical metaphor' (Martin & Rose, 2007). This is often referred to as 'cause *in* the clause' or 'buried cause'.

Jenny makes considerably more use of such forms of logical metaphor than do Ollie and Zoe, who draw on grammatical resources congruently to make causal relations visible. Earlier in this chapter, we noted how these younger writers demonstrated varying capacities to package logical relationships within and between their clauses. As the youngest writer, Zoe's arguments are characterized by explicit additive connections between the propositions of her clauses and sentences. Ollie as an upper primary student compressed more meanings into his simple, single clause sentences through use of longer nominal groups and prepositional phrases. In addition, he uses complex sentences in which clauses are linked in a relationship of Enhancement, largely through the logic of time, manner or place. Jenny's Exposition not only draws on a much higher proportion of lexically dense (though grammatically simple) sentences to package multiple ideas, but combines this with forms of logical metaphor to cumulatively build the propositions of her argument through sophisticated logico-semantic connections within and between her clauses.

Written analytical expositions in the secondary school: an interpersonal focus

We have demonstrated how our stratified model of language can help track the lexico-grammatical resources that writers exploit to connect their argumentative propositions in more or less explicit logical relationships at text, paragraph and clause level. As they shape the logic of their arguments, writers are simultaneously making decisions about their relationship with their putative readers, whether this be teachers or a broader audience. Here, they draw on Interpersonal resources which account in various ways for the relative power of the writer in relation to the audience; and the degree of solidarity or the extent to which the writer or can assume that their readership is 'onside'.

Drawing on our Interpersonal toolkit, we have already seen how Ollie exploits a wider range of MOOD choices than does Zoe, creating the illusion of negotiating his proposal with his implied readers through a series of rhetorical questions. While his choices from the APPRAISAL system position his readers through a strong and explicit appeal to emotion, Zoe's tend to draw on Inscribed Appreciation and Judgement resources in a simpler appeal to logos and ethos. The evaluations of both young writers are explicitly inscribed in attitudinal lexis, and are dichotomous in their positive and negative loadings both of which are highly graduated throughout. Both writers strategically use personal pronouns to build intersubjectivity with an implied readership and Ollie uses some Projection choices to enlist the support of various reported authorities.

Finding the right kind of evaluative stance with the reader can be challenging for student writers as they present their own opinions and evaluations with authority. We can see how, in order to persuade her putative 'expert' audience (i.e. her teacher), Jenny has adopted an 'expert' stance herself as she objectifies various opinions, claims and evaluations through which her arguments are built. Evaluative vocabulary, it will be recalled, refers to the sets of resources which express positive and negative attitudes in terms of feelings, judgements and opinions (Martin & White, 2005, p. 53). The pressure to establish objective and impersonal relationships in Expositions can result in a preference for evaluating things rather than people. In Jenny's text, explicit evaluation is not made of children's behaviour in using mobile phones but of phenomena such as consequences of behaviour (e.g. a <u>negative</u> impact; if the radiation is <u>powerful</u> enough). From a rhetorical perspective, such an evaluative stance contributes to appeals to 'logos'. A process of accumulation occurs in two sentences from Jenny's opening paragraph, reproduced again below:

> However, there is evidence that *mobile phones themselves can be dangerous*. Mobile phones can have *a negative impact* on children's health and lead to a decrease in the cognitive and communicative skills.

Jenny's nominalization 'the negative impact' in the second sentence above is a grammatical transformation of the prior clause 'mobile phones can be dangerous'. This is a powerful strategy for positioning Jenny's audience to agree with her opinion because it presents the negative evaluation as already agreed upon or shared. Her use of adjective 'negative' above to describe impact is an example of explicit evaluative vocabulary, where attitude is inscribed within the wordings. In addition to such explicit evaluations, implicit evaluative expressions, such as allusion, evocative vocabulary and metaphor realize a powerful rhetorical role. Allusion to shared cultural values is particularly evocative as the associated attitudes are typically deeply felt and complex. For example, in referring to the student who had her exam essays rejected because they were written in the shorthand of text messaging, Jenny is drawing on cultural understandings about the importance of examinations.

Evaluation can also be invoked or amplified through a range of grammatical resources referred to as GRADUATION. Resources for grading meanings used by Jenny include grading adverbials (e.g. 'do not *fully* understand'), graded core vocabulary (e.g. '*negative* impact') and indirect graders such as listing (e.g. 'memory loss, headaches and possibly cancer'). We saw how Ollie tends to use direct forms of grading to amplify his emotive vocabulary as his argument progresses such that his emotional appeal is most highly graduated in his conclusion. Jenny draws on more implicit forms of GRADUATION throughout as she evaluates the evidence in support of her arguments, demonstrating her capacity to present an opinion while maintaining the objective tenor that is valued in more mature expositions.

Resources for expanding and contracting argumentative positions

As a sub-set of interpersonal resources, we now focus on those rhetorical resources for expanding and contracting argumentative positions. Since their goal is to change the minds or behaviours of readers, successful writers of expositions need to show their awareness of the possible positions their audience may hold – even when they are not immediately present. In this way, they establish a dialogue (Bakhtin, 1953/1986) with their readers, expanding space for other opinions and contracting that space to create consensus. In the Australian Curriculum for English for example (www.australiancurriculum.edu.au/English/Curriculum/F-10), at Year 5 level, students are required to "understand how to move beyond making bare assertions and take account of differing perspectives and point of view" while at Year 7 they learn "how evaluations about a text can be substantiated by reference to the text and other sources". By the time they reach the middle years of secondary school, students are expected to be able to accumulate arguments and show that they have considered the possible positions the audience might hold. This means introducing and evaluating authoritative evidence to support the preferred position, as well as acknowledging and rebutting other positions. Despite appearing impersonal and objective, dialogue with an audience is essential to more analytical forms of argument, and involves opening up or expanding space for other opinions and then contracting that space to create consensus.

Expanding resources include modality to temper opinions and show the writer or speaker's awareness that even the most authoritative evidence may be questioned. In the opening sentence of paragraph 3 of Jenny's text, for example, the underlined expressions allow for dialogue with those of her audience who support the use of mobile phones:

> <u>It is also possible that</u> use of mobile phones <u>could</u> have an effect on children's ability to think and concentrate.

In addition to straightforward grammatical resources for expressing modality, such as modal verbs (e.g. could, may, must), modality can also be expressed through indirect grammatical resources such as modal adjectives (e.g. responsible), modal nouns and modal phrases and clauses (e.g. it is possible that …). Jenny uses such indirect expressions to make her opinions seem more objective and difficult to argue against, further demonstrating a capacity for effective persuasion in academic contexts that Ollie and Zoe are still to learn.

Closely related to modality are the expanding resources of Attribution. Sources referred to in analytical expositions are typically generalised (Martin & White, 2005) and we see Jenny, as did Ollie, citing broad categories such as 'scientists' or 'evidence'. Jenny however, is further able to specify other sources of attribution to strengthen her arguments (e.g. 'Recent studies by scientists in Washington show …', 'a study undertaken by Monash University suggests …'). The status of the sources can also be adjusted through the use of evaluative vocabulary and grading of nominal groups (e.g. '*recent* studies') and verbal groups like 'suggest' are more graduated than that of 'show'.

Another rhetorical resource frequently deployed in argument is Concession, which involves summarising or referring to an argument which is counter to the position of the writer and then rebutting that argument. This is a strategic device because it appears to open space for other positions and suggests open-mindedness or objectivity. However, as we see in the second sentence below from Jenny's third paragraph, it is in fact ultimately a contracting resource, because the audience is left with the writer's own argument, rebutted on her terms:

> *While scientists do not fully understand the effects of performing two different types of tasks at the same time,* there is evidence that mobile phone use in children was associated with faster and less accurate responses to certain cognitive tasks

This example further shows how the Textual resource of grammatical Theme contributes to persuasion. Foregrounding the concession (bolded in the above sentence) in first or theme position is a powerful way of ensuring that the audience is left with the position held by the writer. For example, Jenny uses the Concessive Conjunctions 'However' (in the third sentence of her opening paragraph) and 'Although' (at the beginning of her concluding paragraph) as a textual Theme to indicate a shift from her expansion to contraction of space.

We see Jenny using fewer of the more directly contracting resources such as rhetorical questions that Ollie used to directly challenge his audience to endorse his opinion (e.g. 'Don't we all deserve a day like this?'); or comment adverbials (e.g. 'Sure you can play a board game ...') which Ollie used to intrude his attitude about issues. Such visibly contracting resources can work in more hortatory expositions such as Ollie's to align audiences around shared values. In more analytical expositions, such resources may appear overly subjective and not in keeping with the preferred stance of presenting an opinion while maintaining an objective tenor. As we shall see in Chapter 7, achieving such a stance is a significant challenge in academic writing and is supported through explicit teaching of rhetorical resources and their effects.

Overall, Jenny's control of rhetorical resources for expanding and contracting argumentative positions distinguishes her exposition as considerably more sophisticated than Ollie's or Zoe's. She has moved beyond making bare assertions as does Zoe and takes account of differing perspectives in more complex ways than does Ollie, as she subtly evaluates authoritative evidence to support her preferred position, while acknowledging and rebutting other positions. Her confidence with such dialogic resources allows her to both open up space for diverging opinions and contract that space to create consensus. Likewise, her capacity to exploit and accumulate more implicit forms of positive and negative evaluation (and graduation of these) throughout her exposition demonstrates her argumentative skill in presenting an opinion while maintaining the objective tenor that is valued in more mature expositions. Her adroit deployment of these interpersonal resources is matched by the sophistication of her argumentative reasoning, most evident in her use of logical metaphor and lexically dense (though grammatically simple) sentences to package multiple ideas in ways that were not yet available to Ollie or Zoe.

Using these aspects of our grammatics toolkit, and focussing on systems for verbal language only, we have been able to undertake a developmental mapping that allows us to identify the rhetorical accomplishments of three writers at three stages of development. Such a toolkit provides an invaluable diagnostic resource for teachers as they plan a persuasive writing curriculum for their students. Just as importantly, it provides a metalanguage that can be adapted for use with students, as we will see further in Chapter 7. Such a metalanguage is just as crucial for the analysis and construction of multimodal forms of persuasion, an issue to which we turn in the concluding section of this chapter.

Expositions: a multimodal focus

Increasingly, in extending their persuasive repertoires in school English, students are learning to strategically select from visual, as well as verbal systems of meaning making. Shannon, an upper primary teacher in one of our research projects scaffolded her students into creating a poster which illustrated their position on the issue of whether children under 13 years of age should be banned from using the social media site, Facebook. As we will see in Chapter 7, Shannon supported her students into constructing not only written Expositions like those of Ollie's above, but multimodal forms that extended the persuasive stance of their written expositions. Once her students had written their expositions on the issue related to Facebook access, they were required to design a poster illustrating an aspect of their argument.

One such poster was produced by Helena in The Grammatics Project. Her three-panel text, reproduced below as Figure 6.1, was designed to "persuade people that under 13s shouldn't be allowed on Facebook because it can hurt people". Helena's explicit intention, as evident in her planning, was to "create a poster showing there's no way of knowing how serious someone is on Facebook". Here she depicts two people having a conversation on Facebook, and one gets hurt because she misunderstood the other's comments. Her poster, like the Zoos Victoria one in Fig 5.1 presented in Chapter 5, draws on verbal and visual resources to persuade us.

Verbally, Helena literally projects what the two girls are typing on-to an enlarged version of the computer screen (top left corner of panel one and top right corner of panel two). The first screen reads "Do you think I'm nice?" and the blond girl's reply in the second frame is projected as "No, you're so mean. I hate you. I never want to see you again". As well as projecting the quoted words, in these first two frames Helena interposes her own evaluative comment on those words ("She's just kidding"), visually enlarged and saliently coloured, to offer an authorial interpretation or evaluation of the projected words. Through these placement and design choices, her authorial comments graphically *elaborate* on the visual meanings of the projected computer screen.

As preparation for designing this poster, Shannon systematically built her students' knowledge of the visual semiotic systems most strongly implicated in

206 'The Wild West': resources (persuasion)

FIGURE 6.1 Helena's poster arguing that 13 year olds shouldn't be allowed on Facebook.

persuasion (we will explore more of Shannon's pedagogy in Chapter 7). She drew on the major systems implicated in interactive meanings in images. Helena's 'argumentative position' unfolds over the three panels of her poster. This triptych form of presenting an argument visually is common in western cultures, where the meaning of one panel relates to the meaning of the others in a kind of inter-visuality.

The system of visual Focalization presented earlier in Figure 3.4 shows something of the subtlety available to artists like Helena in suggesting a view for the reader. She offers us Mediated Observation of the two girls at their computers, presenting an over the shoulder shot of each of them. As viewers, we see them from the back and have access to their own preoccupations. In terms of Social Distance and the option presented earlier in Figure 3.2, it is clear that Helena has decided to represent each domestic tableau from a mid-shot perspective, which creates Social Distance between viewer and depicted characters, enhanced by the depiction of the girls as having their backs to the viewer. This detachment is reinforced in her choice of Subjectivity options, where we only see the backs of the girls, though in a relationship of equality, since presumably the gaze of the viewer would be on the same plane as the gaze of the depicted character. Intersubjectively, the viewer is aligned with the gaze of each girl. Despite having limited contact with the figures in the poster, the viewer is positioned 'along with' each of these girls in turn, viewing their computer screens and their projected meanings. As we saw above, the words on their screens are literally projected into a more salient space in the real estate of the frame, in a semiotic act analogous to that of verbal projection. Taken together, in terms of the rhetorical appeal underpinning these first two panels, Helena's interpersonal design choices of Mediated Observation, Social Distance and (aligned) Equality could be seen as analogous to that of logos. The choices give us a disinterested viewpoint, able to 'see what is going on' as if from an observer stance.

In stark contrast, in her third panel, Helena's intersubjective appeal is much more visibly based on Pathos. She selects Contact, rather than Mediated Observe, for Focalization, with a close up of the first girl whose direct gaze towards the viewer constructs a more empathic engagement with the viewer, who registers her distress immediately. This appeal to Pathos is reinforced in two other design choices. Firstly, contrasting with the more distant whole-body representations of the girls in the first two frames, in the third frame Helena opts for Personal Distance, showing a close-up head and shoulders image of the dark-haired girl. This choice of intimate social distance signals a more empathetic engagement between viewer and image character, compared with the more remote and 'appreciative' engagement inherent in the two 'mid shot' perspectives of the first two panels. As the meanings of these design choices accumulate across each of her three panels, Helena demonstrates a capacity to juxtapose appeals to logos and pathos in a powerfully persuasive multimodal text.

Using a toolkit that describes just one set of design choices related to the interpersonal metafunction, we have been able to evaluate the persuasive impact of Helena's composition. Again, such a metalanguage is a powerful one for teachers as they plan their curriculum to include effective forms of multimodal persuasion and provides a diagnostic resource for tracking students' development in these increasingly important modes of persuasion. We explore each of these issues more fully in Chapter 7.

References

Andrews, R. (2005). Knowledge about the teaching of (sentence) grammar: The state of play. *English Teaching: Practice and Critique*, 4(3), 69–76.
Andrews, R. (2010). *Argumentation in higher education. Improving practice through theory and research*. New York: Routledge.
Australian Curriculum Assessment and Reporting Authority (ACARA) (2012). *Australian curriculum: English*. Version 3.0. Sydney: ACARA. Retrieved from www.australiancurriculum.edu.au/English/Curriculum/F-10.
Bakhtin, M. (1953/1986). *The dialogic imagination: Four essays*. (M. Holquist, Ed., C. Emerson & M. Holquist, Trans). Austin, TX: University of Texas Press.
Cajkler, W. & Hislam, J. (2002). Trainee teachers' grammatical knowledge: The tension between public expectations and individual competence. *Language Awareness,* 11(3), 161–177.
Christie, F. (1993). The 'received tradition' of English teaching: The decline of rhetoric and the corruption of grammar. In B. Green (Ed.), *The insistence of the letter: Literary studies and curriculum theorizing* (pp. 75–106). London: Falmer Press.
Christie, F. (2002). *Classroom discourse analysis*. London: Continuum.
Christie, F. (2004). Revisiting some old themes: The role of grammar in the teaching of English. In J. Foley (Ed.), *Language education and discourse: Functional approaches*, (pp. 145–173), London & New York: Continuum.

Christie, F. (2005). *Language education in the primary years.* Sydney: University of New South Wales Press.

Christie, F. (2010). The ontogenesis of writing in childhood and adolescence. In D. Wyse, R. Andrews, & J. Hoffman (Eds.), *The Routledge international handbook of English, language and literacy teaching* (pp. 146–158). London: Routledge.

Christie, F. & Derewianka, B. (2008). *School discourse: Learning to write across the years of schooling.* London: Continuum.

Cicero (n.d.). Di inventione (C.D. Yonge, Trans). Retrieved from http://classicpersuasion.org/pw/cicero/dnv1-1.htm.

Clark, U. (2010). The problematics of prescribing grammatical knowledge: The case of England, In T. Locke (Ed.), *Beyond the grammar wars: A resource for teachers and students on developing language knowledge in the English/literacy classroom* (pp. 38–54). New York & London: Routledge.

DeStigter, T. (2015). On the ascendance of argument: A critique of the assumptions of academe's dominant form, *Research in the Teaching of English*, 50, 11–34.

French, R. (2012). Learning the grammatics of quoted speech: Benefits for punctuation and expressive reading. *Australian Journal of Language and Literacy*, 35(2), 206–233.

Green, B. (2009). English, rhetoric, democracy; or renewing English in Australia. *English in Australia*, 43(3), 35–44.

Green, B. (2017). English as rhetoric? Once more with feeling ... *English in Australia*, 52(1), 74–82.

Halliday, M. A. K. (1993). Towards a language-based theory of learning. *Linguistics and Education*, 5(2), 93–116.

Halliday, M. A. K. & Matthiessen, C. (2004). *An introduction to functional grammar* (3rd edition). London: Edward Arnold.

Hancock, C. & Kolln, M. (2010). Blowin' in the wind: English grammar in United States schools. In T. Locke (Ed.), *Beyond the grammar wars: A resource for teachers and students on developing language knowledge in the English/literacy classroom* (pp. 21–37). New York & London: Routledge.

Harper, H. & Rennie, J. (2009). "I had to go out and get myself a book on grammar": A study of pre-service teachers' knowledge about language. *Australian Journal of Language and Literacy*, 33(1), 22–37.

Hillocks, G. (1984). What works in teaching composition: A meta-analysis of experimental treatment studies. *American Journal of Education*, 93(1), 133–70.

Hillocks, G. (2010). Teaching argument for critical thinking and writing: An introduction *English Journal*, 99(6), 24–32.

Humphrey, S. (1996). *Exploring literacy in school geography.* Sydney, Australia: Metropolitan East Disadvantaged Schools Program.

Humphrey, S. (2010). Modelling social affiliation and genre in the civic domain. In A. Mahboob & N. Knight (Eds.), *Applicable linguistics* (pp. 76–91). London: Continuum.

Humphrey, S. (2013). Empowering adolescents for activist literacies, *Journal of Language and Literacy Education*, 9(1), 114–135.

Humphrey, S. (2017). *Academic literacies in the middle years: A framework for enhancing teacher knowledge and student achievement.* New York & London: Routledge.

Humphrey, S., Love, K. & Droga, L. (2011). *Working grammar: An introduction for secondary English teachers.* Port Melbourne, Victoria: Pearson.

Humphrey, S., Droga, L. & Feez, S. (2012). *Grammar and meaning.* Newtown, Australia: Primary English Teaching Association Australia.

Kinneavy, J. (1993). *Elements of writing: Complete fifth course.* Austin, TX: Holt.

Klein, P. & Unsworth, L. (2014). The logogenesis of writing to learn: A systemic functional perspective. *Linguistics and Education*, 26, 1–17.
Kolln, M. & Hancock, C. (2005). The story of English grammar in United States schools. *English Teaching: Practice and Critique*, 4(3), 11–31.
Kress, G. (1985). *Linguistic processes in sociocultural practice*. Oxford, UK: Oxford University Press.
Louden, W., Rohl, M., Gore, J., Greaves, D., McIntosh, A., Wright, R., Siemon, D. & House, H., (2005). *Prepared to teach: An investigation into the preparation of teachers to teach literacy and numeracy*. Mount Lawley, Western Australia: Edith Cowan University.
Love, K., & Macken-Horarik, M. (2009). *Obama, Rudd and a grammar for rhetoric in the National English Curriculum*. Paper presented at the Bridging Divides AATE/ALEA Conference, Hobart.
Love, K. & Sandiford, C. (2016). Teachers' and students' meta-reflections on writing choices: An Australian case study. *International Journal of Educational Research*, 80, 204–216.
McCormack, R. (2003). *Common units: Politics and rhetoric*. Paper presented at the Indigenous Minds Forum, Batchelor Institute, Darwin, NT.
Macken-Horarik, M. (1996). Literacy and learning across the curriculum: Towards a model of register for secondary school teachers. In R. Hasan & G. Williams (Eds.), *Literacy in society*, (pp. 232–278). London: Longman.
Martin, J.R. (1985). *Factual writing: Exploring and challenging social reality*. Victoria: Deakin University Press.
Martin & White (2005). *The language of evaluation*. London: Palgrave.
Martin, J. R. & Rose, D. (2007). *Working with discourse: Meaning beyond the clause*. (2nd edition). London: Continuum.
Martin, J. R. & Rose, D. (2008). *Genre relations: Mapping culture*. London & Oakville: Equinox.
Moon, B. (2012). Remembering rhetoric: Recalling a tradition of explicit instruction in writing. *English in Australia*, 47(1), 37–52.
Moore, J. & Schleppegrell, M. (2014). Using a functional linguistics metalanguage to support academic language development in the English language arts. *Linguistics and Education*, 26, 92–105.
Myhill, D. (2009). Becoming a designer: Trajectories of linguistic development. In R. Beard, D. Myhill, J. Riley & M. Nystrand (Eds.), *The Sage handbook of writing development* (pp. 402–414). London: SAGE.
Myhill, D., Jones, S., Watson, A. & Lines, H. (2013). Playful explicitness with grammar: A pedagogy for writing. *Literacy*, 47(2), 103–111.
National Governors Association Center for Best Practices (NGA Center) (2010a). *About the standards – Common Core Standards*. Retrieved from www.corestandards.org/about-the-standards.
National Governors Association Center for Best Practices (NGA Center) (2010b). *Common Core State Standards for English language arts & literacy in history/social studies, science, and technical subjects*. Retrieved from www.edweek.org/media/draft_standards_for_reading_writing_communication_7-14-09.pdf.
Perera, K. (1984) *Children's writing and reading: Analyzing classroom language*. New York: Blackwell.
Sangster, P., Anderson, C. & O'Hara, P. (2012). Perceived and actual levels of knowledge about language amongst primary and secondary student teachers: Do they know what they think they know? *Language Awareness*, 22(4), 1–27.
Schleppegrell, M., (2004). *The language of schooling: A functional linguistics perspective* Lawrence Erlbaum Associates, Mahwah, NJ.

Thomas, D. & To, V. (2016). Nominalization in high scoring primary and secondary school persuasive texts. *Australian Journal of Language and Literacy*, 39(2), 135–148.

Toulmin, S. (1958). *The uses of argument*. Cambridge, UK: Cambridge University Press.

Weekes, T. (2014). *From dot points to disciplinarity: The theory and practice of disciplinary literacies in secondary schooling* (Unpublished doctoral thesis). University of New England, Armidale, Australia.

7
MOVING SOUTH
Teaching persuasion in classrooms

The previous chapters have examined the grammatics of persuasive texts, with an emphasis on the place of analytical expositions in school English. Chapter 5 explored the potential of a functional grammatics in the study of persuasion, with special focus on types of rhetorical appeal such as pathos, ethos and logos. Chapter 6 looked closely at grammatical resources that produced particular rhetorical effects and how these 'appear' in students' writing at different stages of development during the middle years of schooling. The two chapters considered grammatical choices revealed by each metafunctional lens: production of a plausible account of an issue through motivated choices for Participants, Processes and Circumstances within Transitivity; interpersonal engagement of readers through apposite selections for MOOD, MODALITY, PERSON and APPRAISAL; and creation of coherent and well signposted texts through adroit management of THEME and NEW. While these resources are relevant to narrative they work differently in each genre. For example, while a narrative might include dialogue to illuminate understanding of a character, an argument will employ citation to include an expert's opinion as supporting evidence. An author might signpost shifts in setting in a narrative through Circumstances of time or place while a rhetor uses signposting to signal a new point in an unfolding argument. Learning how the 'same' grammatical resources work to achieve different purposes and effects is a crucial task for English teachers, especially if they are to foster academic language learning. There is an increasing array of published materials emerging to support the work of the profession in this process (see for example, Brisk, 2015; Butt, Fahey, Feez & Spinks, 2012; Christie & Derewianka, 2008; Derewianka & Jones, 2012; Gibbons, 2015; Humphrey, Droga, & Feez, 2012; Humphrey, 2017).

In this chapter, we draw once again on strategies from the teaching and learning cycle (TLC) outline in outlined in Chapter 1 and presented in Chapter 4 for narrative. Our goal here is to show how teachers can operationalize a functional grammatics in teaching persuasion in primary and secondary classroom contexts. Building on the material outlined in Chapter 6, we show how teachers can operationalize the grammatics, using it to enhance the work they do in different aspects of persuasion. Once again, we draw on the practical experiences and resources of teachers who participated in The Grammatics Project and shared their learning so generously with us. Many of these were keen to investigate the potential of the functional grammatics for implementing a new national curriculum with a vastly expanded role for grammatical knowledge in teaching of English. Most were keen to ensure that their work on 'essays' produced visible learning outcomes for students and so they concentrated on expository writing. We follow their lead here and focus on ways in which teachers can work with students to build logical, plausible arguments that engage readers powerfully. The period in which we worked in schools seemed to coincide with issues related to digital literacies and in particular to social media and its affordances and dangers for young people. In this chapter, we take up some of the issues that exercised the teachers and students working with us in 2012 in particular. Students' analysis and composition of multimodal persuasive texts are the subject of our first scenario and demonstrate how one teacher, Chris, drew on interactive systems to teach his students how to present an issue in compelling ways in images through management of resources for FOCALIZATION, SOCIAL DISTANCE and ATTITUDE.

As in Chapter 4 which offered different scenarios for teaching narrative, Chapter 7 presents three scenarios from primary and secondary contexts related to teaching of persuasion. Each scenario is adapted from work in real classrooms by teachers in The Grammatics Project as they adapted functional grammatics to meet the needs and interests of their students and the demands of the curriculum for Foundation to Year 10 (ACARA, 2012). Because Australian teachers must generate goals for learning in line with curriculum requirements, we insert content descriptions from the Australian curriculum for English (AC:E) in each unit and show how a functional grammatics is oriented to these goals.

Scenarios in teaching a grammatics for argument

The scenarios we provide to illustrate how the grammatics toolkit might be implemented in the primary and secondary contexts involve the work of a primary teacher working with a composite Year 5/6 group and a secondary teacher working with a mixed ability year group.

Both teachers have been working to build their students' understandings of written argument, the results of which can be seen in Ollie's text "Video games: good or Bad", and Jenny's text about mobile phones. Both are keen to improve their students' ability to structure texts effectively, to engage readers in more nuanced ways and to develop the evidence base for their claims through effective use of Projection, Mood and Modality.

In scenario 1, we meet Chris, a Year 5/6 teacher. In developing written argument with his students, Chris has noted that they are able to use PERSON reasonably well (for example, choosing inclusive pronouns such as 'we' and 'us' in aligning readers). While he thinks that a more nuanced and subtle use of MODALITY could modulate expression of what appeared to be bald claims, Chris decides that teaching other resources are a higher priority at this point. At text level, Chris is tired of the 'firstly, secondly, thirdly' structure that his students typically follow. He needs to review earlier work on alternative ways of signposting arguments in Expositions. He wants his students to experiment with inclusion of a 'narrative hook' as an interesting way to frame an argument rather than the more traditional statement of thesis or issue. As his students will soon be moving to secondary school, using meatier nominal groups to 'pack in' more information is also a priority so that Expositions will be more 'written like'. Interpersonally, Chris wants students to use citation more effectively and to consider the relevance and status of sources in their reporting and quoting of authorities. Inclusion of rhetorical questions and other Appraisal resources will also be considered in his modelling of Exposition.

Chris is a teacher with an interest in the power of images to persuade viewers. His ongoing work with Year 5/6 students occurs as scenario 2. Following the work on interpersonal resources in Exposition, Chris wants his students to produce a poster that will involve them in making choices from FOCALIZATION, SOCIAL DISTANCE and ATTITUDE. This is far from a 'tack on' as he plans to show students how these systems related to and indeed build on those they have learned about earlier in relation to Exposition. He plans to show students how their written arguments can be augmented through appropriate visual choices in their accompanying poster. While this area of visual semiotics is new to him, he feels that the parallels between meanings of words and pictures can be made tangible for students and enrich their understandings of interpersonal grammatics, especially as they learn to use it in multimodal compositions.

In scenario 3, we meet our second teacher, Jamie, who works with Year 8 students in a high-need school where students often struggle with the literacy demands of academic learning. Jamie has noticed that students tend to make bald claims in their arguments and to rely on relatively weak forms of evidence in backing these claims. Her students use rhetorical questions for the most part quite successfully, but she wants her students to concentrate on crafting strong Declarative statements. This is in part to ensure they can structure sentences well through awareness of the role of Subject and Finite verb but also to see how these are ordered in Declaratives, Interrogatives and Imperatives. This work will build students' awareness of how interactive choices contribute to a more nuanced assessment of the likelihood or necessity of different outcomes and the strength of opinions and viewpoints. Overall, Jamie hopes to improve her students' ability to find evidence in arguments for a speaker or writer's point of view, and to estimate the strength of a position based on close analysis of choices for MOOD and MODALITY.

The teaching and learning cycle (TLC) outlined in Chapter 4 guides our teachers' approaches to planning and implementation, with some adaptations to address analysis and composition of images in multimodal texts. As we did in Chapter 4, we use the key stages of the TLC to illustrate the progression of teaching of persuasion, with some difference of emphasis in each scenario. To recall, the four key stages involve:

- *Building the context for work on argument*: understanding the role of argument in the culture, including the combined impact of verbiage and image in multimodal texts;
- *Modelling the structures and features of texts:* use of model texts to focus explicitly on the structure and grammatical features of written and multimodal texts that seek to persuade others to take a particular view on matters of importance;
- *Guided practice*: pedagogic strategies that support students' work on texts in a given genre, often through joint construction of texts or parts of texts;
- *Independent composition and reflection:* approximating the structure and features of a genre through independent composition of a text (or part of a text).

The selection of suitable mentor or model texts for classroom work is of crucial importance. When discussing print-based arguments with students, teachers aim to ensure that students are mindful of the social purpose or function of the mentor text, the big question or issue animating the unit of work and, if possible, the prototypical staging of the genre. When working with argument, teachers also consider how a text generates a stance on an issue, the kinds of 'evidence' used to support the argument, citation of the views of various stakeholders, and the use of ethical, emotional or logical appeals to persuade readers of the validity of a certain position. Similarly, when discussing images in multimodal texts, teachers engage students in discussions of how visual choices position viewers to identify, appraise or respond to depicted figures. Typically, the texts used in such discussions will be advertisements or posters promoting a commercial product, an issue, a cause or an event.

Beyond important initial discussion of the context of texts selected for study, teachers invite students to consider a larger question or issue that is the focus of the unit of work. These will vary of course, depending on the context and goals of the teachers. In this book we relate the metafunctions to overarching questions like the following: how does a text create a plausible and valid account of an issue? (Ideational lens); how does the text attempt to persuade its audience to believe or act in a particular way? (Interpersonal lens); and how is the text organized? (Textual lens). Having access to mentor texts that exemplify the form, function and pattern of focal resources in play is important to the effectiveness of a unit of work. But just having access to model texts is not enough; students need to know how to 'take from the model'. Strategies like Joint Construction support learners' ability to 'appropriate' wordings or image choices in texts that have been selected to focus their attention. They are exposed to choices in a model (identifying them); they discuss these using a functional metalanguage (describing their function) and they infer their significance (interpreting the patterns). In sum, they are scaffolded into focal choices without being expected to manage these independently too early in the learning process.

Let's now examine how Chris, in the first instance teaches about written exposition, and second how he supports his student to compose a persuasive multimodal text.

Scenario 1 – exposition in a primary (Year 5/6) classroom

Chris intends to examine argument at two points in the year. While both explorations will involve salient rhetorical devices in written Expositions, the second phase of work will serve as a springboard into composing multimodal persuasion. Chris often returns to the teaching of a particular genre over the course of the year to review and consolidate students' understandings but also to allow a dimensional stretch in their learning. As outlined above, Chris has already identified areas in which he thinks his students' writing of Exposition might be developed, to move past the 'firstly, secondly, thirdly' form of signposting they are now using. His first goal is to review different ways of signalling a change of direction in an Exposition. This focus is appropriate for students in Year 5 given the Australian curriculum for English (AC:E) requirement that students 'understand that the starting point of a sentence gives prominence to the message in the text and allows for prediction of how the text will unfold' (ACELA 1505).[1] Chris is also keen for his students to experiment with engaging introductions to arguments. In this unit, he will introduce them to the 'narrative hook' that situates an Exposition in problems of human experience, a common feature of many news and current affair programs he and the students have been watching.

Chris has noticed that his students tend to use prosaic, even awkward approaches to citation in providing evidence for their views. They need to quote and report authorities proficiently – whether through direct or indirect speech; and they need to make more discerning choices about which authorities are relevant to particular claims in arguments. The AC:E requires that by the end of Year 4, students will have investigated 'how quoted (direct) and reported (indirect) speech work in different types of text' (ACELA 1494). This learning outcome is a crucial one to meet as the students prepare to move into high school English.

Finally, Chris hopes to expand his students' repertoires of evaluative meaning. To this end, he decides to explore different ways of expressing attitudinal meanings using the appraisal resources of AFFECT, JUDGMENT and APPRECIATION along with strategies for amplifying or softening attitude. As part of this, he wants to ensure his students can appreciate the role of MOOD in engaging an audience – using Interrogative Mood to produce rhetorical questions, for example. In all these tasks, he hopes to fulfil the AC:E expectation that students in late primary school will 'understand how to move beyond making bare assertions and take account of differing perspectives and points of view' (ACELA 1502). All of these goals will contribute to addressing the big issue that animates the two phases of his work with Year 5/6 students – how to build powerful arguments that shape readers views effectively. Chris maps out his goals for his first foray into argument in Table 7.1.

TABLE 7.1 Chris's planning for work on exposition

Big question for this unit of work: How do we build powerful arguments that shape readers' views effectively?	
Textual lens on written Expositions	Signposting stages of an argument effectively [ACELA 1505].
Experiential lens on establishing an argument in different ways	Establishing an argument through a scenario – learning to use a 'narrative hook'.
Interpersonal lens on citing the views of authorities	Using quoting or reporting verbs appropriately [ACELA 1494].
Interpersonal lens on attitudinal vocabulary	Developing a richer vocabulary of words of AFFECT, JUDGMENT and/ or APPRECIATION; Learning how to Amplify or soften attitudinal choices.
Interpersonal lens on engaging audiences through statements, questions, imperatives	Exploring the workings of MOOD; a focus on rhetorical questions [ACELA 1502].

These goals shape the investigations of persuasion that Chris and his students pursue in the weeks to come. The different lenses on the meaning ensure that he and his learners can link what they do with grammar to the rhetorical tasks of argument.

Building the context for work on exposition

Chris sets his students the task of finding examples of arguments to share with the class. They are quite familiar with the Severn Suzuki's speech (see Chapter 5) that formed part of earlier work in a unit on the environment, and regularly read and view educationally focused texts that present views about current world and social events for students. He suggessts that they examine newspapers that regularly include opinion pieces written at a level suited to his students. Given this background, and the inclusion of Expositions as one of the genres assessed under the national testing of writing regime, the students are quite familiar with types of text, their generic structure of Thesis/Position Statement, Arguments and supporting reasons/ evidence, and Restatement of the position. Chris uses the whiteboard to present Expositions by Zoe, Ollie and Jenny (discussed in Chapter 6) to explore alternative ways of signposting arguments in the topic sentences of Expositions. Table 7.2 presents these choices in italics.

Chris reads the three Expositions to students and underlines each of the topic sentences as he goes, asking students to identify the signposting of the argument in each case. They talk about differences between the choices made by Zoe, Ollie and Jenny and how effective they are for the arguments in each text. He points out how Jenny's arguments are more abstract than those made by Ollie and certainly Zoe and they discuss alternative ways of introducing the arguments in each case. He asks children to think about what a signpost does for a traveller who is unfamiliar with territory. They think about the function of signposting in writing and why

TABLE 7.2 Different approaches to signposting of arguments in three Expositions

Zoe's signposting	Ollie's signposting	Jenny's signposting
Argument 1 *Firstly*, playing computer games can hurt your eyes.	Argument 1 *Firstly*, video games can help with school work.	Argument 1 *The most important danger of mobile phones to children's health* concerns the emission of radiation which could lead to cancer.
Argument 2 *Moreover*, playing computer games kills your time.	Argument 2 *In addition to this*, a lot of the video games such as the DS are super lightweight and easy to carry around.	Argument 2 *It is also possible* that use of mobile phones could influence children's ability to think and concentrate.
Argument 3 *Last but not least*, playing computer games makes you forget about everything.	Argument 3 *To continue*, your kids would never be bored.	Argument 3 *In addition to the effects on cognitive skills*, scientists have also raised concerns about the effects of mobile phones on the communication skills of children and teenagers.

it is important. Chris reminds students that this is one of the strategies that make arguments persuasive and that they are going to experiment with it in their writing of Expositions later in the unit.

When he is confident that students know what to look for and why this is important, he asks students to select one of the written texts they have brought to class to annotate for structure and signposting. If these are short and accessible enough, they can work with a partner on their selected text or they can work on one selected by Chris (if theirs is too difficult to annotate). Chris asks each pair to:

- Decide on the social purpose of the argument – what it aims to achieve.
- Annotate their selected text for stages (if these are clear); highlight sentences that contain the issue in contention; number key arguments; and then identify wordings that signpost the arguments made in each paragraph of in each text.
- Discuss with their partner how effective the arguments are and whether the text is well structured and signposted.
- Rate each text out of ten based on how effectively they think the author has persuaded them and identify some reasons why they have given the text this ranking.

Once completed, student pairs form a group of four to share and compare their examples. While the focus here on purpose, structure and signposting is quite simple, it serves to engage the students in reviewing their current understandings of Expositions at the text level. These annotated texts are then displayed in the classroom, along with ratings out of ten for effectiveness and reasons for the rating given.

Chris will return to the question of rating later, once students have been taught about the resources he has identified for his unit focus.

In bringing this work on the context of argument to a close, Chris builds up a class list of points about what makes an Exposition effective – what persuades them to a particular viewpoint or line of action. The students are asked to add points to the list as the unit unfolds.

Modelling features of Exposition

As noted above, the students in Chris's class have adopted an almost perfunctory approach to Exposition. They tend to rely on the 'five paragraph' structure: they introduce the issue and preview arguments in a rudimentary way, elaborate on arguments over three paragraphs and end with a concluding paragraph. Their signposting strategies have become formulaic, perhaps under the influence of national testing regimes that tend to reward routine accomplishment. This may have worked well for them in earlier days, but it is time to expand the repertoire.

For teaching purposes, Chris selects a newspaper article entitled 'Teachers lament faltering pens' which examines the declining standard of secondary students' handwriting, suggesting that a reliance on technology is to blame (written by Elisabeth Tarica and published in the Sydney Morning Herald on 26/03/2012, copy available at www.smh.com.au/national/education/teachers-lament-faltering-pens-20120323-1vp04.html). While this might not be a particularly exciting topic, it does relate directly to the students' experience and highlights an issue of relevance to the field of digital technologies and how young people physically manipulate print in this context. The article has a clear structure and examples of several the linguistic features which Chris wants to teach. He begins his modelling session with a question to students: Who finds handwriting easy? Do you write by hand more quickly than you can text? Following a show of hands on each question, he introduces the first paragraph of the article:

> Once penmanship was an art and handwriting a skill developed through endless practice. Now teachers say cursive handwriting is disappearing from secondary schools, leaving many students unable to write quickly or fluently. The finger is being pointed at technology.

He establishes partner groups and gives each pair a copy of the first paragraph. He then posts probe questions related to Ideational meaning on the board and asks students to think and then talk about the answers:

Ideational Probe Questions

- What is the Issue or Thesis?
- How is it established (e.g. through a bald claim, a scenario or a reported claim made by others)?
- Are the arguments to follow previewed explicitly or not?

Following time to discuss and annotate the extract, Chris gathers the students as a group to collate their ideas, this time asking students to come and annotate an enlarged copy for the group to see. Normally, he would continue to examine the article in its entirety, pointing out the grammatical features and involving them in rhetorically oriented learning activities. But this time, he wants to pause and have the students think about using a scenario as an introduction. Working with his students, Chris models an alternative introduction to the text and then discusses with the students the impact that this might have on the reader:

> "Ok everyone," says the teacher, "time to begin your writing task." Jake lifts the lid to his laptop and smiles as he begins to work. Across the classroom, the soft tap, tap, tapping on keyboards can be heard as the students start to compose. "No – stop everyone!" commands the teacher. "You have to handwrite this one." There is dead silence in the room. What? Handwrite? I don't even have a pen.

Chris returns to the probe questions and asks the students if their revised introduction provides similar responses to these questions. Chris stresses the point that not every Exposition needs to follow the same structure to be effective. They talk about the effectiveness of each opening paragraph.

Following this short joint construction, the students are set two tasks:

- In pairs, the students work to create their own introductions using a scenario for the article about handwriting which they then share with small groups or the class if possible.
- In pairs, the students return to the texts they annotated previously and write a new introduction using a scenario. Each pair shares their revised introductions with another pair, asking them to respond to the probe questions as they do. Their readers give them feedback on the effectiveness of their revised introductions.

What Chris is doing through these activities is alerting students to alternative ways of presenting a position statement or Thesis. Through reviewing the newly written introductions using the Ideational probe questions, he is providing a clear guide for the students to determine the issue and writer's stance. In doing so, the students are mindful that the use of a scenario has a clearly defined purpose in the Exposition – it functions to set a scene relevant to the issue being explored, to bring it to life in ordinary human experience.

Who says so? The work of citation using reporting verbs and phrases

Establishing and substantiating arguments within an Exposition are areas which students on the cusp of secondary schooling need to master. Like many young people, Chris's students are quite happy to voice an opinion. Quite often, this is a personal viewpoint but it is not always supported by evidence. To address this, Chris involves his students in a series of tasks that build their background knowledge of a field. Typically, this involves researching a topic and recording facts that might be used, and related arguments that might be developed. This time, Chris wants his students to cite the words of appropriate experts to establish a more informed, authoritative stance. Drawing on their familiarity with the topic of computer games, Chris asks students to decide who might be an appropriate authority to interview and cite on the following claims:

Who to cite?

- Children like playing computer games.
- Children neglect homework because of the time they spend on computer games.
- Playing computer games is bad for your eyes.
- Playing computer games means you tend not to exercise.

This prior work on the appropriateness of authorities to consult is important if students are to "take account of differing perspectives and points of view" on issues (ACELA 1502) and to decide on which perspectives to include as they seek to support their claims.

In this work on point of view, Chris is now looking at Exposition through an interpersonal lens. Returning to the news feature, "Teachers lament faltering pens", Chris reads through the complete article with students. He then introduces them to the notion of using the opinions of 'experts' to support ideas and asks them to find examples within the text where this occurs, highlight the status of the 'authority' and the 'evidence' they provide. His students refer to Projection resources as 'quoting' and 'reporting' verbs, which is the familiar metalanguage used by teachers in many Australian schools. Some of these examples are set out in the Table 7.3, with quoting verbs highlighted in italics, reporting verbs underlined and sensing verbs in underlined italics.

Examples of quoting and reporting verbs used in citing 'authorities'.

The students then engage in a discussion of the impact of the views of this range of authorities. Chris asks the students to return to the text, this time to look for the ways in which the views of the authorities are introduced and highlights the following:

- Verb choices which reveal the opinions, for example, quoting verbs such as 'says,' 'states', and sensing verbs such as 'has noticed', 'suspects';
- Direct quotes and why these experts might be quoted directly; and
- Indirect or reported speech and why these experts are not quoted directly.

Chris suggests that students refer to these in a general way as reporting verbs. Having introduced the notion of citation and the grammatical forms of reporting verbs and phrases such as 'according to' or 'In Jones' view', Chris provides his students with

TABLE 7.3 Examples of quoting and reporting verbs used in citing 'authorities'

The authority	Status of the authority	Example of views cited by authorities
Ross Huggard	Vice-president of the Victorian Association for the Teaching of English A senior English and literature teacher with 35 years of experience in the classroom	Illegible handwriting has become serious problem for teachers *according to* … *reports* that sometimes students cannot even read their own handwriting "They write things and you're having a terrible time deciphering them," he *says*.
Grace Oakley	Associate Professor at the Graduate School of Education at the University of Western Australia	*has noticed* a decline in undergraduate handwriting over the past 10 years
Gabrielle Leigh	President of the Victorian Principals Association	*suspects* that by the time students get to high school, little classroom time is devoted to helping those struggling with poor handwriting
A spokesperson	For the Australian Curriculum and Assessment Authority	*states* the national curriculum supports the teaching of cursive handwriting

a list of possibilities they might use in their own texts. Table 7.4 below is adapted from work by Humphrey, Love and Droga (2011) that grammatics teachers such as Chris found helpful.

Chris builds up a class list of reporting verbs and phrases and encourages students to add to this list as they find new ones in the articles they are examining. In this way, he expands their repertoire in citing of authorities, later deciding to talk to the students about which reporting verbs suggest agreement on the part of the writer (e.g. establish, prove, show) and which ones suggest disagreement (e.g. claim, claimed to show, assume) and which ones are more neutral (e.g. state, report, suggest).

TABLE 7.4 Reporting verbs and phrases (source: Humphrey, Love & Droga, 2011, p. 93)

Grammatical Forms	'Say'	'Think or feel'	'Find'
Reporting verbs	(Saying verbs) state, say, report, tell, announce, write, stress, argue, respond, claim, suggest, prove, claim, show	(Sensing verbs) think, feel, believe, reckon, assume	(Action verbs) find, demonstrate, discover (that), show
Reporting Phrases	According to Jones; (Jones, 2000:34)	In Jones' view	

Making the point – statements and rhetorical questions

Using different MOOD choices – Declaratives, Interrogatives and Imperatives – opens up the ways in which the writer might construct different propositions or proposals. Chris wants to focus on the use of a combination of statements and rhetorical questions that clearly express the writer's point of view. The argument about the "demise of students' handwriting" that he has been using has examples of clear statements but includes no rhetorical questions. Rather than introduce a new text at this point, Chris involves the students in the following tasks:

- Students find examples of statements that clearly present the author's view, for example, "Illegible handwriting has become a serious problem", "By the time students arrive in high school, many dump the cursive style they have been taught in primary school", "Fast forward to exams and that's a real issue because they cannot write so many words as other people can".
- As part of his review of their knowledge of Subject and Finite verbs, Chris asks the students to underline the Subject and verb in each clause, including dependent clauses like "By the time students arrive in high school, || many dump the cursive style [[they have been taught in primary school]]" and clauses where the Subject is ellipsed, as in "(We can) Fast forward to exams".
- Then students consider what happens to the Subject and Finite verb when a writer poses a question, as in "Has illegible handwriting become a serious problem?" and "Do many students dump the cursive style taught in primary school?" But there is a further issue to explore here.
- In a rhetorical question, the answer is assumed to be obvious. So, Chris takes some statements like these and models the writing of a related rhetorical question, for example, "Fast forward to exams and that's a real issue because they cannot write so many words as other people can" could become "How can students write enough in exams?" or "Don't you think students need to be able to write properly in exams?" Chris explains that we call these kinds of questions 'rhetorical questions' because we do not expect an answer but use them to present the reader with a particular stance. Students write their own examples of rhetorical questions for the article which are shared with the class.
- Together, pairs of students select parts of the text to insert some of the rhetorical questions the students have composed. Chris asks the class to consider the impact of the inclusion of the rhetorical questions on readers and whether they enhance the impact of a persuasive piece of writing.

For or against – gradable positive or negative Attitude

As discussed in some detail in Chapter 6, APPRAISAL choices are used to persuade readers of a particular stance. This is not a new area for Chris's students as they have already considered the ways in which attitudinal choices can be intensified or softened in narratives. The intention here is to show how these resources can be deployed for persuasive purposes. Chris reminds students that some words 'bump up the volume' on attitudinal words whilst others lower it. Some suggest a positive attitude whilst others give the words a negative spin.

Using statements highlighted in the previous task, the students are asked to highlight words which explicitly alert the reader to the stance taken by the author:

- "*Illegible* handwriting has become a *serious problem*", "By the time students arrive in high school, many *dump* the cursive style they have been taught in primary school", "Fast forward to exams and that's a *real issue* because they cannot write so many words as other people can".
- Together, the students identify the types of words which explicitly carry this negative meaning (Inscribed Attitude) – *evaluative adjectives* (e.g. illegible, serious), *evaluative verbs* (e.g. dump), *evaluative nouns* (e.g. problem, issue). The students use coloured markers – red for positive wordings and blue for negative wordings to see if there are any patterns (e.g. of contrast) becoming obvious in stretches of the text and hence revealing the stance of the author on 'the demise of handwriting' (a word which is itself loaded with attitude).
- Chris points out more implicit examples of Attitude, such as 'cannot write so many words as other people can' (Invoked Attitude). At this stage in their development, most of his students will tend to use the more explicit forms of attitude in their writing but Chris wants to introduce them to more subtle ways of making a point and thus to enhance their ability to comprehend choices like these as they read articles like this.

Guided Practice – pair work on earlier texts

Chris has now used three lenses on meaning to explore the stages and features of Exposition and how they work. Textually, his students considered different ways of signposting stages in an Exposition and signalling the points to be made in each paragraph. Experientially, they experimented with the inclusion of a scenario as an alternative means of establishing an issue. Interpersonally, students identified, described and explained the use of reporting verbs in citation of experts, looked at rhetorical questions and APPRAISAL in spinning a viewpoint in different ways. In the guided practice stage of the TLC, Chris invites students now to return to the texts they had collected and reviewed earlier and to apply their new knowledge of grammatics to this re-appraisal.

One of their first activities was to find examples of Expositions in newspapers, environmental magazines and local campaign newsletter and to annotate the texts, identifying social purpose, the issue at stake, key arguments and signposting words. He also asked them to rate the effectiveness of the texts on a scale of 1–10. Building on the knowledge about language they have acquired, Chris now asks students to re-evaluate their effectiveness, this time looking for patterns of the features across the text. He provides the following probe questions to guide their work:

Textual probe questions

- Does the text preview arguments in the opening paragraph? How?
- What do you notice about signposting of arguments in the course of the text?
- Are they varied and effective?

Ideational probe questions

- What is the issue or thesis? How is it established (e.g. through a bald claim, a scenario, rhetorical question)?
- What is the writer's position on the issue? How do you know?

Interpersonal probe questions

- What do you notice about evaluative words in the text? Look for words or phrases which appeal to emotions, make judgments about people or show appreciation of things.
- How are the arguments made? Are they made through the use of strong statements? Are they made through Rhetorical questions? Where do these occur? What impact do they have?
- Are the views of others, including authorities, quoted or reported to support a claim? Are these the appropriate experts to cite? Why? At what points of the argument does happen? How well do they work?

Students share their evaluations with each other, noting the ways in which the highlighted grammatical features are present, or not, and the effectiveness of their use.

Some students finish this work earlier than others so Chris gives them a challenge: he asks them to examine salient interpersonal choices in a text such as a letter from a refugee mother (see www.theage.com.au/act-news/every-day-i-worry-a-refugees-plea-to-bring-her-children-to-safety-20160920-grk9ia):

- Identify words or groups of words that reveal attitude in this text and make a chart showing how the meaning might be 'turned up' or 'turned down'. The chart below is an example of one group's work after reading the article entitled 'A refugee's plea'. Table 7.5 below is an example of the kind of words students doing this extension activity might find.

In a discussion around negative attitudinal resources used in the article, one of Chris's students highlight two words 'refugee' and 'future' as being particularly negative within the context of the article. When pressed to explain why, the student replies, "I cannot imagine that (being a refugee) is a positive thing, and your future is not determined … for her, the future is negative". Such comments show that the student is attuned to the meaning of language choices in context, and how young

TABLE 7.5 Grading of core vocabulary

Graded meaning (turning the volume down)	Core meaning (+ve or –ve)	Graded meaning (turning the volume up)
shock	horror (-ve)	terror
unwell	sick (-ve)	critical condition, diseased
sobbing, whimpering	crying (-ve)	bawling, screaming, wailing
yelling	screaming (-ve)	shrieking
upset, crying, unhappy	miserable (-ve)	depressed, sorrowful

readers and writers of arguments can exercise control over their interpretation and the kinds of meanings they want to make.

Independently composing an Exposition

After all this work, it is now time for the students to write their own exposition. This time, Chris decides to give his students a timed task, which will mean that they will not have time to research the topic and will need to draw on their own knowledge. In preparation for the task, Alex reviews the language resources they have been focussing on before providing them with the prompt 'Playing video games is good for you'. The students are given a short time to plan the response. In Figure 7.1, we see Ollie's plan (see Chapter 6 for copy of his complete response and analysis of its features).

When talking about his writing of this Exposition, Ollie can identify the various rhetorical features he employed, and how they worked to make his text so persuasive. He comments on the impact of his introduction, how 'the narrative is good and awesome and the first statement (sic)'. He also has a very clear idea of his stance and purpose. As he explains in his interview with researchers from The Grammatics Project:

> What I was trying to do as a writer was saying not all videogames are bad. Some of them are bad, I can agree with that, but like the brain games, it can help improve your brain strategy … and I was just trying to persuade people by saying that there is good and bad games [sic].

Importantly, his audience is clearly in view. As Ollie explains, 'I based it around parents and I tried to be like a little bit smart and for the parents.' He is aware of the resources he has used and can provide examples of these in his text when prompted:

> I did the rhetorical questions. … Don't you want your kids to learn having fun, and do you want to clean up that annoying mess, and do you want to be a bad parent? … I did citations … "Experts suggested that tired parents are bad parents" and also that "videogames have stated that some video games can help improve your brain".

Planning space

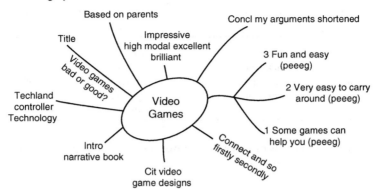

FIGURE 7.1 Ollie's plan.

Throughout this discussion, Ollie reveals ways in which he knowingly appropriated the grammatical resources highlighted to him. Ollie's 'metatalk' is evidence not only of his ability to talk about his own writing in meaningful and purposeful ways, but also of a capacity to reflect on and verbalise his reasons for the writerly choices he has made. Like others in Chris's class of Year 5/6 students, Ollie is a knowing rhetor. Students know more about the structure and features of Exposition as a key genre of academic learning. The point for Chris is to have expanded their repertoires so that the students are aware of what is possible, what is valued and how this can improve their writing of Exposition.

Scenario 2 – multimodal composition in the primary classroom

Having established some strong understandings about the grammatics of written Exposition, Chris returns to the genre later that year with his Year 5/6 class, this time with the intention of helping his students compose a multimodal poster. It makes sense to first have his students compose a written Exposition, a genre they recently examined and then to move from here to explore systems analogous to those they have looked at in verbal texts but now in images – Chris adapts resources from within systems of FOCALIZATION, SOCIAL DISTANCE and ATTITUDE for purposes of students' analysis of internet images on Facebook (see Kress & van Leeuwen, 2006 and Painter, Martin, & Unsworth, 2013 for a full account of these resources). The focus on these systems has been prompted through recent discussion with his students on the topic of cyber-bullying via Facebook. Because his students are familiar with social media like this, Chris decides to explore more systematically the way images position viewers to feel, see and judge things. In this goal, he is fulfilling the Australian curriculum requirement (ACARA, 2012) that Year 5 students "explain sequences of images in print texts and compare these to the ways hyper-linked digital texts are organized, explaining their effect on viewers' interpretations" (ACELA 1511).

Having already provided an account of how Chris worked with his students to write an Exposition in Scenario 1, a brief outline of this work will be given here with an extended focus on his work with visual grammar.

Reviewing written Exposition – Should kids be allowed on Facebook?

Chris has found an online article in the Guardian entitled "*Should kids be allowed on Facebook?*" The article addresses a topical issue related to Mark Zuckerberg wanting to open up the social-networking site to children under 13, an issue about which Chris's students hold firm opinions. The article presents both sides argued by two parents, with one parent, Joanna Moorhead, arguing for the affirmative, and the second, Jenni Russell for the negative.[2] Chris sees the presentation of two opposing views as a way to alert his students to the role of pathos as in emotional appeals.

Working in pairs, the students read through the two texts using the same (or adapted) probe questions from the previous work on argument to guide them. Students write their responses on the table as well as annotate the texts as appropriate. On completion of the task, responses are shared with the class and collated by the teacher (see Table 7.6). Through this work, Chris wants to build the students' field knowledge, while at the same time reviewing the grammatical features of written Exposition they examined in the previous unit. In this activity, he focusses only on experiential and interpersonal lenses on the argument.

The task provides the students with several entry points for writing their own response to the question: "Should kids be allowed on Facebook?". Chris later draws on this analysis for composing a multimodal text. This provides students with time

TABLE 7.6 Compilation of responses to probe questions on the Facebook article

Probe question	*Joanna's response*	*Jenni's response*
What is the issue or Thesis? How is it established (e.g. through a bald claim, a reported claim, a scenario, rhetorical question)?	The introduction makes a bald claim to the effect that use of Facebook by children will not be altered by a "country's decision-makers", links to a scenario of children "tapping furiously like all their mates" to find out what is going on around them.	Jenni begins with an appeal hoping that that Zuckerberg will be stopped, and makes the bald claim that dropping the age for Facebook users will "expose children to emotional pressures and public scrutiny they can't yet handle".
What is the writer's position on the issue?	Children are already using Facebook and will continue to do so. Parents need to help them just as they do in other situations	A significant by-product of Facebook is cyberbullying. This is a problem "no one knows how to fix".

TABLE 7.6 Continued

Probe question	Joanna's response	Jenni's response
What arguments are previewed?	Children experience a range of different situations for which they need parental guidance Facebook is about connecting with others – experiencing this early in life will prepare them for when they are older.	Facebook is complex – children need to manage image in what is a public space – many adults using Facebook have problems doing this.
What kinds of evidence are used to support the author's position (e.g. real-life examples, research statistics, traditional authorities, common-sense or theories)? How persuasive is it?	Mostly common sense – along the lines that parents usually provide guidance for foundational life experiences and can do so for Facebook use.	Mostly common sense – the emphasis is on children not having skills to make sophisticated judgments which even adults struggle with; provides an example from personal experience.
What do you notice about evaluative words in the text? Look for wordings that appeal to emotions, make judgments or show appreciation of things.	"Parents like me *worry* … but the *important* thing to realize is"; "just as you teach them rules for staying *safe* when they're out and about alone, so you teach them rules for *staying safe online*"; "we supervise … we *trust*"	"those huge attractions have their *dark* sides"; "it's *hard* enough … it's too *cruel*…"; "What goes on Facebook can be there *forever*"
How are arguments made? Are they made through strong statements or rhetorical questions? Where do they occur? What impact do they have?	Mostly strong statements but strategic use of rhetorical questions – one occurs as final comment – "Why, when we're trying to educate them in useful skills on other fronts, hold them back on this one?"	Declarative statements – no use of rhetorical questions.
Are views of others, including authorities, quoted or reported to support a claim? At what points of the argument does this occur? Are the authorities appropriate to the claims?	No one is cited or quoted, but there is the suggestion that evidence exists that hundreds of thousands of children are using Facebook	No one is cited or quoted but one personal anecdote is included to support the claim that Facebook impacts on adults' lives.

to map out key points that they might include in their own written expositions. The students are then asked to write their own responses, of which one, written by Anna, is reproduced below (see Text 7.1). While researching a topic is important to building field knowledge, scrutiny of grammatical choices deepens students' understanding of meaning making as the young writer below demonstrates.

Should Under Thirteens Be on Facebook

Everyday kids under 13 are using facebook, so why stop them? Every child needs to learn how to connect online with their family and friends. Connecting is something that every child needs to learn to help them in the future because in future generation everybody will be interacting online. Although kids shouldn't be on facebook it teaches them to be safe online and not to talk to strangers. Facebook also kids connect with there friends that go to different schools.

Communication is something that all the kids are using facebook for, to communicate with old friends, talk to the family or just to see what's going on. Kids love using this site because there is instant messaging, video calling, status updates and uploading photos. Facebook is a great site for when kids leave primary school so they can still catch up with their good friends, that's not all facebook is great for it is great because you can message and video call friends that are overseas. One of my sister's friends went to England and they were putting up status updates, uploading photos and checking into places.

I know every parent worries about their child and wants to know what they do online. Then again you have to trust your child as they grow up. Parents stated that cyber bullying only affects a minority and you can help your child if they are getting cyber bullied. Also bullying doesn't just happen online it can happen anywhere. It was reported that you are more likely to get bullied at school than online. Alternatively if you are scared about what your child is doing online you can teach them to be safe online.

Just because your kids could be prey for lunatics online doesn't mean you cant teach them to be safe, for instance, you could add you child, check there profile regularly and teach them to be safe whilst on facebook. If you were teaching your child to be safe online whilst on facebook they would know not random friend requests', if you were really worried about you could ask for there password.

To conclude my following reasons above, I think facebook is an excellent social media network that is great for connecting with family and friends. If you teach your children to be safe online, tell a parent if your getting bullied then facebook would be a great site for under 13s

TEXT 7.1 Anna's Facebook exposition.

Composing a multimodal text

Satisfied that his students have a good sense of written Exposition at this point, Chris now considers how he might extend their understandings of persuasion to support composition of a multimodal text. It makes sense to keep the topic of children's use of Facebook for this work. Chris begins by examining some images on Facebook pages about topics they have been investigating, such as cyberbullying. He uses these to generate exploratory discussion, inviting students to talk about whether the images suggest connectedness or conflict (bullying) and what makes them think one way or the other. Following this discussion, he then moves into more systematic work on FOCALIZATION and the other systems like SOCIAL DISTANCE and ATTITUDE in images. Chris sets out his goals for the sequence of lessons to follow which focus on how images position viewers and either encourage or perhaps challenge cyber bullying. Table 7.7 provides a snapshot of these goals for this mini-unit.

To provide the students with ready access to each of the systems and their subsystems, Chris uses the systems of interactive meaning presented earlier to explore images in print and digital texts with his students (see Figures 3.2 and 3.3). These will be made readily available to the students through display in the classroom, with individual copies given to each student.

Building shared understandings about images in advertisements

To begin, Chris needs to establish some core understandings about how choices in images work to build a persuasive rapport with viewers. He gathers several images of people and animals from magazines, newspapers and websites to share with the class. He selects images that illustrate well options for FOCALIZATION, SOCIAL DISTANCE and ATTITUDE. For example, he chooses images that show people at close range, with a direct and frontal gaze at viewers as well as images that show people at a distance, using oblique angles and high and low vantage points. He chooses images that are high in emotional content and those that are low, including images that would normally be regarded as neutral for ATTITUDE such as tables, figures,

TABLE 7.7 Chris's planning for teaching of visual grammatics

Big Question: Does Facebook encourage cyber bullying? If so, how do images contribute to this? Can Facebook be used to challenge cyber bullying? How?

Persuasive focus: Interpersonal Lens	*System focus*
How interactive meanings and Focalization are used in images to build solidarity between the viewer and represented participants. How they can be used to challenge behavior?	FOCALIZATION SOCIAL DISTANCE ATTITUDE

maps, etc. His goal is to have access to a range of images that are highly contrastive and suggest very different interactive meaning potentials.

He presents a selection in the first instance as PowerPoint images and asks for students' responses to these. At this point, Chris wants his students to respond with their 'common-sense' understandings of the images. He nevertheless provides some guiding questions to help students begin to tune into interpersonal meanings. Students watch the images and talk about their response to the following questions:

- How are you positioned in relation to the person in the image? Are they looking at you or someone else? Are you positioned at the same level as this person? Can you see all of them? Part of them? Are they close? Distant? Why do you think the artist has chosen to represent them in this way?
- What can you tell about the person's feelings from the image(s)?
- What can you tell about his or her character? Do they look like someone/ something you know? Someone you can trust? What is it about the image that makes you think that?

Later, asking students to work in small groups, he presents each group with two or three selected images, and asks them to annotate them using the above questions as a guide.

The students report back to the group about their images, with Chris noting their interpretations for all to see on a copy of each image. He asks them to comment on the persuasive effect on them as viewers of the depiction choices in the images both separately and in combination.

Modelling visual choices

Returning to the images, Chris introduces the students more systematically to the choices for each system. He works first with options for FOCALIZATION, then SOCIAL DISTANCE and ATTITUDE. He uses the image of the gorilla in the campaign to recycle mobile phones (Figure 5.1) as one example and illustrates and explains the choice of Focalization – Contact: Invite, where the gorilla's head and eyes are turned from the side. He asks students if they have seen pictures with similar kinds of gaze, perhaps even asking them to demonstrate the look of the gorilla themselves. While many of the advertisements also have language components and make use of logos, these appeals are not in focus here. Chris does however deal with verbiage incidentally, as it comes up in children's responses and in a rudimentary way. Chris follows a similar process to teach each of the visual systems.

He explains that as in written texts, choices in visual texts are meaningful. They are shaped by the artist's interests and purposes. Once the students have been exposed to examples of different choices, they are ready to consider the options in a more abstract way. Here Chris introduces each option, concentrating on one subsystem at a time, elaborating on each choice and illustrating this through images.

Chris makes sure that he not only names each choice but highlights its impact. That is, he identifies the choice (e.g. "*Contact is when the participant is looking directly at you either by a frontal gaze – Contact: Direct – or with head/eyes are turned from the side – Contact: Invite*"); he describes how it works (e.g. "*Contact builds the relationship between the image participant and viewer*"); and he explains its likely effect on viewers (e.g. "*The gorilla is looking at you side-on to appeal to you to help protect its world. It is really an invitation to help, isn't it? A kind of appeal to your emotions*").

As he begins to deal with visual ATTITUDE, Chris again ensures that he uses a strategy of identifying the choice (What's there), describing its function (how it works) and then explaining its effect on viewers (why the artist has made this choice or what the effect is). For example, he says, "*If you look at this image, it's Involvement because the head of the gorilla is turned towards you, but as the body is not, it is Detachment. This combination of Involvement and Detachment allows the gorilla to appear as if he is appealing to you for help, that he needs your help. The gorilla might look more threatening if he were facing you directly.*"

The students are then set a task:

- Find two different advertisements to compare and contrast. Use the table below to record your ideas. Think about how the choices help you respond to the image. Be prepared to share your ideas with the group.

Table 7.8 displays the framework that could be used to support children's analysis. Pairs of students share with another pair before the class regroups, using a jigsaw strategy. Each group then contributes their impressions of each image with the class in a follow up discussion. As students respond, Chris guides their discussion, using prompt questions and recasting responses using the visual metalanguage. He shifts from questions about what is chosen, naming the choices and then talking about why these choices might have been made and what the effect is on the viewer. As students begin to proffer insights on these issues, he affirms and elaborates on these for the others, modelling the kind of interpretation he is looking for. Here it is important to guide the students to consider how choices combine to persuade the viewer. There is no expectation that the analyses will make use of all the metalinguistic terms at this point, but Chris presses the students to use some terms as appropriate to encourage them to use the system diagrams. Discussions of how Facebook images could function to make young people feel either embarrassed or confronted might emerge at this point and would serve as a launching place for the work to come next.

TABLE 7.8 Comparison of advertisements

	Image 1	Effect on viewer?	Image 2	Effect on viewer?
FOCALIZATION				
SOCIAL DISTANCE				
ATTITUDE – INVOLVEMENT				
ATTITUDE – POWER				

Guided practice – altering a visual text

Chris is keen to begin work on the Facebook poster, so decides on a quick task that will involve the students in jointly constructing a visual text using the new understandings. He asks them to return to one of the images they analysed earlier and make two or three changes to the choices there, drawing a version of what the new image could look like. Pairs of students then exchange their altered images and comment on the persuasive meaning potential of the changes. This new meaning is then compared to that in the previous analysis to consider the impact that the changes have made. Chris selects one or two of the revised images and invites the students to discuss the choices that have been made and the effect they have on interaction with viewers. As needed, Chris provides the necessary prompts, or re-casts the students' explanations and comments using the metalanguage to help explain the semiotic choices.

Independently composing an advertisement

Preparation for the multimodal poster addressing the Facebook issue has involved several tasks, beginning with the students researching and writing an Exposition arguing either for or against children under thirteen being able to use Facebook. The students have also been introduced to the systems of FOCALIZATION, SOCIAL DISTANCE and ATTITUDE which they will be able to draw on as they compose their poster, and the joint construction of the storyboard for the video has provided them with a focussed planning opportunity which requires them to talk about and explain choices and their intended impact.

This time, Chris wants each individual students to plan his/her poster and provides them with a template to do so. He wants them to detail the choices from the three systems that they intend to use in their poster and reminds the students of the resources they have at their disposal. In Figure 7.2 below, we see Helena's plan. It is the precursor to the Facebook image presented in our previous chapter. In this multimodal composition, Helena has taken a different stance to the one she took in her written exposition, stating that she felt that projecting a negative view opened up more opportunities for her to exploit the visual meanings available through choices from the systems.

The co-patterning of choices from the three systems set out in Helena's plan contribute to building the increasing stress and anxiety of the Facebook user progressively across the images. Helena's selections include:

- In Image 1 and Image 2, Attitudinal choices of Detachment and Equality and Social (SOCIAL DISTANCE) position the viewer as an 'along with' observer and therefore able to read the computer screens along with the represented participant (enlarged in the boxes to the left of each panel).
- In Image 3, there is dramatic shift to Direct Contact, Personal distance and Subjective Involvement, with the distress of the recipient of the unpleasant comment clearly evident.

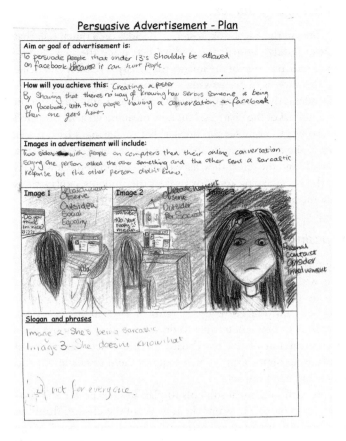

FIGURE 7.2 Helena's persuasive advertisement plan.

The final poster (presented earlier as Figure 6.1) exemplifies Helena's capacity to make salient choices from three systems of visual grammar in her persuasive text to compose a text which carries a clear message

By the end of this unit of work, the students have been introduced to semiotic choices in visual texts and have planned and composed a multimodal text around a familiar issue. They have related their work on the images to the big question of whether Facebook is a source of cyber bullying or can be used to challenge this kind of thing through more considered interventions by students, 'speaking back' through visual texts to others who seek to demean young people. The teaching has been purposeful, contextualized and focussed. It is clear that work on the visual systems has been sufficiently rigorous to challenge the students, and Chris is mindful that further opportunities to use these in interpreting and composing texts are needed. However, as Helena's plan and composition suggest, image analysis has enabled Helena and her class maters to make conscious decisions about how to craft a multimodal text which will align with her intended viewers to draw them in intersubjectively. They will now be more conscious and hopefully more considered users of multimodal texts like this.

Scenario 3 – Mood and Modality in a secondary classroom

Year 8 teacher Jamie is concerned about her students' ability to craft effective arguments – in oral and written language. She teaches a class of mixed ability students, many of whom are reluctant to write extended texts and often assume that strong and categorical claims are a sign of rhetorical strength. As they move into the later years of secondary schooling, she is keen to introduce students to resources that enable them to adjust the strength of their claims. Too often, they tend to directly confront their readers with overly strong modal verbs such as 'should' and 'must', thinking that this is the only way to assert a point of view. She sees MODALITY as a powerful resource for ensuring greater objectivity in claims her students make and crucial for accessing academic language demands of other subjects in the social sciences, in history as well as English. It is a resource that her students are not yet using effectively. She wants students to be able to distinguish between levels of MODALITY to offer more subtle choices, and thus modulate a stance to convince readers to share views more effectively. While she is quite conscious that the force of an argument also comes through in attitudinal language choices, her teaching focus will be on modal choices which she will relate to the crafting of effective statements. In this endeavour, Jamie is guided by the AC:E content requirement that students "Understand how modality is achieved through discriminating choices in modal verbs, adverbs, adjectives and nouns" (ACELA 1536). Because many of her students struggle with grammar, she has designed a scheme of work that will enable them to identify modal verbs, adverbs and nouns, describe their 'strength' and value and interpret their contribution to the impression of subjectivity or objectivity in different arguments. She hopes that students will see the importance of attention to modals if they can link this work to being taken seriously in their arguments.

She sets out her goals for the sequence of lessons (see Table 7.9).

Jamie's special focus is interpersonal so she sets out the probe questions that will focus her students' attention on MOOD and MODALITY choices in the Expositions they read first then later compose:

TABLE 7.9 Jamie's teaching plan for argument

Big question: How do we ensure people take our claims seriously when we argue?	
Exposition focus: Interpersonal Lens	*Grammatics focus*
How word choices express obligation and possibility	Modal verbs, adverbs and nouns
How arguments might be made through statements, imperatives or questions	Mood choices – declarative, interrogative and imperative.

Interpersonal probe questions for argument

- What use is made of *modal verbs, adverbs, adjectives and phrases* in this text?
- How well do they work? Remember that in some kinds of argument, high value modals are powerful and in others they are less so.
- Are arguments made through the use of strong statements? How? At what points? For what purposes?

Modelling modality choices

Jamie begins by introducing her students to MODALITY choices which might be used throughout an exposition. She explains that modality can be used at different levels for varying impact:

- *High modality* – we sound very convinced and passionate. We use high modality when we want to <u>make</u> people agree with us or clearly state our position.
- *Medium modality* – we want to sound more reasoned and logical, less emotional but still quite definite.
- *Low modality* – we are inviting people to agree with us. Low pressure may be more subtle persuasion.

Jamie designs a table detailing the choices available to realize modality at the different levels (see Table 7.10). To avoid a reliance on modal verbs, the table aligns meaning across different word classes, which opens up a selection that students might draw on at different points. Jamie is quite conscious of not simply providing a table like this without any related teaching. She introduces one word class at a time, beginning with modal verbs, names it, describes its purpose and uses examples in texts to explain how it works.

TABLE 7.10 High, medium and low modality choices

	VERB	*ADVERB*	*ADJECTIVE*	*PHRASES OR CLAUSES*
High modality	must should will shall	certainly absolutely definitely	certain definite	It is obvious Everyone knows It is essential to
Medium modality	will would can should	probably usually generally	probable usual likely	I think/believe In my opinion
Low modality	may could might can	possibly perhaps maybe sometimes	possible	I guess It suggests that It seems

Jamie looks for two articles on the internet about the use of iPads in the classroom presenting different views on the same topic. Providing her students with a copy of the articles, she sets the following questions to guide their reading of each text in pairs, reminding them that they should make use of the tables which provide examples of high/ medium / low modality:

1. Who is the writer of the article?
2. List the points that are made.
3. Highlight words of high modality.
4. Highlight words of low modality.
5. Is there a pattern of low or high modality in the article?

The students report back to the group, with Jamie highlighting patterns of modality choices on a copy of each text for all to see. Through this task, Jamie helps her to students to identify words which express different levels of modality, describe how these choices work in the context the text, and explain the points at which the choices are made and for what effect. The students can see a pattern in the use of modal verbs in particular, where the authors began with low modality choices shifting to high modality as the arguments progressed.

Her next activity focusses on distinguishing between choices that express degrees of *possibility* and those that express degrees of *obligation* where high modality demands or insists, and low modality suggests or hints. In groups, students are asked to put statements in order and to consider which statement they would most like to hear/ least like to hear. This task requires students to distinguish between levels of modality and consider the impact of statements in terms of possibility and obligation at different levels of modality.

Task 1a: Put the following in order from 1–9, from those you would most prefer someone to say (1) to one you would least prefer them to say (9)

Statement
I might give you a present
I should give you a present
I would give you a present
I will give you a present
I must give you a present
I can give you a present
I may give you a present
I could give you a present
I shall give you a present.

Task 1b: Put the following in order from 1–9, from most commanding (1) to least commanding (9)

Statement
Students should stop talking
Students might stop talking
Students will stop talking
Students must stop talking
Students can stop talking

The students discuss their choices in small groups before returning to the whole group. Through the discussion, Jamie can support their understanding about the distinction between possibility and obligation as well as how the choice of modal verbs impacts on the strength of each assertion.

Sharing the load – Guided practice using modality

Jamie is mindful of the need to balance the time teaching about language and providing students with the opportunity to write and practise what they have learned in meaningful ways. Given the time constraints of scheduled classes in secondary English, it is not always feasible to have students write an entire essay, so Jamie makes certain that she includes short, focussed tasks at different points in her sequence of lessons. While there are other aspects of Exposition which require attention, this short and sharp focus on MODALITY works well for Jamie and her students at this point. The guided practice stage of her teaching is based on pair and small group work focussing on the sentence and paragraphs:

- Your topic sentence is 'The children of the twenty-first century live in a different world. It has a fifth dimension – cyber space – and it is changing their lives'.

Task 2 Write two or three sentences to follow the topic sentence using modal verbs to express obligation and possibility.

- Include modal verbs at one level – high modality, medium modality or low modality.
- Compare your group's sentence with that of another group. Rank the statements in terms of the force of the statement.

Task 3 Using the same topic sentence, write five sentences this time using modal verbs, adverbs, adjectives and/or phrases. You must use some form of modality in every sentence.

- Compare your sentences with another group's. Use the following questions to guide your comments:
    - What use is made of modal verbs, adverbs, adjectives and phrases and clauses?
    - How well do they work?
    - Are arguments made through the use of strong statements?

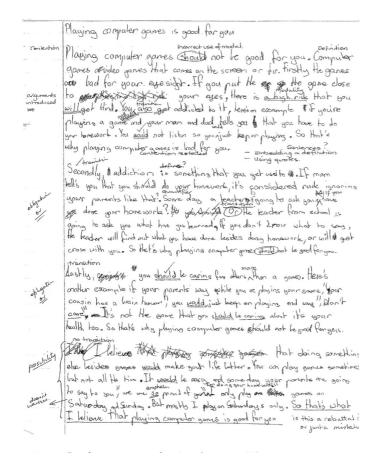

TEXT 7.2 Sam's response to the timed prompt 'Playing computer games is good for you'.

Task 4 Jamie explains how MODALITY can be used to balance different perspectives within one sentence. Using the same topic sentence, she models how the inclusion of varying levels of modality can be used to present how different groups might respond to technology:

The children of the twenty-first century live in a different world. It has a fifth dimension – cyber space – and it is changing their lives.

- The old-fashioned cling to the security of the written word, but the young trust in cyber space.
- The old-fashioned *might* cling to the security of the written word, but the young *will* trust in cyber space.
- It *might* be okay for the older generation to be technophobic, but to survive the younger generation *must* be techno-experts.

Students use the models to write their own sentences and share with the group.

Independent composition of an argument

Jamie sets her students a timed writing task in response to the prompt 'Playing computer games is good for you'. They have already done some work building up field knowledge of the topic and it is also an issue that is quite often raised in the media. In the example below written by Sam (see Text 7.2 on the previous page), we see Jamie's annotations of the student's work, with her comments attending to several areas but highlighting points where the student has attempted to use modality, sometimes successfully, and other times not. The clear and defined teaching focus has worked to support the student in his composition and the teacher in her initial assessment of his writing and impact of her teaching.

Conclusion

The teaching scenarios presented in this chapter featuring Chris and Jamie have outlined ways in which a functional grammatics might be implemented to support students' interpretation and composition of persuasive texts in primary and secondary classrooms. How teachers take up the grammatical options available and operationalise them in ways which progressively scaffold their students to interpret and compose print based and multimodal texts is not only dependent on pedagogic knowledge but very much aligned to their knowledge about language and image. Beginning with the establishment of clearly defined, grammatically informed curriculum goals, strong understandings about persuasive meanings which establish plausible, logical arguments which engage their readers through written Exposition can be established through explicit teaching and modelling. Similar practices can be implemented to explore resources that realize meanings in visual and multimodal texts. As illustrated through the scenarios, an interpersonal lens can be applied to both verbal and multimodal texts to explore semiotic choices in tangible, contextualized ways. The possibilities presented in this chapter are just that – possibilities, and there are of course, other ways in which functional grammatics could be deployed in these contexts

Notes

1. In the AC:E, (ACARA, 2012) curriculum content related to Language is indicated with the acronym, ACELA, with special focus number following this (e.g. ACELA 1494 and ACELA 1495). The acronym for literature is ACELT (e.g. ACELT 1605) and for literacy is ACELY (e.g. ACELY 1704).
2. The article was first published on Wednesday 25 May 2011 15.30 EDT, and is available via the link https://www.theguardian.com/technology/2011/may/25/should-children-be-allowed-on-facebook)

References

Australian Curriculum Assessment and Reporting Authority (ACARA) (2012). *Australian curriculum: English.* Version 3.0. Sydney: ACARA. Retrieved from www.australian curriculum.edu.au/copyright.

Brisk, M. (2015). *Engaging students in academic literacies: Genre-based pedagogy for K-5 classrooms*. New York: Routledge.

Butt, D., Fahey, R., Feez, S. & Spinks, S. (2012). *Using functional grammar: An explorer's guide* (3rd edition). South Yarra: Macmillan Education Australia.

Christie, F. & Derewianka, B. (2008). *School discourse: Learning to write across the years of schooling*. London: Continuum.

Derewianka, B. & Jones, P. (2012). *Teaching language in context*. Melbourne: Oxford University Press.

Gibbons, P. (2015). *Scaffolding language, Scaffolding learning: Teaching English language learners in the mainstream classroom* (2nd edition). Portsmouth, NH: Heinemann.

Humphrey, S. (2017). *Academic literacies in the middle years: A framework for enhancing teacher knowledge and student achievement*. New York & London: Routledge.

Humphrey, S., Love, K. & Droga, L. (2011). *Working grammar: An introduction for secondary English teachers*. Port Melbourne, Victoria: Pearson.

Humphrey, S, Droga, L. & Feez, S. (2012). *Grammar and meaning*. Newtown, Australia: Primary English Teaching Association Australia.

Kress, G. & van Leeuwen, T. (2006). *Reading images: The grammar of visual design*. London & New York: Routledge.

Painter, C., Martin, J. R. & Unsworth, L. (2013). *Reading visual narratives: Image analysis of children's picture books*. Sheffield; Bristol, CT: Equinox.

8
TRACKING EAST
Exploring narratives of many kinds (and modes)

Introduction

In Chapters 5 and 6, we have illustrated how persuasion, like narrative, is not only fundamental to subject English but diverse in its manifestations. Its structures and purposes can range from the forms of written Exposition valued by the academy, to the multimodal forms of argumentation increasingly required by contemporary language arts curricula, to the study of online forms of persuasion which exploit, and are exploited by, young people in their everyday lives through social media platforms such as Blogs, Facebook and Instagram. In Chapter 7, we have seen how teachers engage their students meaningfully in the analysis and construction of varied forms and modes of persuasion, supporting them to identify and deploy a range of verbal and visual semiotic resources for varied school purposes. The textual diversity of the forms of persuasion we have explored in the everyday, civic and academic domains applies just as much to narrative, as we have seen in Chapters 2, 3 and 4, and presents both exciting and challenging opportunities for teachers seeking to use a metalanguage that encompasses visual as well as verbal resources. In this chapter, we take an excursion deeper into new and emerging territory, as we explore visual and verbal choices and their interplay in the multimodal texts that are increasingly part of contemporary curricula. We strategically focus on narrative semiosis in this chapter, considering the challenge of intra- and inter-textuality across various modes, while making the ramifications for study of persuasion evident.

The challenge of diverse multimodal narratives

If narrative is ubiquitous in subject English, it is also diverse in its manifestations. But there are commonalities across the diversities. Stories differ in generic structure (though they always involve a complication of some kind); they diverge in subject matter (though they always involve a problem in human experience and an attempt by one or more individuals to resolve this); the attitudes expressed and invoked will differ but always involve evaluation of one kind or another. And, finally, of course, being so fundamental to cultural life, they vary across media. The richness of narrative texts with their structural variation, topics, stances and orchestration in different modes enlivens the work of English. On any one day, children may be exposed to anecdotes, moral tales, detective stories, ballads, short stories, comics and short or long movies.

But this plenitude can be a challenge too, especially if we need to tease out common threads of meaning across different texts, to explore both similarities and differences in texts that jostle for attention. And really, we have only begun to open the 'Pandora's box' of narrative semiosis with our exploration of words and pictures. Feature films use sound effects, music and *mise en scène* to build narrative worlds and engage viewers emotionally. Graphic novels use text panels and layout, dialogue and thought bubbles and different forms of character representation to work their magic. Digital narratives can draw on a wide range of still and moving image resources as well as sound music and hypertextual links to generate narrative worlds. These can often shift to communicate a highly layered and dynamic visual experience.

The textual diversity increasingly part of the curriculum in school English is both exciting and occasionally overwhelming for teachers keen to explore this in systematic ways. How do they compare versions of a traditional tale like *Goldilocks and the Three Bears* or *The Three Little Pigs* or perhaps contemporary texts like the Harry Potter novels and the popular film series that followed? The demands on a functional grammatics that aims to support work of this kind cannot be underestimated. Our metalanguage needs to show how combined visual and verbal choices (as only two of semiotic modes in play in many texts) open up different interpretive possibilities for readers or viewers. Having access to a common terminology that enables us to relate choices in terms of the meanings they realize is a crucial task for a functional grammatics.

The *inter*-textual challenge is one thing; another can more properly be considered *intra*-textual. As our excursions into multimodal texts like picture books have shown, we need to explore the contribution of all choices in texts (including the visual ones) to the creation of higher order meaning – what we call second order semiosis in our earlier chapters. In earlier chapters, we drew on analogies between dimensions of meaning in language and images to explore similarities and differences between modes in multimodal texts. Interactive meanings can be approached from the point of view of intimacy and detachment, emotional engagement or angle of vision (gaze) and these apply as much to verbal as to visual modes of narration. A key strategy here has been to draw on the likeness between kindred resources whilst bringing out differences in forms of realization.

Of course, images work differently from language and our descriptions need to attend closely to the distinctive character of their manifestations. Both difference and commonality are important to analysis of multimodal texts. This means sensitive attunement to details of colour, shape, detail and the arrangements in images on a page and to details of action, character and setting in wordings. But it also means moving between image and verbiage to explore their mutual interplay – how they work together to create themes, attitudes and aesthetic responses. This can be quite crucial to overarching meaning. For example, the short novel, *Fantastic Mr Fox* is primarily written. We don't need the images to make sense of the story and its characters. Yet, the images do confirm the impression made by wordings – the foxes are brave, resourceful and good and the farmers are rapacious, ridiculous and bad.

However, in some multimodal fiction, the relationship between image and verbiage is not one of synonymy but of tension, irony, even contradiction. We need to work carefully with the images, even just to understand the diegesis properly. For example, in the illustrated short story, *Grandad's Gifts* (Jennings & Gouldthorpe, 1992), introduced in Chapter 4, the image of young adolescent, Shane, viewed through a keyhole, suggests the boy is being observed long before the text reveals the presence in his late Grandad's wardrobe of the fox skin stole that, later in the story, gradually shows signs of returning to life. Then at the end of the story, when Shane has been exposed as having disobeyed his father in opening the door of the wardrobe, which had always remained locked, he says:

> I didn't care what he said or what he did. I was happy in a way I had never been happy before. I picked up the two glass eyes that lay rejected on the floor.

There is a dissonance here between image and language, as the image (shown as Figure 4.8) does not show happiness or defiance at all. It is a high angle view of Shane looking up, presumably at his father, with a downcast look of sadness, or perhaps remorse or even foreboding. So, in this case it is the divergence between the AFFECT shown in the image and that represented in the language that conveys how it is only possible for Shane to experience this happiness and defiance secretly, without disclosing his experience of the supernatural transformation of the fox skin stole into a blue-eyed fox.

In this book, we have not given serious attention to modes like typography or layout, both of which are crucial to a full appreciation of texts like Tann's narrative, *The Lost Thing*. But a beginning must surely be made on this work and its implications for English drawn out carefully. Our concern with both the intertextual and intratextual dimensions of the challenge is not fanciful. In fact, it is now embedded in curriculum requirements such as those of the Australian curriculum (ACARA, 2012). As early as Year 2 (when they are approximately 7 years of age), children are now expected to "identify visual representations of characters' actions, reactions, speech and thought processes in narratives, and consider how these images add to or contradict or multiply the meaning of accompanying words" (ACELA 1469). Then, in Year 4, building on this in study of literature, they will "discuss *how* authors and illustrators make stories exciting, moving and absorbing and hold readers' attention by using various techniques" (ACELT1605).

In this context, children's enjoyment of 'the total world of the story action' – what is often called the 'diegesis' (Bordwell & Thompson, 1990, p. 56; Genette, 1980) – becomes a preliminary (but limited) part of narrative appreciation. Students need to know 'what is going on' in a text if they are to engage with it to a preliminary extent. Still, there is more to their potential enjoyment of a narrative (at least if it is worthy of study) if children have access to a metalanguage that supports this. In shifting their attention from diegesis (story) to narrative semiosis (techniques shaping story), they require ways of talking about narratives that treat them less as 'windows' on human experience and more as optics that bring certain aspects of experience into view. This means exploration of *how* texts invite relatedness to experience in readers and of the shaping power of the composition in this process. A semiotic reading places teachers and children in a new analytical role, orienting them towards the 'how' of literary craft rather than just the 'what' of a story.

Tracking east into the field of intratextual and intertextual relations in verbal and multimodal texts, we are in new territory in English. Some would argue that we are well outside the legitimate purview of a grammatics, even one oriented to meaning, choice and multimodality as ours claims to be. But the East is the place where the sun appears and should be a place of enlightenment and re-creation. That is the spirit in which we approach our work on the interplay of visual and verbal choices within texts and on the transformations of meaning that students undertake in their written responses, their visual translations and their multimodal interpretive work. Although we consider the challenge of intra- and inter-textuality from the point of view of narrative semiosis, the same issues emerge in relation to persuasion. However, our emphasis in this chapter is on narrative as one site in which these issues can be explored with ramifications for study of persuasion considered in passing. Each section of this chapter considers texts in some kind of uptake of another text. It might be a response to a narrative image, a reading of the relationship between image and verbiage on a page, a linkage between earlier and later parts of a narrative, a visual representation of a verbal text or indeed, as in our final student text, a multimodal interpretation of a classical text like Shakespeare's *Macbeth*. Our focus in all these excursions is on the necessity for, and potential of, a relational approach to grammatics – an orientation to different connections between one form or one meaning and another, whether this is realized through verbal or visual means.

Section 2 considers the interplay of different semiotic modes on single pages of *The Great Bear* and how this shapes students' written responses to questions about point of view. We consider an intratextual focus here. Section 3 moves beyond the page to think about the larger 'canvas' of a multimodal text and what the tools might offer students' interpretation of unfolding meanings in a picture book like *The Tunnel*. Section 4 extends the purview of functional grammatics even further and considers intertextual relations between different versions of the 'same' story – in particular *The Lost Thing* (in book and movie version). Here we acknowledge the importance of the two orders of meaning that a carefully crafted literary text makes available – the diegetic order of characters and events that change little in each version (especially if the text is highly important culturally) and the semiotic order that shapes readers' interpretations of literary significance.

Section 5 considers multimodality from the point of view of creative work by students themselves and kinds of understandings that emerge from their transformations of narrative choices. We consider a visualization by two young students: the first is a visualization of an early event in Tim Winton's *Blueback*; the second is an animation by a student who was exploring the possibilities of point of view in rendering events from the familiar nursery tale, *Humpty Dumpty*. Our conclusion highlights the implications of our forays into multimodality for a contemporary grammatics for English.

The Great Bear

We first introduced aspects of *The Great Bear* by Libby Gleeson and Armin Greder (1995) in Chapter 2 in relation to foreshadowing through visual Circumstantiation (see discussion of Figure 2.2). This is a powerful tale not just in its own right but because it is open to a variety of interpretations. The dancing bear spends her days in a cage and her nights performing for a circus crowd in villages visited by the circus troupe. It is clear she is the victim of the villagers who taunt her as she dances, assaulting her with sticks and stones. One fateful night, after another harrowing episode of human cruelty, the bear decides to stand up for herself. At this point in the book, the words disappear and the reader tracks only the images, attempting to infer the nature of her final action. The enigma of this final action has been a source of endless speculation on the part of students in The Grammatics Project, as will be seen.

The Great Bear is a powerful literary picture book that works (in the first half of the text) through the interplay of economical poetic writing, a dominant coloured picture and a faint line drawing of the bear on the bottom left hand of the page. The following double-page spread in Figure 8.1[1] highlights the interplay of each of the three semiotic modes.

In a relational approach to grammatics, we consider how readers endeavour to make sense of each set of choices on this page. Children might begin by working out what people represented in the colour image are doing (Are they circus performers, for example?), perhaps moving between music making and repeated commands, "Dance, bear, dance". From here, they might wonder about the faint drawing of the turning bear and what s/he is doing. If asked how this drawing is linked to words on the page, they might point to the words "She looked around". If asked about repeated patterns in the words on the page, they might notice recurring words like "clash, clash, clash". Because the drawing of the bear in the left-hand corner is so faint, we can assume that this is a rendering of the bear's response to the clash of cymbals. It is an indistinct drawing of the bear, suggesting a creature at the mercy of the crowd. Read in concert with the coloured picture of unsmiling

FIGURE 8.1 A double-page spread from *The Great Bear* showing the circus players.

circus players, the insistent commands in the verbiage and the faint drawing, the bear can be plausibly construed as a victim of the crowd and of her intolerable situation generally.

This impression is only underscored as we turn the page to find the villagers poking a large stick at what can only be the bear (see Figure 2.2 earlier).

Once again, in Figure 2.2 we find the same insistent language displayed in short lines down the left side of the double page spread. There are no human agents in each sentence, even though the dominant image represents the villagers as highly agentive. This time, the faint line drawing of the bear enacts the pain of a creature attempting to avert her attackers. Her body lists as she leans away, facing 'us' and thus inviting contact. In terms of action, the vector created by the bodies of the crowd and intensified by the stick held forward by the leader of the crowd creates a unified 'V' shape that implicates the viewer. If asked "Why are we looking down on the people in this image?" the answer must surely be 'because we are invited to take the position of the bear'. If we consult options for interactive meaning presented in Figure 3.2, we can say that we are involved with the villagers (in their frontal aggressive stance) and positioned above with perceptual (if not actual) power. We are looking down on them as if we are the bear, seeing what she sees.

To understand the shift in power that occurs in *The Great Bear* at this point, we need to combine the description of viewer power (through the high angle viewpoint the artist has selected in the coloured picture) with analysis of focalization (see Figure 3.3). Verbally speaking, the narrator does not give the reader access to the bear's point of view. The words are either voiced by the narrator telling the story (e.g. "Trumpets blast, drums roll") or by characters within the story – the circus performers or the villagers ("Dance bear dance"). In other words, we do not 'see with' the bear through internal focalization in the language of the text. Visually speaking, however, we are invited to identify with the bear through a choice for highly mediated Contact.

In The Grammatics Project, students were asked questions about some of the double-page spreads including those above. In response to a question about the image presented in Figure 2.2, "Why are we looking down on the people in this picture?", almost all readers from Years 4–10 recognized that they were 'occupying' the position of the bear. While some could technicalise their responses, most remained intuitive in their reading (Unsworth & Macken-Horarik, 2015).

If we take the written answers to this question from Year 4 children (approximately 10 years of age) in three different schools, it is clear that they inferred the meaning of the artist's depiction of point of view in the images above.

Text 8.1 shows that Kian, has read the power dynamic in the image.

> In the picture we are looking down on them as we are the one with power.

TEXT 8.1 Kian's response to the question on point of view.

Michele sees the choice as shaped by the bear's view (Text 8.2).

> We are looking down on the people because the image is actually seen by the bear.

TEXT 8.2 Michele's response to the question on point of view.

And Jacqueline communicates the same understanding in Text 8.3.

> Because we are looking though the bear's eyes.

TEXT 8.3 Jacqueline's response to the question on point of view.

Except for Kian's response which refers to viewer-power in the image, the children appear to grasp the significance of the choice without explaining how they know this. Prior to their introduction to a metalanguage for exploring point of view, most were unable to reason about choices along semiotic lines, even if they could recognize their implications. As will be seen, once introduced to the grammatics in the context of work on picture books, these children were better able to marshal explanations of the effects of particular images and wordings in these texts. The grammatics gave them access to a precise metalanguage that supported their reasoning.

A key affordance of a relational approach to grammatics is its capacity to yoke recognition of formal choices to awareness of their function and to relate both to larger patterns of significance (second order semiosis). In multimodal texts like picture books, advertisements and comics, this larger significance is inferred through the "inter-animation of words and pictures" (Lewis, 2001, p. 35). This is a key idea in semiotics, as Roland Barthes expressed this in his work on the 'rhetoric of the image',

> Text and image stand in a complementary relationship; the words, in the same way as the images, are fragments of a more general syntagm and the unity of the message is realized at a higher level, that of the story, the anecdote, the diegesis.
>
> *(Barthes, 1977, p. 41)*

However, what gives a text its unity is not something that can be decided by fiat. As Michael Halliday has acknowledged, "what is 'above' the text depends on one's perspective, on the nature of the inquiry and the ideology of the inquirer. There are different higher-level semiotics and often different levels of meaning within each" (Halliday, 1978, p. 137). In exploring possible and the plausible interpretations of texts, particularly those like the enigmatic picture book *The Great Bear*, we need to look closely at what readers say and write about them. After all, it is the reader who infers narrative significance, whose interpretive work produces the 'unity' of the message at a higher level.

The kinds of coherence that children assign to narratives, especially those that feature an enigma like many of those we introduced to teachers and students in The Grammatics Project, can vary significantly. It is in students' interpretive processes that we find evidence of this interplay. Lewis speaks of the crucial role of such processes of interpretation in analysis of what they call 'inter-animation':

> If we say with Meek that 'pictures and words on a page interanimate each other', we cannot mean that anything physical is happening. We can stare at the page for as long as we like but the pictures and words will stay quite still and determinedly leave each other alone. The only relations they share on the page are spatial ones and if any animating gets done, it is because an active, meaning-seeking reader is at work.
>
> *(Lewis, 2001, p. 55)*

If we consider the third page in our sequence from *The Great Bear*, it is clear a moment of crisis has occurred in the narrative. Early intimations of a shift in power, produced through the gaze that the artist has inscribed for us 'as the character' are fulfilled in the dramatic configuration of word and picture in the following double page spread in Figure 8.2.[2]

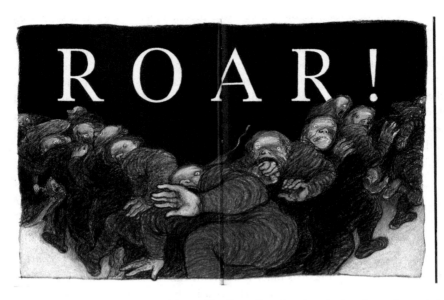

FIGURE 8.2 Double-page spread from *The Great Bear* showing the bear's turning point.

Now it is the bear who 'speaks', as only a bear can. The dramatic V-shaped vector created by the phalanx of terrified villagers positions us as the bear because it is only from this position that it would be possible to see these participants as we do. It is clear also from the salience and size of the typeface and the exclamation mark that a turning point has been reached in this narrative. But how do we infer the significance of the turning point? What is the 'higher order unity' discerned by students? If we consider students' answers to the question posed in relation to this page – "Roar! Why is this one word so important to what the story is about?" – we discern something of students' interpretive work, their reasoning about the 'why' beneath the 'what' of the interplay between image and verbiage on this page.

Alex in Year 4 (see Text 8.4) explains that the roar is an expression of the bear's anger.

> Because the bear was angry and upset

TEXT 8.4 Alex's reading of the significance of the one word 'Roar' in the story.

Neha in Year 7 relates the roar to the sequence of events in the story as well as to the fury of the bear (Text 8.5).

> The word 'Roar!' is very important because it shows that the bear is no longer accepting the fact that he has to dance in front of a crowd to entertain them and get poked. She is furious with them and starts to roar.

TEXT 8.5 Neha's reading of the significance of the one word 'Roar' in the story.

Tom in Year 10 relates the roar to the unfolding climax of the narrative and to the breaking point of the bear (Text 8.6). He demonstrates awareness of the intimate connection between genre structure and experiential meaning.

> This one word depicts the climax of the story and the breaking point of our bear, it shows that the line that the people crossed was also the line to push the bear over the edge.

TEXT 8.6 Tom's reading of the significance of the one word 'Roar' in the story.

The inferencing students undertake is itself relational but the readings produced from this and the account of second order semiosis vary in important ways. They may see the 'roar' as an expression of the bear's feelings (Alex), of the logic of events (Neha) or the climax in narrative arc (Tom). It is interesting to note that interpretation develops less in a linear than in a culminative way. Each response in our sequence of three above subsumes earlier ones. They are in fact supervenient on them, dependent without being able to be explained by lower levels of interpretation. Whilst Alex notes only the bear's feelings, Neha takes this for granted but sees the bear's emotions as part of a wider focus on the logic of events and what the roar 'shows' of the bear's turning point. For Tom, it is narrative structure that is criterial. This student widens the frame to focus on the crisis in the genre betokened by the 'roar'. He refers to 'the breaking point of the bear' at this point in the event sequence. It is a feature of high-end interpretations that they include but transcend more rudimentary accounts, necessarily becoming more complex and abstract in the course of this development (see Macken-Horarik, 2016b for further exploration of these trends in students' interpretive practices).

The value of narratives like *The Great Bear* is that they facilitate different kinds of interpretive work by students. There is an enigma at the heart of this narrative and readers must leap (much as the bear does) beyond the diegesis to discern the implicature of the verbal silence at the end of the text. In this picture book, as in many others, the front and end papers are crucial to sense making. And the grammatics must endeavour (or we with it) to inform our interpretation of the interplay between the words (and the final silence), the images (both faint and coloured) and the endpapers and their cosmological signifance.

This is more than a task for a narrative grammatics of course. It applies equally well to the study of persuasion. Multimodal texts that appeal for help in saving baby seals or African gorillas depend for their effectiveness on the interplay of image and verbiage (and indeed layout and typography) and a grammatics adequate to this also needs adaptation to the task of modelling the crucial interplay within the text and of the uptake by readers of these in their interpretations of the messages.

The Tunnel

We encountered some of the images from *The Tunnel*, by Anthony Browne (1989) in Chapter 2. This is a story about sibling rivalry and ultimately of the power of love in healing differences between siblings. The differences between Jack and Rose are starkly portrayed from the outset. Whilst Rose prefers to stay "inside on her own reading and dreaming", Jack plays "outside with his friends, laughing and shouting, throwing, kicking, roughing and tumbling". The pictures only confirm the impression of two opposing worlds. They depict Rose reading her book of tales as she relaxes in a window nook, lies in her bed while Jack kicks his ball in a waste yard outside with his friends. In the Orientation to the narrative, each sibling is introduced as 'different' in every way. When their mother forces them both outside to "be nice to each other just for once", neither Rose nor Jack express enthusiasm for the enterprise. But when Jack ventures into a tunnel, he leaves his soccer ball behind, whilst Rose clutches her book of fairy tales looking at him disappear into the darkness. Although we know from his physical and verbal behaviour what Jack is like, we do not 'see with' him. Our point of view is mediated through the pictorial choices of the composer. As we saw in Chapter 2, an understanding of Focalization enables us to interpret both what is happening in Figure 2.3 and to share Rose's point of view rather than being positioned 'as the character'. Our view subsumes hers, enabling us both to see her and to see what she sees. The 'over-the-shoulder' view can be seen as aligning us strongly with the focalising character's point of view (Unsworth, 2006, pp. 95–97). This is appropriate to the depiction of the one who must confront her fears and find and rescue her brother Jack. The image that follows this one in Figure 2.4 shows Rose disappearing into the tunnel, leaving her book of fairy tales (and her dependence on fantasy) behind. The point of view offered by these images aligns readers intersubjectively with Rose.

A thematic interpretation of literary texts, even short and relatively accessible ones like *The Tunnel*, means not only looking closely at choices made by an author or artist but seeing them as motivated by higher order concerns (Macken-Horarik, 2006). A symbolic reading of the abandoned book of fairy tales (for Rose) or the soccer ball (for Jack) puts pressure on the grammar. In our responses to the choices, we will tend to produce clauses that assign qualities to things (e.g. 'She *was* frightened') or relate concrete details to abstract significance (e.g. 'The black background *represents* her mental state' or 'This one word *depicts* the climax of the story'). In functional grammatics, the key resource here is the Relational Process which serves to "characterize and identify" things (Halliday & Matthiessen, 2004, p. 210). These processes are inherently semiotic (Matthiessen, 1991) because they enable us to relate forms to meanings through symbolic verbs like 'show', 'express', 'represent', 'depict', 'signify', 'reveal', 'illustrate' and symbolize'.

In our project, these verbs began to appear in the oral and written responses of students following teachers' interventions in text response in 2013. These emerged in part at least as a result of our approach to interpretation, based on the stratified model of language that informed our workshops. When it comes to interpreting images, the first level or 'landing place' involves recognition of colour, gaze and vectors, amongst other choices. In many classrooms, teachers asked students to look closely at 'what' choices had been made. At times, their naming of these were more technical; at other times, less so. Teachers encouraged them to describe these in detail, noting how they worked, tuning into a mood generated by colour palette, exploring the point of view invited by a gaze, noting the salience of a highlighted figure or the action generated by a vector. In this respect, they endeavoured to describe images carefully, giving them appropriate weight in classroom discussions. As Abousnnouga and Machin (2010) have observed in their semiotic study of war monuments, description can be under-valued in the rush to work out what things 'mean'. As project teachers moved upwards and outwards from particular pages to patterns across the text as a whole, they discussed the significance of repeated, contrasting or changing choices. They were moving into the 'why' of choices. This meant exploration of questions like "Why do we see a change in colour palette at this point in *The Tunnel*?" or "Why is the girl shown as she is here?" and so on.

Developments in students' written responses were often striking, as if they had discovered (or been shown) a portal into symbolic meaning – the 'why' beneath the 'what'. In one of the tasks we gave students, we asked them to write about why the image of the girl in Figure 3.3 from *The Tunnel* is shown as it is. This page presents Rose standing outside the tunnel waiting for her brother to re-emerge. Jacqueline (in Year 4) responded as follows in Text 8.7.

> The girl is the main focus on the page and the background image is in the shape of the tunnel.

TEXT 8.7 Jacqueline's response to the question about Rose.

Kian (in the same year but a different school) foregrounded the impact of the image on the reader. Text 8.8 presents his written response to the same question:

> The first image forces you to empathize with the sister Rosie because the black background makes you feel as if the darkness is overwhelming Rosie and her facial expression really shows that she may burst into a stream of sadness.

TEXT 8.8 Kian's response to the question about Rose.

Perhaps predictably, as a secondary school student, Neha (in Year 7) produced a more detailed response (Text 8.9).

> The girl is shown to be sad, frightened and almost in the state of crying. The image of the girl is shown as it is because she is frightened and nervous about his brother being in the tunnel for so long. The black background represents her mental state where she feels lost and frightened about her brother not coming out.

TEXT 8.9 Neha's response to the question about Rose.

All the responses demonstrate awareness of what Kress (2010) calls 'interests' shaping choices in an image like this. The task of students is to recognize and interpret choices for point of view, facial expression and the black tunnel-shaped background as motivated. In order to do this, they have to deploy the grammar of Relational Processes and symbolic verbs like 'show' and 'represent'. These resources enable students like Neha and Kian to construe symbolic meaning – a crucial feature of semiotic readings (Unsworth & Macken-Horarik, 2015).

But it was in the interview data that this capacity to explore higher order meanings was most evident. In a final interview between one of the authors (Carmel Sandiford) and two Year 10 students, it became clear that Hazel and Laila could now use their analysis (and by implication grammatics) to interpret the symbolic significance of events in *The Tunnel*. Laila begins with what she notices about the unfolding narrative and then shifts gear to comment on the impact it has on her and what the reversal of roles means for the two characters. Tellingly, her gaze shifts not only 'upwards' to higher order meanings but 'outwards' to incorporate the whole gestalt of the text. A moving feature of this interview is how closely the interactants – Carmel, Laila and Hazel – track one another in their dialogue. The interpretation of *The Tunnel* is clearly a joint effort:

Interviewer: Is there anything else you would like to say about *The Tunnel* – the work you've been doing? Go on, Laila – you've got an idea.
Laila: There was just one thing I noticed. I guess it just symbolizes when the brother went into the tunnel.
Interviewer: Yes …
Laila: … the next time we see him as a stone in the dark, magical forest I guess which is what you normally see in fairy tale books, right?
Interviewer: Very good.
Laila: Yes, it just kind of makes me feel like the brother and the sister somehow are … how do you say it? No, they kind of get the feel of what the other …
Hazel: Okay …

Laila:	Yes, what the other's world is like. Like how the brother is so energetic and adventurous and like how the girl would not normally do that. This time she went into the tunnel on her own into this adventure and the boy, who doesn't have anything to do with the fantasy stuff, with the fairy tale, fantasy, monsters and witches, now we see him in the girl's world in this magical forest turned into stone.
Interviewer:	That is so clever, Laila. You are so clever.
Laila:	I'd thought of that when I read the book. Pretty good.
Hazel:	I think also it shows that they were able to experience emotions that the other one would face in that like the same situation because he's running … normally he seems so brave and everything to his sister but when he's frozen in stone, you can see on his face that he's really actually scared looking back and he's running really fast and he's frozen in that position and in the tunnel, Rose is actually being the brave one and going in to get her brother.
Interviewer:	It's like a role reversal. It's wonderful.
Laila:	That's it.

A grammatics to support students' interpretive work will structure their noticing, offering a fresh view of choices that may have been taken for granted in a diegetic reading. It will (and perhaps should) fall away as students no longer need the scaffolding it provides. Awareness of the text as an aesthetic construct that shapes interpretation is a crucial feature of the semiotic reading. A short story, a graphic novel or a movie may feature the same story (more or less the same diegesis) but the interpretive possibilities of each version will vary. Once again, we need access to frameworks that reveal commonalities (e.g. storyline or situation) and differences in versions (e.g. degree of empathy invited for a character, attention to verisimilitude, symbolism). In the next section, we consider how different versions of the same story can be approached using the grammatics and what this offers teachers keen to explore the effects of choices in texts that work with familiar material.

The Lost Thing[3]

The experience of ostensibly the same story in multiple paper and digital media formats is a substantial and increasingly routine aspect of literary culture for a broadening age range and social spectrum in the community, as a multi-media re-versioning of established literary works bridges into popular culture. Increasingly, younger generations expect to encounter stories that are simultaneously accessible in various formats. Although adults may note differences between different versions of classic narratives like JR Tolkien's *The Hobbit*, Jane Austen's *Pride and Prejudice* or Thomas Hardy's *Far From the Madding Crowd*, younger audiences appear less aware of the significance of differences between book and movie versions of stories such as *Stellaluna* (Cannon, 1993, 1996) or *The Little Prince* (de Saint-Exupery, 2000a, 2000b). As Unsworth has observed:

> There appears to be a tendency for children to elide any differences between the various versions of the story, especially in relation to animated versions of picture books. This may be partly because the animations are very true to the original drawings in the depiction of characters and also, since the stories are quite short, omissions of aspects of the story are usually not an issue.
>
> *(Unsworth, 2013 p. 17)*

But the differences between book and animated versions of such stories do call for closer inspection, particularly if we are to address the 'constructedness' of narratives and account for ways in which grammatical and visual resources work together in such constructs. For some of the children interviewed in The Grammatics Project, the print and film versions of stories tended to blur together. One Year 4 student we interviewed talked about the story of *The Lost Thing,* first introduced earlier in Chapter 2. But Daki is not clear about whether she is talking about the original picture book by Australian author Shaun Tan (Tan, 2000) or the animated movie (Ruhemann & Tan, 2010).

Daki: ... and I think he actually found the lost thing so that he could open up and actually not be lost himself ... that's why ... that's the purpose of the lost thing in him. ... I think.

Interviewer A: And was that in the book or the movie that you are talking about? Or did you look at both?

Daki: Well we had the book, but we watched the movie as well.

Interviewer B: Yes, so maybe that's the movie because I don't remember the ending of the book being like that. That's interesting. So, you've done the book and the movie.

Daki: Well we had a look at the book. Yeah, but mostly the movie.

Daki's interpretive response for which there is ample, clear and explicit evidence in the movie portrayal of story is less plausible when it comes to the picture book. Her conflation of the two versions of the story highlights the need to teach students more about how resources of image and language are deployed to make meaning but also how variation in such deployment constructs differences in meaning. Using two (or even three) versions of the 'same' event in a story can throw such differences into relief and draw attention to the constructedness of texts and their influence on our interpretation. We return briefly to the narrative and to the image presented earlier in Cahpter 2 as Figure 2.1 to explore a little of these differences and their effects.

In the picture book *The Lost Thing* (Tan, 2000), there are no images where the gaze of the characters is directed straight out toward the reader, so there is no 'contact' between the depicted characters and the reader. Nearly all the images are long-distance views, with only three images that are middle-distance views, and no close-up views at all, so the social distance between the reader and the depicted characters is generally quite remote. The depiction style used to represent the characters visually can be categorized as 'minimalist' as opposed to 'generic' or 'realist' (Painter, Martin & Unsworth, 2013; Welch, 2005). In broad terms, the minimalist style for a human character is one that uses circles or ovals for people's heads, with dots or small circles for eyes, and does not need to maintain accurate facial or body proportions. Painter *et al.* (2013) suggest that this style is indexical of what they call 'appreciative' engagement, with limited emotional involvement. The generic style they see associated with an 'empathic' role for the reader, recognizing something of themselves and others in the characters, and the realist style is considered to support a 'personalizing' engagement of the reader, responding to characters as 'real' individuals. The minimalist images in *The Lost Thing* construct a role of appreciative engagement for the reader.

In terms of options for Focalization presented earlier in Chapter 3 as Figure 3.4, the visual point of view in the book is overwhelmingly Unmediated Observation. Viewers are positioned as outside observers, looking on but essentially detached. After the boy has taken the lost thing home, in the book there is a one-page depiction of him feeding the lost thing. The image shows him on top of a ladder dropping objects from a box into the raised top 'lid' of the lost thing. The image shown earlier in Figure 2.1 is quite a long view showing the full height of the lost thing and a full view of the boy and the high ladder he is standing on to reach the top of the lost thing. It is also an 'observe' image, since there is no gaze from either of the characters directed toward the reader. The text at the bottom on the page reads:

> I hid the thing in our back shed and gave it something to eat, once I found out what it liked. It seemed a bit happier then, even though it was still lost.

This combination of depicting style, relative distance and unmediated observation resists reader identification with the characters as individuals. Even if the salient red colouring and stance of the lost thing (tilted forward to meet the boy) helps us to see him as benign and we engage with the events through first person narration, we remain at a distance.

The tension between the alignment of the reader and the character of the boy as the first-person narrator, and the distancing of the images reflects the treatment of the relationship between the boy and the lost thing. The boy believes he should be concerned about the abandonment of the lost thing by society, but he does not establish any interpersonal closeness with it. He goes 'against the grain' of his social milieu in his attempt to help the lost thing find his home. Subtle changes in the language and very significant differences in the images from the book to the movie remove this tension and the grammatics makes it possible to look at the choices that re-shape the interpretive possibilities of the movie version.

In the animated movie (Ruhemann & Tan, 2010), the images construct a very different pseudo-social relationship with the viewers. There are more mid-distance and close-up views of the characters for instance. Sometimes the main character of the boy looks directly out at the audience whilst the viewer is frequently positioned to have a point of view 'along with' one of the characters and on several occasions as if he or she *was* one of the characters. While the story events are almost exactly equivalent in both versions, and the narration varies only moderately, the visual depiction in the movie significantly affects the interpretive possibilities. The movie substantially maintains the minimalist depiction style of the book, but the closer social distance, more frequent contact images, and particularly the mediated point of view 'along with' and 'as' the depicted characters shift the reader/viewer engagement from *appreciative* to *empathic*, and visually accentuate the boy as a focus for interpretive issues concerning difference, conformity, acceptance and interpersonal outreach. While an exhaustive comparison of point of view in the book and movie versions cannot be presented in this chapter, it is possible to reveal something of the differences in point of view by looking at shots from the same event in the story and compare these with corresponding sections of the book.

In the movie, the narration maintains the sequence about the boy hiding the lost thing in the back shed and it seeming happier after eating. It is faithful to this aspect of the book's diegesis. However, in the movie, all the intervening information about giving it something to eat after finding out what it liked is rendered through images only. And the level of detail in treatment of this sequence is strikingly different from that in the book. Perhaps most important, however, are changes in point of view in the movie. For example, in the subsequent shot from the movie presented as Figure 3.5, we see the ladder being positioned against the side of the lost thing. Unlike the point of view in the corresponding moment in the book, here we are positioned looking down on the ladder. We see only the ends of the large front 'claws' of the lost thing. This would be what the lost thing sees when carrying out this action. So, the point of view for the movie viewer is 'as' the lost thing. In the following shots, we move between the point of view 'as' lost thing and that of the boy and this communicates a strong intersubjective rapport not only between the lost thing (whose consciousness is rendered through Focalization) and the boy, but between these characters and the viewers.

This brief foray into the co-patterning of visual choices in book and movie and the way that their differences generate distinctive forms of alignment or detachment in the viewer has said nothing of other semiotic resources (but see Barton & Unsworth, 2014 for treatment of music in book and movie versions of *The Lost Thing*). The opportunities for a more comprehensive engagement with intertextuality now abound in subject English. There are increasingly accessible multimedia versions of literary picture books in various filmic formats and new computer-based approaches to the use of multiple story versions in school English curricula (Jewitt, 2002, 2006; Unsworth, 2006; Unsworth, Thomas, Simpson & Asha, 2005). The advantage of learning about these systems through analysis of what Unsworth (2013) calls 'transmedia narratives' is that they frequently provide alternative perspectives on ostensibly the same story situation, so children are able to develop a critical understanding of the interpretive difference that can result from different semiotic choices (Mills, 2011).

Critique is crucial, especially given the sheer taken for granted-ness of such narratives and the availability of different versions enables teachers to bring into relief choices that might pass below the threshold of consciousness if not drawn to children's notice. But design is another 'way in' to metasemiotic knowledge (Kress, 2000, 2010). Producing short animated films that experiment with resources for representing characters, action and point of view can teach students so much. It involves a composer's rather than just an analyst's knowledge. Happily, students can now use animation software such as Moviestorm (www.moviestorm.co.uk) or Muvizu (www.muvizu. com) to construct their own films. Transforming meanings through visualization of verbal texts, through short animated versions of traditional tales or through multimodal genres can be a powerful learning experience for students. We turn to this aspect of grammatics in the East for a brief foray into this domain.

Transforming meanings

In his inaugural address for the London Institute of Education in 1995, Gunther Kress posed key questions facing educators as they attempted to produce an English curriculum for an unstable future. In the course of this lecture, Kress explored the movement into writing of children from different countries and made what is an important claim for our purposes in this chapter. He said, "What we make available to the child is a central factor in what the child will and can do" (Kress, 1995, p. 12). Certainly this insight has been borne out in our work with teachers and their students in the grammatics project. Those teachers who took up and transformed for themselves semiotic tools introduced in workshops on verbal, visual and multimodal semiosis were in a much stronger position to makes these visible and accessible for students. And students in their turn took these up, 'metabolising' them in ways we could not have imagined. It will be clear from the written data presented above that students who were attentive to what their teachers made available to them incorporated many of these resources in their own writing and talking. The metalanguage was not only 'turning up' in their writing and talking but appeared to re-shape their ways of thinking about images and their contribution to higher orders of meaning in multimodal texts.

It is fascinating to watch children as they work with semiotic resources drawn to their attention by a teacher aware of how these resources work. They might read a story and borrow its language, adapting it to their own purposes in a new narrative; they might produce a drawing depicting the experiential world of a narrative in a fresh way or transform a narrative into different kinds of meta-text, perhaps a poster or a trailer encouraging audiences to see a play or movie. In all these adaptations of narrative, we see the 'interests' and 'agendas' of rhetors at work. In fact, experimenting with the resources identified and studied in a text by composing a text that utilises these resources is a powerful way to deepen awareness of design. In their paper on writing in multimodal texts, Bezemer and Kress (2008, p. 174) propose that the concept of design is important for 'giving shape to the interests, purposes, and intentions of the rhetor' in relation to available semiotic resources. For them, the rhetor does not 'use' resources so much as make and re-make them in the act of producing signs. They exploit the possibilities of resources, aware for example, that "images do not have words, just as writing does not have depiction" and "forms of arrangement differ in modes that are temporally or spatially instantiated". The implications of these differences are as follows:

> These differences in resources mean that modes can be used to do different kinds of semiotic work or to do broadly similar semiotic work with different resources in different ways. That is, modes have different affordances – potentials and constraints for making meaning.
> *(Bezemer & Kress, 2008, p. 171)*

This is a powerful perspective to adopt in adapting grammatics to the interpretive and productive tasks of school English. It puts semiosis – meaning making – at the heart of English and calls for attention not only to the affordances of different modes but the ways in which students exploit this in acts of meaning.

In the remaining part of this chapter we touch briefly on three different acts of multimodal translation undertaken by students in their interpretation of narratives: a visualization by a ten year old reader of the moment in the novel *Blueback* where Abel Jackson plunges into the water early one morning; an experiment with point of view in an adaptation of the traditional nursery tale of Humpty Dumpty; and a poster produced to advertise an upcoming performance of *Macbeth*.

Finn's "Blueback"

Ten-year-old Finn listens to a reading of the first chapter of *Blueback* (Winton, 1997) and produces an image based on the moment where Abel Jackson, the protagonist, enters the water on the reef where he and his mother are to fish for abalone. In order to compare this image to the meanings made in the novel, we reprise the two paragraphs that orient us to Abel's experience of the world beneath the dinghy:

> He fell back into the water with a cold crash. A cloud of bubbles swirled around him, clinging to his skin like pearls. Then he cleared his snorkel – phhhht! – and rolled over to look down on the world underwater.
>
> Great, round boulders and dark cracks loomed below. Tiny silver fish hung in nervous schools. Seaweed trembled in the gentle current. Orange starfish and yellow plates of coral glowed from the deepest slopes where his mother was already gliding like a bird.

Finn's drawing is presented as Figure 8.3 below. It depicts the boy in the water beneath the boat bobbing above him. Bubbles of air rise from his snorkel as he gazes out from his mask at the fish and other sea creatures beneath him. Another figure (presumably Abel's mother) swims away from him. Abel seems to hang in space, absorbed by the life forms in this underwater world. His arms are open in a

FIGURE 8.3 Finn's drawing of the world beneath the boat.

gesture of awe, perhaps even welcome. There is a stillness about this drawing, as if a moment in time is captured.

There is both more and less in this visual transformation of the verbal description of the scene. Certainly there are more creatures than are represented in the verbiage (an eel, crabs, starfish, large as well as small fish). More subtly though, there is more information about the location of each element in the drawing relative to one another. Because of the visual affordances of images, Finn is able to position the sea creatures in space so we apprehend their relationship to one another 'at a glance'. The upward curving frame line at the base of the drawing seems to cradle or contain the teeming life of this underwater kingdom and directs our reading path. Our gaze moves around the space traced by the rocks at the bottom of the image, shifting from one creature to the other, sideways to the oblique figure of the mother swimming away from Abel and then upwards to the jaunty boat bobbing on the surface of the water. We contemplate Abel's world rather than participating in it. The 'less' in this image has to do with the actions of the characters (Abel's falling back, clearing his snorkel, rolling over and his mother's gliding)., temporal links between these (e.g. Then) and figurative language comparing the mother to a bird, for example. In some ways though, the visual representation has its own metaphoric meaning, captured in some ways by our use of words like 'cradle'.

As a result of the temporal nature of the verbal mode, the descriptive phase from *Blueback* positions us to experience what happens dynamically – a series of events. This contrasts with the synoptic view of the boy in his environment which we see 'at a glance' in the drawing. Both forms of representation need to render the space of the underwater world but do so in different ways. Winton, the author, deploys Circumstantiation to locate us in space, particularly through prepositional phrases like '*into* the water', '*on* the world underwater' and '*in* the gentle current'. More subtly, he exploits evocative Processes to suggest a cathedral-like depth and beauty in this underwater world. The boulders and dark cracks 'loom' below, the silver fish 'hang in space' and the seaweed 'trembles'.

We present the passage again, with Circumstantial meanings underlined and Processes and Comparative epithets that evoke spatial depth in italics:

He *fell back* INTO THE WATER WITH A COLD CRASH. A cloud of bubbles swirled AROUND HIM, clinging to his skin like pearls. Then he cleared his snorkel – phhhhht! – and rolled over to *look down* ON THE WORLD UNDERWATER.

Great, round boulders and dark cracks *loomed* below. Tiny silver fish *hung* in nervous schools. Seaweed trembled IN THE GENTLE CURRENT. Orange starfish and yellow plates of coral *glowed* FROM THE deepest SLOPES where his mother was already *gliding* like a bird.

The space is awe inspiring for Abel and the two representations communicate aesthetic appreciation in distinctive ways. The affordances of image enable Winton to represent the experience as seen by Abel and Finn to transform this into a visual contemplation of the underwater world in which Abel floats.

Visualization of this kind can be achieved without explicit induction into the possibilities of the mode, simply through exposure to the work of others and lots of practice with drawing as Finn does often. But if children largely take up the resources that we make available to them, as Kress has observed, it is clear that pedagogies that open these up are more likely to enable them to explore their potentials in knoweldgeable ways, guided by instruction. Both differences and similarities between texts in each mode can be explored through semantically rich terms like Circumstantiation which are relevant to the resources used to represent setting along with other aspects of the context in narrative.

Rali's Humpty Dumpty

In a research project involving one of our authors, children in Year 4 were introduced to interpersonal resources such as focalization in the course of their work on multimodal authoring. Teachers introduced students to point of view through a 'View, Deconstruct, Demonstrate, Do and Reflect' pedagogic cycle (Chandler, O'Brien &

Unsworth, 2010). The children were asked to play with alternatives in transforming nursery rhymes like *Humpty Dumpty*. In a somewhat hyper-real visual rendition of point of view in *Humpty Dumpty*, one student called Rali experimented with Focalization, in particular with the possibilities of the view 'as' Humpty Dumpty.

The title image in Figure 8.4 depicts Humpty at a distance sitting on the bridge in a precarious way. In technical terms, this is an instance of Unmediated Contact.

The first shot in Rali's animated movie in Figure 8.5 presents the scene as Humpty would see it, sitting on the bridge with one white leg emerging from the image as he gazes down on the scene below from his precarious position.

Composition of this sort involves high level conceptual work. Rali has had to do some solid thinking not only in sequencing of shots but in representing the relative size of buildings as they would appear from different heights and distances.

Shot 2 presented in Figure 8.6 shows Humpty as he begins to fall (jump?) from the bridge. It includes all the detail necessary to achieve continuity with earlier shots and to represent the position not of Humpty now but of the observer watching on in horror. It is interesting to speculate here about why Rali has decided to emblazon the bridge with the coats of arms of the king. But it is clear that this is the crisis point for Humpty and that, as an egg, his fate is probably sealed.

In Shot 3 presented in Figure 8.7, the king's men gather round Humpty, presumably to put him back together again. But in a contrast to the point of view rendered as Humpty falls, after his plunge to the ground, we see 'as' Humpty, his gaze 'upwards' at one of the knights picking him up by one of his legs. Again, Rali is

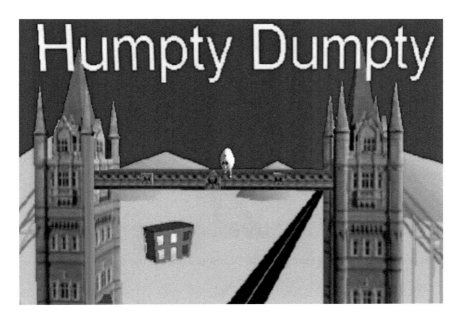

FIGURE 8.4 Title Image of Humpty Dumpty.

FIGURE 8.5 Shot 1 showing Humpty's view from the top of the bridge.

FIGURE 8.6 Shot 2 showing Humpty as he begins to fall from the bridge.

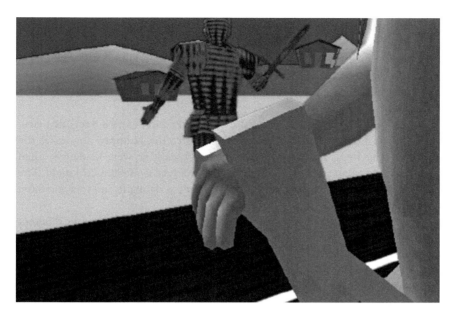

FIGURE 8.7 Shot 3 revealing a view of the knight from below.

FIGURE 8.8 The final shot showing the view of the knight and hen from Humpty's coffin.

posing and resolving problems of relative size in the buildings around Humpty as well as point of view. Or rather, he is attempting to resolve problems of representation that are entailed upon his decision to let us see 'as' Humpty. The red farm house is now presented as it would be seen from close to the ground whereas in the earlier ones shown at a height, we see more of the roofs of houses, naturally because we would see them from above.

Perhaps most daring of all, Rali's final shot presented in Figure 8.8 reveals a view (in some ways horrifying) from inside Humpty's coffin. Humpty now takes the form of a cooked egg, and we see what he would see if he were sentient – a hen with something of an ironic tilt to the head and a heavily armoured knight. The effect is both poignant and humorous and represents a dramatic end to a tale often told without drama.

Apparently Rali produced this short film in several drafts, trying out different Focalization options for shots before settling on one or other. The sheer range of viewpoints Riley is able to manage is an indication of his uptake of resources and the exuberance of his experiments with viewer affiliation. As a researcher investigating possibilities of multimodal authoring in classrooms, Annemaree O'Brien comments on the catalytic power of Riley's problem solving for others:

> This student's creative and thoughtful decisions about viewer affiliation in each shot and across the story became the catalyst for demonstrating to students how viewer position could be manipulated for narrative purposes and in particular for influencing the way the viewer related interpersonally to the depicted characters.
>
> *(Chandler, O'Brien & Unsworth, 2010, p. 132)*

Producing texts that work with narrative techniques gives students the opportunity to experiment (as composers) with choices that others like picture book artists or film makers often take for granted. The process of working with these choices, reflecting on gains and losses of one or the other choice, makes reflection on their potentials and their limits more visible and hopefully more accessible to analysis (Kress, 2005). We return to the potential of projects such as this in our final chapter.

Julian's Macbeth

As students progress in English, they need to grow in their capacity not just for semiosis but for meta-semiosis. Meta-semiosis is simply reflection on the process of making texts and is powerful for the more abstract work of interpretation on which English increasingly turns in the senior years of study (Macken-Horarik, 2016a, 2016b). It often involves experiments with affordances of different modes as we have seen, though experiments with writing are the principal activity. But it also involves reflection on and explanation of how these work. In our grammatics project, we encouraged teachers to use a three-step process in their work on multi-modal texts: *identification* of what choices have been made (e.g. closeness or distance of a represented figure); *description* of how the choice works (e.g. how the choice works to align viewers personally, socially or more distantly with a figure); and *interpretation and explanation* of the broader significance of contrasts in closeness/distance for alignment with this figure in a text.

In one NSW secondary English classroom, students were invited to interpret themes in filmic versions of *Macbeth* in either movie trailer or a poster promoting an upcoming performance of the play. Julian's poster shown as Figure 8.9 depicts the play in a dramatic representation of a stylized hand dripping with blood pointing directly below to a skull gazing blankly out at the viewer as rivers of blood course down its bony cheeks and through its teeth.

This is a strongly centred image and the vertical vector and direction of the blood generates an unavoidable downward movement in our reading path. While we moved 'around' Finn's drawing (presented as Figure 8.3 above), taking in details in the sweep of our reading path, here there is only really one path to take. Our gaze is directed down the vector created by pointing finger towards the skull and from

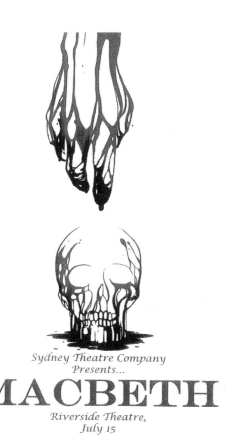

FIGURE 8.9 Julian's poster advertising Macbeth.

there to information about the upcoming performance of *Macbeth*, which is the site of salient information for potential audiences.

Julian's visual work is impressive enough but the meta-level account of his work is perhaps more powerful, especially given the importance of this kind of work for interpretive practices in English. His teacher asked him to explain the choices he had made and why he made them in a written rationale. This is presented as Figure 8.10

Macbeth Poster Analysis

The poster for the theatre production of *Macbeth* uses a number of techniques to engage and focus the viewer's attention. Specifically, the use of symbolism and a strong vector that direct attention and foreshadow the text. There are also different fonts and colours utilised in the advertisement.

The most prominent and obvious technique used in the *Macbeth* theatre advertisement is the use of a vector in the salient image. There is a strong vector created in the flow of blood down the hand and through the skull which points to the text at the bottom of the page. This creates a very vertical 'top-to-bottom' reading order. It also focuses the reader's view firmly on the title *Macbeth* along with the other important information provided. This vector is the most obvious method used within the poster advertisement for *Macbeth*.

Another feature used in the poster advertisement for *Macbeth* is the use of symbolism. This symbolism is used in both the colours utilised and in the salient image itself. The dark red on the white background represents the tarnished purity that is Macbeth. It shows the violence and death at his hands and unending strive for power. It also provides an impacting contrast between the text and images and the background. These colours and images provide an insight to the plot of *Macbeth* and make the poster advertisement clear and easily read.

The poster advertising the theatre production for *Macbeth* also employs several techniques specifically within the text. It uses a minimal amount of text so as not to overwhelm and lose the reader within an overload of information. A large, impacting font is used for the word *Macbeth* to place importance and priority on the title over the other information which is written in a smaller, softer font. These fonts used place the emphasis on the key information while ensuring key information is remembered by the reader.

The poster advertisement for the theatre production of *Macbeth* uses a number of techniques to effectively provide information to the reader. It uses a range of fonts, colour and images as well as techniques such as vectors and symbolism to give an indication of the plot and themes of the play and to focus the viewer's attention.

FIGURE 8.10 Julian's rationale explaining choices made in his poster.

If we take the first three paragraphs of this rationale, it is clear that Julian has taken up constructs presented and explored during class work on experiential and textual meanings made in images. For example, he notes the role of vectors and of visual salience in guiding the reading path of viewers. Julian has incorporated these terms into his response text effectively, representing in his rationale the three-step process his teacher Annette had taught him to use. In his second paragraph, he identifies the choice employed in his poster using the technical terms appropriately ("the use of a vector in the salient image"); he then describes its role in the image, showing that the vector is "created in the flow of blood down the hand and through the skull which points to the text at the bottom of the page". This elaborating move is crucial because it unpacks the choice, showing how it is realized in the image he has produced. Finally, Julian highlights the intended effect of this choice on the viewer – the creation of "a very vertical 'top-to-bottom' reading order".

We found in our research in The Grammatics Project (as in the project associated with Rali's text) that pedagogic tropes of this kind were helpful for teachers keen to give their students 'rule of thumb' processes in their analysis of images and of literary texts more generally. Julian's rationale moves from the 'what' of recognition to the 'how' of elaboration and from there to the 'why' of intended effect and thus recreates in writing the methodology employed in classroom learning. It is an example of the portable tools of analysis employed in a multimodal grammatics and one more instance of the relational approach necessary if we are to employ the metalanguage and the knowledge base effectively in twenty-first century English classrooms.

In this chapter, we have considered a range of texts in various modes that reveal ways that students have taken up and transformed knowledge shared in The Grammatics Project. In many ways, we have failed to do their work justice because it often overturned expectations and transcended the limits of the tools we provided to teachers and which teachers provided to their students. But the East is a place of surprises anyway, and a region inviting further exploration with the aid of a grammatics at an interface with disciplinary practices. The inter- and intra-textual explorations we have pursued here in relation to narrative can be applied to persuasion. In our final chapter, we offer a brief summation of the territory we have visited with the aid of the compass points and point to some of the semiotic journeys that beckon teachers and students (and indeed semioticians) in twenty-first-century classrooms.

Notes

1   Text © 1995 Libby Gleeson Illustrations © 2010 Armin Greder. From THE GREAT BEAR by Libby Gleeson, illustrated by Armin Greder. Reproduced by permission of Walker Books Ltd, London SE11 5HJ: www.walker.co.uk.
2   Text © 1995 Libby Gleeson Illustrations © 2010 Armin Greder. From THE GREAT BEAR by Libby Gleeson, Illustrated by Armin Greder. Reproduced by permission of Walker Books Ltd, London SE11 5HJ: www.walker.co.uk.
3   This discussion of *The Lost Thing* builds substantially on work in Unsworth (2013).

References

Abousnnouga, G. & Machin, D. (2010). Analysing the language of war monuments. *Visual Communication*, 9(2), 131–149.

Australian Curriculum Assessment and Reporting Authority (ACARA) (2012). *Australian curriculum: English*. Version 3.0. Sydney: ACARA. Retrieved from www.australiancurriculum.edu.au/copyright.

Bezemer, J. & Kress, G. (2008). Writing in multimodal texts: A social semiotic account of designs for learning. *Written Communication*, 25(2), 166–195.

Cannon, J. (1993). *Stellaluna*. Orlando, FL: Harcourt brace.

Cannon, J. (1996). *Stellaluna*. San Francisco, CA: Livingbooks/Random House/Broderbund.

Barton, G. & Unsworth, L. (2014). Music, multiliteracies and multimodality: Exploring the book and movie versions of Shaun Tan's *The Lost Thing*. *Australian Journal of Language and Literacy*, 37(1), 3–20.

Barthes, R. (1977). Introduction to the structural analysis of narratives. *Image, music, text* (S. Heath, Trans., pp. 79–124). New York: The Noonday Press.

Bordwell, D. & Thompson, K. (1990). *Film art: An introduction* (3rd edition). New York: McGraw-Hill Publishing Company.

Browne, A. (1989). *The tunnel*. London: Julia McRae Books.

Chandler, P., O'Brien, A. & Unsworth, L. (2010). Towards a 3D digital multimodal curriculum for the upper primary school. *Australian Educational Computing*, 25(1), 34–40.

Genette, G. (1980). *Narrative discourse* (J. Lewin, Trans.) Ithaca, NY: Cornell University Press.

Gleeson, L. & Greder, A. (1999). *The great bear*. Sydney: Scholastic.

Halliday, M. A. K. (1978). *Language as social semiotic: The social interpretation of language and meaning*. Edward Arnold.

Halliday, M.A.K. & Matthiessen, C. (2004). *An introduction to functional grammar* (3rd edition). London: Edward Arnold.

Jennings, P. & Gouldthorpe, P. (1992). *Grandad's gifts*. Ringwood, Victoria: Puffin Books.

Jewitt, C. (2002). The move from page to screen: The multimodal reshaping of school English. *Visual Communication*, 1(2), 171–196.

Jewitt, C. (2006). *Technology, literacy and learning: A multimodal approach*. London: Routledge.

Kress, G. (1995). *Making signs and making subjects: The English curriculum and social futures (an inaugural lecture)*. Institute of Education: University of London.

Kress, G. (2000). Multimodality. In B. Cope & M. Kalantzis (Eds.), *Multiliteracies: Literacy learning and the design of social futures* (pp. 182–202). New York & London: Routledge.

Kress, G. (2005). Gains and losses: New forms of texts, knowledge and learning. *Computers and Composition*, 22 5–22.

Kress, G. (2010). *Multimodality: A social semiotic approach to contemporary communication*. London: Routledge.

Lewis, D. (2001). *Reading contemporary picture books: Picturing text*. London & New York: Routledge.

Macken-Horarik, M. R. (2006). Hierarchies in diversities: What students' examined responses tell us about literacy practices in contemporary school English. *Australian Journal of Language and Literacy*, 29(1), 52–78.

Macken-Horarik, M. R. (2016a). Grammar in wonderland: What might a re-imagined grammar look like in contemporary school English? *mETAphor*, 1, 4–9.

Macken-Horarik, M. R. (2016b). Building a metalanguage for interpreting multimodal literature: Insights from systemic functional semiotics in two case study classrooms. *English in Australia*, 51(2), 85–99.

Matthiessen, C. (1991). Language on language: The grammar of semiosis. *Social Semiotics*, 1 (2), 69–111.
Mills, K.A. (2011) "I'm making it different to the book": Transmediation in young children's print and digital practices. *Australasian Journal of Early Childhood Education* 36(3), 56–65.
Painter, C., Martin, J. R. & Unsworth, L. (2013). *Reading visual narratives: Image analysis of children's picture books*. London: Equinox.
Ruhemann, A. & Tan, S. (Writers) (2010). *The lost thing* [DVD/PAL]. Australia: Madman Entertainment.
de Saint-Exupery, A. (2000a). *The little prince*. London: Penguin.
de Saint-Exupery, A. (2000b). *The little prince. (CD ROM)*: Tivola.
Tan, S. (2000). *The lost thing*. Sydney, NSW: Lothian.
Unsworth, L. (2006). *E-literature for children: Enhancing digital literacy learning*. London & New York: Routledge/Falmer.
Unsworth, L. (2013). Re-configuring image-language relations and interpretive possibilities in picture books as animated movies: A site for developing multi-modal literacy pedagogy. *Ilha do Desterro: A journal of English language, literature in English and cultural studies*, 64, 15–47.
Unsworth, L. & Macken-Horarik, M. (2015). Interpretive responses to images in picture books by primary and secondary school students: Exploring curriculum expectations of a 'visual grammatics'. *English in Education*, 49(1), 56–79.
Unsworth, L, Thomas, A., Simpson, A. & Asha, J. (2005). *Children's literature and computer based teaching*. London: McGraw-Hill/Open University Press.
Welch, A. (2005). *The illustration of facial affect in children's literature*. (Unpublished BA Hons coursework paper). University of Sydney.
Winton, T. (1997). *Blueback*. London: Picador.

9
ENVOI

The problems of grammar reprised

In Chapter 1 we acknowledged three problems that frustrate a re-imagined grammar in school English and our intention to address these through functional grammatics. First, we identified the image problem that grammar has accrued over time which makes it hard to think about in new ways. Correctionist approaches to grammar have resulted in an over-emphasis on errors, with a tendency to focus on 'problems in expression'. An idealised model of the standard has often led to self-consciousness or even shame about a regional or class dialect exposed to scrutiny and judgement in a classroom. And traditional grammar has often meant (certainly for those of us old enough to remember this) parsing and analysis of concocted wordings conducted seemingly without relevance to tasks of interpretation and composition. Grammar has taken on an 'aura of unhappiness' for many because of this history.

Second, we identified a knowledge problem for many English teachers in Anglophone countries like England, Scotland, Australia, New Zealand and the United States. Several studies reviewed in Chapter 1 have identified a pattern of 'weak linguistic knowledge' in the profession that not only creates a preoccupation with grammatical forms but limits consideration of conceptual and higher order matters and leads to 'sterile teaching divorced from the realities of language in use' (Myhill, Jones, Lines & Watson, 2012, p. 142). Where teachers are anxious about their ability to identify particular grammatical forms, they are less likely to be open to exploration of the possibilities of grammar. Building a deep and relational approach to the study of grammar is a clear and pressing task for the profession.

Third, we alluded briefly to the 'distractor' problem of public discourses that treat grammar (or the lack of it) as a symptom of problems in the school system, in teacher preparation and even in the wider society. As researchers like Cameron (1995),

Myhill (2000) and Locke (2009) have noted, media 'panic' tends to erupt in periods of curriculum change. In an era of instability in which current accounts of grammar are clearly insufficient to meet contemporary challenges, it is easy to seek archaistic relief in old ways of dealing with change and grammar becomes a surface for these longings and for the imaginary stability that going back to 'basics' might bring. Media discourses that circulate at times of change *are* a problem for English, and for a re-imagined approach to grammar because they divert attention from highly challenging work in English that requires full attention – study of literary texts (and indeed literariness itself), of rhetorics of persuasion and of digital literacies. A little over a decade ago, Gunther Kress was asked to clarify his claim that English had entered a period of 'radical instability'. He responded as follows:

> The frames around (secure) knowledge have disappeared; it is now acceptable for seemingly serious people to talk about 'intelligent design' and to insist that it be taught in schools. Text-books present core curricular knowledge in image rather than in writing: as with glaciers, the frames around stable means of representing are softening, melting, disappearing. Cultural diversity produces profound challenges to canonical forms of all kinds.
>
> *(Kress, 2006, p. 27)*

In a period of tumultuous change, it is necessary to re-imagine grammar and to do so in ways that put creative semiosis at the centre of our theory of grammar, to focus doggedly on the contribution this can make to crucial disciplinary practices of English. These must necessarily include more traditional work on literary interpretation and new challenges of digital literacies, with the knowledge base of the profession continuing to expand to undertake this work.

The preceding chapters of our book offer an elaborated response to these problems through a functional grammatics in two domains of practice – narrative and persuasion. We spend a little time in the next section reviewing our responses to problems articulated above and ways in which work with teachers influenced these. In the final section of this chapter we comment on the potentials and limits of our toolkit.

What we did about the problems

Our first move was to propose a distinction between metalanguage and language. Taking inspiration from Halliday we argued that functional grammatics could be conceived in principled ways as an intellectual resource for investigating grammar (Halliday, 2002). Earlier studies developing a functional grammatics for primary school students, in particular, work by Geoff Williams (2004, 2005) and later Ruth French (2012), highlighted the potential of this approach for students at all levels of school English and inspired us to explore its possibilities for work on narrative and argument. Once the need for this distinction was established, we proceeded with the assumption that a functional grammatics could shed light not just on problems in grammatical usage (thus serving a correctionist impulse) but on processes of meaning making (enabling new approaches to grammatical study). Although we did not deny the importance of grammatical knowledge for correcting problems in expression, we argued for a grammatics attuned to all dimensions of student semiosis – difficulties, achievements *and* grammatical innovations such as we find in texting, googling and tweeting. This was the orientation we adopted in The Grammatics Project as in this book. We hope that teachers come to see grammar as a site of creative endeavour, where sense making of different kinds is the goal rather than correct use of the rules.

The impact of The Grammatics Project on the work of students and teachers was a key focus of several chapters in this book. For example, Chapters 3, 6 and 8 showcased some written, visual and multimodal work samples produced by students during their encounter with functional grammatics. The teachers who guided the production of these (and other like) texts were the focus of pedagogy chapters and appeared in teaching scenarios related to narrative (Chapter 4) and persuasion (Chapter 7). The practices they adopted are from the teaching learning cycle (TLC) that is a feature of Sydney School literacy research (Humphrey, 2017; Martin & Rose, 2008; Rose & Martin, 2012).

Our work with teachers in very different contexts meant that we needed to adapt often highly abstract principles of functional grammatics to requirements of the (then) new Australian curriculum for English (AC: E) and to needs and starting points of teachers working in very different primary and secondary classrooms. The principles of functional grammatics presented in detail in Chapters 1, 2, 5 and 8 are the outcome of our effort to relate these to the curriculum content and to make them as accessible and practical as we could. We revisit briefly the principles of metafunction, stratification, system and rank and how we adapted these to address problems we identified in English.

The principle of *metafunctions* was central to work with narrative and persuasion. In the context of disciplinary practices related to literature and rhetoric, a grammatics is in a service role. It is not, nor can it ever be, the whole 'story' when it comes to these, but it does ground investigations of patterns of how grammatical choices are configured to produce what we called, following Hasan (1985), 'second order semiosis'. We described *metafunctions* as semantically differentiated lenses on meaning. In working with teachers, we described them as interface categories for interpreting narrative craft – plot, character, point of view and literary theme. In the realm of persuasion, they shed semantic light on rhetorical appeals to logos, ethos and pathos in persuasive arts. In our view, they served to deepen interpretation of narrative (Chapter 2) and persuasion (Chapter 5).

Because the metafunctions are portable, we can use them as optics for exploring different kinds of meaning in images, drawing on Kress and van Leeuwen (2006) and on Painter, Martin and Unsworth (2013). In The Grammatics Project, the principle of metafunctions enabled us to relate material realizations in form to higher order literary or rhetorical abstractions like representation, point of view and evaluation. The principle of metafunction was vital to our work at the interface with the 'true north' of disciplinary practices in English.

The knowledge problem identified earlier was perhaps the thorniest of all and we needed to adapt the principles of stratification, system and rank to build grammatical knowledge in systematic ways. Many of the teachers involved in our project expressed concern about gaps in their knowledge of grammar. Some admitted they had difficulty even identifying grammatical constituents like nominal groups, verbal groups and even clauses. They may have done powerful work in interpreting literary texts or arguments but felt 'out of their depth' when it came to grammar. This lack was felt most acutely by secondary teachers, though a few who taught English as an additional language/ dialect (EAL/D) expressed confidence with parts of speech and other terms associated with traditional school grammatics. They were however, less adventurous in exploring higher order meanings, often tending to stay 'close to the ground' in work on grammar in classrooms.

Resolving the challenge of different kinds of knowledge amongst teachers led us to conceptualise levels of language identified in the principle of *stratification* as 'landing places' on which we do different kinds of grammatical work. On the lower landing place, we identify grammatical constituents (perhaps bracketing them according to form and perhaps function). On a slightly higher level we describe or gloss the function of constituents in wordings either using the metalanguage of systemic functional grammatics (as in Mental or Material Process) or less technically (as in sensing verb or doing verb). As we acknowledged in our pedagogy chapters, it was important that teachers felt free to use the curriculum metalanguage as this was the mandatory framework for teaching of grammar. At the highest landing place, we integrate functional analysis into interpretation of patterns of meaning in texts. At this level, the grammatics yields to concerns of text or 'discourse semantics' (Martin, 1992). But it is important that teachers can 'step up' from the grammar basics, as it were, to understand how form-function and pattern can be related. In our view, even if we begin with discourse semantics, teachers still need to be able to recognize and label grammatical forms that undergird their acts of interpretation. This task of exploring the implications of a stratified model of language and indeed of semiotic resources more widely has only begun but we discovered powerful moments of insight into the significance of this principle in interviews with teachers. This excerpt from an interview with Year 4 teacher Alice at the end of the first year of the project shows that she is integrating her ability to identify forms (like verbs) with awareness of their function (saying, sensing) and linking this, even if this is rudimentary, to interpretation of their larger role in discourse (dialogue, feeling). For a woman who trained as a Visual Arts teacher, this knowledge made Alice feel 'more of an English teacher':

> When we look at a book I say to the kids "Okay, what sort of verbs is dominating in this passage?" And they'll go "Oh, it's saying verbs. There's dialogue happening". So, that sort of thing. We talk about sensing verbs. "Oh we know how that person is feeling so it tends to be internal" and that sort of thing

> ... I feel like I'm becoming more of an English teacher and less of a creative arts teacher.

As Halliday argues, a grammatics that will be adequate to the workings of grammar needs to be informed by different viewpoints (Halliday, 2008). Attention to the view 'from above' highlights the meaning of a choice whereas the view 'from below' attends to forms that realize meanings (make them real). Perhaps most challenging for a profession without a strong basis in knowledge of grammar is the view 'from around' which takes into account systems of choice of different kinds and their mutual interaction. We considered this issue in Chapter 3 in relation to Interpersonal meaning. All three viewpoints are relevant to a strengthened knowledge of grammar in the profession and to the ability to show how this work can enhance learning for students.

Because teachers often lack awareness of grammatical constituency (Christie, 2004), we found the principle of *rank* helpful for showing teachers how groups and phrases were built from nouns, verbs, prepositions and other word classes (see Macken-Horarik, Sandiford, Love & Unsworth, 2015 for discussion of this issue). As Chapter 3 outlined, it is important to know how to chunk wordings into functional constituents. Without a sense of rank, we simply cannot make grammatically useful decisions about how to group the words we need to describe. Dealing with intermediate units of description such as groups and phrases allowed teachers in The Grammatics Project to highlight the role of constituents in larger syntagms like clauses and clause complexes. An understanding of the formal 'shape' of a constituent like a prepositional phrase or a dependent clause is necessary if students are to explore patterns of signposting in texts. This is the necessary ground on which analysis of Circumstantiation in a written narrative is based. In The Grammatics Project, we discovered that we needed to give the principle of *rank* far more attention than we had anticipated. It was still not enough however, and some of the teachers reported in their final interview that they wished they had more than a few days 'on the sentence' to develop secure understandings of its grammatical constituents.

The notion of choice is crucial to school English and has been important to our exploration of meaning-making systems in this book. Again, the work of others has been inspirational. In relation to verbal texts, the *Introduction to Functional Grammar* has been a crucial resource (Halliday & Matthiessen, 2004). In Chapter 2, we explored the role of Mood and other systems like Polarity in realizing interaction in grammar. The heuristic of the system network was extended to visual semiosis, building on Kress and van Leeuwen (2006) and Painter *et al.* (2013). A key affordance of the system is that it displays differences that 'make a difference' to meaning. Although it was originally developed for grammatical description, as John Bateman has observed, it 'actually offers a general formalism for capturing structured collections of alternatives' (Bateman, 2014, p. 36). For us, as for teachers in The Grammatics Project, it offers a powerful way of exploring 'choice' in a principled way. In short, it is a way of systematising choices.

Negotiating the terrain in English – potentials and problems of grammatics

Building on insights from Geoff Williams, we assumed that a grammatical toolkit useful to English should provide teachers and students with "intellectual tools for reflecting systematically on language" (Williams, 2004, p. 263). The intellectual potential of a functional grammatics makes it worth the investment. In deploying it in tasks of interpretation and composition, teachers and students working with us could exploit the 'mimetic power' of the metalanguage. While we have accepted the need to distinguish between 'grammatics' (as theory) and grammar (as practice), this does not mean that the metalanguage is unrelated to the phenomenon it names. Within the domain of Transitivity, for instance, the grammar of action is analysed in terms of Actors, Material processes and Goals whilst the grammar of thought is analysed in terms of Sensers, Mental processes and Phenomenon. This grounding makes the grammatics 'good to think with' about all modes of semiosis – verbiage, image and multimodal communication. This analogical potential was clear to Halliday in later years of his reflection on the issue:

> When I first used the term 'grammatics', I was concerned simply to escape from the ambiguity where 'grammar' meant the phenomenon itself – a particular stratum in language – and the study of that phenomenon; I was simply setting up a proportion such that grammatics is to grammar as linguistics is to language. But over the years since then I have found it useful to have 'grammatics' available as a term for a specific view of grammatical theory, whereby it is not just a theory about grammar but also a way of *using grammar to think with*.
>
> *(Halliday, 2002, p.416, emphasis added)*

If English is a subject in need of re-definition, the concept of grammatics offers one way of exploring its possibilities. It has been imaged as territory that calls for clearly articulated intellectual and semiotic co-ordinates. We developed a theoretical compass to help us find our way through its (often unfamiliar) terrain. The 'true north' of the discipline calls for a grammatics oriented to disciplinary practices at all levels and stages of schooling. The 'deep south' is the terrain in which teachers attempt to focus and build students' literacy repertoires through scaffolding pedagogies. What we called the 'wild west' is the terrain – perhaps the thickets – of grammatical knowledge and of the analogous use of this to explore visual meaning. It is the territory we have only begun to probe in this book. Finally, the 'Far East' terrain is the field of dreams, the challenge of new literacies, new ways of making and reading texts. Figure 9.1 re-presents the heuristic that guided both our foray into the different terrain and principles that guided our work on this book. We insert the chapters relevant to each compass point onto the figure.

Like any heuristic, our compass is just *that* – a conceptual representation for locating ourselves in unfamiliar and complex territory. Like the map, it is not the

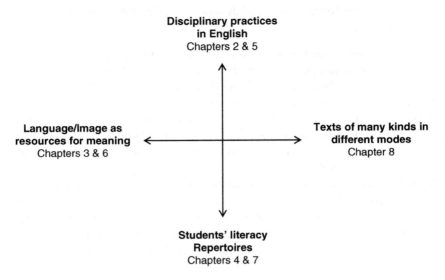

FIGURE 9.1 The compass points guiding excursions with grammatics.

territory. English is both a disciplinary potential and an 'actual reality', unfolding in ways not accessible to the best heuristic. We used the compass as a metaphor for orienting teachers in coherent ways to key points in the discipline. While our adaptation of categories developed to account for language to description of images is in many ways problematic, it has nevertheless been an interesting experiment. It has enabled us to shed light on students' work using a functional grammatics that a mute acceptance of its limits might not have revealed. As Chapter 8 attempted to show, the tasks facing students as they engage with literary picture books, graphic novels and movies calls for a grammatics that is at least aware of the need for such engagement.

A compass is a traditional tool for finding direction in unfamiliar territory. Perhaps more appropriate in a global age might be a global positioning system (GPS). But the compass is simpler to depict and allows us to move more easily between one point and another. There are problems with any metaphor, just as there are limits to any toolkit. A tool is not the construct we build with its aid. The shovel is not the plant that grows in the hole we have dug. The building cannot be equated with the tools that are used to construct it – including the scaffolding that supports it. With the tumultuous changes occurring in the wider communicational environment, especially in the field of digital literacies, there is no way that any toolkit can encompass the interpretive, explanatory or theoretical work needed in the field of semiotics. Even so a flawed enterprise can yield powerful insights.

This book has in many ways offered an account of the insights we produced in attempting to re-imagine grammar through functional grammatics, guided as we were by the compass points. We want to sincerely thank the teachers and students who helped us to do this and whose efforts gave us heart to continue to use the grammatics to 'think with' about key challenges of contemporary school English.

References

Bateman, J. (2014). *Text and image: A critical introduction to the visual/verbal divide*. London & New York: Routledge.

Cameron, D. (1995). *Verbal hygiene*. London: Routledge.

Christie, F. (2004). Revisiting some old themes: The role of grammar in the teaching of English. In J. Foley (Ed.), *Language education and discourse: Functional approaches (*pp. 145–173). London & New York: Continuum.

French, R. (2012). Learning the grammatics of quoted speech: Benefits for punctuation and expressive reading. *Australian Journal of Language and Literacy*, 35(2), 206–233.

Halliday, M. A. K. (2002). On grammar and grammatics. In J. Webster (Ed.), *The collected works of M. A. K. Halliday: Language and linguistics (Vol. 3)* (pp 384–417). London: Continuum.

Halliday, M. A. K. (2008). *Complementarities in language*. Beijing: The Commercial Press.

Halliday, M. A. K. & Matthiessen, C. (2004). *An introduction to functional grammar* (3rd edition). London: Edward Arnold.

Hasan, R. (1985). *Linguistics, language and verbal art*. Geelong, Victoria: Deakin University Press.

Humphrey, S. (2017). *Academic literacies in the middle years: A framework for enhancing teacher knowledge and student achievement*. New York & London: Routledge.

Kress, G. (2006). A continuing project: English for a period of radical instability. In B. Doecke, M. Howie & W. Sawyer (Eds.), *Only connect: English teaching, schooling and community* (AATE Interface Series), (pp. 27–30). South Australia: Wakefield Press.

Kress, G. & van Leeuwen, T. (2006). *Reading images: A grammar of visual design* (2nd edition). London & New York: Routledge.

Locke, T. (2009). Grammar and writing: The international debate. In R. Beard, D. Myhill, J. Riley & M. Nystrand (Eds.), *The Sage handbook of writing development* (pp. 182–193). London: Sage.

Macken-Horarik, M., Sandiford, C. Love, K. & Unsworth, L. (2015). New ways of working 'with grammar in mind' in school English: Insights from systemic functional grammatics. *Linguistics and Education*, 31, 145–158.

Martin, J. R. (1992). *English text: System and structure*. Amsterdam: Benjamins.

Martin, J. R. & Rose, D. (2008). *Genre relations: Mapping culture*. London & Oakville: Equinox.

Myhill, D. (2000). Misconceptions and difficulties in the acquisition of metalinguistic knowledge. *Language and Education*, 14(3), 151–163.

Myhill, D., Jones, S. , Lines, H. & Watson, A. (2012). Thinking grammar: The impact of embedded grammar teaching on students' writing and students' metalinguistic understanding. *Research Papers in Education*, 27(20), 139–166.

Painter, C., Martin, J. R. & Unsworth, L. (2013). *Reading visual narratives: Image analysis of children's picture books*. London: Equinox.

Rose, D. & Martin, J. R. (2012). *Learning to write, reading to learn: Genre, knowledge and pedagogy in the Sydney School*. London: Equinox.

Williams, G. (2004). Ontogenesis and grammatics: Functions of metalanguage in pedagogical discourse. In G. Williams & A. Lukin (Eds.), *The development of language: Functional perspectives on species and individuals* (pp. 241–267). London: Continuum.

Williams, G. (2005). Grammatics in schools. In R. Hasan, C. Matthiessen & J. Webster (Eds.), *Continuing discourse on language: A functional perspective (Vol. 1)* (pp. 281–310). London: Equinox.

INDEX

Abousnnouga, G. 39, 253
abstraction 187, 187t, 197
Accelerated Literacy 20
action orientation 78
Actor 6
advertisements 170–1, 230–1, 232t, 233–5
affect 87, 88, 127, 129–36, 152, 153, 191, 215
allusion 202
analysis, first and second level of 36–7, 176; first order semiosis 63, 151, 165; second order semiosis 63, 67, 274
analytical exposition 178–80
anaphora 163
Andrews, R. 2
'Apology to the Stolen Generations of Australia, The' (Rudd) 155–65, 176, 180
appraisal: inscribed 45–6, 87–8, 92, 130, 151, 191, 223; invoked 45–6, 97, 130; narrative and 75, 81, 86–96; persuasion and 151–2, 155, 157–8, 161, 164, 180, 191–3, 222
appreciation 87, 127, 130, 137, 191–2, 193, 215
argument: building context for work on 214; description of 11; independent composition of 240; interpersonal probe questions for 236; teaching a grammatics for 212–41; teaching plan for 235t; types of 179; written analytical exposition and 183–5, 187, 188, 195–6
argumentative positions 203–5
Aristotle 146, 179, 180

attitude: evaluation and 89t; image-viewer relations and 24; multimodal texts and 226, 230–2, 233; narrative and 87–8, 91–3, 96, 117–18, 125; persuasion and 151, 152, 191, 212, 213; positive or negative 222–3
attitudinal Epithets 52
attribution 203
Australian Curriculum for English (AC:E) 8, 19, 97, 106, 124, 177, 194, 203, 212, 215, 235, 274

Barthes, R. 32, 35, 249
Bateman, J. 276
Bednarak, M. 86
Behavioural Processes 59–60, 86
Bezemer, J. 259
Blueback (Winton) 15, 33, 45, 47, 84–6, 97, 246, 260–2
Briggs, R. 165
Brown, F. 33, 41–3, 50, 58
Browne, A. 54, 83–4, 88, 252
Browne, B. 167
Bruner, J. 20
Bush, G. 4

Cameron, D. 4, 272–3
cause 51
cause and effect 200–1
character 117–18
characterization 51–5, 62t, 110–12, 114t
'Children Overboard' affair 166
Cicero 147, 154, 159

Circumstances 47, 62, 67, 189, 191, 211: in creation of setting 57; of location 51, 109; of location in Time or Place, Manner, Cause, Condition, Extent, Role and Matter 51, 186; of place 110
Circumstantial meanings 110
circumstantiation 50–1, 62*t*, 189, 262, 276
citation 219–21
Classifiers 52, 53
clause: complex/expanding 7, 16; embedded 17; simple 6, 16;
close-up 77
cohesion 44
Common Core State Standards (CCSS) 179
compass metaphor 25–6, 26*fig*, 277–8, 278*fig*
Complement 6
complex sentences 16–17
Complication Stage 39, 41
compound sentences 16–17
concession 204
condition 51
conjunctions 16, 81, 190, 200
connectives 145
Contact 76, 83
Content (Wh-) Interrogative 72*t*
'contextualized grammar' 4
co-ordinating conjunctions 16
core vocabulary 225*t*
creativity 19–20, 22–3
Cullis-Suzuki, S. *see* Suzuki, S.

Dahl, R. 33, 40–1, 42*t*, 45, 50, 59–60, 87, 106, 112, 137; *see also Fantastic Mr. Fox* (Dahl)
debate 178
Declarative 72*t*, 75*t*
Declarative Mood 24, 71, 142–3, 150, 157
deliberative argument 179
description 15*t*, 267–9
design, concept of 259
detachment 77
dialogue 79–80, 110–12, 112*t*, 114*t*, 203
diegesis 56, 245
'Di Inventione' (Cicero) 154
direct Contact 83
direct quoting 192, 215, 220–1
Disadvantaged Schools Program 102
disciplinary literacies 20
disciplinary practices 11–13, 26*fig*
discourse, free indirect 93–4, 137
discourse semantics 9, 81, 87, 275
discussion 178
Donnelly, K. 4
Droga, L. 221

Elaboration 7, 47, 91, 92, 97, 153
ellipsis 70
embedding 17
empathic engagement 258
endpapers 251
Enhancement 7, 47, 189–90, 200, 201
Environmental Children's Organization (ECO) 148–9
epideictic argument 179, 180
ethos 146, 150–2, 155, 156, 159, 161, 166–7, 171, 191
evaluation 39, 41, 89–90*t*, 202, 203
evaluative moments 60
Expansion 47, 188, 199
experiential lens 107, 108*t*, 113*t*, 125
experiential meanings 46
explanation 15*t*, 200, 267–9
Expositions: building context for work on 216–18; description of 11; ideational probe questions for 218–19, 224; independently composing 225–6; interpersonal probe questions for 224–5; modelling features of 218; multimodal focus on 205–7; in primary classroom 215–26; role of, in schooling 178; textual probe questions for 224
expository essay 178, 181–2
Extension 7, 47, 189
extension work 115
extent 51
eye level 77

Facebook article 226–7, 227–8*t*
Facebook assignment 205–7, 227–9, 233–5
Fantastic Mr. Fox (Dahl): action-reaction patterns in 33; attitude and 91; characterization and 51; image and 244; interactive systems of choice in 69–71; interpersonal meanings and 45; loading and 87–8; material processes and 57, 58–60; mood and 73; orientation stage of 40–1; stages of 42*t*; student reactions to 137; teaching plan for 107*t*; teaching scenario and 106–12; theme and 48–9, 144, 145; viewpoints in 43
Farnan, N. & Fearn, L. 33
Feez, S. 20, 22*fig*
Fejo, N.N. 159–62, 165
Finite verb 6, 15, 70, 73, 82–3
first person narration 69
focalization: advertisements and 170–1; description of 13; evaluation and 89*t*; Facebook assignment and 206–7; image-viewer relations and 24; interactive

systems of choice and 69, 76, 77*fig*; interactive systems of choice in 69; interpersonal lens and 36, 54; in *The Lost Thing* 257; multimodal texts and 226, 230–1, 233, 247–8, 252; narration versus 93–5; narrator voice and 117; persuasion and 212, 213; in *The Tunnel* 85–6; unmediated 83; visual 83, 84*fig*; in *The Weapon* 43; *see also* point of view
forensic argument 179, 196
foreshadowing 125
Forster, E.M. 56
Foxspell (Rubenstein) 125, 135–6
free indirect discourse 93–4, 137
French, R. 273
functional approaches 4–10

gaze 83
generic structure 39
generic style 54
Genette, G. 60
genre: grammatics and 39–44; meaning and metafunctions and 44–50; written analytical exposition and 183
Gleeson, L. 51, 246
goal 6
Golding, W. 35
Gore, A. 147
Gouldthorpe, P. 124
Graduation 87, 90*t*, 91, 92, 96, 152, 180, 202
grammar: grammatics versus 5–6; re-imagining of 1–2, 3, 273; teachers' knowledge of 2–3; as term 5
'grammar wars' 4
grammatics: grammar versus 5–6; of images 76; potentials and problems of 277–8; systemic functional 4–10
Grammatics Project, The 5, 9 274–5, 276
Grandad's Gifts (Jennings & Gouldthorpe) 106, 124–34, 127*fig*, 128*fig*, 131*fig*, 133*fig*, 134*fig*, 137, 244
Granpa (Burningham) 36–7, 61
Gray, B. 106
Great Bear, The (Gleeson & Greder) 51, 52*fig*, 77–8, 245, 246–52
Greder, A. 51, 246
guided practice 103–4, 123, 135–6, 214, 223, 233, 238–9

Halliday, M.: on complexity of language 18, 47; on content stratum of language 13–15; on contextual variables 12; on embedding 17; on Golding 35; on grammar 3, 5, 7; on grammatics 6, 7, 276, 277; on interpretation 249; on logogenesis 144; on maps 68; on metafunctions 45; on mood 72; on projection 93; on stratification 81; on systematic functional grammar 24; on textual meanings 48; trinocular vision and 14, 62, 74, 82
Hancock, C. 2, 7
Hasan, R. 36–7, 39, 63, 67, 274
Hayes, D. 19
high angle 77–8
Hillocks, G. 179, 196
hortatory Exposition 178, 180
Humphrey, S. 20, 22*fig*, 145, 177–8, 221
Humpty Dumpty 246, 262–6
Hunger Prevention Campaign 171
Hutchins, P. 36–7
Hyram and B (Caswell & Ottley) 61

ideas, projection of 93
ideation 81
ideational lens: narrative and 50–62; probe questions related to 62*t*, 180*t*; textual lens versus 179; on written expositions 186–93, 197–201
ideational metafunction 44
identification 15*t*, 266–9
image: grammatics of 76; interactive systems of choice in 76–9; language and 67–8; rhetoric of 249; stratification in 81–6; *see also* multimodal texts
imperative Mood 72–3, 142–3, 150
'implied reader' 79
Inconvenient Truth, A 147
independent writing 20, 22*fig*, 105*fig*, 124; independent composition 214
indicative Mood 72–3
inferred mediation 83
information: structure 145; waves of 145
Inheritors, The (Golding) 35
inner worlds 118–19, 118*fig*
inscribed judgement 151, 167
inscribed mediation 83
instantiation 194
interaction 69–71, 79–80
inter-animation 249
internal focalization 13, 94
interpersonal lens 49, 70*t*, 107, 126*t*, 181, 181*t*, 201–2
interpersonal metafunction 44, 45, 68
interpretation 15*t*, 267–9
interrogative/interrogative mood 24, 70, 72*t*, 150, 190–1

Introduction to Functional Grammar (Halliday & Matthiessen) 7, 276
invited Contact 83
invoked attitude 87, 91, 151, 191, 223
involvement 77

Jakobson, R. 50
Janicka's dialogue 80
Jeffers, O. 54
Jennings, P. 68, 91–3, 116–18, 124–5, 128, 129
Johnston, K. 19
joint construction of text 103–4
Jones, S. 137
judgement 87, 151, 191–2, 193, 215

King, S. 56, 109
knowledge orientation 78
Kolln, M. 2
Kress, G. 60, 67, 76, 94, 141–2, 254, 259, 273, 274, 276

landing places 15, 275
language: image and 67–8; stratification in 81–6
language orientation 109
learning outcomes, reflection on 104
lexical cohesion 145–6
Lines, H. 137
literate discourse 106
loading 87, 152, 191
Locke, T. 273
locutions 93
logical meanings 47
logical metaphor 201
logogenesis 144, 155–64
logos 146–7, 152–5, 156, 162, 166–7, 171, 179, 191, 202, 207
long shot 77
Long Walk to Freedom (Mandela) 164–5, 168
Lost Thing, The (Tan): affect and 88; description of 37–9; opening of 43; point of view and 94–6, 95*fig*; setting of 51; temporal unfolding in 61; top-down views in 78; versions of 245, 255–9; visual aspects of 244
Love, K. 221
low angle 77
Luke's Way of Looking (Wheatley) 36–7, 45

MacBeth 266–9
Machin, D. 39, 253
Malcolm, K. 40
Mandela, N. 164–5, 168

manner 51
marked theme 48–9
Martin, J.R.: discourse semantics and 81; on genre pedagogy 44; on graduation 87; on grammar 9–10; on inscribed appraisal 45; on interactivity 86–7; language and image and 86, 147, 274; on logogenesis 164–5; periodicity and 48–9, 145; on reactions 33; school-based research of 178; on social processes 39; on *The Weapon* 43, 43*t*
material process 6, 24, 46, 57–8, 60–1, 86, 186–7, 188, 198
matter 51
Matthiessen, C. 5–6, 9–10, 47, 72, 93
Maus (Spiegelman) 36
meaning, transforming 259–60
mediated observation 206–7
mental Process 6, 13, 24, 60, 61, 86, 92, 160–1
metafunction: application of 12–13; narratives and 44–50; portability of 274–5; as theoretical resource 12; uses of 9
metalanguage 8–9, 34–5, 277
meta-semiosis 266
mid shot 77
minimalist style 54
Modality: description of 82; dialogue and 79; high 236–7, 236*t*; low 236–7, 236*t*; medium 236–7, 236*t*; modelling choices for 236–8; persuasion and 143, 150–1, 155, 180, 191, 192–3, 203, 213, 235–9, 236*t*; in secondary classroom 235–41
modelling text 119, 121–3
modulation 150
"moment of truth" structure 43
Mood: attributes of 1; choices for 72*t*, 96; declarative 24, 71, 142–3, 150, 157; imperative 72–3, 142–3, 150; indicative 72–3; interactive systems of choice and 72–5; interpersonal lens and 86; interrogative/interrogation 24, 70, 72*t*, 150, 190–1; managing 79; options for meaning in 76*fig*; persuasion and 142–3, 150, 151, 155, 157, 162, 164, 180, 190–3, 213, 222; polarity and 75*t*; in secondary classroom 235–41
Moorhead, J. 227
multimodal composition, in primary classroom 226–35
multimodality 81
multimodal texts: composing 230; diverse 242–6; The Grammatics Project and 10; metalanguage and 8–9
Myhill, D. 3, 4, 137, 273

narration 93–4
narrative composition, managing interaction in 79–80
narrative hook 185, 187, 213, 215
narratives: building context for work on 103, 118–19, 128–9; composition of multimodal 135–6; description of 11; ideational lens and 50–62; independent composition of 104; independent composition of multimodal 136; investigating grammatics for 32–66; joint construction of 103–4, 113*t*; modelling features of 103, 108–9; modelling structure of 103; multimodal 242–6; multimodal interpretation and text creation 124–36; objective 69; perspectives on 43*t*; resources for meaning in 67–100; scenarios in teaching grammatics for 104–36; subjective 69; teachers' notes on 40*t*; teaching, in classrooms 101–40; teaching in primary classroom 106–15; teaching in secondary classroom 115–24; ways of reading 12
narrative semiosis 245
narrative viewpoint 116–18, 120–1*t*, 121–4, 122*fig*
narratology 35–6
narrator 36
narrator voice 117
naturalistic style 54
negotiation 87
New 145, 154, 154*t*, 155, 163
9-11/9-11 165–6
'No Child Left Behind' 4
Nodelman, P. 60, 76
nominalization 188, 197–8, 202
non-finite verbs 16–17, 73

Obama, B. 164
Object 6
objectivity 69, 76, 77*fig*, 78, 171
obligation 237–8
O'Brien, A. 266
observe image 83, 94
On Writing (King) 109
Orientation stage 39, 40–1, 80, 106, 107–8, 109, 113–14
O'Toole, M. 81
Ottley, M. 36–7
outer worlds 118–19, 118*fig*

Painter, C. 9–10, 61, 257, 274, 276
parallelism 154–5

participant depiction 51–5, 62*t*
Participants 46, 51–3, 153–4, 155, 160, 162, 186–7, 189, 197, 200
pathos 146–7, 152, 155, 156, 158, 161, 166–7, 171, 191, 207
PEEL structure 196, 199
periodicity 145
Person 151, 155, 157, 164, 180, 192–3, 212–13
Personal Distance 207
perspective 53*t*
persuasion: description of 11; interface of grammatics and 141–75; multimodal forms of 165–72; resources for meaning in 176–210; social distance and 171, 206–7, 212, 213; teaching in classroom 211–41; *see also* rhetoric
phases 156
Pietersen, H. 168
plotting 54, 56–62, 62*t*
point of view 93–6, 116–18, 120–1*t*, 121–4, 122*fig*, 206–7, 247–8, 257–8, 276; *see also* focalization
Polar (Yes/ No) Interrogative 72*t*, 75*t*
Polarity 24, 75*t*, 79, 96, 150
position 183–5, 195–6, 219
position reinforcement 183, 195–6
possibility 237–8
Pratt, M.L. 43
Predicator 70
process 46, 52, 54, 56–62, 62*t*
projection 13, 93, 188, 192, 199

Quirky Tails (Jennings) 91–3
quoting 192, 215, 219–22, 221*t*

rank, principle of 16, 18, 276
reference 145
reflection 104, 124, 214
relational processes 46–7, 57–8, 60, 86, 153, 188, 198, 252–3
repertoire development 18–23; students, building repertoires of 18–23, 26*fig*
Resolution Stage 39, 41
rhetoric: in broader civic domain 164–5; grammatics and 148–55; of the image 249; logogenesis and 155–64; *see also* persuasion; rhetorical approach to communication 141–2; 'rhetorical grammar' 4; rhetorical questions 190–1, 215, 222
role 51
Rose, D. 33, 44
Rosie's Walk (Hutchins) 36–7

Rudd, K. 144–5, 147, 155–65, 176, 180
rule of three 154–5
Russell, J. 227

salience 145
scaffolding pedagogy 20–1, 102–3, 214
semantic drift 35
semiotic resources, organization of 13–18, 26*fig*
sequencing 61
setting 50–1, 62*t*, 109–10
signposting 144, 145, 161, 184, 196, 215, 216–17, 217*t*
situation 54
Slattery, L. 4
small group work 129–35
social contexts, complexity of 10
social distance: interactive meaning and 76–7, 77*fig*, 83; in *The Lost Thing* 256; multimodal texts and 226, 230–1, 233; *see also* persuasion
social esteem 87, 88
social media 141–2
social sanction 87, 88
speeches, study of 177–8
Stevens, W. 35
stratification 13–16, 15*t*, 18, 68, 81–6, 97, 199, 201, 275
Stuck (Jeffers) 54
Subject 6, 15, 73, 82–3
subjectivity 69, 70, 76, 77, 77*fig*, 83, 171
subordinating conjunctions 16
Suzuki, S. 144–5, 148–55, 180, 216
'Sydney School' 5
systemic functional theory 6–7, 81

tagged Declarative 75*t*
tags 73, 73*t*, 96
Tan, S. 36–7, 51, 94, 256
teaching-learning cycle (TLC) 20–1, 22*fig*, 102–4, 105*fig*, 211–12, 213–14
teaching plans: for argument 235*t*; for exposition 216*t*; for *Fantastic Mr. Fox* (Dahl) 107*t*; for multimodal narrative 126*t*; for visual grammatics 230*t*; for *The Weapon* 119*t*
Tense 73
text-based teaching learning cycle 20–1, 22*fig*
text connectives 184–5
text orientation 109
texts: exploring 23–5, 26*fig*; modelling features structures and features of 214;
see also expositions; multimodal texts; narratives
textual lens 49, 144–6, 146*t*, 180–1
textual meanings and metafunction 44, 48
Theme 48, 144–5, 154, 154*t*, 155, 163
thesis statement 183–5, 186–7, 219
third person narration 69
Tin Pot Foreign General and the Old Iron Woman, The (Briggs) 165
topic sentences 216
Transitivity 6, 24, 33, 47, 57, 67, 155, 187*t*, 191
transmedia narratives 258
tricolon structures 154–5, 158–9
trinocular vision/view 14–15, 62, 74; view 'from above' 14–15, 74–5, 82, 266, 276; view 'from around' 14–15, 74–5, 82, 276; view 'from below' 14–15, 74, 82, 265, 276
Tunnel, The (Browne) 54, 55*fig*, 78, 78*fig*, 83–4, 85*fig*, 88, 245, 252–5
two-level process of analysis 36–7

Unbearable (Jennings) 125
'Unhappily Ever After' (Jennings) 68, 91–3, 97, 106, 116–19, 116*t*, 137
unmediated observation 257
Unsworth, L. 86, 167–8, 255–6, 258, 274

van Leeuwen, T. 9, 39, 60, 67, 76, 94, 274, 276
vectors 60
verbal Process 24, 60, 93, 156–7, 188, 198
verbal texts, interactive systems of choice in 69–76
Victory speech (Obama) 164
viewer power 247–8
visual choices, modelling 231–2
visual grammatics, plan for teaching 230*t*
visual text, altering 233
Vocative 70
Voice: passive 161; active 161
Voices in the Park (Browne) 88
voicing 89*t*, 93
Vygotsky, L. 20

Watson, F. 137
Way Home (Hathorn & Rogers) 51
Weapon, The (Brown): action-reaction patterns in 33; characterization and 51–3; description of 41–3; free indirect discourse in 137; interactive

systems of choice and 71, 73; as mentor text 105; perspectives on 53*t*; plotting and 57–8; point of view in 94, 120–1*t*; setting of 50; teaching plan for 119*t*
Wheatley, N. 36–7
White, P. 45, 86, 87
Williams, G. 273, 277
Winton, T. 15, 33, 45, 84–6, 262
World Wildlife Fund 166–7

written analytical Exposition: importance of 178; in primary school 183–93; in secondary school 193–202; *see also* Expositions
written Expositions, in schooling 182–93

Zoo (Browne) 88, 90, 167
Zoos Victoria poster 142–3, 143*fig*, 165, 231–2
Zuckerberg, M. 227

Helping you to choose the right eBooks for your Library

Add Routledge titles to your library's digital collection today. Taylor and Francis ebooks contains over 50,000 titles in the Humanities, Social Sciences, Behavioural Sciences, Built Environment and Law.

Choose from a range of subject packages or create your own!

Benefits for you
- Free MARC records
- COUNTER-compliant usage statistics
- Flexible purchase and pricing options
- All titles DRM-free.

Benefits for your user
- Off-site, anytime access via Athens or referring URL
- Print or copy pages or chapters
- Full content search
- Bookmark, highlight and annotate text
- Access to thousands of pages of quality research at the click of a button.

REQUEST YOUR FREE INSTITUTIONAL TRIAL TODAY

Free Trials Available
We offer free trials to qualifying academic, corporate and government customers.

eCollections – Choose from over 30 subject eCollections, including:

Archaeology	Language Learning
Architecture	Law
Asian Studies	Literature
Business & Management	Media & Communication
Classical Studies	Middle East Studies
Construction	Music
Creative & Media Arts	Philosophy
Criminology & Criminal Justice	Planning
Economics	Politics
Education	Psychology & Mental Health
Energy	Religion
Engineering	Security
English Language & Linguistics	Social Work
Environment & Sustainability	Sociology
Geography	Sport
Health Studies	Theatre & Performance
History	Tourism, Hospitality & Events

For more information, pricing enquiries or to order a free trial, please contact your local sales team:
www.tandfebooks.com/page/sales

The home of Routledge books

www.tandfebooks.com

PGMO 04/25/2018